PLUMES
from Paradise

This book is dedicated to the memory
of the late Sir Serei Eri GCMG KStJ

Poet, Writer, Broadcaster, Teacher,
Defence Secretary, Diplomat,
Museum Trustee and former Governor-General

PLUMES
from Paradise

Trade cycles in outer Southeast Asia
and their impact on New Guinea and
nearby islands until 1920

PAMELA SWADLING

With contributions by Roy Wagner and Billai Laba

SYDNEY UNIVERSITY PRESS

This edition published in 2019 by Sydney University Press

First published in 1996 by the Papua New Guinea National Museum
PO Box 5560 Boroko, National Capital District, Papua New Guinea
in association with Robert Brown and Associates (Qld) Pty Ltd
PO Box 1299 Coorparoo DC, Queensland 4151. Australia.

Sydney University Press
Fisher Library F03
The University of Sydney NSW 2006
AUSTRALIA
sup.info@sydney.edu.au
sydney.edu.au/sup

National Library of Australian Cataloguing-in-Publication data

Creator:	Swadling, Pamela, author.
Title:	Plumes from paradise : trade cycles in outer Southeast Asia and their impact on New Guinea and nearby islands until 1920 / Pamela Swadling ; with contributions by Roy Wagner and Billai Laba.
ISBN:	9781743325445 (paperback)
	9781743325469 (ebook: epub)
	9781743325452 (ebook: PDF)
	9781743325476 (ebook: mobi)
Notes:	Includes bibliographical references and index.
Subjects:	Feather industry–New Guinea.
	Feather industry–New Guinea–History.
	Birds–Conservation–New Guinea.
Other Creators/	Wagner, Roy, author.
Contributors:	Laba, Billai, author.

Cover design by Miguel Yamin

Contents

Conventions followed

The Malay Archipelago is the old geographic term for the Indonesian Archipelago. In order to avoid confusion between old and modern political boundaries, the term Indonesian, rather than Malay is used for current and historic residents of what is now the Indonesian Archipelago.

Geographical place names as well as species have had variant spellings over the years. Where possible the current spelling is used.

Turtle shell is used rather than the misleading trade name tortoiseshell for the shell of marine turtles such as the hawkbill turtle.

The standardisation of monetary values has not been possible. British sterling equivalents are given for other currencies when they are known.

Place names and their spellings have changed since written records began in eastern Indonesia. A question mark before a place name indicates that the location in brackets may be the one referred to in the cited text.

Acknowledgements

This book has taken over a decade to research and write. There were periods when the project became overwhelming and I was disheartened. To all those colleagues and friends who gave their time to provide encouragement and constructive comments I am truly grateful. I particularly wish to thank Jack Golson along with Chris Ballard, Mark Busse, Tim Curtin, Frederick Errington, Deborah Gewertz, Harry Jackman, Mary LeCroy, Robin Torrence and Peter J. White.

I also wish to acknowledge the help of Father John J. Tschauder S.V.D. for locating and translating various German texts. Other German translations were made by Philip Holzknecht, Father Theo Aerts, Sylvia Ohnemus and Claire Smith. Dutch material was translated by Adri Govers, Tim Bruwer and Marsha Berman; Danish by Tim Bruwer and Indonesian by J.H. Siregar and Jack Zieck.

For various forms of help, I also wish to thank: Bryant Allen, Wally Ainui, Clive Alexander, the late Arnold Ap, Peter Bellwood, Michele Bowe, Jennifer Broomhead, Geoffrey Bundu, Joe Chan, Ian Craven, Tony Crawford, Frances and Tony Deklin,

Robert Depew, Tom Dutton, Soroi Marepo Eoe, the late Anthony Forge, K.W. Galis, Rick Giddings, Anton Gideon, Ian Glover, Mclaren Hiari, Stalin Jawa, Charlotte Kamaya, Stuart Kirsch, Navu Kwapena, Nancy Lutkehaus, Roy Mackay, Herman Mandui, Wilma Marakan, Mary Mennis, James Menzies, Bill Mitchell, Douglas Newton, Andrew Pawley, William S. Peckover, Philippe Peltier, Harry Persaud, Simon Poraituk, Dan Potts, Jan Pouwer, Judith Robertson, Peter Sack, J.W. Schoorl, Dirk Smidt, Dorota Starzecka, James Urry, Gabor Vargyas, Michael P. Walters, Paul Wanga, Virginia-Lee Webb and Jack Zieck.

For photo archive and other library assistance I wish to thank the staffs of the American Museum of Natural History; Australian Museum Library, Sydney; Bijdragen tot de Taal-, Land- en Volkenkunde, Leiden; the British Reading Room and Newspaper Library of the British Library, London; Ethnographical Museum, Budapest; Frobenius-Instituut, Frankfurt (Main); Fotobureau, Koninklijk Instituut voor de Tropen, Amsterdam; the Linden Museum, Stuttgart; the Metropolitan Museum of Art, New York; the Mitchell Library, Sydney; Museum of Far Eastern Antiquities, Stockholm; Photo Archives, Rijksmuseum voor Volkenkunde, Leiden; Wildlife Conservation Society, New York; the PNG National Museum Library; the PNG National Archives; the New Guinea Collection and Interloan Department of the Michael Somare Library of the University of Papua New Guinea, and the New Guinea Collection and Interloan Department of the PNG National Library.

Every effort has been made to trace copyright holders and obtain permission, but this has not been possible in all cases. Any omissions brought to our attention will be remedied in any future editions.

The Wenner-Gren Foundation for Anthropological Research in New York provided funds to purchase copies of this publication for Papua New Guinea's universities and public libraries.

New edition

Our increased understanding of New Guinea's prehistory has required some revisions to the text. The rest of the publication remains as first published.

Pamela Swadling
2019

Figures

Plates

Tables

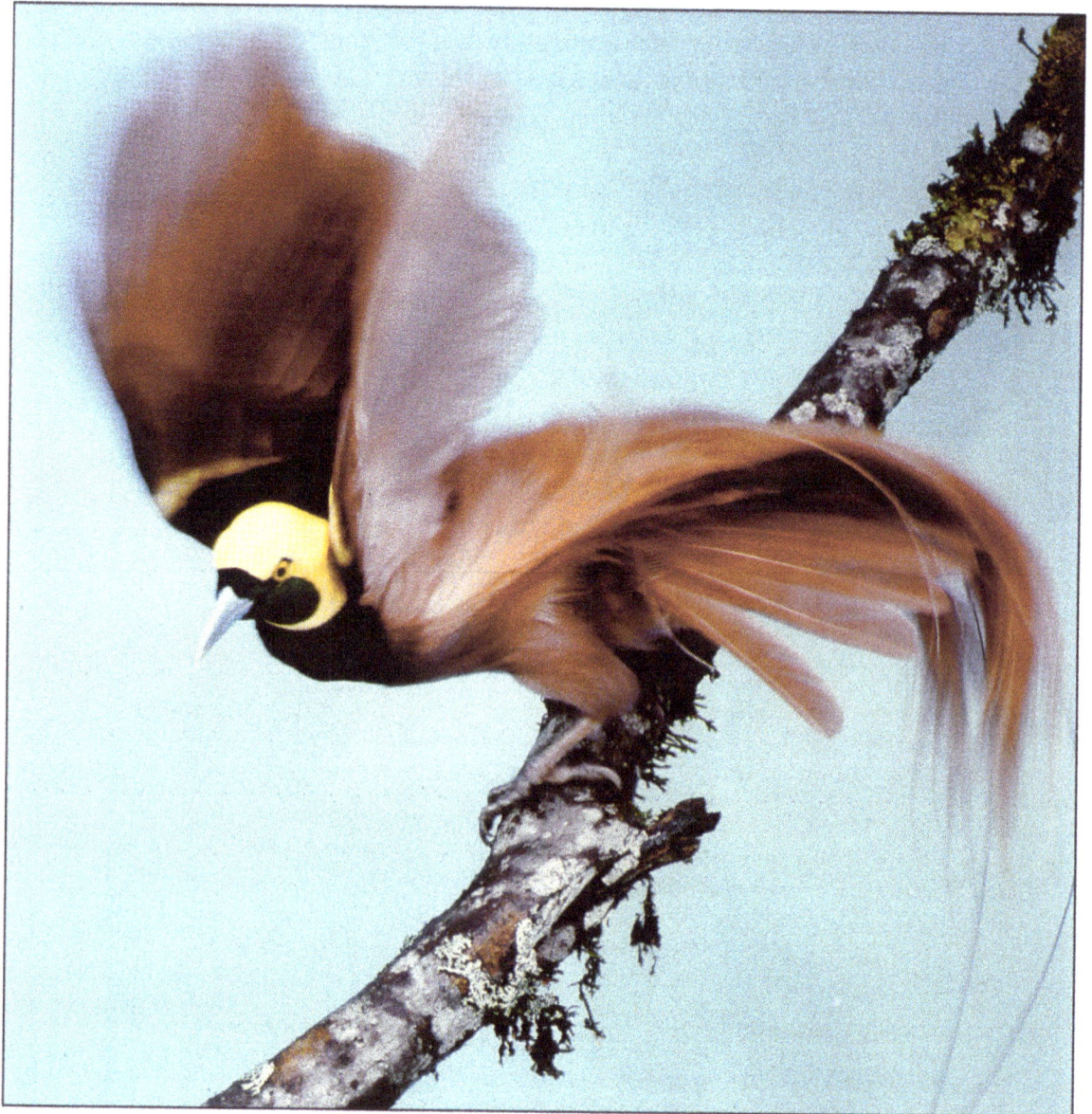

Plate 1: The Raggiana Bird of Paradise features on both the national crest and flag of Papua New Guinea, the only country where it is found. **Photo:** Courtesy of William S. Peckover.

1

Introduction

The natural resources peculiar to New Guinea and nearby islands have provided attractive trade items for distant markets for thousands of years. This book describes the export histories of bird of paradise skins,[1] spices, sandalwood, aromatic barks, damar (a gum used for lighting before mineral oil became available), pearls, trepang (edible sea slugs also called bêche-de-mer), and copra from prehistoric times until the 1920s. All of these products have gone through at least one, in some cases two trade cycles of boom and bust. The history of these cycles and the changing trading relationships they stimulated contribute to our understanding of the foundations of the present political economy of outer Southeast Asia.

During the various trade cycles, trading relationships provided opportunities for the exchange of new products and ideas. New Guineans, for instance, probably gave the world sugarcane. Some introductions to New Guinea were of only local consequence, whereas others such as the sweet potato led to major socioeconomic changes in the remote highlands of the interior. The varied nature of these interchanges played a role in giving each area its own history, and in part they explain the complex history behind the cultural diversity of New Guinea.

The first people to settle New Guinea some 50,000 years ago came from Southeast Asia. For much of their history these settlers and subsequent migrants remained part of outer Southeast Asia. By 4,000 years ago a chain of trading transactions, which allowed products to move from one community to the next, linked New Guinea and Asia. This was when early domesticated banana and sugarcane varieties from New Guinea were dispersed to Asia and beyond. Shortly before 2,000 years ago this trade was generating sufficient interest to support the activities of long-distance specialist traders from Asia.

Bird of paradise skins were the main product sought by the first specialist traders and as a result were the first product from New Guinea to go through a trade cycle of boom and bust. This cycle began just prior to 2,000 years ago and ended about 250 AD. It ended because spices and aromatic barks and woods displaced plumes as prime luxuries in Asia. After the boom, plumes continued to be traded as a subsidiary product of the spice trade.

By 300 AD the Spice Islands and Timor had overtaken New Guinea as the focus of Asian trade. As New Guinea became more isolated it was less influenced by the changes taking place in Southeast Asia. This explains why today we generally consider Southeast Asia and New Guinea to be different geographic areas with their own distinctive customs and ways of life.

By 1400 AD many aspects of Javanese culture, including sultanates, had been introduced to the Spice Islands. The world demand for cloves, nutmeg and mace was growing and began to attract increasing international interest, especially in Europe. The first cloves and nutmegs from the Spice Islands to reach Europe came via the Middle East. As their use increased, a desire arose amongst Europeans to obtain direct access to these products by finding their source. A Portuguese expedition was finally successful in locating where they were produced in 1512.

The power and wealth of the sultanates started to decline when the Dutch began to seek control over the Spice Islands. In their efforts to impose a monopoly on spice trading the Dutch disrupted established trading networks. The Dutch East India Company soon found the overheads of policing a spice monopoly and restricting production financially crippling. They tried to overcome this problem by diversifying their interests in other products and areas. For instance, they tried to participate in the massoy trade of southwestern New Guinea, but were unsuccessful. By 1650 the inability of the Dutch to maintain economic prosperity in the Moluccas had transformed the region into one characterised by raiding and retribution. Raiding continued until the Dutch began capturing the perpetrators by using steam-powered boats in the 1850s.

Having decided that New Guinea had little economic potential, the Dutch promoted the Sultan of Tidore as suzerain on their behalf. This relieved them of having to administer New Guinea and its offshore islands themselves, but still protected the eastern flanks of the Dutch East Indies from other mercantile powers. The Dutch choice of the Sultan of Tidore, rather than Ternate and Bacan was probably related to their perception that Tidore would make the best lackey.

The area put under the Sultan of Tidore's control was extended as the Dutch perceived a growing interest by other powers in the Pacific. In 1704 the Dutch proclaimed that the Sultan of Tidore controlled the Western Papuan Islands off the western tip of New Guinea; by 1848 the borders of his putative rule had been extended to the proximity of the current international border between Indonesia and Papua New Guinea.

Bird of paradise skins were unknown in Europe before the sixteenth century. By the nineteenth century increasing numbers were reaching Europe. European milliners soon appreciated their beauty and began to use them and the feathers of other wild birds to decorate hats. Fashionable women in the Western world developed a passion for wearing such hats. By the turn of the century contemporary commentators were comparing the increased hunting of wild birds to a 'gold-rush' and it was feared at the time that many birds would become extinct. Never before had so many species and such large numbers of birds been slaughtered for plumage. By the time the European plume boom ended in the 1920s. the search for bird of paradise skins over the millennia had probably brought more New Guineans into contact with foreigners than any other product. As a result these plumes have adorned heads in Asia and the Middle East, including China, India, Nepal, Persia and Turkey, as well as Europe, North America, Australia and New Zealand.

The European plume industry and conservationists were soon locked in debate with both sides claiming the high moral ground. As with the current biodiversity debate, conservationists were outraged over the likely extinction of species in the name of development, just as the prohibition of their activities was unacceptable to those whose livelihood was dependent on the plume trade.

Very different policies were adopted to deal with this problem by the colonial powers in New Guinea. Although London was one of the main world feather markets, Australia prohibited plume hunting in Papua in 1908. The Germans did their best to protect the birds, as well as reap the economic benefits of the plume boom since it funded economic development on mainland New Guinea. They introduced protective measures such as hunting permits, closed seasons and conservation areas. The plume trade also provided much needed revenue for Dutch New Guinea. In 1909 the Dutch introduced hunting licences and imposed a hunting season. They believed that the birds would survive as only fully plumed males were shot for the plume trade. This meant that males with immature plumage were able to breed and thus ensure the survival of the birds. The outcome of these policies subsequently influenced the conservation measures adopted for protecting birds of paradise in West Papua and Papua New Guinea.

The isolation New Guinea experienced after 300 AD explains how it became the last unknown and the 'land of the unexpected.' There was of course in western New Guinea some indirect contact with world trade systems through Bacan in the Moluccas, and later contact through Chinese, Seram Laut and Bugis traders. In what is now Papua New Guinea the resumption of contact with world trade systems was gradual. It can be seen to have begun with the proposed Seram Laut damar traders on the Trans Fly coast from 1645–1790; trepang fishing in the 1830s and later pearling in Torres Strait in the 1860s; copra in the New Guinea Islands in the 1870s and Ternate plume and shell traders on the north coast in the 1880s. Dutch, German and British colonial interests led to the division of New Guinea amongst these colonial powers in the 1880s. In 1884 colonial rule in German New Guinea (later the Mandated Territory of New Guinea) and British New Guinea began to lay the foundations for the modern independent state of Papua New Guinea.

It is only in recent times that New Guinea has begun once again to be orientated towards Asia. Dutch New Guinea, now West Papua, became part of Indonesia in 1969. Since independence new trade and social links have begun to reintegrate Papua New Guinea with Asia.

The organisation of this book

Both geographical and chronological considerations have influenced the chapter organisation of this book. Chapters 2 to 5 cover the history of spice and plume trading. Spices are presented first. The following three chapters (3–5) are concerned with plume acquisition by Asians, Europeans and New Guineans as well as the growth of the conservation movement.

Chapters 6 to 13 examine specific regions of New Guinea and nearby islands. They are organised geographically with an eastwards progression. The final chapter integrates the contents of all the chapters into a chronological framework. It starts with the foundation period of inter-island trade. This is followed by a series of trade cycles which are driven by changing world markets and their related trade contacts.

The first trade cycle is concerned with specialist Asian traders seeking plumes, the second with Asians and subsequently Europeans after spices, the third with Asians and Europeans supplying marine products to China, and the fourth with Europeans acquiring copra, plumes, pearls and minerals. These trade cycles are not discrete entities in time, but changes in emphasis with some products continuing and others discontinuing from one cycle to the next.

The contributions by Roy Wagner, from the University of Virginia in the United States, and Billai Laba, of the Department of Environment

18

and Conservation in Port Moresby, present new information on the distribution, character and nature of likely Indonesian trade with the Trans Fly coast of Papua New Guinea. Their contributions supplement material presented in Chapter 9 and bring a new dimension to Torres Strait studies.

Note

1. The term skin is generally used because the entire bird is skinned and prepared so that its plumes are shown to best advantage.

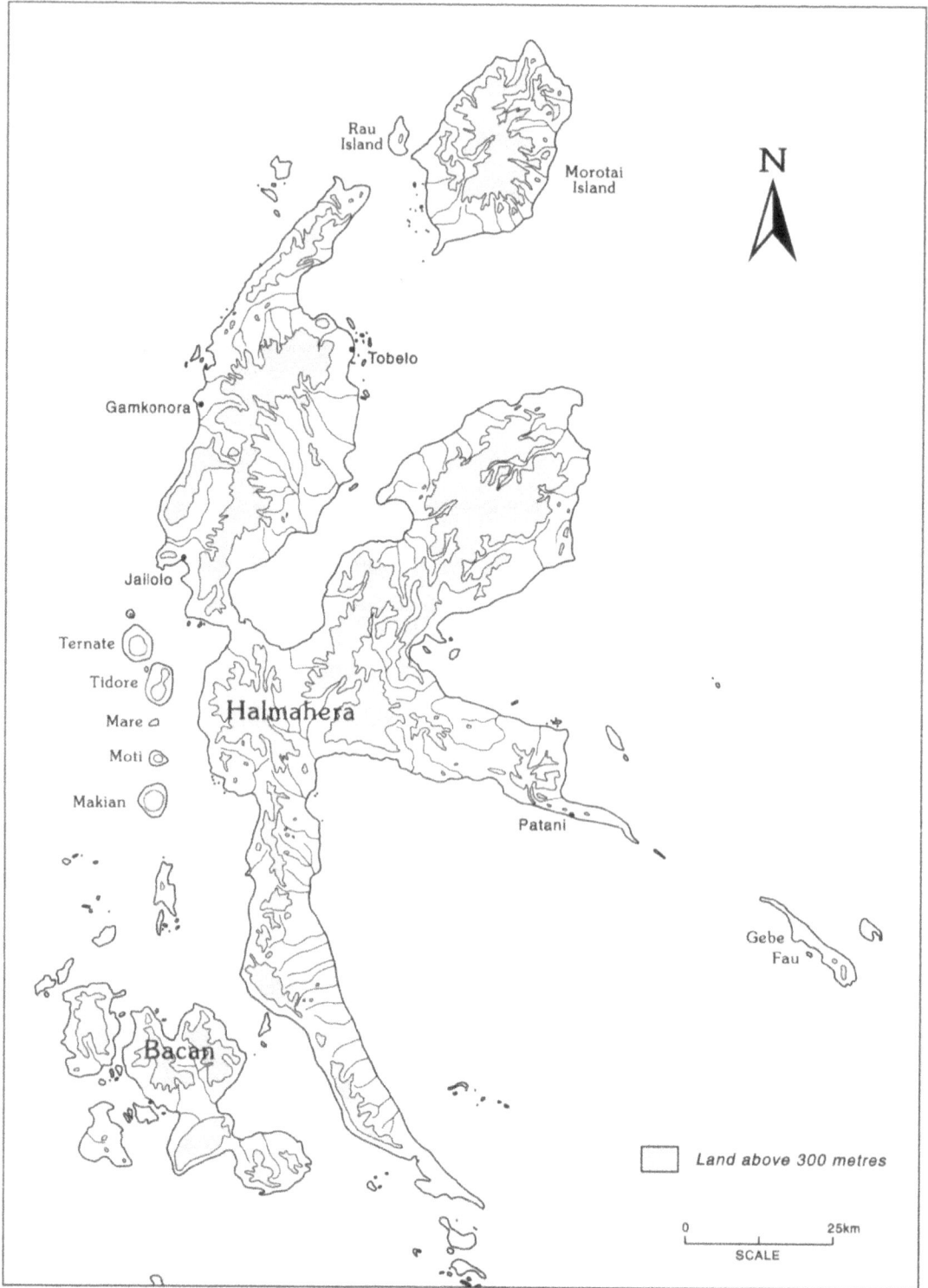

Figure 1: The Moluccas were originally the five small clove producing islands of Ternate, Tidore, Moti, Makian and Bacan.

2

The rise and decline of the Spice Islands

Introduction

Spice trading began in prehistoric times during the foundation period of inter-island trade and continued as a subsidiary activity in the first trade cycle when specialist Asian traders sought plumes from New Guinea. During the second trade cycle spices became the prime product acquired by Asian, and subsequently European traders. Unrealistic expectations, poor management of spice production and marketing, and greed brought about the economic decline of the Spice Islands. As a result the inhabitants of the Spice Islands found themselves forbidden from growing the spices their ancestors had domesticated. The declining prosperity of the region led to raiding and acts of retribution. Later some Spice Islanders participated in the supplying of marine products to China during the third trade cycle and plume trading during the fourth.

Clove and nutmeg production and use

Cloves were first cultivated on the five small volcanic islands which became known as the Moluccas. Individually named Ternate, Tidore, Moti, Makian and Bacan (Figure 1), these islands are located off the western coast of Halmahera some 400 kilometres from the western tip of New Guinea. This is not that far, in fact closer than a direct flight from Port Moresby to Madang. Along with the islands in the Banda group (Figure 2) the five islands became known as the Spice Islands and remained the only source of cultivated cloves and nutmeg until the sixteenth century.

Today the people on Ternate and Tidore as well as many of those on Moti, Makian and Bacan speak languages related to those spoken on the Bird's Head of New Guinea.[1] Until detailed archaeological and linguistic studies have been made we can only ponder the extent to which this common linguistic heritage was brought about by trade. However, current information suggests that this is a likely explanation as the Bird's Head and the Moluccas have been important trade centres respectively for plumes and cloves.

The use of cloves seems to have begun earlier and been more extensive than nutmegs and mace. By means of a chain of trading transactions cloves were traded to India and the Middle East[2] long before they became important in China. Indian records indicate that cloves were traded to the Indian subcontinent before the birth of Christ. Somewhat later a Roman, Pliny the Elder, refers to cloves in 70 AD.[3]

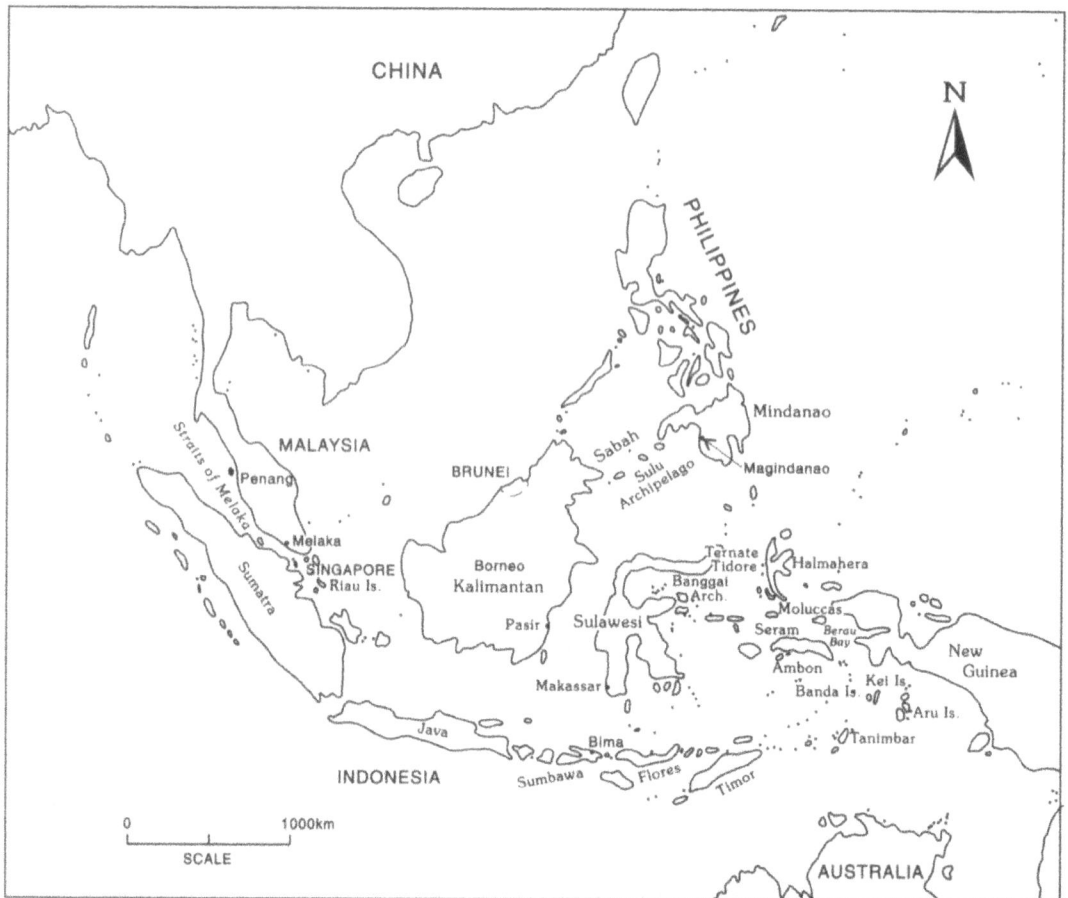

Figure 2: Southeast Asia

The introduction of Hindu-Buddhist cosmological ideas and the concept of a divine ruler to Southeast Asia from the Indian subcontinent about 300 AD led to a marked increase in the use of spices and aromatic woods. From this time the demand for spices and aromatic barks and woods in Asia grew whilst that for plumes declined.

The aristocracy in Europe were using cloves as a cooking ingredient by the Middle Ages (500–1500 AD). By the late Middle Ages nutmegs were also being used. The first reference to nutmegs in Europe occurs in the twelfth century. They were initially used as a fumigant as well as a spice.[4]

In the thirteenth century cloves were still a scarce luxury commodity in Europe and Asian traders operating west of Java were largely ignorant of their source. They generally assumed that these spices were a product of Java.

During the fourteenth century the Majapahit kingdom of Java extended its influence as far as the Moluccas in order to obtain a regular supply of spices. Majapahit maintained its authority by levying tribute until its decline in the fifteenth century. This contact with Java stimulated the development of a number of kingdoms (sultanates) in the Moluccas, such as Ternate, which became commercially and politically important. The sultans were able to provide traders with large quantities of cloves as they received a large part of each clove harvest as tribute. This gave them a dominant role in the spice trade. The spice traders, who mainly came from abroad, won favour and good terms by assisting the sultans to promote their own interests. The accumulating wealth and regal splendour of these sultans became widely known.

By the fifteenth century the Moluccas were known to Arab traders as *jazirat-al-mulk*, the land of many kings. The Portuguese pronunciation later gave us Moluco and Moluccas in its plural form.[5] When cloves were grown on Ambon and Seram the name Moluccas came to refer to a larger area.

The favoured route to the Spice Islands was via the Sunda chain which includes Timor. Merchants either obtained all the spices they wanted at the nutmeg and mace producing islands of Banda, which also served as an entrepôt for the Spice Islands as a whole, or continued on to the clove producing Moluccas. The established route to the Moluccas was via Ambon and western Seram.

In 1512 the Portuguese became the first Europeans to visit the Spice Islands. They reported that cultivated cloves were only produced on the five islands of Ternate, Tidore, Moti, Makian and Bacan. Portuguese estimates made in the early sixteenth century suggest that 600,000 to 1,200,000 kilograms of cloves were harvested each year.[6]

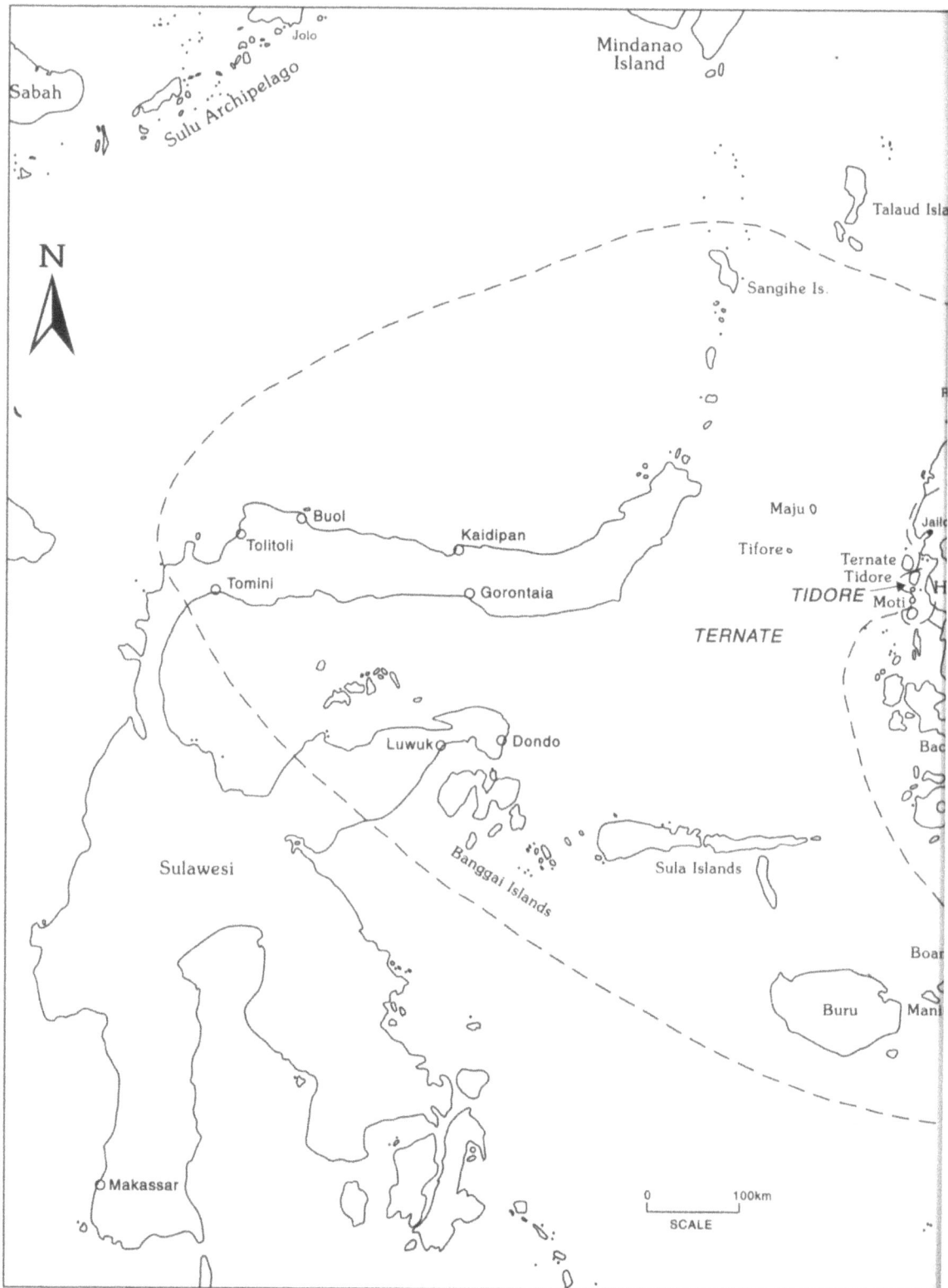

Figure 3: The subjected territories of the Sultans of Ternate, Bacan, Tidore and Jailolo in the early sixteenth century.

TERNATE

BACAN

JAILOLO

TIDORE

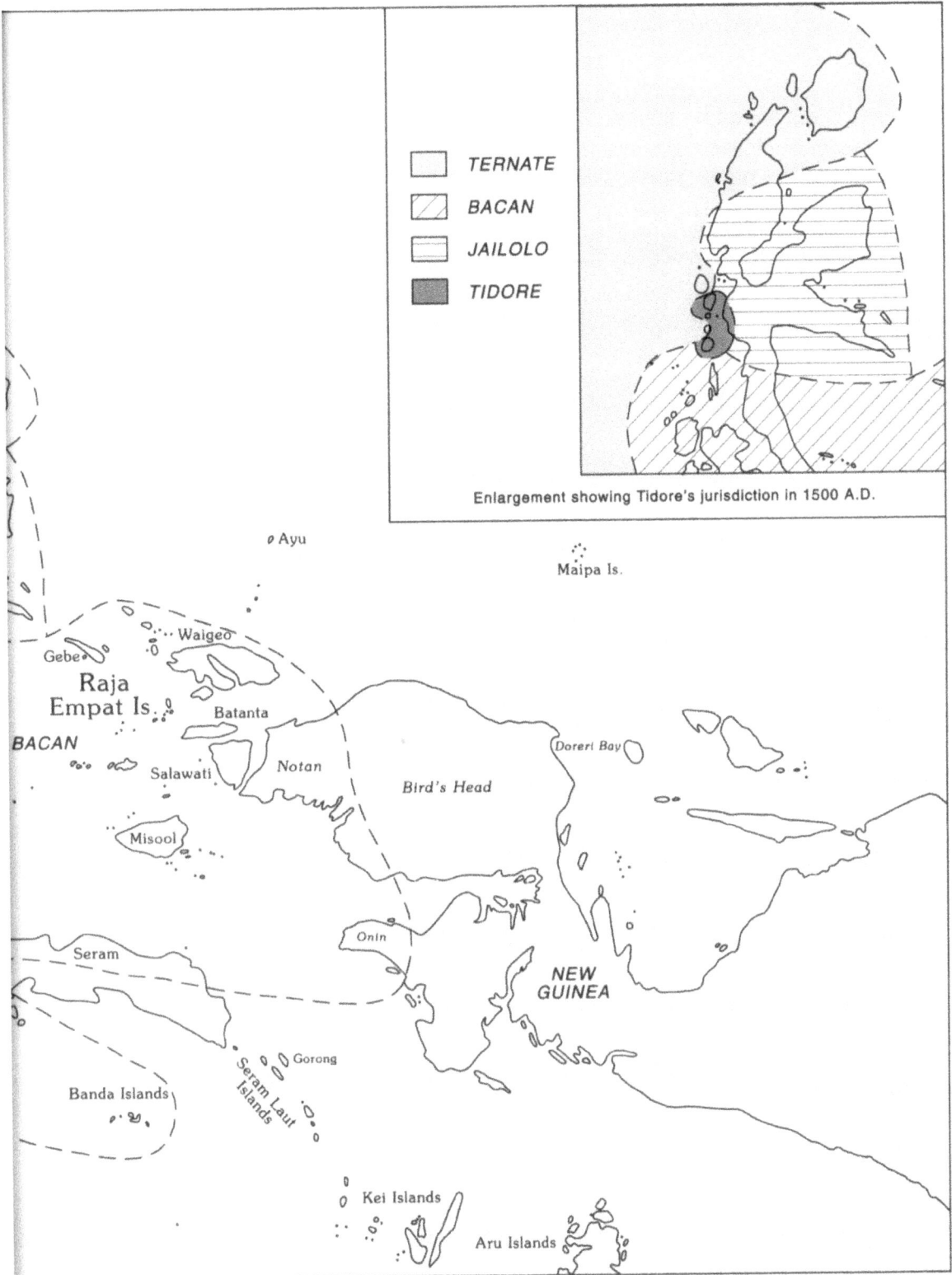

Enlargement showing Tidore's jurisdiction in 1500 A.D.

ο Ayu

Maipa Is.

Waigeo

Gebe

Raja
Empat Is.

Batanta

BACAN

Salawati

Notan

Doreri Bay

Bird's Head

Misool

Onin

Seram

NEW
GUINEA

Gorong

Banda Islands

Seram Laut
Islands

Kei Islands

Aru Islands

With current average yields of two kilograms per tree[7] this would require stands of 300,000 to 600,000 trees.

Moluccan traditions claim that cultivated cloves originated on Makian.[8] Moti also seems to have been a long-term producer, whereas Tidore was more recent than Ternate, and Bacan had only begun ten years before the Portuguese arrived in 1512.[9]

Wild clove trees are common in the lower montane forests of many islands in the Moluccas and New Guinea. Unlike cultivated trees, wild trees have larger and less aromatic flower buds and leaves. Their essential oil content is also less and it has a different composition. They are also more variable, more vigorous as juveniles and more resistant to *matibudjang* disease than cultivated cloves.[10]

Many people can recognise cloves, nutmeg and mace on the spice rack, but know little about the way they are grown. Cloves are the unopened flower buds of *Eugenia caryophyllus*, a tree which grows from seed to a height of 7–12 metres under plantation conditions. In the Moluccas during the time of the Dutch clove monopoly, clove trees did not begin bearing until they were 15 years old;[11] but under favourable plantation conditions they now bear after 6–8 years. They continue producing for as long as 50–60 years.

The flower buds are harvested by climbing the trees and picking the buds growing on the tips of the branches when they are fully grown but unopened. The bud is then green or beginning to turn red. Whole inflorescences are picked by hand and the buds rubbed off and dried in the sun as quickly as possible. This produces the hard, dark brown flower buds we know as cloves.[12] Each tree yields about two kilograms of cloves a year with the peak harvest being from June until September.[13]

Nutmeg is the seed of *Myristica fragrans* and mace is its seed aril or covering. Nutmeg seeds are produced by the female trees of *M. fragrans* which are grown in the shade of kanari (*Canarium commune*) trees.[14] In the Moluccas during the time of the Dutch spice monopoly, nutmegs usually took 10 years to come into bearing, earlier fruiting was considered to indicate an inferior tree.[15] Today under favourable plantation conditions they begin bearing when 4–6 years old. They grow to a height of 8–12 metres. Some male trees are kept for fertilisation and the rest are usually felled.

The seeds are either gathered by hand from the trees or collected after they have fallen to the ground. The aril is removed from the seed, pressed and then dried in the sun to produce mace. The seeds also have to be dried.[16] The cultivated nutmegs from Banda are described as being round, whereas the wild nutmegs collected from the Aru Islands, Halmahera, and Berau Bay (MacCluer Gulf) in New Guinea are long in shape.[17]

At present any account of the spice trade in eastern Indonesia is solely dependent on historical records. Archaeology has yet to reveal its side of the story. An archaeological study of the history of exotic goods in the Spice Islands, particularly foreign ceramics, glass beads and other non-perishable goods, as the world demand for cloves and nutmegs grew will undoubtedly enhance what can be reconstructed from historical records.

The socioeconomic and political situation in the Spice Islands in 1512

The Moluccas: cloves

When the Portuguese arrived in the Spice Islands in 1512 there were four sultanates – Ternate, Tidore, Jailolo and Bacan.[18] The political and economic infrastructure of these sultanates was hierarchical. Their nature was clearly influenced from Java, just as today Papua New Guinea has a largely Australian infrastructure and towns such as Jayapura in West Papua reflect the Indonesian way of life.

Unlike in the clove producing islands where power was in the hands of sultans, in 1512 Banda had no single ruler. Authority was autonomous. Decisions were made by councils of *orang kaya* (village elders). In each village they were responsible for organising ceremonies and allocating rights to the nutmeg groves.[19]

Figure 4: A *korakora*. Raiding *korakora* were crewed by 100–300 men.

Source: Röding 1798 reproduced in Horridge 1981.

In the sixteenth century most of the islands between Sulawesi[20] and New Guinea were subjugated by the Sultan of Ternate or the Sultan of Bacan, who was aligned with him (see Table 1 and Figure 3). The number of men the Sultan of Ternate is reputed to have been able to summon at this time is quite astounding. His authority was maintained by keeping a large fleet of paddle-propelled vessels (*korakora*) in the waters between Sulawesi and New Guinea (Figures 4 and 5).[21] These were crewed by slaves. The Sultan obtained these men either as tribute willingly or unwillingly given. When villages failed to pay tribute they were raided and men were seized to work as slaves for the Sultan.

Table 1: The subjected territories of the Sultan of Ternate that provided him with militia at the beginning of the sixteenth century.

	militia available
Ternate	3,000
Moti (Motir) [part of Moti was also under Tidore]	300
Maju and Tifore (Myo and Tyfory)	400
Bao and Jaquita (northern Halmahera)	1,000
Bata China (northern Halmahera)	10,000
Veranulla (near Ambon, Amboina)	15,000
Boana (Buana) and Manipa	3,000
Buru (Bouro)	4,000
Sula (Xula)	4,000
Luwuk (Labaque), Sulawesi	1,000
Dondo, Sulawesi	700
Tomini (Tornine), Sulawesi	12,000
Gorontalu and Ilboto, Sulawesi	10,000
Kaidipan (Kydipan), Sulawesi	7,000
Tolitoli (Tetoli) and Buoi (Bohol), Sulawesi	6,000
Sangihe (Sangir)	3,000
Gazia (? location)	300
Japua (? location)	10,000
Total	**90,700**

Source: Forrest 1969: 34 (first published 1779).

The use of paddles more than sails allowed surprise attacks when seasonal and available winds were unfavourable for a chosen destination. In contrary winds the use of paddles made *korakora* much swifter than European sailing boats. Their speed in these circumstances meant that they frequently outperformed European shipping until the 1850s when steam vessels came into use.[22]

The *korakora* ranged in size from small vessels to large ones of up to 10 tons.[23] The paddlers sat on platforms stretched across the outrigger booms as shown in Figures 4 and 5. Large raiding vessels had four platforms with fifty paddlers on each side of the *korakora*. Fighting men rode on a superstructure of platforms raised over the hull.[24] *Korakora* were so well suited for Moluccan conditions that they were used also by European visitors such as Forrest and by Dutch naval patrols based at Ambon.

Tidore's jurisdiction was small at this time. It consisted of part of Moti and Halmahera and the important clove island of Makian. This island had the best harbour in the Moluccas. Makian was a major export centre exporting not only its own cloves but those from other

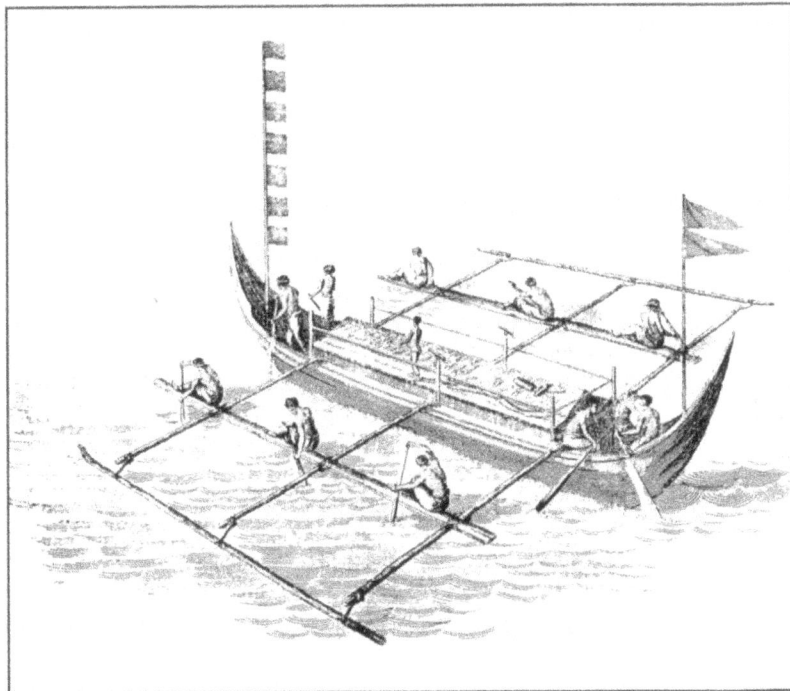

Figure 5: A Moluccan *korakora*.

Source: Forrest 1969: Plate 4 (first published 1779).

islands as well. Despite all these geographical advantages, the people of Makian were subordinate to the Sultan of Tidore, whose island had no harbour suitable for long distance vessels.[25]

Early Portuguese accounts report that Bacan first started cultivating cloves about 1500. They also mention that this sultanate had good ports and was active in trade.[26] The nature of this trade is not stipulated, but probably involved massoy bark from Onin, as well as bird of paradise skins from the Raja Empat Islands, Bird's Head and Onin (Figure 3). This would explain why it was the Sultan of Bacan who presented five Lesser Bird of Paradise skins to the Spanish expedition in the Moluccas in 1521.[27]

Curiously the Portuguese also report that Bacan along with Tidore and Ternate were net importers of foodstuffs. Rice had been supplied from at least the twelfth century.[28] In Bacan's case this was probably a luxury, presumably paid for by massoy bark and bird of paradise skin exports, as early Dutch accounts indicate that food was plentiful there.[29] In the early fifteenth century most rice imports came from Java and Sumbawa. Ternate obtained its sago from Moti, the Morotai and Rau Islands of northern Halmahera as well as Seram and Ambon.[30]

Banda Islands: nutmeg and mace

The Banda Islands were the sole suppliers of cultivated nutmeg and mace when the Portuguese arrived in eastern Indonesia in 1512. Nutmegs were cultivated on Great Banda (Lontor), Neira, Ai, Run and Rozengain (Figure 6). The women of these islands did most of the cultivation.[31]

Intermarriage with Javanese and Malay merchants established on the coasts of Great Banda and Neira was accepted by the Bandanese.[32] A Dutch source reports as many as 1,500 Javanese in the Banda Islands in 1609, with the total Bandanese population being 15,000 people.[33] Islam had been introduced some thirty years prior to the arrival of the Portuguese in 1512, but is reported to have been limited to those involved in trade, most likely individuals with Javanese and Malay connections.[34]

The Bandanese grew only nutmegs, coconuts and some fruit on their tiny islands. They were dependent on trade, mainly with the Aru and Kei Islands, for sago which was their staple food. In exchange for sago they gave coarse textiles from the Sunda Islands brought to Banda by Javanese and Malay traders. The Bandanese also obtained bird of paradise skins from the Aru Islands as well as parrot skins from a wider range of localities. These dried birds were sought by Bengali merchants in Melaka (Malacca) who supplied them to other Indians, as well as Persian and Turkish traders (see Chapter 3 below).

The spice trade: merchants, transactions and shipping

The Asian clove trade was based entirely on barter. In addition to foodstuffs, favoured imports in the Moluccas and Banda in 1512 were cloth, metalwork and porcelain. Since the possession of these items was a matter of considerable prestige, they also became incorporated into ceremonial exchanges.

The Javanese and Malays provided a number of products in exchange for cloves, nutmeg and mace. These included rice, cummin, Javanese and Cambaya cloth,[35] porcelain, copper, quicksilver, silver, vermilion and Javanese metal gongs. The Chinese provided blue Chinese porcelain dishes and cups, silver, iron, Chinese coins, ivory and beads. Other goods included iron axes, swords and knives from the Banggai Archipelago traded at Ternate, gold from northern Sulawesi and from other places coarse native cloth and bird skins.[36] The Portuguese maintained the barter trade in which cloves were exchanged for goods, whereas the Dutch introduced payment in money.

At the time of Portuguese contact, it is reported that at least eight junks a year visited Banda and the Spice Islands. A wholesale trade was carried out by the captains and supercargoes of these vessels.

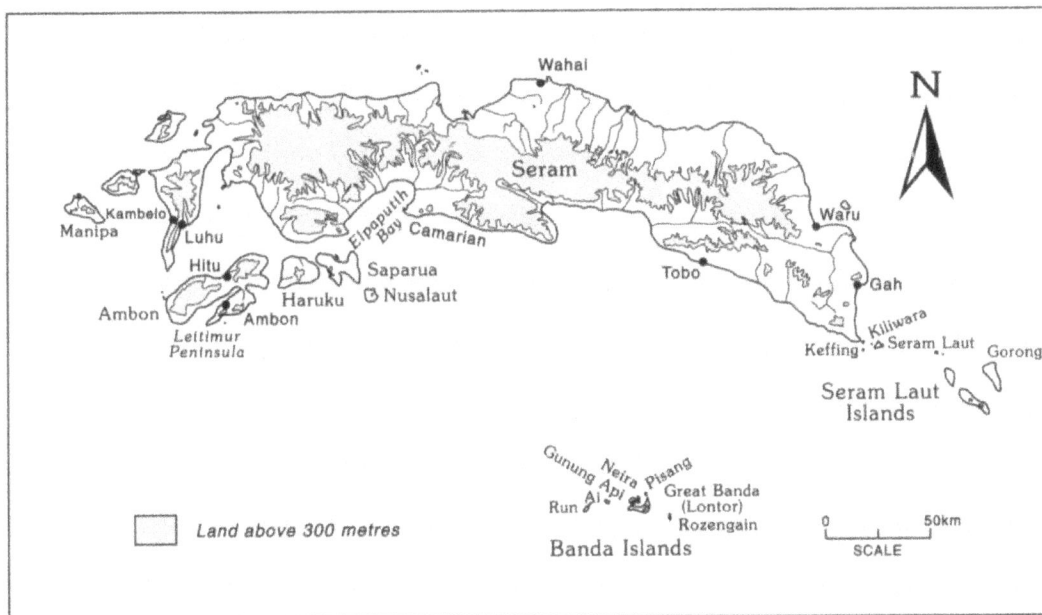

Figure 6: Seram, Banda and Seram Laut Islands.

Other merchants travelling as passengers or crew members carried out their own transactions. Large profits could be made as the prices obtained for spices in Melaka were almost ten times their cost in the Spice Islands.[37]

The wealth of the Sultan of Ternate clearly indicates that he carried out a lucrative trade with these merchants. It is likely that the patronage he gave to each ship's captain and supercargo was comparable to that later recorded as given to the Sultan of Sulu. This sultan and his prestigious *datu* (notables) usually imposed a customs duty of up to 10 percent of a cargo's value. In addition to this customs duty the sultan and his *datu* expected to receive trade goods on credit. These were often repaid in goods with highly inflated prices. This brought the overall presents and exactions received by the Sultan and his *datu* to at least 30 percent of the total value of a ship's cargo.[38] With such returns, there was no incentive for the Sultan of Sulu and his *datu*, nor presumably the Sultans of Ternate and Tidore, to contemplate the risk of shipping products to markets themselves. It was easier to let the merchants do the work and receive the material largesse they brought. By this means the sultans accumulated considerable wealth.

When the Portuguese reached Banda early in 1512 they found that this small group of islands served as the entrepôt for the spice trade in eastern Indonesia. In Banda they were able to obtain not only locally produced nutmegs and mace, but also cloves imported by Bandanese and other regional traders. The inhabitants of Ternate, Tidore, Moti, Makian and Bacan harvested the cultivated cloves growing on their islands, but left the task of exporting them to others.

The Bandanese were the only group in the Spice Islands with vessels large enough to take profitable cargoes to Java and Melaka. These boats were built in Banda for this long distance trade. Pires, a Portuguese scholar who visited Melaka in 1511–1515, reports that there was a *shahbandar* (harbourmaster) in Melaka who looked after Bandanese interests.[39]

The Kei Islanders were also known for their boat building, but they only made prau suitable for regional use. The largest vessel they built was the paddle-propelled *korakora* used in local trade and warfare.

It seems curious that the Bandanese developed long-distance craft, but had no kingdoms; whereas islands such as Ternate, Tidore and Bacan developed kingdoms, but had no long-distance merchant fleets. It has been suggested above that the quantity of presents and exactions the sultans and their notables were able to obtain, from the captain and supercargo of each vessel, played a part in discouraging them from contemplating shipping their own spices.

However there was probably another factor behind Banda's development as an entrepôt. This was the ability to sail and return from Banda via the Sunda chain to Melaka in six months, compared with a year to go to and return from the Moluccas. Such a time advantage would have encouraged the development of Banda as an entrepôt and further discouraged the Moluccan sultans from undertaking such voyages. Traders could leave Melaka in January or February, return from Banda in early July and be back in Melaka by August. If they continued on to the Moluccas, they had to leave Banda in May and wait in the Moluccas until January when suitable winds allowed them to return to Melaka. It was also possible to reach the Moluccas by way of Brunei in only 40 days. This route was less profitable than the southern route which also allowed stops in Java and the Lesser Sundas, especially Timor, for sandalwood.[40]

Local inter-island trade

Within eastern Indonesia there was also inter-island trade. Specialised goods were traded by means of local prau (*korakora*). In New Guinea pottery was produced in the Jayapura and Sentani region; at Dorey, and on Roon and Japen in Cendrawasih Bay; on Mare Island near Tidore; probably on the Misool and Waigeo Islands; at Arguni, Sekar and elsewhere in Onin; as well as in the Banda, Kei and Aru Islands; and in the Ambon, Haruku and Saparua Islands off southern Seram.[41] Shell bracelets were made in Gorong (Goram), cloth in west Seram and prau in the Kei Islands. In addition many island groups were dependent on imported food. For instance, sago, the staple of the Bandanese, was imported from the Kei and Aru Islands.

Relations between the Spice Islanders and 'New Guinea'

The Moluccan sultans appointed rajas in their domains. Four raja became renowned in the islands off the western tip of New Guinea, hence the name Raja Empat (four rajas). These rajas were resident on the four main islands of Misool, Salawati, Waigeo and Batanta (or ?Gebe).[42] The Raja Empat Islands were also referred to as the Papuan Islands. In 1602 a clear difference was made between Papua, namely the Raja Empat group, and the mainland of New Guinea.[43, 44] By 1684 stretches of coastline south of Berau Bay (MacCluer Gulf) were known respectively as Papua Onin and Papua Kowiai.

The Sultan of Bacan was aligned with Ternate and reigned over the Obi Islands, northern Seram, the Raja Empat group (the Papuan Islands) and Onin. He also had contact with Notan, the western part of the Bird's Head.[45]

Relations between the Spice Islanders and Europeans until 1599

As soon as the Portuguese captured the Malaysian port of Melaka in 1511, they despatched three ships to the fabled Spice Islands. With the assistance of Malay pilots, these Portuguese ships reached Banda in 1512 having travelled via Java and the Lesser Sundas. Two ships returned to Melaka laden with cloves and nutmegs obtained from Banda. The crew of the third vessel continued on to Ambon and the Moluccas in a local vessel after their ship was wrecked. They then returned to Melaka, except one member, Francisco Serrao, who remained on Ternate until his death in 1521.

When the crews of the first Portuguese ships to visit the Spice Islands returned to Portugal, they obtained huge profits on the cloves and nutmegs they had purchased. By acquiring them directly, they had cut out all the middlemen who would have profited each time the spices changed hands on their long route to Europe. At that time merchants returning to Melaka from the Moluccas were able to sell their cloves at an almost tenfold profit. In times of scarcity, profits of one hundred and two hundred and forty times were obtained in India and Lisbon respectively.[46] This profit margin was irresistible to the Portuguese and other European powers.

After the Portuguese captured Melaka in 1511 there was a short-term decline in the number of Javanese and other Asian traders coming to the Moluccas. This was a matter of concern to the Sultans as they were dependent on foreign traders to export their cloves and obtain goods and foodstuffs in return.

Portuguese squadrons visited the Moluccas in 1513 and 1518, but established no settlements. In 1521 two ships of Magellan's Spanish expedition stopped at Tidore for six weeks. In 1522 the Portuguese returned to establish a permanent settlement. They built a fort on Ternate with the Sultan's blessing. The Sultan expected that these new traders would interact with him in the same way as Asian traders. He did not comprehend that their intentions were to obtain a monopoly over the spice trade and proselytise Christianity.[47] His perception was that the Portuguese would assist him in his local struggle for power.[48]

Although the Bandanese village elders resisted all attempts by the Portuguese to establish a base in their islands, they did agree in 1522 to conclude a treaty with the Portuguese government. This aimed to control the inflation in nutmeg prices resulting from the trading activities of independent rather than official Portuguese traders.[49]

Soon afterwards the Spanish established friendly relations with Tidore. This led to the Portuguese making a treaty with Ternate which gave the Ternatians a higher price than they received from other traders. It became a requirement that Portuguese ships had to be filled before other traders could be supplied with cloves. This led to a competitive struggle between the Portuguese and the Spanish and their associated Moluccan protégés.

To offset these Portuguese requirements the Spanish offered producers on Tidore and elsewhere eight times as much as the Portuguese. This was not well received by the Portuguese. Unlike the Portuguese, the Spanish had lower costs in the Moluccas as they did not maintain a permanent presence.[50]

Spanish–Portuguese competition for spices in the first half of the sixteenth century sent clove prices up. Asian traders continued to come for spices and the Sultan of Ternate and his notables continued to provide a large share of their cargoes.

Attempts by Portuguese government officials to stop private trading by Asians and independent Portuguese traders were unsuccessful. The Ternatians blocked such proposals by refusing to provide the Portuguese government officials with food unless they were free to sell cloves to whomsoever they wished.[51]

Despite the presence of Europeans and the efforts of the Portuguese to impose a monopoly, the Bandanese continued to obtain spices from the Moluccas. When Ternate came under Portuguese control they obtained their cloves from Tidore. The Portuguese soon found themselves in

Plate 2: The ruins of the old Portuguese fort called Tololo on Ternate. It was built in the sixteenth century.

Photo: Courtesy of Fotobureau, Koninklijk Instituut voor de Tropen, Amsterdam.

conflict with Tidore when they tried to examine the cargoes of Bandanese ships, as part of the enforcement of their spice monopoly.

The increased prices offered by the Portuguese and Spanish resulted in more people tending wild stands and establishing cultivated stands. The high returns to be obtained from cloves encouraged their introduction to other islands. On Seram and Ambon they were planted where vessels stopped for water and provisions on their way to and from the Spice Islands. As with cloves, the increased prices for nutmegs resulted in people establishing new cultivated stands as well as collecting nuts from wild stands. Nutmegs were introduced to Gorong, Seram and other islands. There was no appreciation by producers that the market could not continue to grow and that over-production would ultimately produce a glut.

In addition relations between the Portuguese and the Moluccans were not turning out as each party had expected. The Portuguese established a number of bases (the ruins of one of their forts are shown in Plate 2). They also introduced changes to the Moluccan way of life and others arose because of their presence. Some of these changes were unacceptable to the Moluccans. This caused resentment and led to uprisings against the Portuguese. Between 1534 and 1574 there were three uprisings.

In 1534–5 the Moluccan sultans sought the assistance of four Papuan rajas to chase away the Portuguese. These were the raja of Vaigama (Waigama on Misool), Vaigue (Waigeo), Quibibi (Gebe) and Mincimbo (?Misool). Their resistance failed and the Papuan Islanders concerned were subjected to a Portuguese show of strength when the Portuguese Governor sent Joao Fogaço there in 1538. Fogaço returned to Ternate with a large quantity of food to supplement the limited quantities they had been able to obtain during the Moluccan resistance to Portuguese domination.[52]

By 1538 considerable quantities of cloves were being exported from Seram (Figure 6). The first clove trees on this island had been planted at Kambelo. The cloves produced were traded to Javanese merchants who supplied foodstuffs and cloth in return. Hitu, a Moslem trade village on Ambon, soon became the export centre. The people of Hitu and their Javanese and Bandanese allies came into conflict with the Portuguese over this clove trade in the 1550s.

In another uprising Tidore and Jailolo with Spanish assistance tried to oust the Portuguese. The Ternatian and Portuguese forces retaliated and in 1551 finally overwhelmed Jailolo. This kingdom played no further part in Moluccan affairs until 1789.

When the Portuguese murdered Sultan Hairun of Ternate in 1570, the Ternatians became determined to rid themselves of the Portuguese.

Led by the Sultan's son, Bab Ullah, and assisted by both Tidore and Bacan, the Moluccan forces overwhelmed the Portuguese who surrendered their fort on Ternate and withdrew to Ambon in 1574.[53] This victory gave Sultan Bab Ullah great prestige and consolidated his influence in the islands between Sulawesi and New Guinea.[54] Meanwhile the Portuguese concentrated their commercial activities on Ambon.[55]

Following an attack by Sultan Bab Ullah, Tidore invited the Portuguese to establish a military post on their island as the Spanish did not maintain a permanent presence. They saw this as a way of not only avoiding political and military domination by the Ternatians but also a means of becoming the centre of the clove trade. Although the Portuguese did establish a fort on Tidore in 1578, Ternate remained the main trading centre.[56]

Drake visited Ternate in 1579. He gives a glowing description of the Sultan of Ternate. The Sultan's entourage consisted of twelve guards with lances and eight or ten notables who walked behind him. The Sultan was sheltered from the sun by a canopy embossed with gold. He wore a gold cloth laplap and a pair of red shoes. On his head was a crown formed from inch-wide plaited gold rings and around his neck there was a gold chain necklace. The fingers of his left hand wore diamond, emerald, ruby and turquoise rings, and on his right hand there was another turquoise ring as well as a ring set with many diamonds. Both Drake and his crew were impressed by the Sultan's demeanour and wealth.[57] The gold, jewels and other luxuries had been obtained in return for cloves. These spices soon attracted other Europeans to the Spice Islands.

The Dutch made their first visits to Ternate and the Banda Islands in 1599. They established good relations on the basis of recognising the Portuguese as a common enemy. The Bandanese leaders sought gifts before trading began. The Dutch complied by providing gifts for the *orang kaya* (village elders) and fees for the *sjahbandar* (harbour master). Even when transactions commenced at two hired houses (Figure 7), the *orang kaya* had to be periodically regratified with tribute – knives, mirrors, kegs of gunpowder, crystal goblets and lengths of red velvet.

In Banda the Dutch sought locally produced nutmeg and mace, and cloves imported from Ambon. This was a prolonged and tedious business as it required dealing with hundreds of people, each with only minute quantities to sell. All sellers wanted also to inspect individually the range of Dutch goods. Both parties did not hesitate to defraud each other as regards quantity or quality. For instance, there were problems with decayed nutmegs and mace on the one hand, and rusted knives, broken mirrors and mildewed textiles on the other.[58] This give and take did not last for long.

Relations between the Spice Islanders and Europeans from 1600 until the 1650s

By 1600 cloves, nutmeg and mace were being overproduced, with large quantities being wasted.[59] The Dutch recognised that the surplus of supply over demand would in time produce a glut. They thus took steps to control production. The steps they took had tragic consequences for the people of the Spice Islands.

In 1602 some Bandanese elders signed a contract which gave the Dutch a trade monopoly in their islands. The Bandanese apparently signed this document because they feared reprisals if they refused. They were horrified when the Dutch began to enforce the agreement.[60] In 1609 the Dutch occupied Neira (Figure 7) and established a fort there, despite strong resistance from the Bandanese.[61]

One consequence of this monopoly was that the Bandanese no longer obtained adequate supplies of rice and sago. Dutch merchants

Figure 7: Sketch of the first Dutch trading post in the Banda Islands which was on Neira Island.
Source: Hana 1978:15 from Commelin 1646.

were unwilling to provide sufficient quantities, since they were interested only in more profitable, less bulky and non-perishable cargoes. To the dismay of the Bandanese, Javanese batik, Indian calicoes, Chinese porcelains and metalwares, etc., were not matched by the heavy velvets, woollens and other products manufactured in the Netherlands.[62]

When the Dutch captured the Portuguese forts in the Moluccas in 1605, they did not consolidate their victory by immediately establishing a settlement. On their return in 1607 they were surprised to find that a joint Spanish–Portuguese[63] fleet from Manila had recaptured one of the old Portuguese forts on Ternate. This gave the Spanish control over south and west Ternate. The Dutch then built with Ternatian help a fort (Plate 3) in east Ternate and a new Ternatian capital was established nearby. In 1608–9 Moti and Makian came under joint Dutch–Ternatian control and the Dutch established a permanent garrison on Bacan in 1609.[64]

This military presence allowed the Dutch East India Company to enforce their policy of a spice monopoly in the Moluccas. They

Plate 3: Gate of the Dutch fort Oranje in Ternate town. The fort dates from 1607.
Photo: Courtesy of Fotobureau, Koninklijk Instituut voor de Tropen, Amsterdam.

instigated a ruthless military campaign against trading vessels from other European trading countries and discouraged Asian traders.

By 1610 Luhu and Kambelo were two of many villages growing cloves on Seram (Figure 6) and clove cultivation and trade was extending eastwards on Seram to Elpaputih Bay. In the same period clove cultivation on the original five clove producing islands had dropped dramatically and by 1623 they were no longer significant suppliers of cloves.[65] This was of no concern to the Dutch as the quantity of cloves grown on Ambon and Seram was double world consumption. Ambon's harvest alone was sufficient to meet the demands of Europe and Asia.

In 1622 the Dutch realised that there was a clove glut and made greater efforts to enforce their trade monopoly. The Dutch trade monopoly brought hardship and despair to the Spice Islands. The rice or sago provided by the Dutch East India Company in exchange for cloves was expensive because Dutch transportation costs were far higher than those of Asian traders. To overcome their food shortages Ambonese and other Moluccans began to harvest local sago palms and fetch sago from distant islands, as well as grow their own rice. This did not please the Dutch East India Company. Any groups caught importing food supplies were punished by the Company, usually by cutting down their spice trees. This led to insurrections, first on Banda and then on Ambon.[66]

The food shortages induced by the Dutch trade monopoly led to fights and population dispersals. Men also left their settlements to avoid military service to their rulers. Conditions were so bad that infanticide was widely practised. By 1620 Bacan's population was a fraction of its former size. This was partly because of epidemics, but also because its menfolk wished to avoid military service. In 1618 Bacan could barely raise enough men to crew two *korakora* with 100–200 men per vessel, whereas formerly this island could raise 6,000 able-bodied men.[67]

The inadequate supplies of food provided by the Dutch resulted in famine. In return for a regular supply of rice the Run Islanders in the Banda Islands (Figure 6) agreed in 1617 that the British could settle on their island.[68] At the beginning of the seventeenth century the British were still endeavouring to participate in the spice trade. They had a number of factories on the shores of India, but had yet to establish fortified trading enclaves. The presence of the British on Run upset the Dutch. Efforts to enforce their supremacy in the Banda Islands resulted in the horrifying conquest of the islands by Jan Pieterszoon Coen in 1621. W.A. Hanna in his book on Banda describes the events that took place as follows:

Coen ... sent out party after party, not only on Lonthor (Great Banda) but on the other islands as well, to burn and raze the almost deserted villages and to harass the refugees wherever they may have taken shelter. Those who did surrender were frequently herded together with those who had been captured. They were then loaded onto troop transports to be shipped off to Batavia, where they were sold as slaves. One consignment totalled 883 persons (287 men, 356 women, and 240 children, of whom 176 died on shipboard). Others died by the hundreds and thousands of exposure, starvation, and disease. When forced onto the heights from which there was no escape, many leaped to their death from the sheer sea cliffs. Coen eventually shortened the period of retribution by ordering a blockade which effectively interrupted the import of vital foodstuffs and prevented the escape by sea of those who still had strength enough to seek sanctuary in distant islands. Some few Bandanese reached Ceram (Seram), Kai (Kei), and Aru, but of the original population of perhaps fifteen thousand persons, no more than a thousand seem to have survived within the archipelago, mainly on Pulau Run and Pulau Ai, where the English presence provided not active protection but some meagre deterrence to atrocities. Another 530 homesick, indigent, and troublesome Bandanese were eventually shipped back from Batavia, where thirteen of their *orang kaya* had been executed when implicated along with certain Javanese in an alleged conspiracy to kill Coen, burn the city, and flee to Banda.[69]

Asian trade with the Moluccas collapsed when Banda was captured and destroyed by the Dutch in 1621. In 1623 the Dutch captured and massacred the staff working in a British factory on Ambon. This resulted in British and other merchants withdrawing from the Spice Islands to Makassar. There the British obtained considerable quantities of cloves, often smuggled from Seram, which they traded in India to their commercial advantage.[70] Some Asian traders continued to operate in clove producing areas not actively patrolled by the Dutch East India Company, but this was a risky undertaking for both traders and suppliers.

Although there were huge stocks, the price of cloves continued to rise until 1632. After this date the price went into continuous decline.[71] In order to reduce production the Dutch East India Company began to destroy clove and nutmeg trees in 1647. They decided to restrict clove cultivation to Ambon and the nearby small islands of Haruku, Saparua and Nusalaut (Figure 6). Nutmegs were only permitted to be grown on the European managed plantations staffed by slaves established in the Banda Islands. The overproduction of nutmeg and mace was no longer a problem as the European planters had to follow Company policy.[72] The cultivation of cloves and nutmeg outside permitted areas was forbidden, and any spice trees found were destroyed and their owners punished.[73] These restrictions gave rise to resentment and an uprising occurred when the Dutch intervened in the ascent of Sultan Mandar Syah to the throne of Ternate in 1648. The Dutch East India Company not only suppressed this uprising, but decreed in contracts with Ternate and Bacan drawn up in 1653, that cloves could not be cultivated in their territories.[74] Clove growing was prohibited in Tidore in 1657. It is ironic that after 150 years of European contact the descendants of the people who had domesticated cloves were prohibited from growing them.

In 1652 a treaty granted the Dutch East India Company the right to destroy as many clove trees as it thought desirable. Nutmeg plantations and sago palms were also felled during these operations and as a result many islands became depopulated. For instance, in 1654 Buru was devastated and parts of Seram were abandoned.[75]

By these ruthless methods the Dutch East India Company obtained a monopoly over the spice trade, but at great expense to the people of the region and to themselves. One of the Company expenses arising from this monopoly was compensation payments to the Sultans for their loss of income. These were paid as annual subsidies, the so-called *recognitiepenningen*.[76] The destruction by the Dutch of large numbers of established clove and nutmeg stands may also have reduced the surviving genetic diversity of these crops.[77]

The failure of the Dutch spice monopoly and the growing China trade

The Dutch East India Company did not make a profit on its Spice Island ventures. Their expenditure on forts and monopoly enforcement activities, such as extirpation, was greater than their profits. By 1650 their policies and activities had transformed the formerly prosperous Moluccas into an economic wilderness and instability quickly became the norm.[78] Raiding and retribution became common until Dutch steam-powered ships made an impact in the 1850s.

When Asian and local trade in eastern Indonesia collapsed after the destruction of the Banda Islands in 1621, Asian and local traders in the Moluccas relocated to Magindanao on Mindanao Island. This port lay midway between the Spanish based at Manila and the Dutch at Ternate.[79]

Ternatians subsequently became involved in the development of Sulu either as slaves or freemen from the mid 1700s until the late 1800s. Sulu depended on a supply of slaves to maintain the workforce collecting trepang, mother-of-pearl and other products for the China trade. Captives were obtained from the Philippines as well as from

Sulawesi and the Moluccas.[80] Alfred Russel Wallace reports a Sulu raid as far south as the Aru Islands in 1857, see Chapter 9 below.

The Bandanese who had escaped to east Seram after the events of 1621 became prominent in obtaining commodities for despatch to China. Initially massoy, bird of paradise skins, pearls and damar were the main commodities obtained. After 1720 trepang became important as well.

In 1750 cloves gave only a profit of three times their cost price. This was a big difference from the huge profits obtained by the first Portuguese ships. Faced with diminishing returns, the Dutch East India Company tried to diversify its interests, while still maintaining a monopoly over the spice trade.[81] The Company was not successful in either endeavour and by the 1770s it faced bankruptcy.

Despite declining profits, the British and French were keen to break the Dutch spice monopoly. Captain Thomas Forrest in 1774–76 made a voyage through the northern Moluccas and to west New Guinea on behalf of the British East India Company. He was looking for opportunities for British settlement in the area and a means of breaking the Dutch East India Company's monopoly on the spice trade.[82]

Some years earlier in 1770–72 several hundred young plants had been collected from remote locations in the northern Moluccas by a French expedition. Sufficient plants survived to allow clove plantations to be established in Mauritius and Réunion. From these islands they were subsequently introduced to Zanzibar in 1818 and Madagascar in 1820. In about 1800 whilst the East Indies were under British control during the Napoleonic wars clove and nutmeg plants from the Moluccas were also established in Malaya and Sumatra.[83]

In 1788 the Governor-General of the Dutch East Indies reported that 2.7 million kilograms of cloves were already stored at Batavia and that it was expected that 750,000 kilograms would be stored at Ambon by the end of the year. He understood there were 1.5 million kilograms stored in Holland and annual sales were only 250,000 kilograms as demand was diminishing rather than increasing.[84]

Spice planting in the Moluccas remained restricted until 1824 and the required delivery of cloves was not finally abolished until 1864.[85] By then the clove market was dominated by non-Indonesian centres. Today the islands of Zanzibar and Pemba off the coast of Africa are the world's largest producers of cloves and most nutmeg and mace comes from Sumatra in western Indonesia and Granada in the West Indies.[86] This trade relocation brings to an end the remarkable story of the rise and decline of the spice trade in the Spice Islands.

New roles for Tidore and Ternate

In 1660 the Sultan of Tidore signed a treaty with the Dutch East India Company which led to him playing a new role as suzerain of 'Papua'. As time passed, and as the Dutch perceived a growing interest in New Guinea by other metropolitan powers, they increased the area designated to be under his control. The role that the Sultan of Tidore played in the political history of this region is the main topic of Chapter 6.

During the colonial period Ternate became economically important as a major plume export centre. In their search for plumes hunters and traders from Ternate and Tidore travelled vast distances within New Guinea. One of the longest documented trips is described in Chapter 11. The next chapter is concerned with when and how plumes were first traded to Southeast Asia.

Notes

1. Collins and Voorhoeve 1981.
2. Giorgio Buccellati, an archaeologist working in Terqa, a site on the middle Euphrates in Syria, claims to have recovered a handful of cloves from a partly overturned jar in a middle-class house dated to the period 1750–1600 BC (Buccellati 1983a: 54; 1983b: 19). Palaeobotanists have not confirmed that this find consists of cloves, but instead view his discovery as some unrelated species (Spriggs 1998).
3. Innes Miller 1969: 50–1.
4. About 4% of the essential oils found in both nutmeg and mace consists of the poison myristicin, so they are toxic at high levels and must be used sparingly (Cobley 1976: 245).
5. Ambary 1980:1.
6. Ellen 1979: Figure 4.
7. Muller (1990a: 18). Further information is needed on yields as an early Portuguese account claims that as much as 70 pounds (35 kilograms) was obtained from each tree after a favourable monsoon (Villiers 1990:95). Once this is clarified and the density of clove trees per hectare is known, it should be possible to assess the reliability of early harvest estimates in terms of the area of suitable clove growing land in these islands amended by observations as to the area under cultivation at the time.
8. Ellen 1979: 54.
9. Meilink-Roelofsz 1962: 98, 155.
10. Wit 1976: 216.
11. Wright 1958: 57.
12. Cobley 1976: 242–3: Wit 1976: 216–7.
13. Muller (1990a: 18)
14. Muller 1990a: 93.
15. Wright 1958: 57.
16. Cobley 1976: 244–5; Smith 1976: 316–7.
17. Wright 1958:19–20; Galis 1953–4: 37.

18. van Fraassen 1981: 2.

19. Ellen 1979: 67.

20. Although the most fertile soils in Indonesia, outside Java and Bali, occur in the Minahasa region of northern Sulawesi (Babcock 1990: 189), the agricultural potential of this area did not give rise to a powerful kingdom. At the time of European contact the area was under the influence of Ternate.

21. Meilink-Roelofsz 1962: 97.

22. Kolff 1840: 4.

23. Forrest 1969: 23.

24. Horridge 1981: 5.

25. Meilink-Roelofsz 1962: 97–8.

26. Meilink-Roelofsz 1962: 98.

27. Stresemann 1954: 263.

28. Ellen 1979: 54.

29. Meilink-Roelofsz 1962: 352, footnote 78.

30. Villiers 1990: 94.

31. Meilink-Roelofsz 1962: 161.

32. Ellen 1979: 67.

33. Villiers 1990: 87.

34. Meilink-Roelofsz 1962: 96–7.

35. From the Gulf of Cambay, Gujarat, India.

36. Meilink-Roelofsz 1962: 99; Ellen 1979: 56–7.

37. Meilink-Roelofsz 1962: 83–4.

38. Warren 1981: 6–7. By comparison merchants had to pay 20 to 30 percent on the value of their cargo as duty (gifts and formal charges) in Canton, but in Melaka it was only 3 to 6 percent (Curtin 1984: 130).

39. Meilink-Roelofsz 1962: 96.

40. Villiers 1981: 733; Villiers 1990: 93. The obsidian from West New Britain in Papua New Guinea found in Sabah was probably traded via the so-called Brunei route (see Chapter 3).

41. Ellen 1979: 53: Ellen and Glover 1974; Schurig 1930; Solheim and Ap 1977; Solheim and Mansoben 1977; Spriggs and Miller 1979.

42. The passage between Gebe and the small island of Fau (Figure 1) was considered to be one of the best and safest anchorages in the Indonesian archipelago. It was frequently visited by whalers and ships using the eastern passage to China in order to obtain water and wood (Earl 1853:66; Kops 1852: 305). In the mid 1850s whalers visited Doreri Bay (Figure 3) once a year (Wallace 1862a: 155). Wahai on the north coast of Seram (Figure 6) was also visited by American and English whalers (Earl 1853: 56).

43. The first European to see New Guinea was Dom Jorge de Meneses, the Portuguese Governor-elect of the Moluccas in 1526. Driven eastwards from Halmahera during a voyage from Melaka to Ternate he sheltered in the Bird's Head area. He learnt that the Moluccans called these islands 'Ilhas dos Papuas'. This was confirmed in 1529, when a Spaniard, Alvaro de Saavedra, reports that the Moluccans called the people of New Guinea Papuas because they are black and have frizzled

hair. He also mentions that the same name has been adopted by the Portuguese (Whittaker et al 1975: 183–4).

44. Early navigators were amazed by the similarity between the people of this large island and those of the Guinea coast of West Africa and began to call the island New Guinea. This officially dates back to when De Retes landed at the mouth of the Mamberamo River in 1545 and claimed the land for Spain naming it Nueva Guinea (Whittaker et al 1975: 186–7).

45. Galis 1953–4: 9: Miklouho-Maclay 1982: 439.

46. Villiers 1990: 93.

47. van Fraassen 1981: 3.

48. Meilink-Roelofsz 1962: 154.

49. Meilink-Roelofsz 1962: 161.

50. van Fraassen 1981: 3–4; Meilink-Roelofsz 1962: 154–5.

51. Meilink-Roelofsz 1962: 155–7.

52. Galis 1953-4: 9.

53. van Fraassen 1981: 4.

54. As soon as the Portuguese were driven out of Ternate in 1574, the Bandanese were once again able to obtain their supplies directly from Ternate and the islands under its influence (Meilink-Roelofsz 1962: 162).

55. Meilink-Roelofsz 1962: 160: Ellen 1979: 59.

56. van Fraassen 1981: 4.

57. Drake 1966: 91.

58. Hanna 1978: 14.

59. Ellen 1979: 67.

60. Hanna 1978: 19.

61. Meilink-Roelofsz 1962: 184.

62. Hanna 1978: 19.

63. The treaty of Zargossa (1529) officially ended Portuguese–Spanish conflict in the Moluccas, but problems continued until 1546. It was not until Portugal became part of the Spanish empire in 1580 that the Spanish and Portuguese collaborated in the Spice Islands (Meilink-Roelofsz 1962: 155). They were finally ousted from the Spice Islands by the Dutch in 1660.

64. van Fraassen 1981: 10-11; Meilink-Roelofsz 1962: 183–4.

65. Ellen 1979: 58–60.

66. Meilink-Roelofsz 1962: 215; Ellen 1979: 65–6.

67. Meilink-Roelofsz 1962: 216–7.

68. Meilink-Roelofsz 1962: 201.

69. Hanna 1978: 54–5.

70. Meilink-Roelofsz 1962: 219–221; Ellen 1979: 65; Curtin 1984: 155.

71. Chaudhuri 1965: 169.

72. Wright 1958: 1.

73. Ellen 1979: 66; Ellen 1987: 42: Meilink-Roelofsz 1962: 218–220.

74. van Fraassen 1981: 11–12.

75. Ellen 1979: 66; 1987: 42.

76. van Fraassen 1981: 11–12.

77. Wit 1976: 216.
78. Ellen 1979: 66.
79. Laarhoven 1990: 165–6,180.
80. Warren 1990.
81. Ellen 1979: 66.
82. Forrest 1969: van Fraassen 1981: 16–17.
83. Wit 1976: 216–7: Wright 1958: 48–9.
84. Wright 1958: 22.
85. Ellen 1979: 67
86. Cobley 1976: 241; Wit 1976: 216–7.

3

The plume trade: the demands of Asian traders and the first birds of paradise to reach Europe

Introduction

Plumes rather than spices appear to be the main product sought by the first specialist Asian traders. When the demand for plumes declined, spices became the most important product. The continued availability of trade plumes during the spice trade cycle attracted European interest. In time this gave rise to a demand for bird of paradise skins by natural history collectors as well as by fashion conscious women during the European plume boom.

Birds of paradise

New Guinea is famous for its variety of spectacular birds. Some eight per cent of the world's bird species are found there,[1] including some of the most beautiful, the birds of paradise (*Paradisaeidae*). No other group of birds has their diversity and splendour of plumage. Some birds of paradise have seasonal filamentous nuptial plumes which are brightly coloured and open on display into fans of colour (Plates 1 and 4). Others have wire-like accessory plumes that extend from the tail, head, back or shoulders. Many species feature brilliant metallic hues, whilst others are distinctive by their extremely long tail feathers.

Thirty-eight of the known forty-two species of birds of paradise live in New Guinea and on its offshore islands (Figure 8). Two of these 38 species, the Magnificent Riflebird and Trumpet Manucode, also occur in Australia. Only four species are found beyond New Guinea and its immediate offshore islands. Of these the Paradise and Queen Victoria's Riflebirds are found in Australia and the Wallace's Standard Wing and the Paradise or Silky Crow in the Moluccas. Birds of paradise do not occur in the Admiralty Islands, Bismarck Archipelago or the Solomon Islands.

The great English naturalist Alfred Russel Wallace observed that New Guinea had a greater proportion of beautiful birds than the rest of

Plate 4: The Lesser Bird of Paradise.
Photo: Courtesy of William S. Peckover.

49

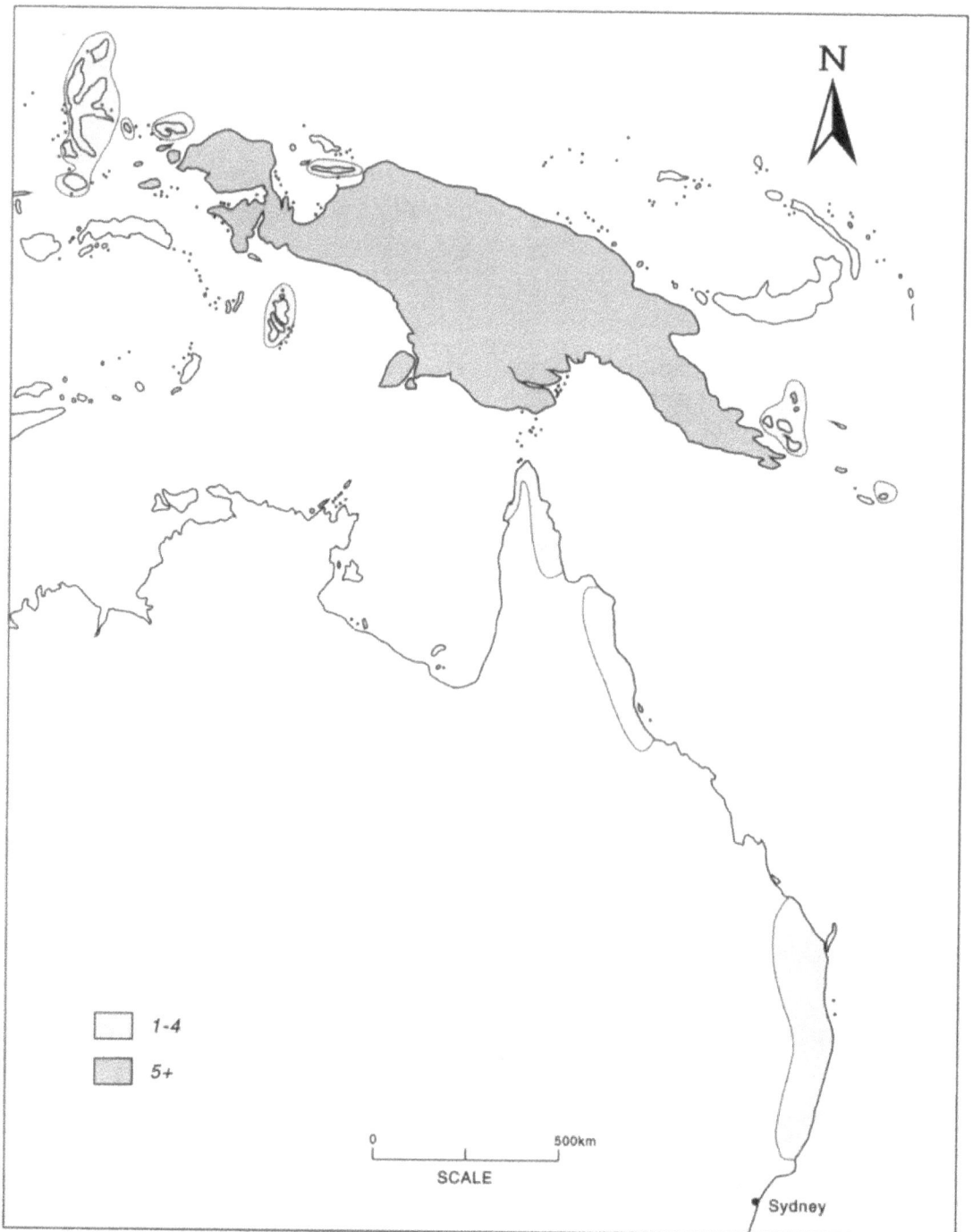

Figure 8: The distribution of bird of paradise species.

Source: Based on Cooper and Forshaw 1977.

the world.[2] He was also so impressed by the birds of paradise that he subtitled his account of eight years' travel in the Malay Archipelago (now Indonesia) from 1854–1862 as travels in the land of the orangutan and the bird of paradise.

The Asian plume trade

Many bird of paradise species have splendid plumes which quickly arouse human admiration and desire. My thesis is that leaders in island communities to the west of New Guinea have long known about these plumes.

Tracking such trade is difficult as plumes do not survive in the ground to be found in archaeological sites. Instead, the story about the plumes trade is initially dependent on the appearance of illustrated plumes/feathers on prehistoric artifacts and then in due course on their mention in historical records.

Some indication as to when the plume trade may have commenced can be based on the appearance of other introductions to Southeast Asia from New Guinea. While substantial trade connections existed in New Guinea by 5,000 years ago, less is known for this period in western Indonesia.

The distribution of certain ceremonial valuables, namely stone mortars and pestles[3] and stemmed obsidian artifacts,[4] indicates that substantial trade connections existed in New Guinea by 5,000 years ago (Figure 9). The obsidian (volcanic glass) artifacts were made from obsidian sources from Lou Island off southern Manus and on the Willaumez and Hoskins peninsulas of West New Britain.[5]

Less than 15 mortars and pestles have been found in West Papua, whereas some 2,000 come the region encompassing mainland Papua New Guinea, New Britain, New Ireland and the island of Milne Bay. As mortars and pestles are found in areas suitable for taro agriculture it is likely that these artifacts were used to make ceremonial puddings comparable to those made in historical times by some communities in northern Papua New Guinea and offshore islands.[6]

There are stylistic similarities in the stone mortar and pestle varieties found in the highlands, also on the shores of the former Sepik-Ramu inland sea, the Madang-Morobe coastline and West New Britain. It is unlikely that these stylistic similarities shared between widely spaced regions arose from independent invention. Rather they indicate the presence of extensive exchange networks. These have allowed ideas and products, such as obsidian and crops, to be exchanged by the social contacts that linked these regions.

It may be significant in terms of an early plume trade that bird pestle and mortar varieties tend to have distributions that link coastal and highlands areas.[7] This pattern is repeated again in the historical records on plume hunting when collectors sought exotic species.

The highest density of bird pestles, with wings folded against their body, extends from the East Sepik-Madang coast up into the western part of the central highlands of PNG whereas most bird mortars with wing features occur from the coastal areas of Vitiaz Strait up into the Eastern Highlands. The other pattern is for isolated finds of bird pestles, with raised wings, to occur along river valleys and their tributaries into the highlands; see Figure 56 in Chapter 14 for illustrated examples.

Isolated raised wing finds have been made in the Lae-Wampar area of the Middle Markam River in Morobe Province, Aikora on the upper Gira River in Oro Province and two finds associated with the Fly River in Western Province; one from Wonia in the Trans Fly and the other from Ningerum on an upper tributary of the Fly River. It is hard to explain the sole distribution of these pestles without seeking some explanation that relates to birds and inland access via major river systems.[8]

The initial domestication of bananas occurred in New Guinea and by about 4,000 years ago they had been dispersed westwards as far as Pakistan. A similar time frame seems the case for sugarcane with its

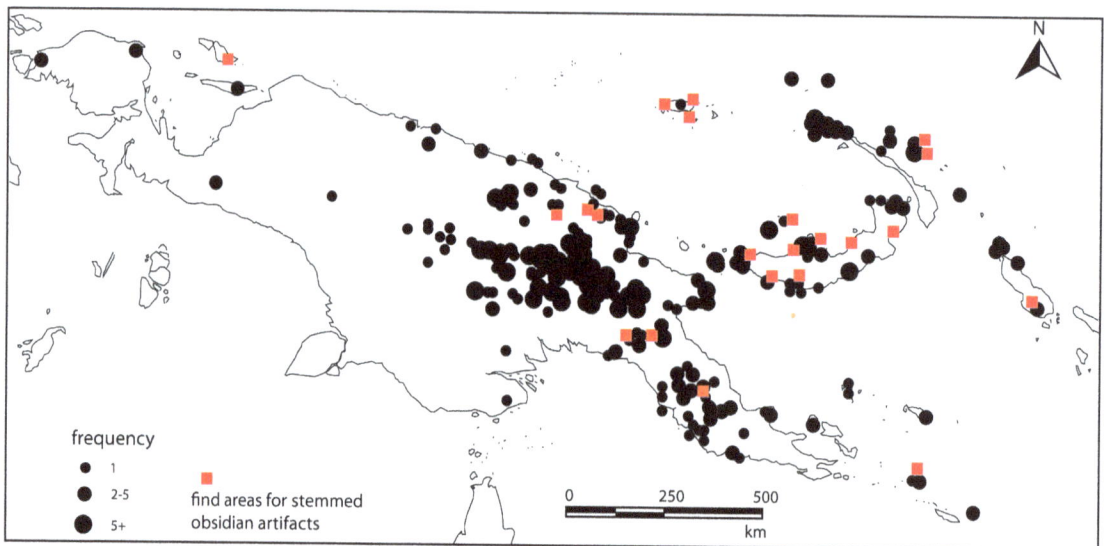

Figure 9: Distrbution of stone mortars and pestles and stemmed obsidian artefacts in New Guinea and nearby islands.

Sources: Based on Swadling database.

initial domestication in New Guinea and then a subsequent down-the-line westward dispersal to Southeast Asia and beyond.

Other New Guinea products were also being traded westwards. Some of the obsidian (volcanic glass) excavated from 3,000 to 2,000 year old deposits in the Bukit Tengkorak rock shelter in Sabah (Borneo) comes from near Talasea on the Willaumez Peninsula in West New Britain Province, Papua New Guinea,[9] a distance of more than 3,000 kilometres.

There is no doubt that attractive birds and their plumes have long been valued in Asia. The earliest record is of peacocks from the Indian subcontinent and Sri Lanka being introduced to Greece via Persia and Turkey by 3,000 years ago.[10]

Chinese chronicles dating from over 2,000 years ago indicate that in China colourful bird feathers, cinnamon and scented woods, ivory, pearls and turtle shell were the main luxury imports.[14] As feathers quickly decay in the ground we cannot expect to find direct evidence of their prehistoric use. However, indirect evidence of such use does survive as illustrations on artifacts from this period which have withstood the ravages of time. These artifacts are described in due course below.

The desire to accumulate rare and beautiful possessions in Southeast Asia increased during the period 2,500 to 2,000 years ago as autonomous villages located on the floodplains developed into centralised chiefdoms, and subsequently into small states. This profound change gave rise to an intensification of agriculture and production as well as ceremonial activities. The accumulation of rare and beautiful possessions became not an end in itself, but a means of demonstrating status. The possession of such goods, which were scarce because of the time required to manufacture or obtain them, ensured their owners respect in these new chiefdoms. Rare feathers became symbolic of high status. The best illustrated case of this transition in mainland Southeast Asia is the culture of the Dong Son warrior-aristocrats of North Vietnam. Their artwork has survived on drums and other artifacts and depicts a high use of feathers. Ranking behaviour in Southeast Asia was further encouraged by the increasing population size of settlements and the growing complexity of long-distance trade networks, especially the stimulation of the new products and novel ideas introduced by the expansion of Indian and Chinese civilization.[15]

These new developments are also reflected in outer Southeast Asia. Just before 2,000 years ago there was an almost simultaneous appearance of metal and glass artefacts (Figure 10) in island Southeast Asia as far as New Guinea. Some bronze artifacts from this period have a specific distribution in this region. These are the Heger type 1 kettle drums and other bronze artifacts with Dong Son motifs. They occur in the island arc extending from Sumatra, Java and the Lesser Sundas to New Guinea (Figure 11). This trade route has a long antiquity and clearly commenced before written records began. It is proposed here that these artifacts were imported by specialist traders seeking feather and other forest products in outer Southeast Asia. The presentation of these exotic bronze valuables to leaders of important local communities would have assisted in establishing alliances ensuring the traders safe passage and assistance in acquiring the products they sought.

Drawings of people wearing feather headdresses commonly occur on the oldest bronze drums recovered in Southeast Asia, including eastern Indonesia. Boats and their occupants are frequently depicted. Most of the warriors and crews of the boats shown on these drums wear

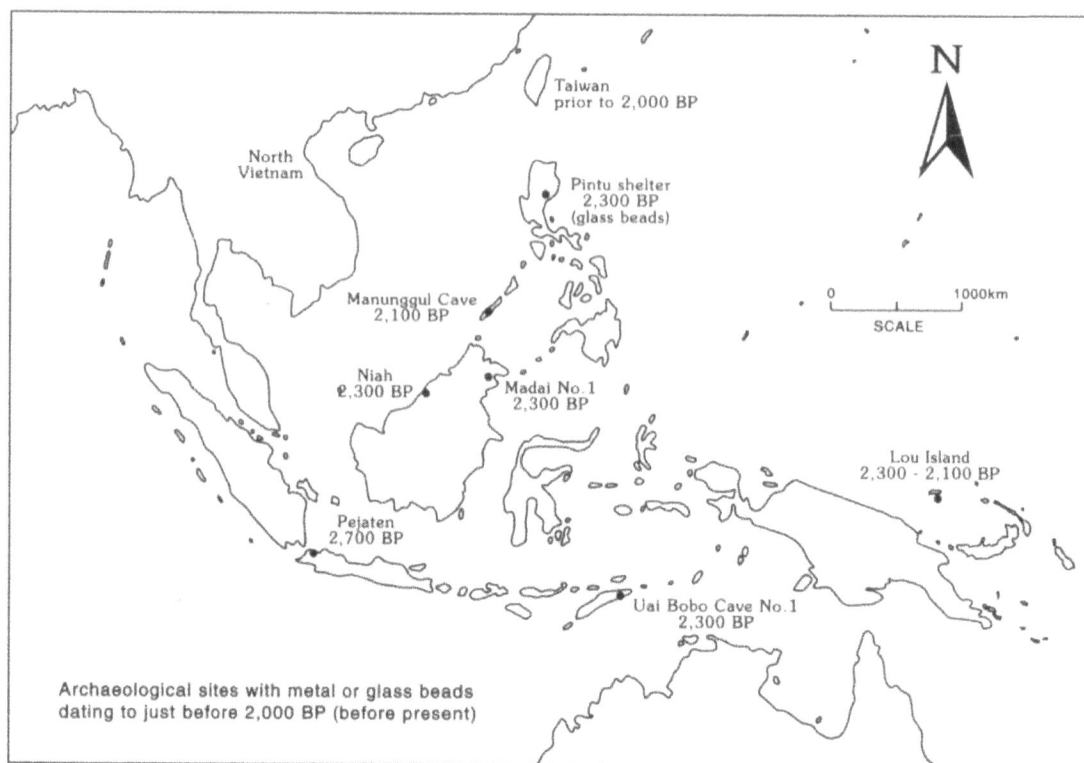

Figure 10: There was a simultaneous introduction in archaeological terms of metal and glass beads from Southeast Asia as far as New Guinea just before 2,000 years ago.

Source: Based on Spriggs 1989.

feather headdresses (Figure 12). In addition the boats generally have bird-head prows and tail-feather sterns.[16] Plumed headdresses also occur on other artifacts. One of the most striking is a ceremonial axe found on Roti Island in eastern Indonesia. The circlets at the perimeter of the headdress shown on this axe could be interpreted to represent the green feathered discs of King Birds of Paradise (Figure 13).

Other decorations on the bronze kettle drums found in outer Southeast Asia indicate that the makers of these drums had links with both China and India. One panel of a drum from Sangeang Island, near Sumbawa east of Bali, shows a raised-floor dwelling with a saddle-roof. Inside this building are people who appear to be in costumes worn during the Chinese Han dynasty (221 BC to 220 AD). Another

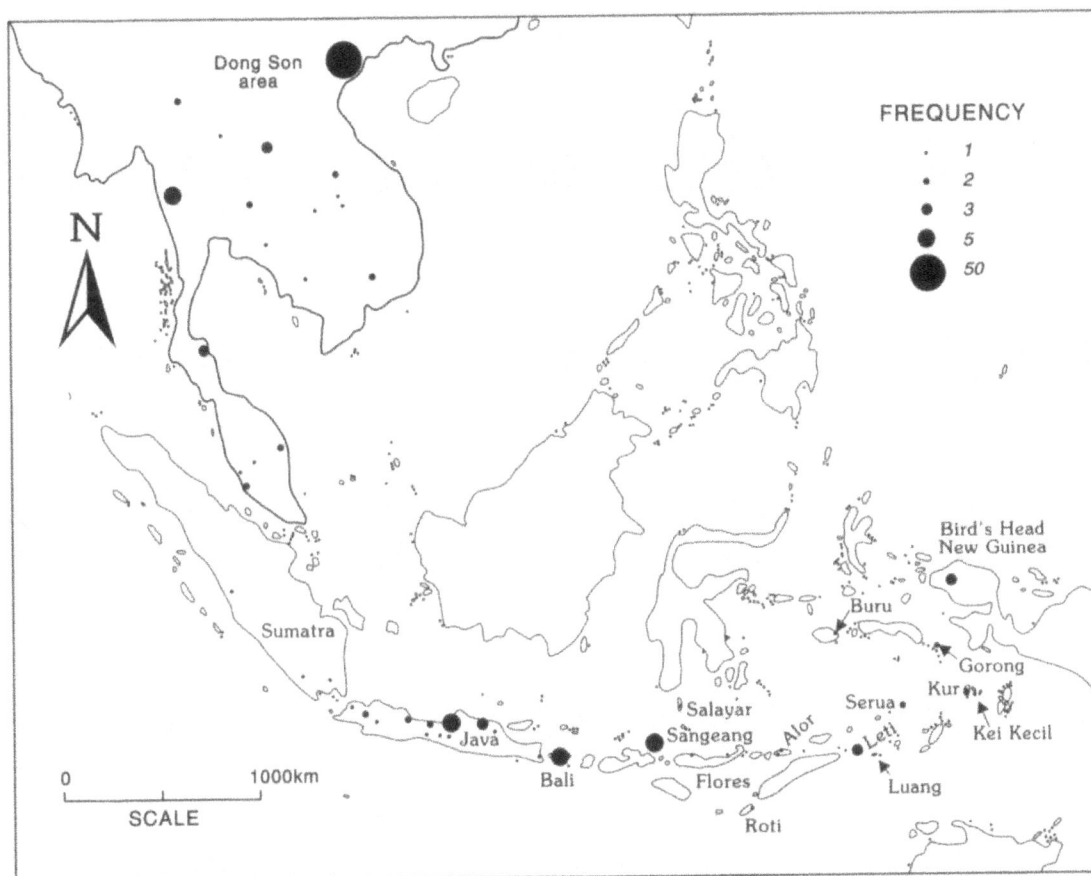

Figure 11: The schematic distribution of early bronze kettle drums (Heger type I) from the Asian mainland to New Guinea.

Source: Based on Bellwood 1978a; Kempers 1988; Spriggs and Miller 1988.

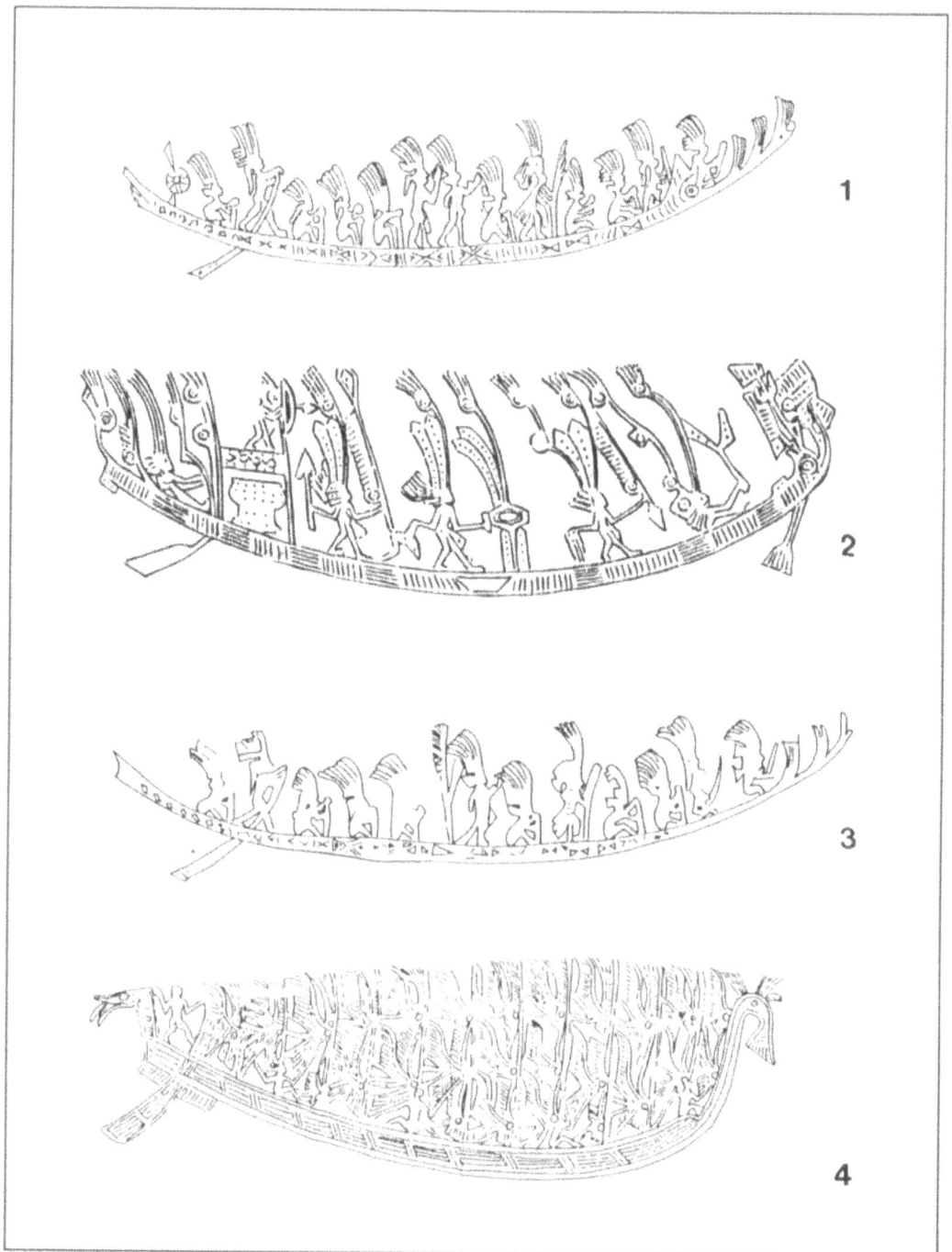

Figure 12: Feathers dominate the attire of the warriors and crew of boats depicted on Dong Son bronze kettle drums. The boats are also decorated with plumes. These illustrations are from drums from the following locations:

1. Yunnan or northwest Vietnam.

2. Ngoc Lu, Vietnam

3. U'bong, northwest Thailand.

4. Sangeang Island, Sumbawa, eastern Indonesia.

Sources: 1-3 from Goloubew 1929; 4 from van Heekeren 1958.

panel of the same drum shows two men in costumes from northwest India; one is sitting astride a horse whilst the other stands in front holding a spear and what may be a mace.[17] Two other remarkable drums are clearly imports from the west. The Salayar drum depicts elephants and peacocks (Plate 5), and a Kei Islands drum not only has elephants, but tigers as well. The natural distribution of elephants, tigers and peacocks does not extend to eastern Indonesia.

The bronze kettle drums found in eastern Indonesia date after the first appearance of these artifacts on the Asian mainland. The motifs depicted on eastern Indonesian Heger type I drums are less naturalistic and more stylised than the oldest drums found on the mainland (see Figures 12 and 14). The available information suggests that those found in eastern Indonesia were made in North Vietnam before 250 AD.[18]

Three large bronze tops from Heger type 1 drums[19] have been found near Aimura Lake in the interior of the Bird's Head of West Papua; see Plate 6. Bronze from one of these drums has been tested. Its composition matches Dong Son alloys rather than later products.[20] Further support for such an antiquity for bronze artifacts in New Guinea comes from the dating of a small tabular bronze artifact found in 2,300 to 2,100 year old deposits on Lou Island in the Manus Province of Papua New Guinea.[21]

The bronze artifacts found in New Guinea with the exception of the small artifact from Manus and one from the Waropen coast of Cendrawasih Bay[22] are restricted to the Bird's Head and Jayapura region. These two areas of western New Guinea have mountainous country where many bird of paradise species are found close to the coast. This is also why the Bird's Head and Jayapura region became important centres for exporting birds of paradise during the European plume boom.

Some of Bird's Head and Lake Sentani bronze finds have Dong Son affinities, namely the decorated ceremonial axe from Ase Island in Lake Sentani and the three drum tops from Aimura Lake on the Bird's Head. Certain finds have parallels elsewhere in Indonesia, whereas others are unique,[23] presumably because they have been produced locally by smelting down disused and broken bronze artifacts. Traders may have smelted down their broken implements in order to make replacements or other needed items while waiting for favourable trade winds to allow them to return westwards. In this respect the undated Jembakaki site on Batanta Island, off the Bird's Head,[24] deserves an archaeological investigation to determine the age of the bronze moulds and remnant raw materials found there.

The green, blue and brown glass bracelets found in the burials excavated at Gilimanuk, an early Metal Age site on Bali,[25] are very

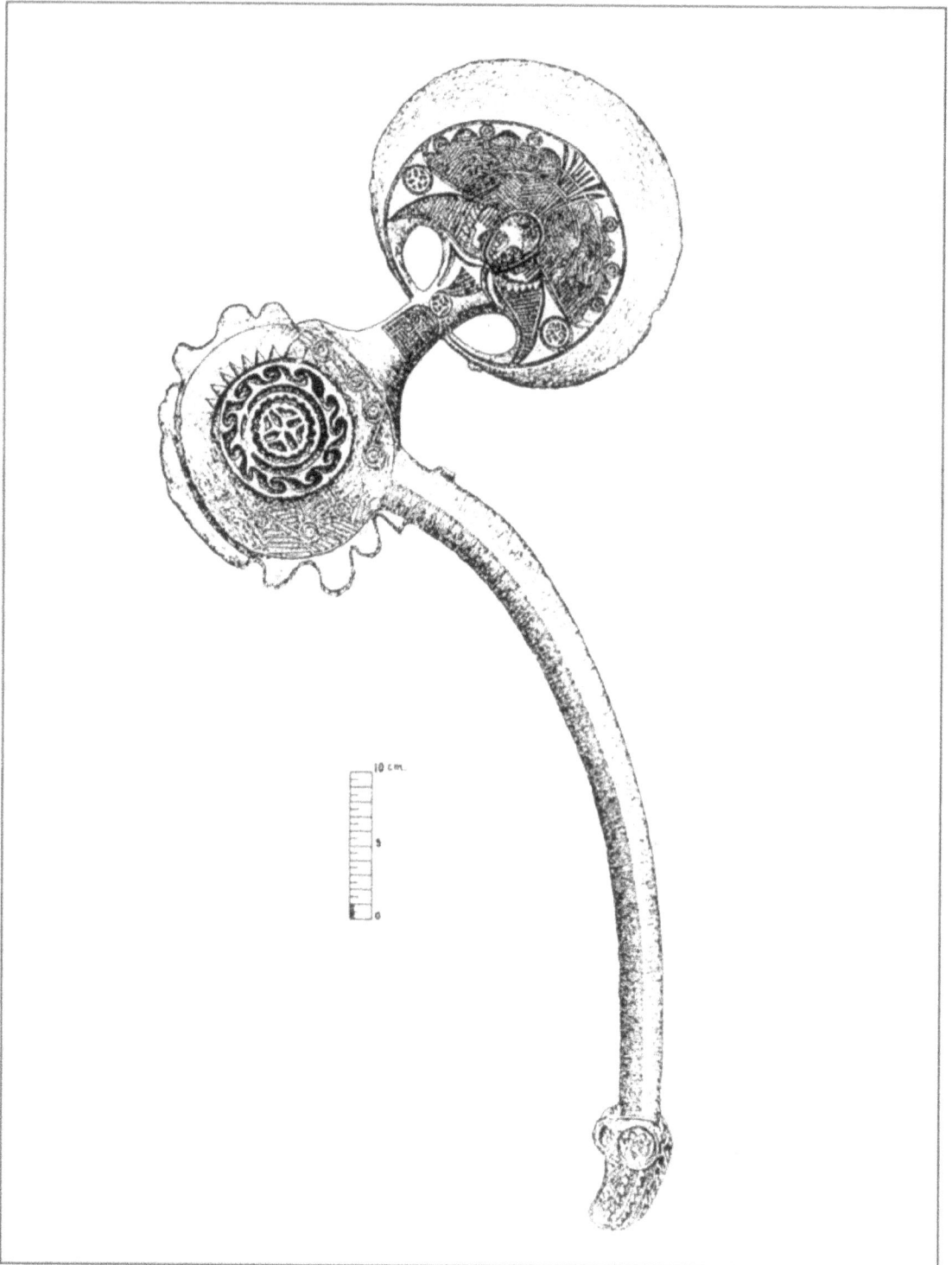

Figure 13: One of the three ceremonial bronze axes from Roti Island in eastern Indonesia with Dong Son motifs showing a human figure wearing a feather headdress.

Source: Van Heekeren 1958.

similar to those used as traditional valuables by the people of Biak Island in Cendrawasih Bay, and on the north coast of New Guinea from Lake Sentani to east of Vanimo. Moreover, George Agogino[26] reports finding bronze artifacts in association with glass beads in two archaeological sites on the north side of Lake Sentani (see Chapter 11 below).

Metal using did not continue in New Guinea, presumably because contact ceased once the Southeast Asian interest in plumes abated. By 250 AD the demise of the culture of the Dong Son warrior-aristocrats and other related groups was occurring as the Chinese state of Wu expanded southeastwards into their territory. The resulting decline of these groups led to a downturn in the Asian plume trade.

In addition, by about 300 AD Indians had not only introduced Hindu-Buddhist cosmological ideas which linked god, ruler and realm, but also a new range of exotic goods. By adopting this cosmological world view, overlords came to claim divine qualities and began to vie with each other for status, followers and supplies of the exotic goods currently in vogue.[27] Forest products such as spices and aromatic barks and woods were now more in demand than plumes.

By 300 AD cloves, nutmegs and sandalwood[28] had replaced feathers as the main outer Southeast Asian trade items sought in Asia and the Middle East. Consequently the Spice Islands and the Onin area of the New Guinea mainland became the new centres supplying these markets, as they were respectively the sources of cloves and nutmegs and massoy bark.

As mentioned above spices appear to have been traded to India and the Middle East long before they were in demand in China. Cloves, nutmegs and sandalwood from eastern Indonesia were probably first traded as subsidiary products of the plume trade. When the demand for these products grew they became more important than plumes. Just as there was a change in products sought from eastern Indonesia, there was also a change in the products supplied in return. For instance, large drums were now out of fashion in Asia and were no longer presented to important leaders in eastern Indonesia.

Although the Asian trade in plumes declined, it did not cease. In Southeast Asia feathers continued to be sought as status items. For instance, they were supplied to the Indonesian kingdom of Srivijaya which existed from the seventh to eleventh centuries and controlled the Straits of Melaka. In the eighth century it is recorded that the Maharaja of Srivijaya, Sri Indrawarman, carried bird of paradise plumes to the Chinese Emperor as tribute.[29]

Plate 5: The Salayar drum from eastern Indonesia depicts elephants and peacocks, which do not actually occur there. Height of drum 92 cm.

Photo: Courtesy of Museum of Far Eastern Antiquities, Stockholm.

Figure 14: Most of the feathers depicted on bronze drums in eastern Indonesia have more stylised versions of feather headdresses than those on the oldest Heger type I drums found on the Asian mainland. Shown here is the Fam drum from the Kei Islands. Part A shows the schematic section of the drum whereas B shows the detail of one of the feather panels.
Source: Spriggs and Miller 1988. Reproduction courtesy of Indo-Pacific Prehistory Association.

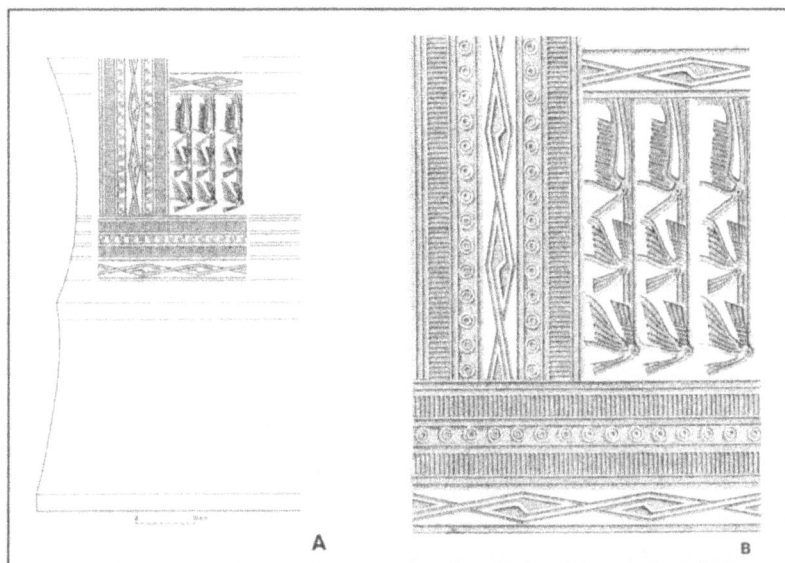

Plate 6: One of the bronze drum tops found at Aimura Lake on the Bird's Head of West Papua. Photo by J.E. Elmberg in article by K.W. Galis (1964).
Source: Reproduction courtesy of Bijdragen tot de Taal-, Land-en Volkenkunde.

The sphere of influence and dominance of trade claimed by the Indonesian kingdom of Majapahit in 1365 is given in an ancient poem, known as the *Negarakertagama*, dating from that year and written in old Javanese by the poet Prapanca. The islands and areas mentioned in eastern Indonesia include Timur (Timor), Seran (Seram), Wandan (Banda), Ambwan (Ambon), Moloko (Moluccas) and Wwanin (Onin) in western New Guinea.[30] At that time it is likely that the massoy producing area of Onin was already a subjected territory of one of the Moluccan sultans, namely the Sultan of Bacan.

Early Portuguese records report that bird of paradise skins were being traded to Persia and Turkey in 1500 AD. The inhabitants of the Kei and Aru Islands in eastern Indonesia brought sago, as well as bird of paradise and parrot skins, to Banda. The bird skins were bartered by the Bandanese for textiles. From Banda they went to Melaka where they were acquired by Bengali merchants, who in turn traded them to Turks and Persians[31] who used them to decorate the headdresses of important officials. In 1546 the plumes worn by the Janissaries of the Ottoman Empire, an elite corps of Turkish troops guarding the Sultan, were described by Belon. His description best fits plumes from birds of paradise.[32] In 1772 M.P. Sonnerat observed that the Dutch also participated in this trade. He reports that they supplied bird of paradise skins to the rich inhabitants of Persia, Surat (in the Cambay Gulf area of Gujarat, India) and the Indies. In these areas the plumes were used to decorate turbans and helmets as well as horses.[33] Beliefs combining the beauty of the birds of paradise with special sacred powers were and remain common in Asia. When the Spaniards reached Tidore in 1521 they learnt that birds of paradise were highly prized by the Moluccans, because the plumes made their men invulnerable and invincible in battle.[34]

It was probably through the activities of Bengali merchants that bird of paradise plumes first reached Nepal. The flank plumes of the Greater Bird of Paradise are a symbol of royalty in Nepal. They are only worn by the King and his senior officials (Plates 7–9). The supply of Greater Bird of Paradise skins declined when hunting became illegal throughout New Guinea in 1931. This was recognised as a real problem prior to the coronation of King Mahendra of Nepal in 1957. It was overcome when the United States of America made a state gift to Nepal of Greater Bird of Paradise skins which had been confiscated by customs officials and handed over to the American Museum of Natural History.[35]

On Bali, bird of paradise skins are still used during certain funerary rites. For the Balinese people feathers represent the transformation of the departing soul as a bird and its departure for paradise.[36]

Plate 7: Bird of Paradise plumes were treasured like jewels in Nepal and only worn by the King and his senior officials. Here the American Ambassador is presenting a member of his staff to the King in the late 1940s. Both the King and his Prime Minister wear crowns adorned with the interwoven flank plumes of the Greater Bird of Paradise. These plumes reached Nepal by a long established trade network which only declined when hunting became illegal throughout Dutch New Guinea in 1931.

Plate 8: Commanding General Kaiser Shamsher Jang Bahadur Rana wears four or more interwoven flank plumes of the Greater Bird of Paradise. At the same ceremony, see Plate 6, the King's crown is adorned with at least six plumes.
Photos 7-8 by Volkmar Wentzel, copyright National Geographic.

Plate 9: King Mahendra of Nepal wearing four or more interwoven flank plumes of the Greater Bird of Paradise at his coronation in 1957. Photo by E. Thomas Gilliard, courtesy of the American Museum of Natural History.

Plate 7

Plate 8

Plate 9

The first birds of paradise to reach Europe were trade skins

Birds of paradise were unknown in Europe until the sixteenth century. In 1522 bird of paradise skins were carried back to the King of Spain by Magellan's circumglobal expedition. Although the Portuguese had reached the Spice Islands in 1512 there is no report that their crews took bird of paradise skins to Europe. The crew of the 1512 expedition were probably too elated with the rewards they would reap from being the first Europeans to discover the location of the fabled Spice Islands to be concerned with attractive feathers, no matter how splendid they were.

The crew of the *Victoria*, the only one of Magellan's ships to survive the first circumnavigation of the world, took five skins of the Lesser Bird of Paradise back to Europe in 1522. These were obtained from the Sultan of Bacan in the Moluccas in November 1521.[37] The crew reported that the Moluccans called the birds *bolon diuata* (birds of God) and claimed that they came from an earthly paradise.[38] This was the beginning of wild speculations and misconceptions about birds of paradise in Europe.

Since trade skins had no feet or wings the Portuguese called them *Passaros de Sol* meaning birds of the sun, whereas the later arriving Dutch gave them the Latin name *Avis paradiseus* or paradise bird. It was initially assumed by many Europeans, since none had seen any live specimens, that the birds lived in the air, always turning towards the sun and never landing on earth until they died, for they had neither feet nor wings. These scholarly speculations caught the imagination of the general public. As a result birds of paradise were painted by artists, sung about by poets and became the topic of edifying contemplation by theologians.

By 1600 ships' crews were bringing Greater, Lesser and King Birds of Paradise skins to Europe. In 1605 Carolus Clusius of Leiden University was able to describe these three species from skins obtained in Europe. This trade did not involve large numbers of skins. For instance, in 1652 it was said that it was as rare to see a shop open on Christmas Day, as to see birds of paradise. They were still rare in England in 1670, but less so in Holland and Germany where collections were being established.[39]

The confusion about the feet and wings arose because of the way New Guineans preserve birds of paradise. As mentioned above, the entire bird is skinned in order to accentuate the beautiful plumes. During this process the legs, skull and coarse wing feathers are usually removed during skinning.[40] Ash is applied to the inside of the skin and a stick is inserted through the mouth into the body cavity. The skin is then smoke dried. As the skin dries it collapses onto the stick which protrudes beyond the bill. Mounted in this way it is easy to incorporate the bird skin into a headdress. When not being worn the skins are usually stored in sealed bamboo tubes or palm leaf wrappings in the rafters so that fireplace smoke protects them from insects.

By 1605 bird of paradise skins with feet had been brought to Europe. The first illustration of a bird of paradise with feet was published in Europe in 1655. Some theologians ignored all this and persisted with the theory that the birds did not have feet. It took time to convert these stubborn doubters. Such views only ceased in 1660 when sufficient numbers of specimens with feet could be viewed in collections.

European scholars continued to conjecture wildly about birds of paradise, unaware that Dutch scholars based in the Dutch East Indies had learnt much about the birds by interviewing Indonesian traders. In the late 1670s many details about birds of paradise were published by Johann Otto Helwig who worked as a doctor and naturalist in Batavia. In 1682 Herbert de Jager, Chief Merchant with the East Indies Company in Batavia, published a description of how birds of paradise were hunted and how their skins were prepared.[41]

The history of how the different species of birds of paradise reached Europe provides an indication of their availability as trade products. The Greater, Lesser, King and Twelve-wired Birds of Paradise were the first to gain the attention of naturalists in Europe. All four were painted from trade skins by Jacob Hoefnagel in 1610.[42]

The great Dutch naturalist George Eberhard Rumphius illustrated three birds of paradise while he lived on Ambon from 1653–1702. These illustrations were later found and published by François Valentijn in 1726. The three species drawn by Rumphius from trade skins before he went blind in 1670 were the Greater, Lesser and King Birds of Paradise. Rumphius also described trade skins of the Arfak Astrapia, Black Sicklebill, Glossy-mantled Manucode and Twelve-wired Bird of Paradise.[43]

Other trade skins were illustrated or painted in Europe from 1734–1782. The Black Sicklebill was illustrated by Albertus Seba in 1734 in his *Thesaurus* and the Flame Bowerbird was painted by George Edwards in 1750. In 1774 the Magnificent Bird of Paradise, the Black Sicklebill (both sexes), the Crinkle-collared Manucode and Western Parotia were illustrated by Le Comte de Buffon in the 25th edition of the *Planches enluminées*. Some years later, in 1782, the Magnificent Riflebird was illustrated by François Levaillant.[44]

A trade skin of the Red Bird of Paradise was among the birds of paradise obtained as battle spoils from The Hague in 1795 and subsequently deposited in the Paris Museum.[45] It was probably also in Paris in 1850 that Edward Wilson purchased a trade skin of the Wilson's Bird of Paradise.[46]

All the brilliantly coloured species found in the area where Asian traders were active (Figure 15) were known to Europeans from Asian trade skins by 1851; see Tables 2 and 3 and Figures 16 and 17. The only birds of paradise which occur in this area and were not obtained by Europeans as trade skins are relatively drab and would not have been sought for their plumes. These species are the Long-tailed Paradigalla, Wallace's Standard Wing, the Buff-tailed Sicklebill, Palebilled Sicklebill, Trumpet Manucode and Jobi Manucode. Judging from the history of their availability as trade skins it would seem that the Greater, Lesser, King and Twelve-wired Birds of Paradise were the main species sought by Asian plume traders.

The Greater Bird of Paradise was the first bird of paradise described scientifically; see Table 2. This was done from a trade skin in 1758. The King and the Flame Bowerbird were also described in that year. Ironically the first bird of paradise to reach Europe, in 1522, the Lesser Bird of Paradise, was not described scientifically until 1809.

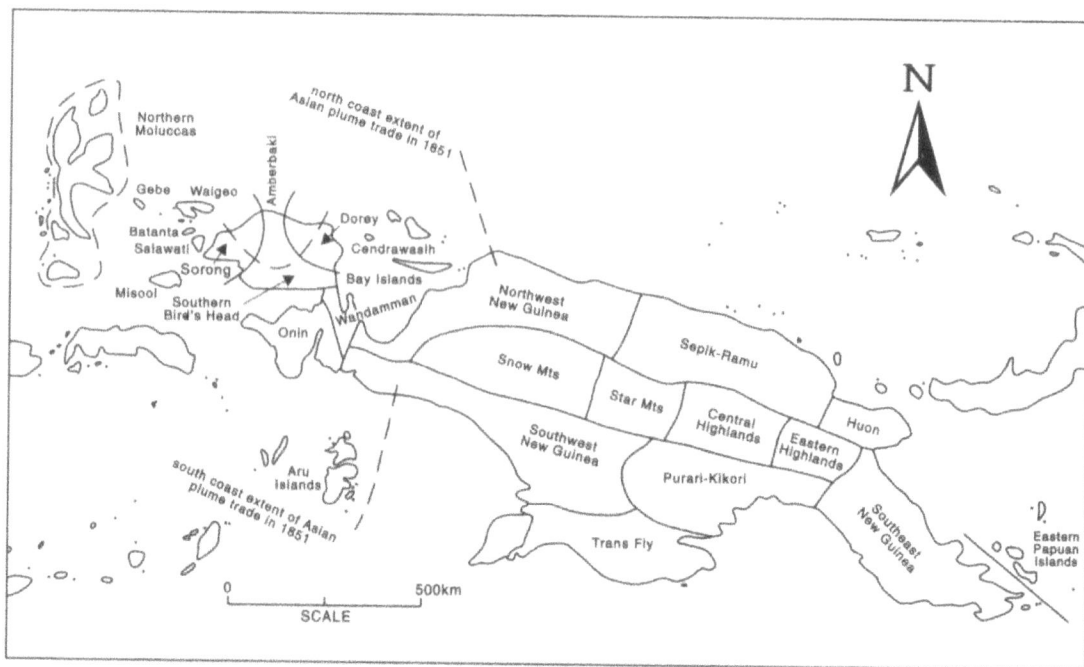

Figure 15: The geographic areas used in Table 3. The hinterlands of Sorong, Amberbaki and Dorey are shown to overlap as it is not known how far plumes were traded in these areas.

Source: Based on Beehler et al 1986: 4.

Table 2: Birds of paradise and bowerbirds identified from trade skins by 1851. They are grouped by distinguishing features.

Birds of Paradise	
iridescent throat, upper breast and crown plumes	
Magnificent Riflebird	*Ptiloris magnificus* (Vieillot, 1819)
flag-tipped wires from tufts on each side of nape	
Western Parotia	*Parotia sefilata* (Pennant, 1781)
erectile cape of feathers springing from nape	
Superb Bird of Paradise	*Lophorina superba* (Pennant, 1781)
filamentous display plumes	
Greater Bird of Paradise	*Paradisaea apoda* (Linnaeus, 1758)
Lesser Bird of Paradise	*Paradisaea minor* (Shaw, 1809)
Red Bird of Paradise	*Paradisaea rubra* (Daudin,1800)
thread-like tail wires	
King Bird of Paradise	*Cicinnurus regus* (Linnaeus, 1758)
Magnificent Bird of Paradise	*Cicinnurus magnificus* (Pennant, 1781)
Twelve-wired Bird of Paradise	*Seleucidis melanoleuca* (Daudin, 1800)
Wilson's Bird of Paradise	*Cicinnurus respublica* (Bonaparte, 1850)
tail long and step-like	
Arfak Astrapia	*Astrapia nigra* (Gmelin, 1788)
tail long and graduated	
Black Sicklebill	*Epimachus fastuosus* (Hermann, 1783)
plumage black glossed purple to green	
Crinkle-collared Manucode	*Manucodia chalybata* (Pennant, 1781)
Glossy-mantled Manucode	*Manucodia atra* (Lesson, 1830)
crow-like	
Paradise or Silky Crow	*Lycocorax pyrrhopterus* (Bonaparte, 1851)
Bowerbirds	
Flame Bowerbird	*Sericulus aureus* (Linnaeus, 1758)

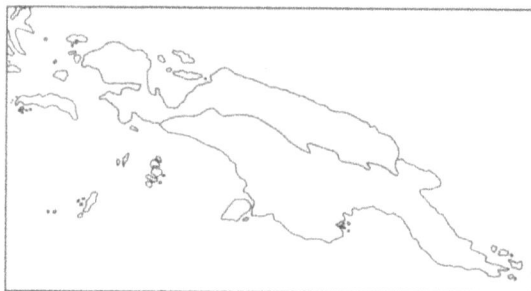

Lesser Bird of Paradise
Known in Europe in 1521
given scientific name in 1809

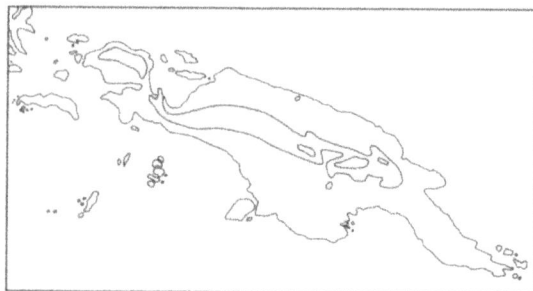

Black Sicklebill
Known in Ambon before1700 / Known in Europe by 1734
given scientific name in 1783

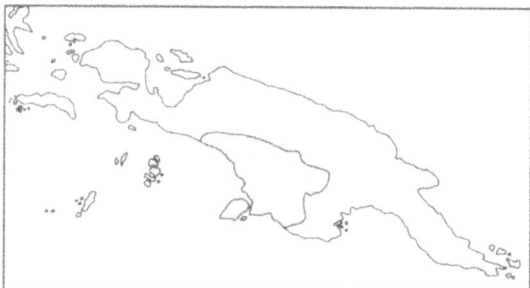

Greater Bird of Paradise
Known in Europe by 1600
given scientific name in 1758

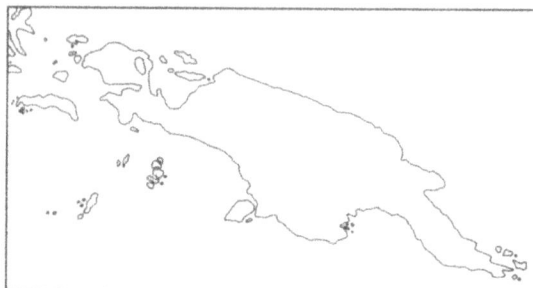

Arfak Astrapia
Known in Ambon before 1700
given scientific name in 1788

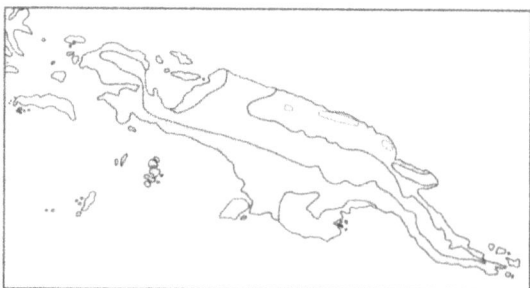

King Bird of Paradise
Known in Europe by 1600
given scientific name in 1758

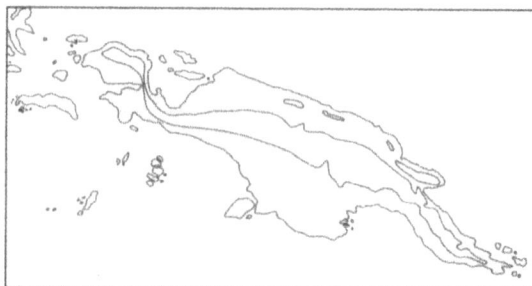

Glossy-mantled Manucode
Known in Ambon before 1700
given scientific name in 1830

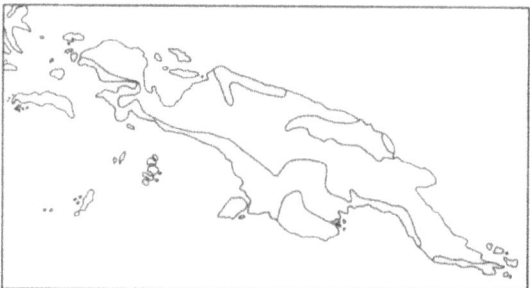

Twelve-wired Bird of Paradise
Known in Europe by 1610
given scientific name in 1800

Figure 16: The natural distribution of birds of paradise which become known to Europeans from trade skins by 1700.

Source: Based on Coates 1990; Cooper and Forshaw 1977.

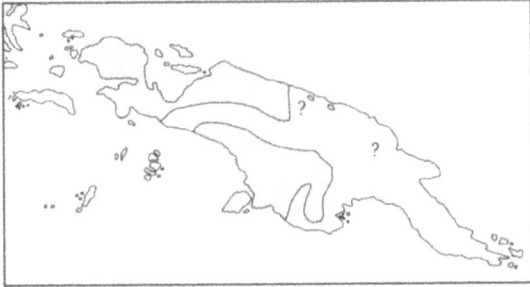

Flame Bowerbird
Known in Europe by 1750
given scientific name in 1758

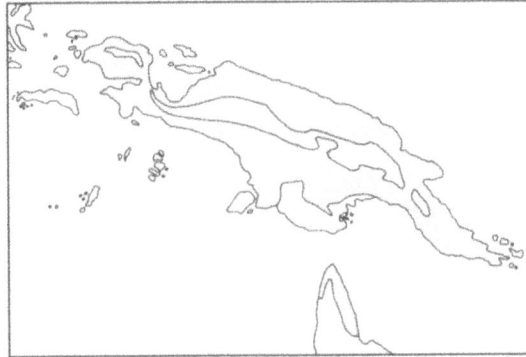

Crinkle-collared Manucode
Known in Europe by 1774
given scientific name in 1781

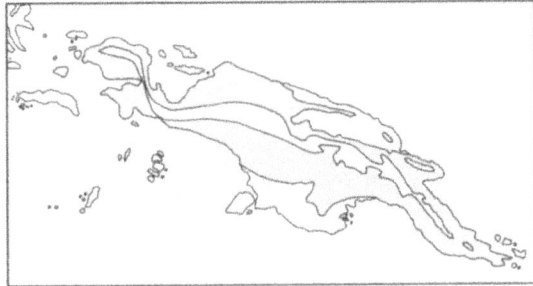

Magnificent Bird of Paradise
Known in Europe by 1774
given scientific name in 1781

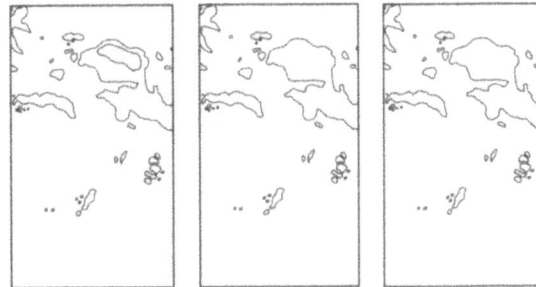

Superb Bird of Paradise
given scientific name in 1781

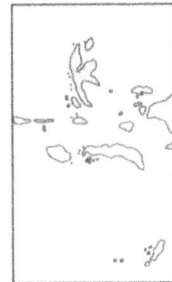

Magnificent Riflebird
Known in Europe by 1782
given scientific name in 1819

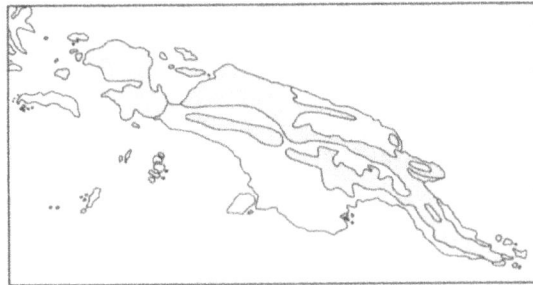

A   B   C

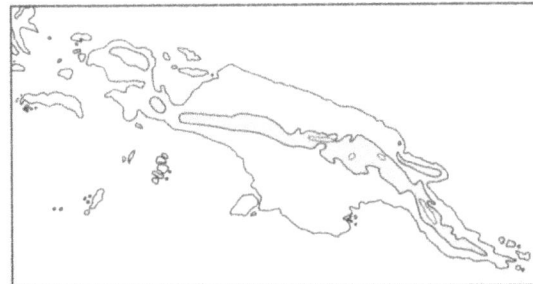

A: Western Parotia
Known in Europe by 1774
given scientific name in 1781
B: Red Bird of Paradise
Known in Europe by 1795
given scientific name in 1800
C: Wilson's Bird of Paradise
given scientific name in 1850
D: Paradise Crow
given scientific name in 1851

D

Figure 17: The natural distribution of birds of paradise which became known to Europeans from trade skins between 1700 and 1851.

Source: Based on Coates 1990; Cooper and Forshaw 1977.

EXTENT OF PLUME TRADE IN 1851

Geographic areas (Figure 5)

Geographic area columns (left to right):
Australia · Eastern Papuan Islands · Southeast New Guinea · Huon · Purari-Kikori · Trans-Fly · Eastern Highlands · Central Highlands · Star Mountains · Snow Mountains · Southwest New Guinea · Sepik-Ramu · Northwest New Guinea · Cendrawasih Bay Islands · Wandammen · Onin · Southern Bird's Head · Dorey hinterland · Amberbaki hinterland · Sorong hinterland · Aru Islands · Misool Island · Salawati Island · Batanta Island · Waigeo Island · Gebe Island · Northern Moluccas

SPECIES KNOWN TO EUROPEANS FROM ASIAN TRADE SKINS BY 1851

#	Species
1	Arfak Astrapia
2	Black Sicklebill
3	Crinkle-collared Manucode
4	Glossy-mantled Manucode
5	Greater Bird of Paradise
6	King Bird of Paradise
7	Lesser Bird of Paradise
8	Magnificent Bird of Paradise
9	Magnificent Riflebird
10	Paradise Crow
11	Red Bird of Paradise
12	Superb Bird of Paradise
13	Twelve-wired Bird of Paradise
14	Western Parotia
15	Wilson's Bird of Paradise

SPECIES REPORTED AFTER 1851

#	Species
16	Blue Bird of Paradise
17	Brown Sicklebill
18	Buff-tailed Sicklebill
19	Carola's Parotia
20	Crested Bird of Paradise
21	Curl-crested Manucode
22	Emperor Bird of Paradise
23	Goldie's Bird of Paradise
24	Huon Astrapia
25	Jobi Manucode
26	King of Saxony Bird of Paradise
27	Lawes' Parotia
28	Long-tailed Paradigalla
29	Lona's Bird of Paradise
30	Macgregor's Bird of Paradise
31	Pale-billed Sicklebill
32	Paradise Riflebird
33	Queen Victoria's Riflebird
34	Raggiana Bird of Paradise
35	Ribbon-tailed Astrapia
36	Short-tailed Paradigalla
37	Splendid Astrapia
38	Stephanie's Astrapia
39	Trumpet Manucode
40	Wallace's Standard Wing
41	Wahnes' Parotia
42	Yellow-breasted Bird of Paradise

Legend:
● species known to Europeans from trade skins by 1851
★ species reported after 1851
? presence uncertain

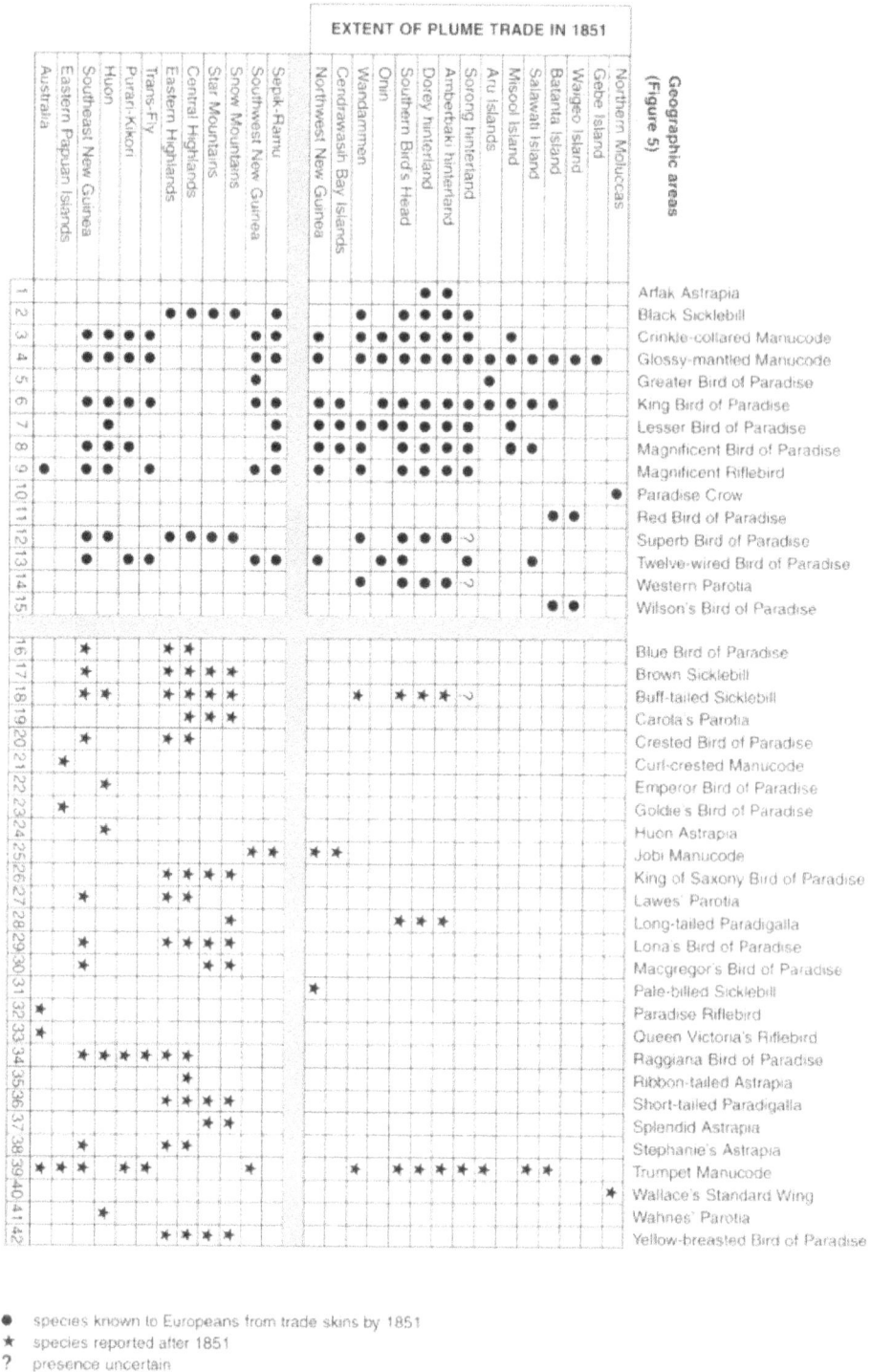

The Buff-tailed Sicklebill, Jobi Manucode, Long-tailed Paradigalla, Pale-billed Sicklebill, Trumpet Manucode and Wallace's Standard Wing were the only species from the areas supplying the Asian plume trade in 1851 unknown to Europeans. These six species are all relatively drab and would not have been keenly sought by plume traders.

Table 3: Distribution of birds of paradise showing species known to Europeans before and after 1851.

Notes

1. Ian Craven (personal communication 1989) obtained this figure by calculating what percentage the 725 known bird species found in New Guinea (Beehler et al 1986) were of the total world population of just over 8,600 (Scott 1989).

2. Wallace 1879: 425–6.

3. Torrence and Swadling 2008; Swadling and Hide 2005; Swadling 2005; Swadling, Weissner and Tumu 2008; Swadling 2013; Swadling 2016; Swadling 2017.

4. Araho, Torrence and White 2002.

5. Torrence and Swadling 2008; Torrence, Swadling, Kononenko, Ambrose, Rath and Glascock 2009.

6. Swadling 1981, 1986.

7. Swadling 2005; Swadling, Weissner and Tumu 2008.

8. There is no reason to doubt the find locations for the Lae-Wampar, Aikora, Wonia and Ningerum bird pestles. The Lae-Wampar (Lae-womba) lived about 20 km upstream from the mouth of the Markham River. It was the first reported by Holtker 1951: 240–241. The Aikora bird pestle was found by gold prospectors in an alluvial terrace of the Aikora River, an upper tributary of the Gira River. It was first reported by Barton 1908. The Wonia bird pestle was collected by C.W. Marshall in 1927 (Specht 1988) and the Ningerum find was collected by the late Herman Mandui of the Papua New Guinea National Museum.

9. Denham 2011.

10. Denham 2011.

11. Bellwood 1989: 149.

12. Unlike peacocks birds of paradise are not easily bred. This means that a regular supply of bird of paradise plumes could not be obtained by breeding, instead the plumes had to be imported. Live birds of paradise were traded, but these were rare and expensive. In 1862 Alfred Russel Wallace paid £100 for two live male specimens of the Lesser Bird of Paradise in Singapore. One bird died after a year, the other survived for two years at the Zoological Gardens in London (Wallace 1986: 557; Preswich 1945).

13. Doughty 1975: 7.

14. Wang 1958: 4.

15. Glover 1990; Higham 1989.

16. Bellwood 1978a: 185.

17. Bellwood 1978a: 222.

18. Kempers 1988; Spriggs and Miller 1988; Spennemann 1985a, 1987.

19. Bellwood 1978a: 222.

20. Elmberg 1968: 125–6.

21. Ambrose 1988.

22. Bintarti 1985.

23. Soejono 1963.

24. Galis 1964.

25. Soejono 1979: 194.

26. Agogino 1979; Agogino 1986.

27. Higham 1989: 357, 361.
28. The sandalwood came from Timor. The best quality white sandalwood supplied to western Indonesia and India still comes from this island.
29. Bachtiar 1963: 55.
30. Rouffaer 1915 cited by Galis 1953–4: 6; O'Hare 1986.
31. Meilink-Roelofsz 1962: 65.
32. Doughty 1975: 10.
33. Sonnerat 1781: 42.
34. Stresemann 1954: 263.
35. Gilliard and Riboud 1957: 146; LeCroy 1985: Ripley 1950.
36. Anthony Forge personal communication 1984.
37. Stresemann 1954: 263.
38. Stresemann 1954: 264; Cooper and Forshaw 1977: 17.
39. Stresemann 1954: 272: Trend 1988: 30.
40. Wallace (1857: 412) reports that the flesh of the Greater Bird of Paradise is dry, tasteless and tough.
41. Helwig 1678, 1679 and Jager ca. 1682, published in 1704 cited by Stresemann 1954: 273.
42. Stresemann 1954: 270.
43. Stresemann 1954: 274–5: Gilliard 1969: 22.
44. Stresemann 1954: 275–6.
45. Stresemann 1954: 277.
46. Gilliard 1969: 211.

4

The plume trade:
the demands of natural historians

Réné P. Lesson was the first naturalist to observe a living bird of paradise in its natural habitat. This occurred in the coastal forest inland of Doreri (Dorey) Bay on the Bird's Head of New Guinea in July 1824, Figure 3. There Lesson saw a Lesser Bird of Paradise in flight. Lesson described his experience as follows:

The view of the first bird of paradise was overwhelming. The gun remained idle in my hand for I was too astonished to shoot. It was in the virgin forest surrounding the harbour of Dorey. As I slipped carefully along the wild pigs' trails through this dusky thicket, a Paradisaea suddenly flew in graceful curves over my head. It was like a meteor whose body, cutting through the air, leaves a long trail of light.[1]

Apart from seeing and collecting specimens of the Lesser and King Birds of Paradise in the forests surrounding Doreri Bay, Lesson reputedly obtained trade skins of the Magnificent Bird of Paradise, Superb Bird of Paradise, Arfak Astrapia, Black Sicklebill, Western Parotia and Flame Bowerbird.[2] In Sydney on his way to France he purchased a specimen of the Paradise Riflebird. This purchase extended the known distribution of birds of paradise to Australia.[3]

After Lesson's success the ornithology of New Guinea became a serious field of research. The Director of the Natural History Museum in Leiden was so impressed by Lesson's achievements that he sent H.C. Macklot and Salomon Müller to collect birds of paradise in New Guinea in 1828. Their expedition was not considered successful as they found only known species in the forests around Triton Bay in southwest New Guinea. They did, however, collect the White-eared Catbird (*Ailuroedus buccoides*), a species of bowerbird, at Lobo near Fort Du Bus in 1828, (Figure 28).[4]

In 1830 Rennesse van Duivenboden founded a family firm in Ternate.[5] One of the main activities of this firm was acquiring new species and selling them to whichever museum paid the most. Any unusual birds of paradise were sent directly to European museums or despatched to one of the great plume dealers, such as Mantou, the Parisian plumassier. These dealers then sold them at premium prices to the patrons of scientific institutions. Over the years Duivenboden and his son made huge profits from this activity. They protected their interests by providing little information about the source of each specimen, and in some cases what was provided was incorrect.

In the late 1840s, John Macgillivray, who collected for John Gould, found the Queen Victoria's Riflebird (*Ptiloris victoriae*) on Barnard Island in northeast Australia. In 1848 he also collected the Fawn-breasted Bowerbird (*Chamydera cerviniventris*) near the tip of Cape York.[6]

From 1854–1862 Alfred Russel Wallace spent eight years in the Malay Archipelago, now known as Indonesia. In the Aru Islands south of New Guinea he was able to observe the Greater Bird of Paradise from March to May 1857. His observations were the first to confirm the 1670s to 1680s reports of Helwig and Herbert de Jager about how the Greater Bird of Paradise was hunted and prepared for the plume trade.

Wallace's observations that fully plumed males gathered and displayed in high trees as mating groups is considered by ornithologists to be his most important contribution to the study of birds of paradise.[7] At last it was known how these birds used their beautiful plumage. He also extended the westward distribution of birds of paradise by finding Wallace's Standard Wing (*Semioptera wallacei*) on Bacan in the Moluccas. Wallace also found the Spotted Catbird (*Ailuroedus melanotis*), a species of bowerbird, in the Aru Islands.

Wallace was disappointed that despite visiting more places and investing more time than Lesson, he was only able to acquire fully plumed, male specimens of six birds of paradise: the Greater, King, Lesser, Red, Twelve-wired and Wallace's Standard Wing.

He could not understand why, apart from the Lesser and some female King Birds of Paradise, he did not acquire in 1858 the other birds of paradise and bowerbirds he believed Lesson obtained during his brief visit to Doreri Bay in 1824. Wallace cites these as being the Magnifica (Magnificent), Superba (Superb), *Astrapia nigra* (Arfak Astrapia), *Epimachus magnus* (Black Sicklebill), *Parotia sexsetacea* (Western Parotia) and *Sericulus aureus* (Flame Bowerbird).[8]

Wallace's achievements stimulated others to follow in his footsteps. Schlegel, the new director of the Leiden Museum, sent three collectors to New Guinea in search of birds of paradise. These were H.A. Bernstein from 1861–1865, D.S. Hoedt from 1863–1868 and H. von Rosenberg from 1863–1873.

Bernstein collected many Black Sicklebills near Sorong and Magnificent and Twelve-wired Birds of Paradise on Salawati. He also found that Waigeo and Batanta Islands were the home of the Wilson's Bird of Paradise. On Morotai Island at the northern tip of Halmahera he was the first European to see the Paradise or Silky Crow in its natural habitat[9] (Figures 1 and 3).

By 1867 the Leiden Museum had the best collection of birds of paradise. The number held of certain species is given below:

Greater Bird of Paradise	46
King Bird of Paradise	25
Wallace's Standard Wing	25 (almost all collected by Bernstein)
Red Bird of Paradise	21 (all collected by Bernstein)
Lesser Bird of Paradise	16
Magnificent Bird of Paradise	15
Wilson's Bird of Paradise	9
Western Parotia	1 (collected by Müller)

Von Rosenberg sent hunters from Andai into the Arfak Mountains of the Bird's Head in February 1870. They returned with the Arfak Astrapia, Superb Bird of Paradise and Western Parotia and a new species of bowerbird, the Vogelkop Bowerbird (*Amblyornis inornatus*).

The evident success of the collectors despatched by the Leiden Museum encouraged others to search for new species. Over the next seventy years this search was to be taken up not only by those who came to New Guinea as natural history collectors, but also by those who came as government officers or were seeking their fortune.

In 1872 Odoardo Beccari, an Italian botanist, and his companion Luigi Maria D'Albertis visited Doreri Bay. From Andai village D'Albertis went into the Arfak Mountains and found the Flame Bowerbird (*Sericulus aureus*). It was previously known only from trade skins. He also observed and shot specimens of the Western Parotia, Superb Bird of Paradise and Black Sicklebill and a new species, the Buff-tailed Sicklebill (*Epimachus albertisi*). Beccari returned to the Arfak Mountains in 1875 and not only saw the species observed by D'Albertis but also a new species, the Long-tailed Paradigalla (*Paradigalla carunculata*).[10]

In 1873 the trader A.A. Bruijn, who was the son-in-law of the Ternatian business magnate, Rennesse van Duivenboden, despatched bird collectors to obtain birds of paradise. They were led by a Frenchman called Leon Laglaize. On Japen in Cendrawasih Bay they found the Jobi Manucode (*Manucodia jobiensis*). The Pale-billed

Sicklebill (*Epimachus bruijnii*) they acquired probably came from the nearby Waropen coast of Cendrawasih Bay.

By the end of the 1870s Dutch pacification was having an impact along the north coast of Dutch New Guinea. From this time onward, we must assume that Indonesians and others were going in ever increasing numbers into inland regions to hunt birds of paradise. By the 1880s bird hunters from Ternate had extended their activities eastwards as far as the Sepik coast of what is now Papua New Guinea (see Chapters 11 and 12).

When D'Albertis went to Australia to convalesce from the rigours of fieldwork in Dutch New Guinea in 1873, the corvette he was travelling on stopped at Orangerie Bay at the eastern tip of southeast New Guinea.[11] Two trade skins of a new species, the Raggiana Bird of Paradise (*Paradisaea raggiana*), were brought out by villagers. On a subsequent expedition in 1876–7 D'Albertis travelled up the Fly River and observed that along the Fly there was some overlap in the distribution of Raggiana and Greater Birds of Paradise.[12]

In 1876 Andrew Goldie came to southeast New Guinea and worked both as a collector of natural history specimens and as a gold prospector. Carl Hunstein, a German adventurer, joined Goldie as his hunter and dissector. They made plant and animal collections which were sold to the Australian and British Museums. Apart from finding many birds of paradise previously known from western New Guinea, they found Goldie's Bird of Paradise (*Paradisaea decora*) and the Curlcrested Manucode (*Manacodia comrii*) on Fergusson Island.[13]

In 1883 Hunstein left Goldie and worked in Southeast New Guinea on his own. He found Lawes' Parotia (*Parotia lawesii*) in the Astrolabe Mountains in 1884. On Mount Maguli in the Owen Stanley Ranges he found the Brown Sicklebill (*Epimachus meyeri*), Stephanie's Astrapia (*Astrapia stephaniae*), the Blue Bird of Paradise (*Paradisaea rudolphi*) and a male of the Streaked Bowerbird (*Amblgornis subalaris*). Goldie had found the female of this species the previous year. These specimens were sold to Otto Finsch when Hunstein met him in Cooktown on the Queensland coast in 1884. Finsch sent them to A.B. Meyer at the Dresden Museum.[14]

Sir William MacGregor, the first Governor of British New Guinea, was interested in natural history. When climbing Mount Knudsford with Karl Kowald in the Owen Stanley Range in 1889 they found the Crested Bird of Paradise (*Cnemophilus macgregorii*) and Macgregor's Bowerbird (*Amblgornis macgregoriae*). Governor Hahl of German New Guinea was also interested in collecting natural history specimens, but did not obtain any new species.[15]

MacGregor's discoveries generated considerable interest in the southeastern ranges. In 1893 Loria's Bird of Paradise (*Cnemophilus loriae*) was found in the Owen Stanley Range by Lamberto Loria, an Italian naturalist. His assistant, Amedeo Giulianetti, accompanied MacGregor to collect in the Wharton Range. They returned with Macgregor's Bird of Paradise (*Macgregoria pulchra*).[16]

Despite considerable effort, similar successes were not quickly forthcoming in German New Guinea. Hunstein joined the New Guinea Company in 1885 and in 1887 took part in the first German Sepik Expedition as a bird collector. No new birds of paradise were found.

In 1888 Hunstein and Stefan von Kotze climbed into the Rawlinson Ranges of the Huon Peninsula from near Finschhafen. There they found the Emperor Bird of Paradise (*Paradisaea guilielmi*) and a subspecies of Raggiana, *Paradisaea raggiana augustaevictoriae*.[17]

Believing that birds of paradise would also be found in New Britain, Hunstein went there in 1888. He was drowned when Ritter Island off West New Britain erupted on the 13th of March 1888.[18]

In 1896 the Yellow-breasted Bowerbird (*Chlamgdera lauterbachi*) was found during the New Guinea Company expedition from Stephansort (Bogadjim) overland to the Ramu River.[19]

Duivenboden's company took full advantage of the rivalry between natural history specimen collectors and played them off against each other in order to obtain higher prices. This was particularly the case with A.B. Meyer at the Dresden Museum in Germany and Baron Walter von Rothschild who established his own museum at Tring in England. Through Duivenboden's company, Meyer obtained specimens of Carola's Parotia (*Parotia carolae*) and the King of Saxony Bird of Paradise (*Pteridophora alberti*) in 1894. A year later Rothschild obtained the Splendid Astrapia (*Astrapia spendidissima*) and the Yellow-breasted Bird of Paradise (*Loboparadisea sericea*).[20]

In 1906 Carl Wahnes discovered Wahnes' Parotia (*Parotia wahnesi*) and the Huon Astrapia (*Astrapia rothschildi*) in the Rawlinson Ranges and Sattelberg Range in German New Guinea.

In 1911 a collector from Rothschild's museum at Tring joined a Dutch military patrol exploring the headwaters of the Eilanden River in southwest Dutch New Guinea. At 2,000 metres on the slopes of Mount Goliath he found the Short-tailed Paradigalla (*Paradigalla brevicauda*). He was also able to document the habitat of four species known from skins obtained by Duivenboden's collectors. These were the Carola's Parotia, King of Saxony Bird of Paradise, Splendid Astrapia and Yellow-breasted Bird of Paradise. As Duivenboden's men did not collect in this part of southwest New Guinea, Mount Goliath was not the source of the type specimens. Their likely source was discovered in 1920 when the Pratt brothers went up the Wanggar River from Cendrawasih Bay into the Weyland Ranges.[21] The source of another species collected by Duivenboden's men continued to remain a mystery for some time. This was the Golden-fronted Bowerbird (*Amblyornis flavifrons*). This mystery was solved when it was found living in the Foja Mountains inland from the north coast of West Papua by Jared Diamond in 1981.[22]

In 1929 the Fire-maned Bowerbird (*Sericulus bakeri*) was found in the Adelbert Mountains by Rollo H. Beck and his wife, and A.L. Rand collected Archbold's Bowerbird (*Archboldia papuensis*) on the slopes of Mount Trikora (formerly Wilhelmina) during the 1938 Archbold Expedition.[23] No more bowerbirds remained to be discovered in New Guinea.

The last bird of paradise to be scientifically named and described was the Ribbon-tailed Astrapia (*Astrapia mayeri*). In 1938 Fred Shaw Mayer received two unusual feathers from a missionary. These had been obtained from a man in Mount Hagen who was wearing them in his hair. He in turn had acquired the feathers by trade from their source area some 130–160 kilometres to the west of the Hagen Ranges. These feathers resulted in the preliminary identification of the species and a complete skin was obtained soon afterwards.[24] It thus took from 1758 until 1939 for natural historians to discover all the birds of paradise and bowerbirds. Subsequent taxonomic work has determined that there are 42 species of birds of paradise. These are listed in Table 4.

Table 4: A list of all birds of paradise, plus those bowerbirds found in New Guinea. They are grouped by distinguishing features.

Birds of Paradise

erect crest	
Crested Bird of Paradise	*Cnemophilus macgregorii* (De Vis, 1890)
Loria's Bird of Paradise	*Cnemophilus loriae* (Salvadori, 1894)
greenish wattles	
Yellow-breasted Bird of Paradise	*Loboparadisea sericea* (Rothschild, 1896)
large orange wattles behind eye	
Macgregor's Bird of Paradise	*Macgregoria pulchra* (De Vis, 1897)
yellow and blue wattles	
Short-tailed Paradigalla	*Paradigalla brevicaudia* (Rothschild and Hartert, 1911)
Long-tailed Paradigalla	*Paradigalla carunculata* (Lesson, 1835)
iridescent throat, upper breast and crown plumes	
Magnificent Riflebird	*Ptiloris magnificus* (Vieillot, 1819)
Queen Victoria's Riflebird	*Ptiloris victoriae* (Gould, 1850)
Paradise Riflebird	*Ptiloris paradiseus* (Swainson, 1825)

flag tipped wires from tufts on each side of nape	
Wahnes' Parotia	*Parotia wahnesi* (Rothschild, 1906)
Lawes' Parotia	*Parotia lawesii* (Ramsay, 1885)
Carola's Parotia	*Parotia carolae* (Meyer, 1894)
Western Parotia	*Parotia sefilata* (Pennant, 1781)
immense blue flanged quill springing from each side of the nape	
King of Saxony Bird of Paradise	*Pteridophora alberti* (Meyer, 1894)
erectile cape of feathers springing from nape	
Superb Bird of Paradise	*Lophorina superba* (Pennant, 1781)
two pairs of long erectile white plumes on bend of wing	
Wallace's Standard Wing	*Semioptera wallacei* (Gould, 1859)
filamentous display plumes	
Greater Bird of Paradise	*Paradisaea apoda* (Linnaeus, 1758)
Lesser Bird of Paradise	*Paradisaea minor* (Shaw, 1809)
Red Bird of Paradise	*Paradisaea rubra* (Daudin, 1800)
Goldie's Bird of Paradise	*Paradisaea decora* (Salvin and Godman, 1883)
Raggiana Bird of Paradise	*Paradisaea raggiana* (Sclater, 1873)
Emperor Bird of Paradise	*Paradisaea guilielmi* (Cabanis, 1888)
Blue Bird of Paradise	*Paradisaea rudolphi* (Finsch, 1885)
thread-like tail wires	
King Bird of Paradise	*Cicinnurus regius* (Linnaeus, 1758)
Magnificent Bird of Paradise	*Cicinnurus magnificus* (Pennant, 1781)
Twelve-wired Bird of Paradise	*Seleucidis melanoleuca* (Daudin, 1800)
Wilson's Bird of Paradise	*Cicinnurus respublica* (Bonaparte, 1850)
tail long and step-like	
Arfak Astrapia	*Astrapia nigra* (Gmelin, 1788)
Ribbon-tailed Astrapia	*Astrapia mayeri* (Stoner, 1939)
Stephanie's Astrapia	*Astrapia stephaniae* (Finsch and Meyer, 1885)
Huon Astrapia	*Astrapia rothschildi* (Foerster, 1906)
Splendid Astrapia	*Astrapia spendidissima* (Rothschild, 1895)
tail long and graduated	
Black Sicklebill	*Epimachus fastuosus* (Hermann, 1783)
Brown Sicklebill	*Epimachus meyeri* (Finsch, 1885)
Buff-tailed Sicklebill	*Epimachus aibertisi* (Sclater, 1873)
Pale-billed Sicklebill	*Epimachus bruijnii* (Oustalet, 1880)
plumage black glossed purple to green	
Crinkle-collared Manucode	*Manucodia chalybata* (Pennant, 1781)
Glossy-mantled Manucode	*Manucodia atra* (Lesson, 1830)

Curl-crested Manucode	*Manucodia comrii* (Sclater, 1876)
Trumpet Manucode	*Manucodia keraudrenii* (Lesson and Garnot, 1826)
Jobi Manucode	*Manucodia jobiensis* (Salvadori, 1876)

crow-like

Paradise or Silky Crow	*Lycocorax pyrrhopterus* (Bonaparte, 1851)

Bowerbirds

Spotted Catbird	*Ailuroedus melanotis* (Gray, 1858)
White-eared Catbird	*Ailuroedus buccoides* (Temminck, 1835)
Golden-fronted Bowerbird	*Amblyornis flavifrons* (Rothschild, 1895)
Macgregor's Bowerbird	*Amblyornis macgregoriae* (De Vis, 1890)
Streaked Bowerbird	*Amblyornis subalaris* (Sharpe, 1884)
Vogelkop Bowerbird	*Amblyornis inornatus* (Schlegel, 1871)
Archbold's Bowerbird	*Archboldia papuensis* (Rand, 1940)
Fawn-breasted Bowerbird	*Chamydera cerviniventris* (Gould, 1850)
Yellow-breasted Bowerbird	*Chamydera lauterbachi* (Reichenow, 1897)
Flame Bowerbird	*Sericulus aureus* (Linnaeus, 1758)
Fire-maned Bowerbird	*Sericulus bakeri* (Chapin, 1929)

Sources: Beehler et al 1986; Coates 1990; Cooper and Forshaw 1977; Gilliard 1969.

Notes

1. Gilliard 1969: 22–23; Stresemann 1954: 279–80.
2. Wallace 1857: 415; 1862a: 154–5.
3. Stresemann 1954: 280.
4. Stresemann 1954: 281; Gilliard 1969: 259.
5. van der Veur 1972: 280.
6. Gilliard 1969: 113.
7. Stresemann 1954: 281.
8. Wallace (1857: 415) was irritated by Lesson's use of French trivial names and his poor documentation as to how and where he acquired his specimens. This has led to some confusion as to what species Lesson actually acquired in Doreri Bay. For instance Gilliard (1969: 22, 423) states that Lesson only observed and shot two species, the Lesser and King Birds of Paradise and obtained trade skins of the Trumpet Manucode, Glossy-mantled Manucode and Flame Bowerbird. This differs from Wallace's understanding of his collection.
9. Gilliard 1969: 93–4.
10. Gilliard 1969: 131–2: Stresemann 1954: 283–4.

11. D'Albertis 1877, 1880; Goode 1977: 55.
12. D'Albertis 1877: 38–9.
13. Gilliard 1969: 445; Stresemann 1954: 284.
14. Gilliard 1969: 250, 445–6: Stresemann 1954: 284–5.
15. Gilliard 1969: 446; Stresemann 1954: 285-6.
16. Gilliard 1969: 446–7; Stresemann 1954: 286.
17. Gilliard 1969: 245; Stresemann 1954: 286.
18. Gilliard 1969: 239, 455; Stresemann 1954: 286.
19. Gilliard 1969: 454.
20. Gilliard 1969: 418; Stresemann 1954: 258–7.
21. Gilliard 1969: 433–4.
22. Aschenbach 1982; Diamond 1982a; Diamond 1982b.
23. Gilliard 1969: 434–5, 453.
24. Gilliard 1969: 153–4.

Plate 10: Coiffures and a hat decorated with bird of paradise plumes from 1830 fashion magazines.

Source: *Townsend's Monthly Selection of Parisian Costumes,* January, February and March 1830. Reproduced by permission of the British Library.

5

The plume trade: the demands of fashion-conscious European women and the growth of the conservation movement

The history of fashionable feather wearing by Europeans

Although the Romans wore ostrich plumes, ornamental plumage did not become popular in Europe until the time of the Crusades (1096–1270). Crusaders reportedly returned with plumes amongst their spoils of war. In the thirteenth century the profession of trading and working in ornamental feathers was introduced into France from Italy. Initially plumes were used to decorate knights' helmets and the hats of high ranking officials. Subsequently cavalier hats trimmed with ostrich plumes became popular in both Europe and Virginia.

Feather wearing remained a male activity in Europe until the late eighteenth century. In 1775 Marie Antoinette started a new fashion. It happened one evening when her husband, King Louis XVI of France, complimented her on the ostrich and peacock feathers she wore in her hair. Soon plume wearing became a fashion amongst the aristocratic ladies of France. It later spread to other European capitals. At royal courts or on other occasions more and more aristocratic women began wearing plumes set in jewelled brooches or in headdress clasps. Although the wearing of peacock feathers gained bad associations when Marie Antoinette and Louis XVI were executed during the French Revolution, plume wearing continued to be fashionable at royal courts in Europe and amongst the well-to-do.[1]

Village-prepared bird of paradise skins were initially used by European milliners. This was the case in the 1830s. When surplus natural history specimens became available to milliners they came to prefer these arsenic-cured skins because of their greater durability. This preference meant that the demand for village trade skins quickly declined. In the 1850s their price fell from two dollars to six pence each.[2] As insufficient quantities were forthcoming from natural history collectors, specialist hunters had to be despatched to obtain and prepare arsenic-cured bird of paradise skins for the European plume trade. Ternate became an important centre supplying these skins to

Europe. As mentioned in Chapter 4, Rennesse van Duivenboden and his son established the main plume firm; other plume merchants based in Ternate included A.A. Bruijn, who became Duivenboden's son-in-law, and J. Bensbach.

The wearing of ornamental plumage in Europe was at first only within the means of people of high status. From the late nineteenth century improving economic circumstances allowed increasing numbers of women to follow the dictates of fashion, and milliners in turn began to gain access to an increasing range of species from all over the world. The demand for plumes increased in Europe and America as more and more fashion-conscious, middle-class, urban women wore the latest styles suggested by fashion houses in Berlin, London, New York and Paris. They were able to follow these fashion trends by subscribing to the growing number of fashion magazines and home journals.[3] This demand by upper and increasing numbers of middle-class European women for hats with spectacular and beautiful plumes brought about the European plume boom of 1908.

Plate 11: A bonnet decorated with a bird of paradise in an 1882 English fashion magazine.
This Pifferano bonnet is made of fine black straw, lined with black velvet and trimmed with black satin strings and a bird of paradise.

Source: *The Queen,* 20 April 1882. By permission of the British Library.

Although plume wearing by aristocratic women dates back to 1775, it was some time before bird of paradise plumes became available to milliners. Fashion magazines indicate that they were being worn by 1830 (Plate 10) and were also popular shortly after Queen Victoria was crowned in 1837. Export and import information indicate that the supply and demand for these plumes increased through the ensuing years and from time to time they featured in fashion magazines. In 1863 bird of paradise plumes were one of the favourite trims on the continent, and they decorated some of the French hats imported into New York in 1875. An English fashion magazine features a bonnet decorated with a bird of paradise in 1882 (Plate 11). Birds of paradise were also popular during the summer sales of bird feathers at Harpers Bazaar in New York in 1896.[4] By 1908 they were one of the mainstays of the plume trade. Plates 12–15 show birds of paradise decorated hats and plume advertisements for 1911–12 and Plate 16 those being worn in 1921.

Plate 12: Hats decorated with birds of paradise appearing in 1911–12 fashion advertisements.
a. Dainty restaurant hat with black Chantilly lace, ermine (weasel) crown and bird of paradise mount.
b. Black velvet hat with large tomato coloured paradise.
c. Hat with silver lace corners and silver tassels with large white paradise plume.
d. French hat, navy in colour with white trim and natural paradise plumage.

Sources: *Millinery*, October, November, December 1911, June 1912. By permission of the British Library.

a

b

c

d

a

STUART SONS
AND CO.

OLD CHANGE, LONDON, E.C.

Manufactories :—

LONDON, LUTON, DUNSTABLE.

Branches :—

Manchester, Liverpool, Newcastle, Glasgow, Dublin, Sheffield.

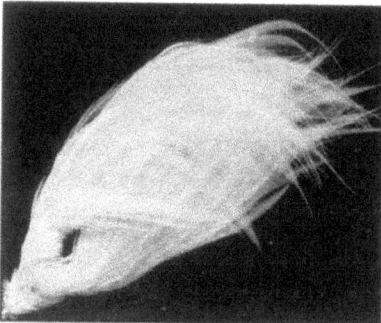

b

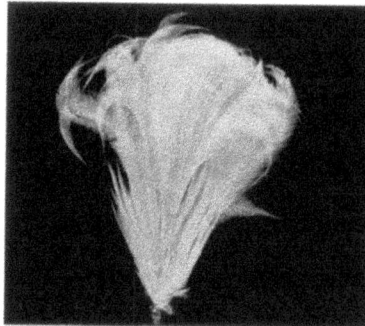

c

Plate 13: Advertisement for paradise plumes by Stuart Sons Company, London, 1912.
a. Dark paradise plumes 260 shillings each.
b. Light paradise plumes 247 shillings each.
c. Light paradise plumes 140 shillings each.

Source: *Ladies wear Trade Journal,* 1912, Vol. 2, No. 12. By permission of the British Library.

Plate 14: Blue ostrich headwear with paradise in centre and mounted bird of paradise.

Source: *Millinery,* January 1912. By permission of the British Library.

Plate 15: Hats decorated with birds of paradise appearing in 1912 fashion advertisements.
a. Painted silk picture hat, lined with olive crepe, with silk ribbon and imitation paradise plume.
b. Dark green tam with folded silk brim and large black paradise.
c. Black hat with rich yellow paradise mount.

Sources: *Millinery*, 1912, Vol. 2, No. 4; *Millinery*, 1912, Vol. 1, No. 11. *Ladies Wear Trade Journal*, London, 1912, Vol. 2, No. 9. By permission of the British Library.

Plate 16: Hats decorated with birds of paradise appearing in 1921 fashion advertisements.
a. Spring wear hat trimmed with a natural bird of paradise.
b. A soft, black fabric hat with sprays of bird of paradise plumes set in tuffs.

Sources: *The Millinery Trades Journal*, London, 1921, March–April. *The Queen*, 1921, 29 January, 1921. By permission of the British Library.

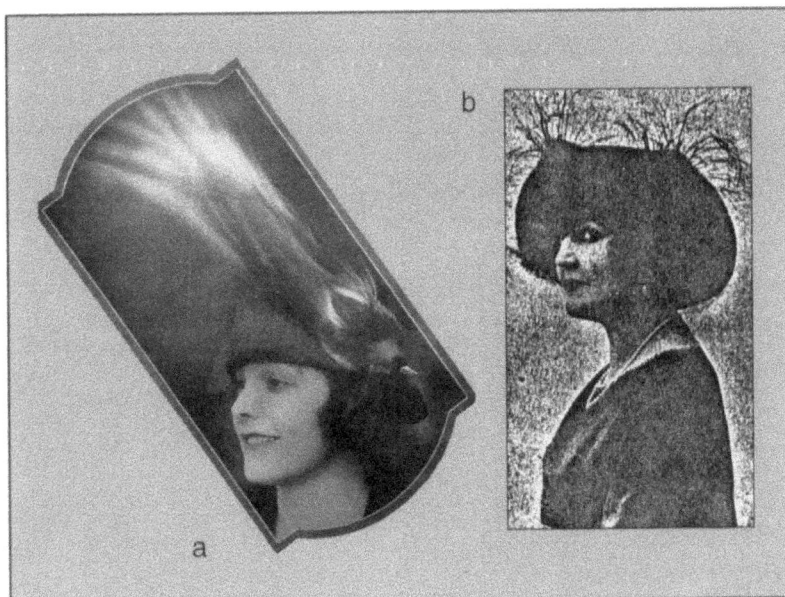

The number of birds killed to supply the Western world

It is difficult to compile meaningful figures and compare plume sales with season to season changes in fashion recorded in the fashion magazines due to the lack of consistency in the statistics on plumage imported into the United Kingdom and the United States during the plume boom. Insufficient categories were recorded, usually only ostrich and other ornamental plumage. The categories used also changed from time to time and included products other than plumes.[5]

Ostrich, egret and bird of paradise were the mainstays of the international feather trade. Before breeding programmes were established ostrich plumes came from Aden, Cape Colony, Egypt, Morocco, Natal and Tripoli. Egret plumes were mainly obtained from Venezuela, Brazil and Columbia, and bird of paradise plumes came from Dutch and German New Guinea as well as from Papua until 1908. Other species became fashionable for certain periods. For instance, in the 1880s and 1890s owl heads, small birds and hummingbirds perched on artificial flowers, and fragile goura sprays on dress hats became popular.[6]

Out of all the plume birds, birds of paradise fetched the highest prices. Table 5 gives the prices of the top twenty bird species on offer in London in 1913.

Table 5: The lower and upper prices of the top twenty bird species on offer in London in 1913.

	prices US $	
Greater Bird of Paradise[1]	lower	upper
Light plumes: medium to large	10.32	21.00
medium to long, worn	7.20	13.80
slightly damaged, plucked	2.40	6.72
Dark plumes: medium to good, long	7.20	24.60
King Bird of Paradise		2.40
Magnificent Riflebird	1.14	1.38
Rubra (Red) Bird of Paradise		2.50
Twelve-wired Bird of Paradise	1.44	1.80
African Golden Cuckoo		1.68
Cassowary plumes, per ounce		3.48
Condor skins	3.50	5.75
Crown Pigeon heads, Coronatus	.84	1.20
Crown Pigeon heads, Victoria	1.68	2.50

Egret (Osprey) skins[2]	1.08	2.78
Emu skins	4.56	4.80
Argus Pheasant	3.60	3.85
Impeyan Pheasant		2.50
Silver Pheasant		3.50
Tragopan Pheasant		2.70
Swan skins	.72	.74
Peacock necks, gold and blue	.24	.66
Golden Pheasant	.34	.46
'Green' Bird of Paradise	.38	.44

Notes:

1. The absence of Lesser Bird of Paradise skins seems an anomaly; perhaps they were grouped with the Greater Bird of Paradise by feather merchants as no one would want to buy something less than the best.

2. By 1913 the wearing of egret/heron plumes was no longer socially correct and this had led to a decline in the prices paid for these plumes.

Source: Hornaday 1913: 124–125.

The feather imports into the United Kingdom from 1872 until 1921 show that there was a considerable demand for feathers in Europe by 1872 (Figure 18). The 1872–1913 figures for feather imports into the United States (Figure 19) illustrate that the fashion of feather wearing commenced earlier in the United Kingdom and Europe than it did in the United States. The feather exports from German and later the Mandated Territory of New Guinea from 1909–1922 (Figure 49) clearly illustrate the initial boom, the intervention of World War I and the resumption of the plume trade until it was outlawed.

Enormous numbers of birds were slaughtered for the feather trade. When one remembers the saying as light as a feather, 50,300 tons of feathers seems an incredible amount. This was the quantity of plumage to enter France between 1890 and 1929.[7]

Conservative estimates calculated from the weight of plumage sold indicate that some 155,000 birds of paradise were sold at London auctions between 1904–8.[8] This is an average of more than 30,000 birds a year reaching London alone. Increasing quantities of plumes were purchased until the outbreak of the First World War. In 1912 one British firm received 28,300 skins in a single shipment. Ernst Mayr, the Alexander Agassiz Professor of Zoology at Harvard University,

£ millions

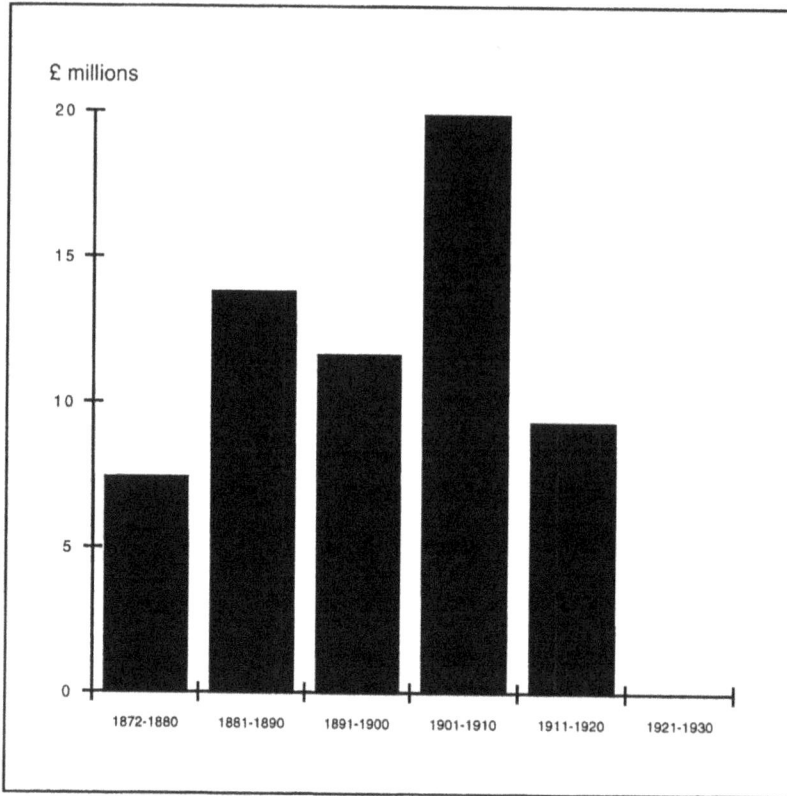

Figure 18: Feather imports into the United Kingdom from 1872 until they were prohibited in 1921.

Source: Based on Doughty 1975: Table 2.

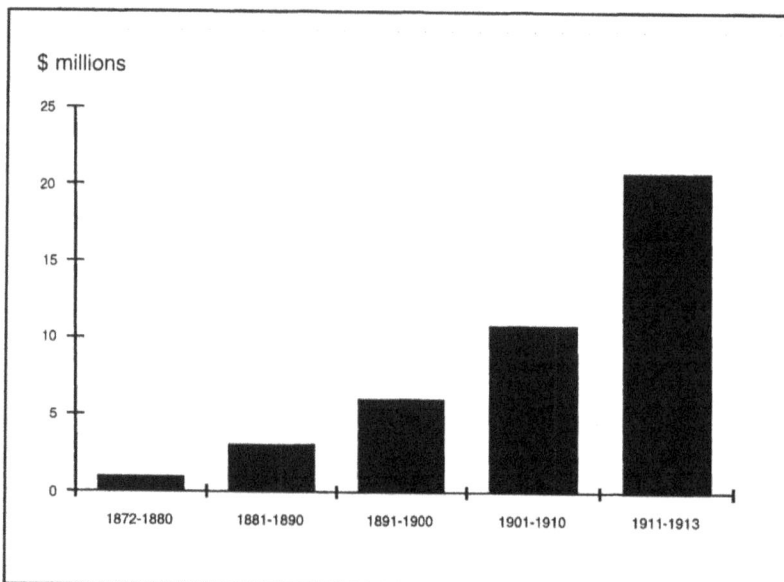

$ millions

Figure 19: Feather imports into the United States from 1872 until they were prohibited in 1913.

Source: Based on Doughty 1975: Table 3.

estimated that in a peak year some 80,000 skins were exported from New Guinea.[9] Mayr's estimate seems reasonable on the basis of the available statistics shown in Table 6. This table gives known figures for 1913. Better statistics will no doubt become available as more records are located.

Table 6: Estimated number of birds of paradise exported from New Guinea in 1913.

region	value £	number of skins	estimated number of skins
German New Guinea	50,277	16,691	
Fakfak & Kokas	40,000	8,000	
Merauke		25,000	
Hollandia			?20,000
Manokwari	40,000	8,000	
Sorong			?5,000
			Estimated total about 80,000

Note
Nielsen (1930) states Merauke exported 25,000 birds valued at 2–2,500,000 kronen in the year before World War I. The Historic Section of the Foreign Office, London (1920) gives the export value of plumes from Merauke as 36,108 florins, using the 1918 exchange rate (see Figure 40 below), the sum of £3,610 for 25,000 birds seems far too low.

Sources: Historical Section of the Foreign Office, London 1920: 26; Cheesman 1938a: 41; Nielsen 1930: 228; Sack and Clark 1980: 156.

Although feather wearing has a long tradition in some parts of the world, never before in human history had so many birds and different species been slaughtered for plumage. The slaughter of some 300,000 albatrosses, gulls, terns and other birds on Laysan Island over several months in 1909 stands out as one of the fastest acts of carnage that occurred, but this was only one such case in the North Pacific. Laysan Island lies some 600 kilometres east of Midway Island in the Hawaiian Islands. The massacre was the work of twenty-three Japanese hunters hired by Max Schlemmer. They would have killed all the birds on the island if they had not been arrested by officers of the United

States government. It was Schlemmer's plan to ship the birds to Japan, thence to Paris which was the main market for seabirds from the North Pacific.[10]

The development of the conservation movement

From the early sixteenth century onwards, laws had been introduced in feudal England to protect certain game birds. This was done because guns were killing more of these birds than the old practice of falconry. Guns also had a marked effect on wildlife in other parts of the world. For example, the use of guns in the United States had by 1850 devastated the bison herds on the prairies and was leading to the extinction of the passenger pigeon.

After 1850, the sight of waving sprays of feathers and the use of wings and stuffed birds on hats upset sufficient members of the public in Europe and America to generate an outcry of outrage and disgust. The plight of many birds was also brought to the attention of the public by ornithologists, scientists, writers and church leaders who used both aesthetic and economic arguments against the plume trade. This opposition to the practice of feather wearing aroused sentiments which are still with us today.[11]

Activists aroused considerable sympathy for their cause by showing how some plumes were obtained by slaughtering parent birds at nesting colonies. They also explained how some of the birds being slaughtered ate insects which otherwise destroyed crops, whilst others, such as robins, were familiar to children from an early age as part of their cultural heritage. Middle-class urban Britons and Americans learnt about the unpleasant aspects of the feather trade from articles about these topics in local and national newspapers. This generated an interest in wildlife, especially birds, and was part of the 'back to nature' movement of the late nineteenth century.

Partly in response to this outrage, and also as a means of providing a regular supply, steps were taken to breed commercially some of the favoured plumage birds. In 1860–1900 the French Société d'Acclimatisation established breeding colonies of pheasants in France and similar projects were undertaken in England and the United States. Ostrich breeding colonies were established before the mid-1860s in the Cape Colony and North Africa and spread in the late 1860s to the United States, Europe, Australia and New Zealand.[12] Ostrich breeding began in Australia in 1869.[13]

In the late nineteenth century prizes were offered to those who could establish a successful egret farm. Some egrets/herons were reared in enclosures. Bird numbers were controlled and their plumage was clipped or plucked regularly. The French Société d'Acclimatisation successfully raised egrets in Tunisia in 1895. Other successes were reported from Argentina, Brittany, Ceylon, India and Madagascar. Despite such efforts the carnage of these birds in their breeding colonies continued.

By the 1880s the mass slaughter of wildlife as well as the widespread destruction of significant natural landscape and cultural monuments was causing concern. In an attempt to address this issue conservation movements were established in Europe and the United States. For instance in 1885 the Plumage League, which later became the Society for the Protection of Birds, was established in England and the Audubon Society was founded in the United States in 1886.

Initially the anti-plumage movement in the United Kingdom was restricted to socially prominent ladies and well-educated people and focused on the propriety of feather wearing. Three duchesses, three earls, a marquess, a viscount and three bishops were vice-presidents of the Society for the Protection of Birds. Servants and friends were discouraged from wearing plumes on moral and religious grounds. In this way the royal family came to support the Society for the Protection of Birds and King Edward VII gave it a royal charter in 1904. The support of Edward VII and Queen Alexandra for the Society meant that its members could no longer be viewed as a faddist minority.[14]

In 1881 protests had commenced in India over the killing of green parrots and other insect-eating birds for their plumes. This led to local governments being given some control over the possession and sale of plumage in the breeding season by the Wild Birds Protection Act of 1887. This proved to be an inadequate measure to control their slaughter. In 1900 a branch of the Society for the Protection of Birds was established in India. The growing outrage over the killing of birds which helped control insect pests resulted in the enactment of legislation prohibiting the shipment of wild birds from British India for the millinery trade in 1902. Despite this legislation, plume smuggling, especially of heron and kingfisher plumage, continued for many years.[15]

When the Society for the Preservation of the Wild Fauna of the Empire was founded in 1903, similar laws to those enforced in India were also implemented in many other British colonies, including Papua and the West Indies. In Papua it became illegal to hunt and deal in birds of paradise, goura pigeons and egrets/herons in 1908 (see Chapter 13). The hummingbird was the main species protected in the West Indies.[16]

As well as establishing agencies to protect wildlife and preserve natural and cultural heritage, steps were taken to protect and preserve significant conservation areas. This led to National Parks being established. The first two National Parks to be declared were

Yellowstone in 1872 in the United States and Tongariro in 1894 in New Zealand.[17]

Legislation was introduced when local species were threatened

In the 1860s there was public outcry over the slaughter of sea birds on Flamborough Head in Yorkshire in England. This led to the passing of an Act for the Preservation of Sea Birds. Despite this early legislation there was never again the same public concern in Britain over the slaughtering of wild birds for millinery purposes.

In England and France, the feather trade lobby successfully delayed the enactment of protective legislation because in each case the local populace was well removed from the slaughter. The London feather trade depended mainly on imported plumes. Some ornithologists thought that if British birds such as robins and swallows had been at stake, the British reaction might have been different. They concluded that the lack of response by the British public reflected their inability to become personally concerned about the brightly coloured birds they had never seen alive.[18]

The interests of the long established and lucrative Paris feather market held sway in France. This meant that the French government was willing to protect endangered species, but was not willing to ban hunting. In accordance with this policy, the millinery industry erected posters in their workshops prohibiting the processing of indigenous French birds and endangered overseas species.[19]

In the United States and Australia increasing publicity was given to the slaughter of sea birds and herons. Personal accounts of the havoc wrought by hunters in heron-breeding colonies in these countries greatly assisted the early passage of protective legislation. Moulted plumes obtained only one fifth to one sixth the price of 'fresh' feathers from slaughtered birds. Most heron ospreys and aigrettes were obtained by killing adult birds during the breeding season when the plumes were in their best condition. When it became known that adult herons were being slaughtered for their plumes even before their chicks could fend for themselves the public was outraged.

The following description of the destruction observed in a breeding colony in Florida after it had been visited by plume hunters in 1897 is one of many:

… our party came one day upon a little swamp where we had been told Herons bred in numbers. Upon approaching the place the screams of young birds reached our ears. The cause of this soon became apparent by the buzzing of green-flies and the heaps of dead Herons festering in the sun, with the back of each bird raw and bleeding … Young Herons had been left by scores in the nests to perish from exposure and starvation.[20]

A disturbing photographic sequence prepared by A.H. Mattingley in 1906 of egret killing in the Murray Basin of New South Wales received widespread publicity in Australia, England and the United States (Plate 17). The photographs showed an undisturbed nesting colony and then the impact of plume hunters on these birds.[21]

The enormity of the slaughter became evident when it was recognised that this was happening in many other countries as well. Between 1899 and 1912 some 15,000 kilos of heron plumes were exported from Argentina, Brazil and Venezuela. More than 80 per cent of this amount came from Venezuela. In order to obtain one kilo of plumes some 800–1,000 small herons as well as 200–300 larger ones had to be slaughtered. These figures indicate that some 12–15 million small herons and 3 to 4.5 million large ones were killed for the plume trade in Argentina, Brazil and Venezuela. Large numbers of herons were also killed in Florida. The growing outrage at this slaughter provided the political climate for the introduction of protective legislation. In the United Kingdom in 1899 Queen Victoria confirmed an order requiring British army officers to replace egret/ heron plumes worn on regimental uniforms with ostrich plumes.[22]

In Florida, herons were given some protection by the Florida Sea and Plume Bird Law of 1877, and this was strengthened in 1891 and 1901. In 1903 the first national bird reservation was set up on Pelican Island in Florida by Presidential Executive Order. Despite such

Plate 17: Photographs of egrets killed for the plume trade being displayed on the streets of London in 1911. The placard carriers were employed by the Royal Society for the Protection of Birds.

Source: Hornaday 1913. Courtesy of Wildlife Conservation Society, New York.

measures it was widely apparent by 1910 that heron populations in Florida were continuing to decline. It was also recognised that this situation would not change as long as hunters could get as much as $80 an ounce for these plumes.[23]

The slaughter of herons in Florida and sea birds on the Atlantic coast was not easily ignored. In 1889 Senator Hoar of Massachusetts introduced a bill which restricted the trade in millinery plumes. It failed to pass. In 1900 the Lacey Act was passed. This legislation made bird protection a concern of the U.S. Department of Agriculture and prohibited interstate traffic in birds killed in violation of state laws. In 1910 the Shea-White Plumage Bill was passed in the State of New York and by 1911 this had curtailed millinery activities in New York city. The importing of wild plumage into the United States ceased when the Federal Tariff Act which included plumage import prohibitions became law on the 3rd of October 1913.[24] This made the United States the second major feather importing country to prohibit such imports. Australia had done so by a proclamation issued under the Commonwealth Customs Act earlier that same year.[25]

The bird of paradise trade

In England members of the Royal Society for the Protection of Birds believed that the fortnightly auctions of plumage in Mincing Lane spelt the end for many species, especially birds of paradise. Considerable publicity was given to Walter Goodfellow's 1907 and subsequent descriptions of the slaughter of birds of paradise in Dutch New Guinea. He believed that the extinction of the Greater, Lesser, Red and Raggiana Birds of Paradise was imminent because hunters were beginning to hunt out the restricted ranges of these species.[26] Sir William Ingram, an English newspaper man and bird enthusiast, decided to ensure the survival of the Greater Bird of Paradise by establishing a colony in the West Indies (see Chapter 9).

Fears about the imminent extinction of birds of paradise were offset by statements that the hunters only shot fully plumaged males and were not interested in drab females or sub-adult males who had the capacity to mate. This was the viewpoint expressed by the Dutch Minister in London when questioned about the wholesale slaughter of birds of paradise in Dutch New Guinea.[27]

Resistance by millinery trade interests

In Britain support from the upper classes for legislation to halt the importation of wild bird plumage for millinery purposes met organised resistance from British trade interests. Until 1921 every bill brought forward was blocked. The first bill aimed at controlling plume imports was introduced into the House of Lords by Lord Avebury in 1908, but it died in the Commons. A number of arguments were advanced as to why a plumage importation bill should not be passed. These included the loss of British jobs and trade for Britain, particularly if the feather trade was required to relocate on the continent. The British plume trade, like the administration of German New Guinea, requested that the industry should be retained as long as plumes were in fashion and in demand.

The feather trade stressed that it was concerned only with common birds and would do all in its power to save rare birds from extinction. Claims that birds were declining and disappearing from their old homes was in their view not the result of plume hunting but the impact of urban growth and agricultural development. It was also claimed by the trade that the bulk of hat trimmings was made up of artificial feathers, especially in the case of egrets/herons, but also in the case of birds of paradise. Plate 15a shows an advertisement for an imitation bird of paradise plume.

In 1917 the United Kingdom Board of Trade passed an importation of plumage regulation. This became the Importation of Plumage (Prohibition) Bill in 1921. The failed 1908 Bill had proposed an end to feather sales. The 1921 Act only prohibited the importation of wild bird feathers; it did not prohibit their possession or sale.[28] Consequently bird protection groups continued to seek restrictions which would prohibit the possession and sale of such feathers. The protectionists believed that customs seizures, and the ensuing small number of prosecutions, represented only a small proportion of the plumes entering Britain.

The plumage laws of the United States were more comprehensive than those of the United Kingdom. Anyone caught smuggling plumes in the United States faced heavy fines.[29] One of the largest seizures of bird of paradise skins occurred at Larendo in Texas in January 1916. Abraham Kallman was caught smuggling 527 skins of the Greater Bird of Paradise into the United States valued at $52,700. He was fined $2,500 and spent six months in jail. The seized skins were donated to museums.[30]

Legislation in New Guinea prohibiting commercial hunting and exporting to supply the European plume industry

Internationally expressed conservation concerns have had both direct and indirect impacts on the protection of birds of paradise in New Guinea. When the market prices for birds of paradise increased during the late nineteenth century and boomed in 1908 different responses were made by the governments of Papua, German New Guinea and Dutch New Guinea. The government of Papua introduced legislation which prohibited commercial bird hunting in 1908 (see Chapter 13). This was the result of the efforts of the Society for the Preservation of the Wild Fauna of the Empire. It was the first legislation to prohibit the commercial hunting and export of birds of paradise plumes in any part of the island.

Hunting was permitted in German New Guinea, but profits were funnelled into the economic development of mainland New Guinea (Kaiser Wilhelmsland). A number of conservation measures including hunting permits, closed seasons and conservation areas were introduced as a means of ensuring not only the survival of birds of paradise, but also the continuation of hunting as long as it was profitable. The profits gained from the sale of bird skins were used to finance the establishment of a number of plantations in Kaiser Wilhelmsland (see Chapter 12). However the German public became outraged over the slaughtering of wild birds, and the introduction of legislation prohibiting the importation of wild bird feathers into both Australia and the United States in 1913 probably encouraged the German government to succumb to conservationist demands and introduce a one year ban on bird of paradise hunting in German New Guinea on a trial basis in 1914. Hunting resumed in the Mandated Territory of New Guinea after the war. It ceased in 1922 when the Australian government brought in legislation prohibiting the export of bird of paradise skins and other plumes.

By the mid 1890s concern was being expressed in the Netherlands about the number of birds of paradise being slaughtered in Dutch New Guinea.[31] The complete ban on hunting imposed in Papua in 1908 may have influenced the Governor-General of the Dutch East Indies to impose a hunting season, from the 1 April to 1 November each year. Hunters were also required to obtain an annual hunting licence costing 25 florins. This decree was made on 14 October 1909.[32] On 16 August 1911 these restrictions were extended to the Sultanate of Tidore and areas under its jurisdiction.[33] This move was probably to cover some legal loophole, as by then this sultanate was largely incorporated within the colonial state (see Chapter 6). The 1911 decree came into force on 1 May 1912.[34] As in German New Guinea, the hunting season coincided with the time the birds were in plumage. This is not surprising as the economy of much of Dutch New Guinea, like that of German New Guinea, was dependent on plume hunting.[35] In Dutch New Guinea, the Marind-Anim region near Merauke was the first area to be closed in 1922. When Britain passed its Importation of Plumage (Prohibition) Bill in 1921, the plume trade went into decline. By the mid 1920s the prices paid for plumes had fallen and the boom was clearly over.[36] Hunting in the rest of Dutch New Guinea was prohibited in 1924, with the exceptions of the western Muyu area which was closed in 1926, Digul in 1928 and Hollandia in 1931 (see Chapters 10 and 11).

The new plume trade in New Guinea

Although there was no longer a European market for plumes after the 1920s, an Asian market remained and a more extensive plume trade developed in Papua New Guinea. For example in the Fly River region of Papua New Guinea the buyers consisted of people from other parts of the country who had been brought into the region to work on government, prospecting and other projects. The local people were keen plume traders. R. Archbold and A.L. Rand report, whilst in the Fly River region in 1936, that their workers exchanged tobacco for plumes on several occasions. Plumes of those species not found at home were keenly sought by these workers. Such acquisitions were considered by their purchasers to be almost as important as the pay they would receive.[37]

In the Wahgi valley there have been remarkable changes in the dominant feathers used in headdresses and bridewealth payments (Figure 20). Prior to the arrival of the first government officers and prospectors in the Wahgi valley in 1933 far fewer birds seem to have been killed, and the Lesser Bird of Paradise seems to have been the main species sought. After 1933 the locally available Raggiana Bird of Paradise became the dominant plume worn and exchanged. Its use peaked in 1950 and by 1970 it was out of favour. Ornithologists working in the Wahgi valley believe that this was a cultural decision rather than one brought about by declining availability. Changing economic and social circumstances provided Wahgi residents with opportunities to obtain more exotic species. From the 1950s it was possible for Wahgi men to travel on plume-buying trips, in many cases in association with employment, to the far western highlands, the far eastern highlands, the interior of the Finisterre Range, the Rai coast, and Sogeri and Woitape in the Central Province.[38] The bird skins and feathers displayed in the Wahgi thus came from distant areas.

By 1965 Stephanie's Astrapia had become the most frequently worn and exchanged plume and this remains the case. Stephanie's Astrapia are not common in the Wahgi valley forests. They are obtained by trade from other areas, especially the Jimi valley, as well as from parts of the Central, Enga and Morobe Provinces.[39]

The use of Black Sicklebill and Lesser Bird of Paradise plumes also increased after 1933 in the Wahgi valley (Figure 20B). The limited availability of the Black Sicklebill has made it the most valuable plume worn in the Waghi valley. By 1990 it was being sold for 40–100 kina a feather whereas Stephanie's Astrapia was only worth 6–50 kina each. These expensive feathers are carefully stored in sealed containers to keep out insects and rats when not being worn on ceremonial occasions (Plate 21). The long tail feathers of the Black Sicklebill and Stephanie's Astrapia are stored in bamboo tubes, whereas smaller plumes are kept in suitcases or other containers.[41]

Figure 20: In the period 1924–1974 there was a change in the main species of birds of paradise exchanged in Wahgi bridewealth payments.

Source: Based on Heaney 1982: 228.

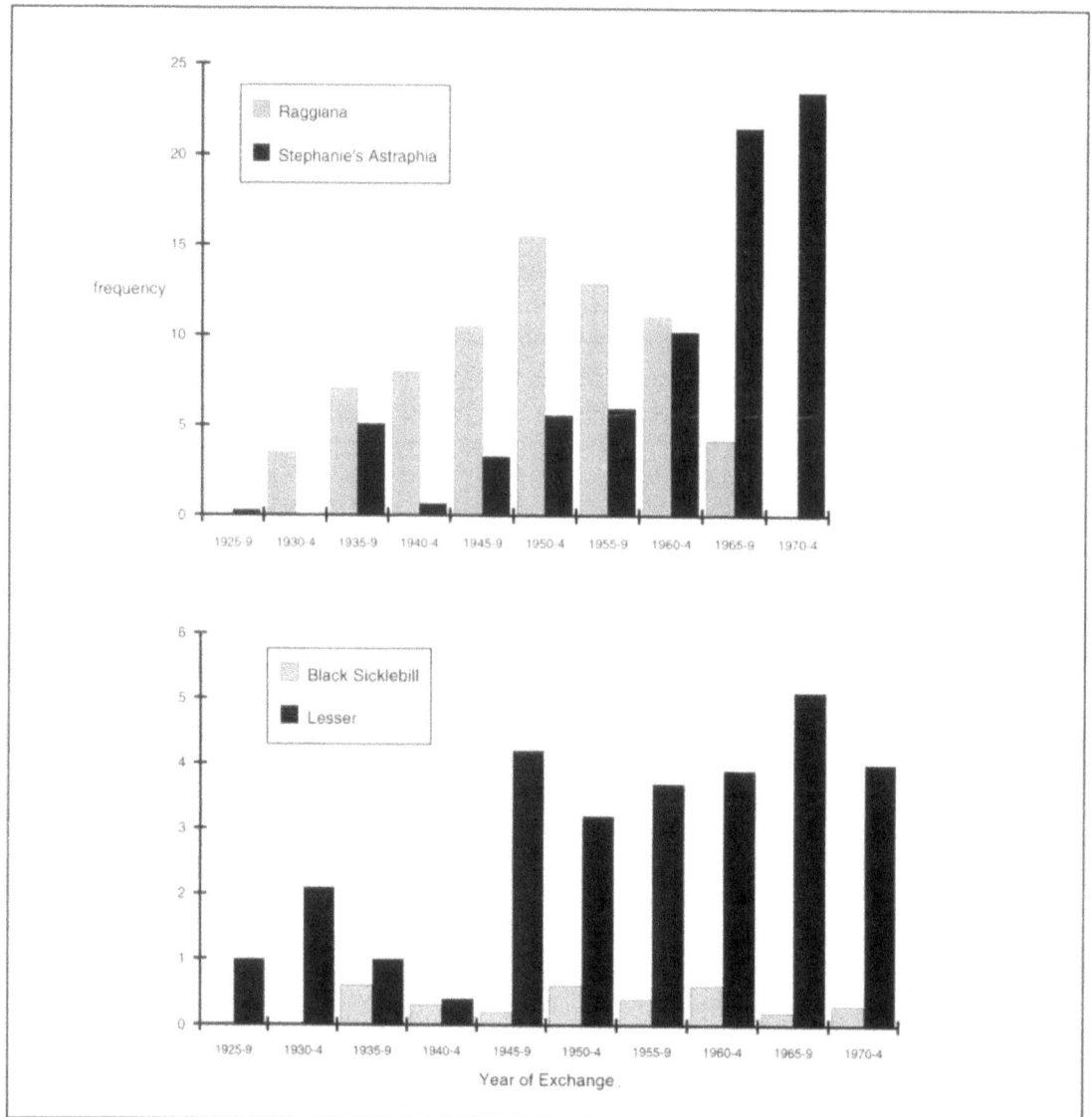

When the Raggiana began to decline in value in the Wahgi and Simbu valleys the plumes possessed by the people living in these valleys were traded to outlying areas. Plates 18–19 show Simbu plume traders at Yaramanda, a Kyaka Engan village on the northern slopes of Mount Hagen, trading Raggiana plumes in 1959. They had come to Yaramanda because they had heard that its residents were preparing to take part in a ceremonial exchange festival which would require them to wear Raggiana plumes. The traders assumed that they would find people there interested in buying their plumes.[40] Plate 20 shows Engan men mainly wearing Raggiana plumes at a dancing ground in about 1970.

As a result of this new plume trade, and the increasing use of guns in Papua New Guinea, some plume supply areas have now been overexploited. For instance, prior to the time villagers began illegally using shotguns the Greater Bird of Paradise and Raggiana Bird of Paradise were common in the Ok Tedi area. By the late 1970s the Greater Bird of Paradise was still common in localities where shotguns had not been used, but the Raggiana appeared to have declined.[42]

In West Papua, A.M. Rumbiak[43] estimates that between 150 and 200 Greater Bird of Paradise were caught in the Bomakia area inland of Merauke each year in the early 1980s. The rapidly inflating prices suggest that the numbers caught were declining. In 1972 a hunter obtained about 1,000 rupiah for a Greater Bird of Paradise skin in the Bomakia area, by 1973–78 the price had risen to 3,000–5,000 rupiah, by 1979–81 it was 5,000–7,000 rupiah and by 1982–3 the price was set at 10,000 rupiah (about 5 US dollars). The Greater Bird of Paradise (*Paradisaea apoda*) commanded the best price, but 1,000–2,000 rupiah were also paid for the more difficult-to-hunt King Bird of Paradise (*Cicinnurus regius*) and Twelve-wired Bird of Paradise (*Seleucidis melanoleuca*). The birds were bought by resident and itinerant traders and government officials in Merauke and Kouh. Some policemen also hunted as well as confiscated birds. In the early 1980s birds were illegally taken out of West Papua by traders, government officials, military personnel, boat crews and pilots.

Protective legislation in New Guinea

In the late 1920s, Ernst Mayr made a number of ornithological expeditions to New Guinea. He observed that no bird of paradise species seemed to have suffered any permanent harm, despite the slaughter of an appalling number of adult males during the European plume boom. This lack of impact had come about because only fully plumed, adult males were killed for the millinery trade.[44]

Their resilience was high because only a few mature males are needed in each generation for mating. This is possible as there are no

Plate 18: Simbu plume traders at Yaramanda on the northern slopes of Mount Hagen in Enga Province In 1959.

Plate 19: The Simbu plume traders (shown In Plate 18) display their Raggiana skins. Both photos by Ralph Bulmer, courtesy of Andrew Pawley.

Plate 20: Raggiana are the dominant plumes worn by these Engan men at a dancing ground.

Plate 21: Men from the Wahgi valley. The main bird of paradise plumes worn are those from Stephanie's Astrapia and the Lesser Bird of Paradise. Also present are Black Sicklebill, Ribbon-tailed Astrapia and the King of Saxony Bird of Paradise.

Both photos: Courtesy of George Holten. Taken in about 1970.

pair bonds and males do not assist with nesting or the rearing of young. Males do not acquire full plumage until four to five years old and are capable of mating before it develops.[45] Consequently the killing of fully plumed, adult male birds of paradise did not have the same devastating impact as the slaughtering of nesting herons.

This is also why birds of paradise have survived despite being hunted by New Guineans for thousands of years. The species most commonly used in headdresses in the Wahgi valley of Papua New Guinea were considered by ornithologists to be still common in surrounding forests in the 1960s. For this reason Thomas Gilliard recommended that traditional methods of hunting be permitted to continue.[46] An attempt by a member of the House of Assembly to introduce legislation in 1965 that would allow the commercialisation of the bird of paradise plume trade was rejected.[47]

In 1966 the Fauna Protection Ordinance of Papua and New Guinea prohibited the killing of protected fauna, including all members of the family Paradisaeidae, namely birds of paradise, bowerbirds, manucodes, riilebirds and trumpetbirds. In 1968 the Ordinance was amended to stipulate that only Papua New Guineans can hunt or keep protected wildlife, and then only if they hunt them for traditional purposes using traditional weapons. The selling, buying or exporting of their skins was prohibited. An amendment in 1974 made it possible for anyone wishing to hunt these species for scientific purposes to do so after they had obtained written government permission. Further legislation was passed in 1976 to control the use of shotguns. The penalty for shooting birds of paradise with shotguns became 500 kina per bird. In 1979 Papua New Guinea became party to the Convention on International Trade in Endangered Species of Wild Fauna and Flora (CITES). This convention controls and regulates the international exportation and importation of all endangered fauna, including all Paradisaeidae.[48]

In Papua New Guinea the visual representation of birds of paradise is widespread in daily life. They feature on the national crest and flag, as well as on coins, stamps and business logos. Moreover, on ceremonial occasions and at *singsing*, traditional dancers continue to wear their gorgeous plumes. Few people are not moved by the splendour these plumes bring to such performances. On the basis of their beauty, as well as the part they have played in the country's traditional ceremonies, birds of paradise have gained a symbolic role in expressing Papua New Guinea's national identity. Today the illegal use of guns, the sale of plumes to other Papua New Guineans and habitat destruction threatens their long-term survival.[49]

In Dutch New Guinea the whole family of the Paradisaeidae was protected in 1931 by a decree proclaimed by the Governor-General.[50] This legislation has been retained by the Republic of Indonesia and is still used to prosecute people caught trading in birds of paradise. This was the case, for instance, on the 16th of January 1992 when a man was caught in Jayapura trying to despatch birds to Java.[51] Likewise in February 1985 a director of a local company was jailed for four and a half years for attempting to smuggle 163 bird of paradise skins out of West Papua through Sorong Airport.[52]

By 1963 the survival of the Greater Bird of Paradise in the Aru Islands was a matter of concern, as they were being threatened not only by hunting for a thriving plume trade, but also by a diminishing habitat.[53] It is now illegal to export bird of paradise skins from the Aru Islands, but a clandestine trade continues. Wildlife officers now fear for the survival of birds of paradise in these islands as their numbers have dropped so low that they doubt whether the populations are viable. Kobroor Island has now been proposed as a nature reserve in order to protect the birds of paradise and other wildlife found in the islands.[54]

While some smugglers are caught others continue to flout the law, encouraged by the large profits to be made by despatching birds to Java.[55] In the 1980s one skin was reported to be worth at least US$30 in Jakarta. Hunting for this trade on the more densely settled south coast of Japen has reduced the numbers of birds of paradise to be found there. Today tourists visiting West Papua wishing to see birds of paradise in their natural habitat are advised to visit the Raja Empat Islands, especially Waigeo and Batanta, and the sparsely settled north coast of Japen.[56]

In 1990 the Republic of Indonesia passed an Act concerned with the conservation of living resources and their ecosystems. This Act prohibits anyone from hunting and trading in birds of paradise. It also stipulates that protected species cannot be transferred from one part of Indonesia to another.[57] The appropriate regulations governing the implementation of this Act are currently being prepared and these should remove any uncertainty about the use of protected species.

Notes

1. Doughty 1975: 1–3, 8.
2. Wallace 1857: 414.
3. Doughty 1975: 3, 6–7,14.
4. Doughty 1975: 22, Table 1. In addition, P. Bleeker in 1856 reports figures for plume exports from Ternate for 1832–54. These are high for the 1830s, low for the 1840s and non-existent for the 1850s. Wichmann (1917: 389) doubts Bleeker's figures. He suspects that many plumes were not registered, as M.D.

and R. van Duivenboden was actively trading in plumes in the 1850s. It is possible that these figures relate to the export of village-prepared trade skins, which Alfred Russel Wallace reports declined in value from two dollars to sixpence in the 1850s (Wallace 1857: 414), and do not include arsenic-cured skins obtained by specialist hunters.

5. Doughty 1975: 24.
6. Doughty 1975: 18–22.
7. Doughty 1975: 124.
8. Doughty 1975: 30.
9. Gilliard 1969: 30.
10. Doughty 1975: 85; Hornaday 1913: 137–142.
11. Doughty 1975: 13, 31–156.
12. Doughty 1975: 7, 9, 18.
13. Scott-Norman 1992: 16.
14. Doughty 1975: 103, 116.
15. Doughty 1975: 61, 158.
16. Downham 1911: 103.
17. Nicholson 1987: 194, 221.
18. Doughty 1975: 80.
19. Brass in Vohsen et al 1913: 236 (German New Guinea colonial document).
20. Pearson 1897 cited by Doughty 1975: 64–5.
21. Anon 1910b: Doughty 1975: 65.
22. Doughty 1975: 12, 74.
23. Doughty 1975: 69–83.
24. Doughty 1975: 158.
25. Mackenzie 1934: 314; Osborn 1913.
26. Doughty 1975: 86.
27. Anon 1910a: 16.
28. Doughty 1975: 117.
29. Doughty 1975: 51–2.
30. Hornaday 1917.
31. Wichmann 1917: 388.
32. Staatsblad van Nederlandsch-Indie 1909, No. 497.
33. Staatsblad van Nederlandsch-Indie 191, No. 473.
34. Wichmann 1917: 388–90.
35. Wichmann 1917: 389.
36. Cheesman 1938a: 40–44; Schoorl 1957.
37. Archbold and Rand 1940: 52-3, 143.
38. Bulmer 1962; Downes 1977; Gilliard 1969: 35–39; Healey 1980: 263; Hughes 1973.
39. Healey 1980. 1986, 1990; Heaney 1982; O'Hanlon 1989: 123; 1993.
40. Bulmer 1962: 16–19.
41. Bulmer 1962: 16; Deck 1990.

42. Bell 1969: 208: Coates and Lindgren 1978: 68–9.

43. Rumbiak 1984.

44. Gilliard 1969: 30.

45. Gilliard 1969: 31–2.

46. Gilliard 1969: 38–39.

47. Gellibrand et al 1966; Schultze-Westrum 1969: 302.

48. Fauna Protection Ordinance of 1966 and 1968 amendment; Fauna (Protection and Control) Amendment Act 1974; Fauna (Protection and Control) Amendment Act 1976; International Trade (Fauna and Flora) Act 1979; Spring 1977: 2.

49. Beehler 1993: Kwapena 1985: 154–5; Peckover 1978. The use of guns to shoot females and immature males also means that traditional conservation measures are being ignored (see Bulmer 1961: 6, 9).

50. Staatsblad van Nederlandsch-lndie 1931, No. 266.

51. Michele Bowe personal communication 1993.

52. Anon 1985.

53. Pfeffer 1963 cited by Cooper and Forshaw 1977: 176.

54. Muller 1990a: 133–4.

55. Anon 1990: Petocz 1989.

56. Muller 1990b: 51. 67. 71. 90–1.

57. Act of the Republic of Indonesia, No. 5 of 1990.

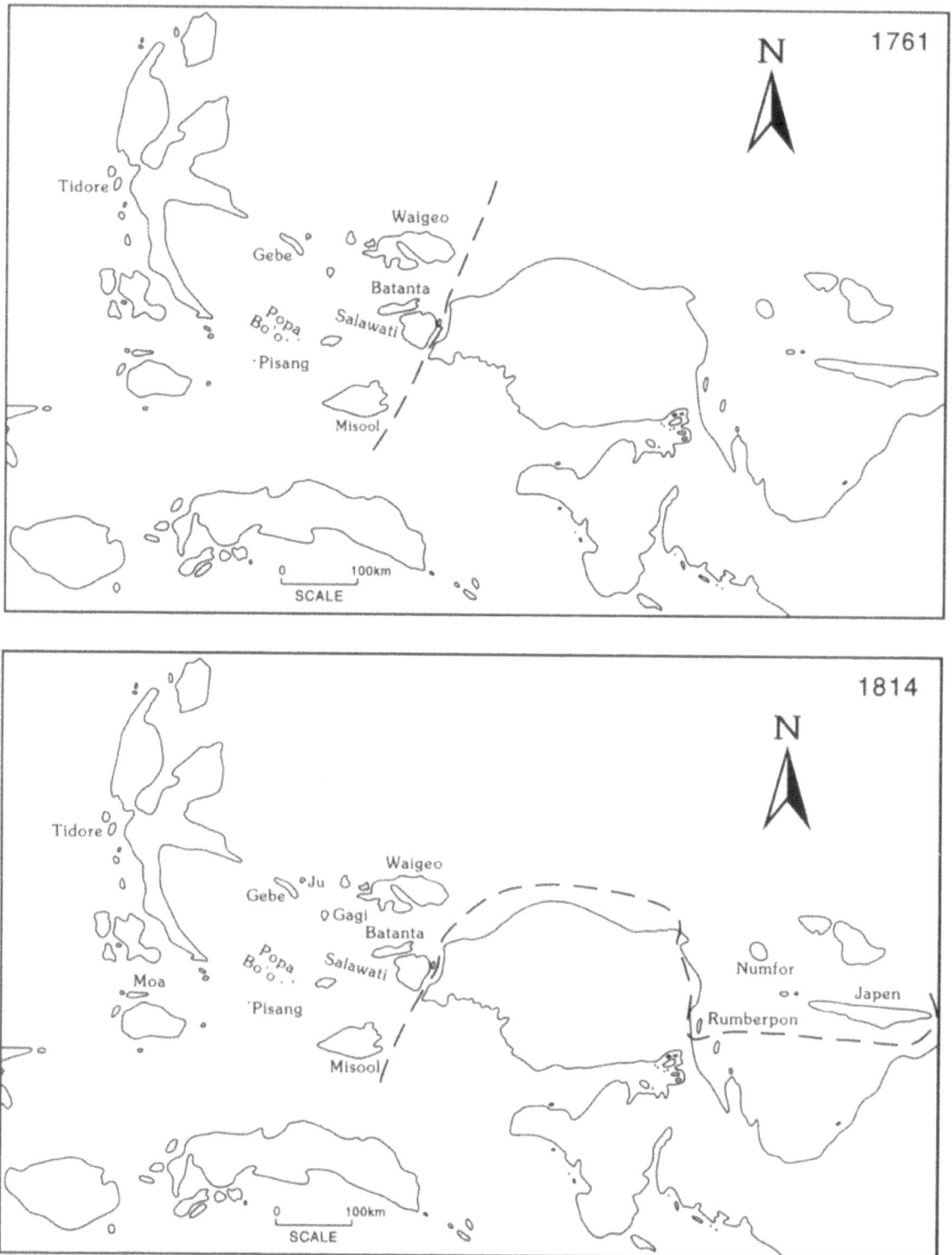

Figure 21: The respective areas of New Guinea designated under Tidore by the Dutch in 1761 and by the English in 1814 (designated areas are named).

108

6

Sultans, suzerains and the colonial division of New Guinea

Introduction

This chapter is the first of the geographical presentations. It provides a history of how one of the Spice Island sultans became the putative suzerain of part of New Guinea. The chapter begins with the demise of the spice trade in the Spice Islands. Trade emphasis then changes to supplying goods to China, then to plumes, copra and other products for European markets. A growing European interest in tropical products resulted in the control of New Guinea being divided amongst the Dutch, German and British governments.

The decline of the Ternatian and Bacan sultanates and the rise of Tidore

As mentioned in Chapter 2, in 1653 the Sultans of Ternate and Bacan were required by the Dutch East India Company to destroy all the clove trees in their territories. They also had to provide the labour for this work under Dutch supervision.[1] To compensate for their lost spice income the Dutch East India Company agreed to pay both Sultans an annual subsidy. A similar arrangement was made with Tidore, but there was a short delay until the new sultan ascended the throne in 1657.

The Dutch East India Company made their first formal treaty with the new Sultan of Tidore after ousting the Spanish-Portuguese representatives from Tidore in 1660. In this treaty the Sultan of Tidore was made responsible for troublesome 'Papua', namely all the islands at the tip of western New Guinea, apart from the islands of the 'Pigaraja'. The latter is generally accepted to mean the Raja of Misool (Figure 21), who remained under Bacan.[2] This was the first of a number of treaties. After 1761 the geographic area encompassed by each new treaty increased as the Dutch perceived a growing interest by other metropolitan powers in the Pacific, see Figure 22.

The choice of Tidore is interesting, as it was the Sultan of Bacan and not Tidore who had real influence in the troublesome Raja Empat

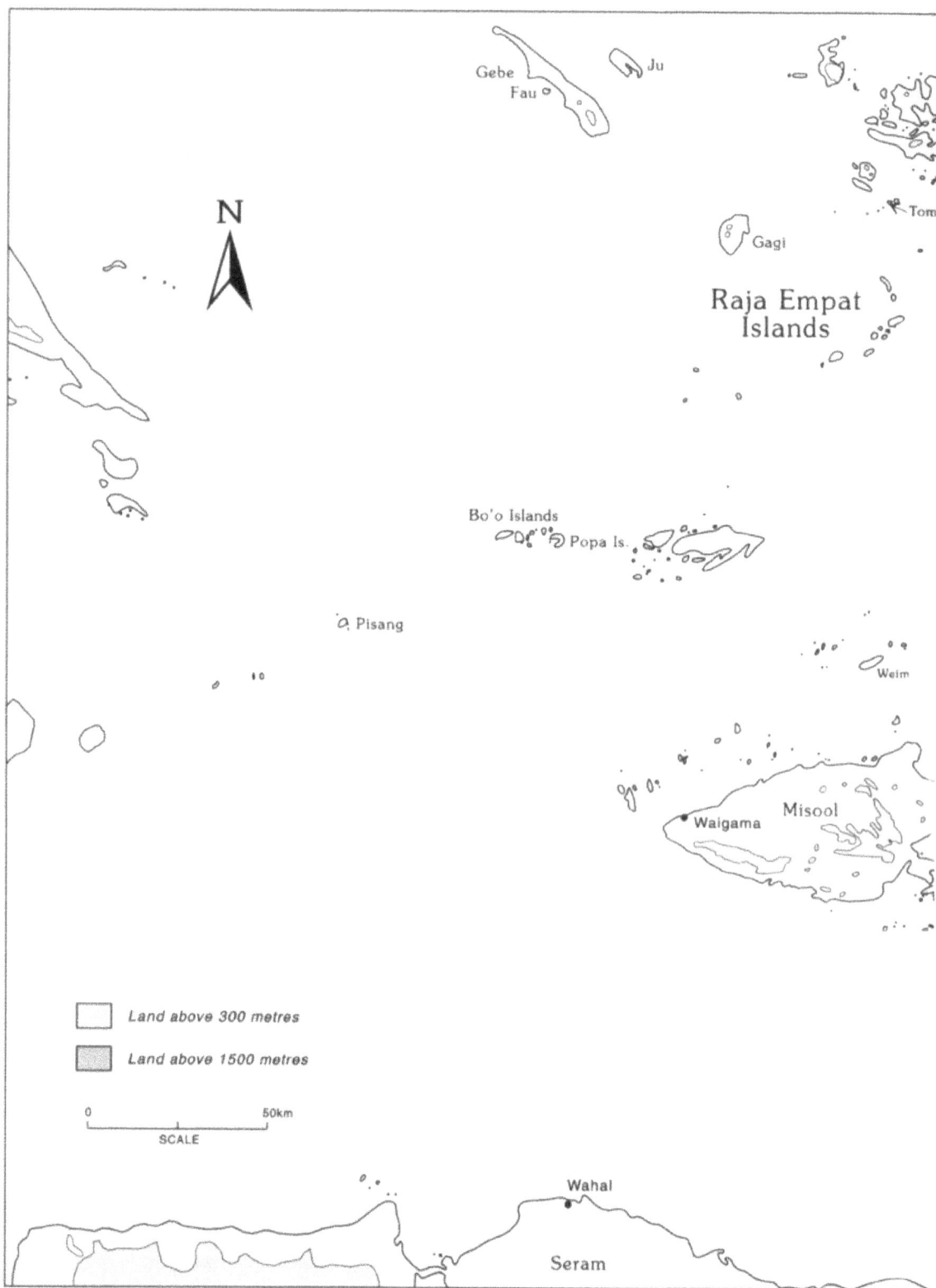

Figure 22: The Raja Empat Islands

Waigeo

Cape of
Good Hope

Mavalibit
Bay

Muka

Besir

Tamrau Mountains

Mega

Sorong

Bird's Head
(Vogelkop)

Semeter

Salawati

Almura Lake

Berau Bay
(MacCluer Gulf)

Rumakai
Hati-Hati
Fatagar

Arguni Is.

ONIN

Fak Fak

Islands. The Sultan of Tidore had no presence in the area. This suggests that other factors drove the Dutch East India Company to select the Sultan of Tidore. He was of course their man as the Dutch East India Company had influenced proceedings when the new sultan was chosen. By ensuring his success, it must be presumed that the Company expected to gain some advantage. Another factor in Tidore's favour was that unlike the Sultan of Bacan, he was not closely associated with Ternate, the sultanate which had given rise to so many rebellions against the Dutch.

The Company expected the Sultan of Tidore to relieve them of the responsibility of maintaining law and order in the unprofitable Papuan Islands. Attempts to find precious metals or spices in New Guinea had been unsuccessful. Many company ships had been despatched to investigate the island's resources, but apart from massoy (see Chapter 8), no profitable products had been found.

A new treaty was signed between the Dutch East India Company and the Sultan of Tidore in 1667. It is vague about the area under the Sultan's jurisdiction. Such vagueness was clearly intentional, as it allowed the Company to make him responsible for all Papuan misdemeanours.[3]

When Keyts visited western New Guinea in 1678 he found no evidence of Tidore's influence. The Governor of Banda also states in 1679 that the Sultan of Tidore did not have to be consulted when dealing with Papuans. However people in the Papuan Islands clearly feared him for his piracy and *hongi* raids.

By 1680 the Dutch East India Company had left trade with New Guinea to the Dutch planters on Banda, but their trading ventures ceased when a number of traders were killed. The treaty of 1667 between the Dutch East India Company and the Sultan of Tidore was renewed in 1689. In 1700 yet another contract was signed. This stipulated that the Sultan had to keep hostilities between the inhabitants of the Papuan Islands to a minimum. In 1703 Tidore's representatives were allowed to travel with Company officials to New Guinea. This was the beginning of a practice which was to continue for the next two centuries.[4]

In 1706 Governor Rooselaar named the following islands as being under the rule of Tidore: Pisang, the 23 Bo (Bo'o) Islands, Popa, Misool, Salawati, Batanta and Waigeo.[5] It is significant that neither Gebe nor the Onin peninsula of New Guinea are mentioned. Later in 1716, the Governor of the Residency of Ternate wrote that the Sultan of Tidore pretends to dominate part of the Bird's Head, but even he admits that the Papuans do not recognise this claim.[6]

Despite the Sultan of Tidore's lack of authority in the Papuan Islands and western New Guinea, the Dutch renewed their contract with him in 1733. It was a far from satisfactory situation: the Sultan of Tidore had neither the respect of the people he was supposed to rule, nor an honest relationship with the Dutch. To obtain influence and intelligence the Sultan sent representatives to the Raja Empat Islands. When the Sultan's representatives were present, these islanders were afraid to make any critical comments about the Sultan to Dutch officials, as they feared retribution.[7]

In 1761 the Dutch Government reassessed the rights of the Dutch East India Company in the eastern East Indies. They were concerned about the growing foreign threat to their spice monopoly. Their apprehensions were correct as a French expedition and subsequent English rule of the East Indies resulted in spice plants being collected and plantations being established elsewhere (see Chapter 2).[8]

In the late eighteenth century the Dutch only allowed Chinese traders from Ternate and Tidore to trade in New Guinea. They were permitted to do so on the grounds that they would not trade in nutmegs. The Chinese were permitted to trade for massoy bark, slaves, ambergris, trepang, turtle shell, pearls, parrots and birds of paradise. In return for these goods they gave iron tools, chopping knives, axes, blue and red cloth, beads, plates and bowls.[9]

It was Dutch policy to give as much power as possible in Papuan affairs to the Sultan of Tidore. By doing so, the Dutch hoped that he would become a local authority who could be held responsible for all Papuan offences. Dutch unification policies also expanded the area under Tidore's jurisdiction. These expansions were not always welcomed by the Sultan. The locals likewise had no say in the matter. According to Thomas Forrest,[10] who was in the Raja Empat Islands and visited Doreri Bay in 1774–5, the Papuans did not like the Tidorese. Despite being supported by the Dutch, the Sultan of Tidore was still unable to assert influence on Onin in 1775 without informing the Sultan of Misool.

The Dutch East India Company's worries about protecting the Moluccas from foreign vessels increased when internal problems began to escalate. The Company tried to stop the Raja Empat Islanders from carrying out plundering raids by punishing their leaders. In 1770 they imprisoned the Raja of Salawati and in 1774 the Company arrested and exiled the Raja of Waigeo.[11] In view of subsequent events these efforts had little impact. Papuan raids continued. There was also an increase in the number of raids from Sulu and Mindanao. The real problem came when a successor to the late Sultan of Tidore had to be chosen. Prince Nuku became angry when he was unsuccessful.

In 1781 Nuku left Tidore and declared himself Sultan of the Papuan Islands. This was the beginning of a guerilla war which lasted for many years. The Papuans sided with the rebellious Prince Nuku. As a result Gebe and Numfor were able to extend their sphere of influence. During these chaotic years Gebe assembled a fleet of 300 praus which went on plundering sea raids.

In 1780 a contract was made between the Dutch East India Company and the new Sultan of Tidore which stated that his authority extended to all the villages on New Guinea. This claim was never repeated in subsequent treaties and was probably made to thwart Prince Nuku. At first things went badly for Prince Nuku. He was defeated by Tidore and lost Salawati in 1789, and in 1790 Misool submitted to Tidore. The relationship between Bacan and the Raja Empat Islands, especially Misool, was now over.

The British were able to enter the waters of the Dutch East Indies legally after the Dutch had signed the Treaty of Paris in 1784. This treaty required the Dutch to allow free navigation in the archipelago. In 1791 John MacCluer sailed past the Bird's Head and explored Berau Bay (formerly MacCluer Gulf). In 1793 he returned with Captain John Hayes and Captain Court to found the first European settlement in New Guinea. These British East India Company entrepreneurs had obtained permission from Prince Nuku before attempting to establish their spice plantation at Doreri Bay. Hayes had a handful of British sailors and Indian soldiers under his command. They built a stockade called Fort Coronation in Doreri Bay (Figure 25) and took possession of the area he called New Albion. The fort had a wooden palisade and was defended by 12 cannons. New Guineans were 'recruited' to plant and tend spices, to harvest local wild nutmegs and cut teak. The venture was not a success. The supply of provisions did not go as planned. There were many deaths from malaria and beriberi, and some men were attacked, captured and sold as slaves. Some of those captured were sold by Numfor islanders on Seram. The base was abandoned in April 1795.[12]

Alternating British and Dutch control of the East Indies

In 1795 the Netherlands were occupied by Napoleon's forces, and thus at war with Great Britain. That same year the British based some of their ships at Prince Nuku's headquarters on Gebe. In 1796 and 1797 Prince Nuku with the assistance of two British ships captured all the government posts in the Moluccas, except Ternate which was not taken until June 1801.

In 1798 Prince Nuku proclaimed a man from Makian island as the Raja of Jailolo. The former Jailolo sultanate had ceased to exist after its sacking in 1551 by Ternatian and Portuguese forces following a combined Tidore, Jailolo and Spanish attempt to oust the Portuguese. Prince Nuku wanted the new Raja of Jailolo to undermine Ternatian support on Halmahera and in this way weaken the combined power of the Dutch and Ternatians. The Raja of Jailolo and all the successors to his title persisted in this endeavour until the last Raja of Jailolo was exiled in 1832. These efforts won support in Halmahera, especially the Tobelo region, the Raja Empat Islands, north and east Seram, Mindanao and the Sulu Archipelago.[13]

The East Indies were returned to Dutch control in 1802 when a peace treaty was signed at Amiens. As the Dutch East India Company had been disbanded in the Netherlands in December 1799, their assets became the responsibility of the Board of Asian Possessions. A colonial government was established when the Dutch resumed control of the archipelago in 1802, but this only lasted until 1810 when another European war began.

During the short Dutch administration, Prince Nuku died at Tidore in 1805. The so-called Raja of Jailolo continued Nuku's pretence to the throne and resisted the Dutch until 1806 when he fled and found assistance in the Raja Empat group.

In 1810 the British regained what they called East India. In 1814 an agreement was made with the legitimate Sultan of Tidore and the Sultan of Ternate before the British Resident. The area of the Sultan of Tidore was described as comprising the islands of Maijtara, Filongan, Mare, Moa, Gebe, Joy (Ju), Pisang, Gagi, Bo'o, Popa, together with the whole of the Papuan Islands and the four districts of Mansary, Karandefur, Ambarpura and Umbarpon (Rumberpon) on the coast of New Guinea (Figure 21 bottom).[14] The latter are thought to refer to the Numfor colonies on the west coast of Cendrawasih Bay and on Japen.[15]

The Dutch colonial government from 1814

The Dutch regained control of the archipelago in August 1814 and reestablished their colonial government. It was not until 1817 that a new treaty was signed with the Sultan of Tidore. The problem of the Sultan of Jailolo remained, but it soon became apparent that he had no real political ambitions and was no more than a pirate.

By 1817 the Dutch Residency of Ternate consisted of the self-governing sultanates of Ternate, Tidore and Bacan, as well as their subjected territories. These included Halmahera and adjacent islands, the Raja Empat group, the Sula archipelago and east Sulawesi. Dealings between the self-governing sultanates and the Dutch colonial government were regulated by contracts drawn-up with the Sultans of Ternate, Tidore and Bacan. Their subjected territories, however, were more or less under the total control of their own rulers. The Dutch considered the overall situation far from satisfactory, but did not instigate changes because of a lack of personnel and finance. This lack of activity reflected the limited economic interest shown by the Dutch in these areas.[16]

Further contracts were signed with Ternate and Tidore in 1824 which reiterated and strengthened the agreements of 1814 regarding their areas of suzerainty.

In 1824 the Netherlands and England came to an agreement that the Dutch had a right to part of New Guinea as stated in the treaty of 1814. It was also agreed that most of the island still remained 'free' in that it was not claimed by any metropolitan power.

In 1828 the Dutch government claimed sovereignty of New Guinea from the Cape of Good Hope on the Bird's Head to 141° east longitude on the south coast (near the current international border with Papua New Guinea) and the lands within (Figure 23 top). This event took place near Lobo in Triton Bay at Fort Du Bus on 24 August 1828. The fort was established by a military detachment dropped off from the *Triton* and *Iris*. The history of suffering experienced by the personnel of this settlement is well known. There was much illness and many died. In the eight years before the fort was abandoned and demolished in 1836, some 10 Dutch officers, 50 Dutch and 50 Indonesian soldiers died.[17]

After 1828 the area under the Sultan of Tidore's authority was not described by the Dutch in any of the contracts made between them. In 1828 Dutch administrative officials began travelling in warships along New Guinea's coastline. In addition to confirming the appointment of headmen on behalf of the Sultan of Tidore, they punished slave hunting and head-hunting. In 1830 Tidore defeated Gebe, the former head-quarters of Prince Nuku. In 1832 the Sultan of Jailolo was sent into exile.

In the 1840s the Dutch government requested information as to the areas where Dutch colonial rule was accepted.[18] This survey started in the Moluccas. In a secret report made in 1848 it was stated that Tidorese rule extended along the north coast of New Guinea until Cape Bonpland at 140°47' east longitude (Figure 23 bottom).

Bruyn de Kops was a lieutenant on the *Circe*, the Dutch man-of-war which accompanied the Tidorese *hongi* fleet on a weather-thwarted attempt to mark the extent of the north coast reputedly now under the Sultan of Tidore.[19] In a secret decision made on 30 July 1848 the notion that Tidorese rule extended along the north coast of New Guinea as far as Cape Bonpland on the eastern side of Humboldt Bay was accepted by the Dutch government, without any further clarification. The Dutch did not make this eastern border public until 1865 and they were also very vague as to what areas came under Tidore's jurisdiction or directly under the umbrella of Dutch rule.

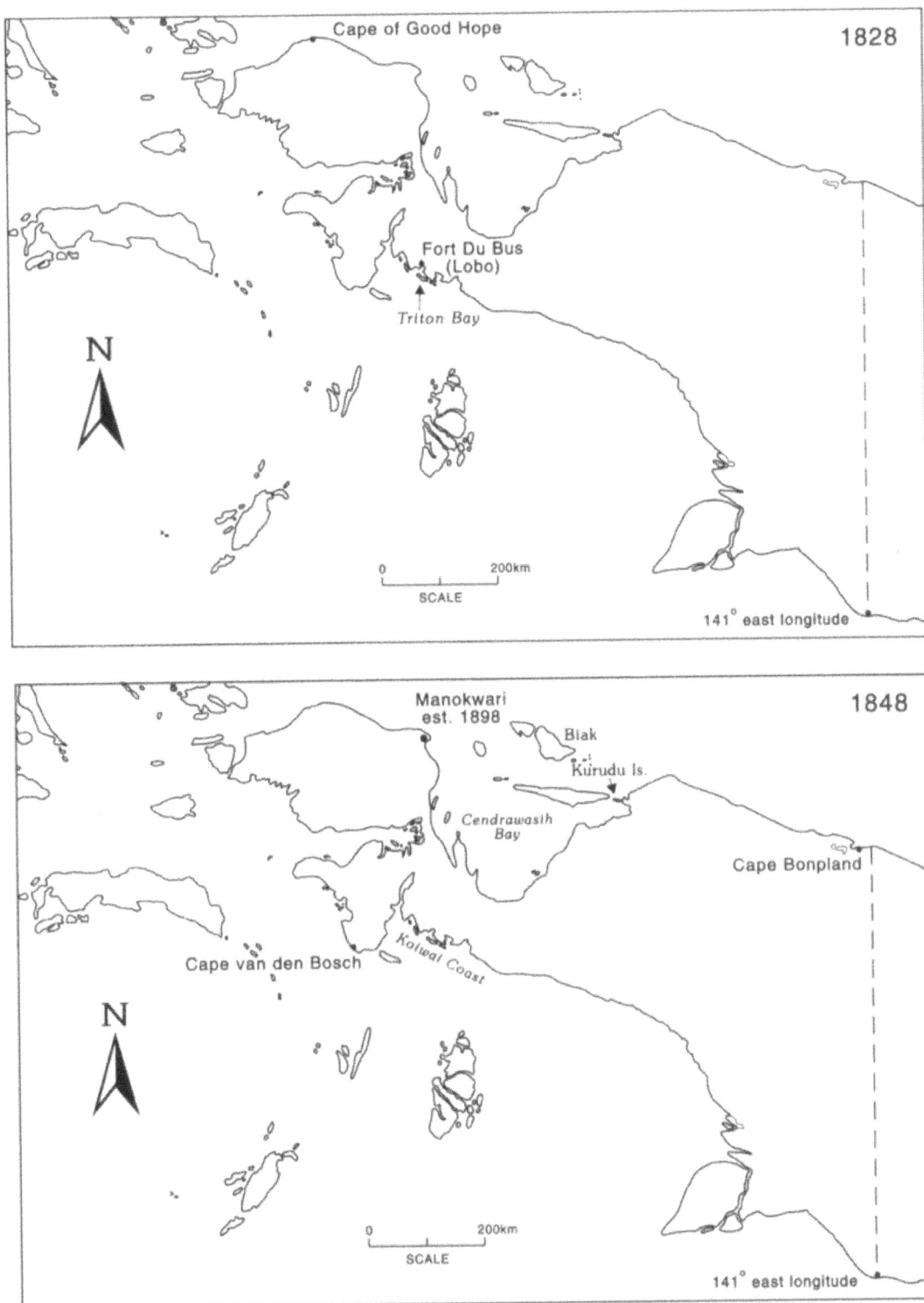

Figure 23: The respective areas of New Guinea designated under Tidore by the 1828 and 1848 treaties between the Dutch and Tidore.

Although he did not interfere with trade, the Sultan of Tidore began to assert his authority, with Dutch backing, over western Dutch New Guinea in 1848. He did this by issuing levies (tribute demands) which were enforced by punitive *hongi* trips of rape and pillage. In New Guinea some of the worst raids were made on the easternmost areas of foreign trade, namely Kurudu Island on the north coast and the Kowiai area on the southwest coast (see Figure 23 bottom and Chapters 8 and 11). When the Dutch authorities forbade *hongi* expeditions, the influence of the Sultan of Tidore in western New Guinea soon ceased.[20]

The tribute demanded by Tidore had to be taken to the Sultan. Dumont D'Urville records that each 'chief in Doreri Bay sent an annual tribute to this Sultan. Their tribute was a slave of either gender, turtle shell and bird of paradise skins.[21] Sometimes this obligation was not met, thus provoking the notorious expeditions of the Tidorese fleets to Cendrawasih Bay. Sometimes fleets from Gebe and east Halmahera would make independent raids claiming to be acting under instruction from Tidore.

When the leaders from Cendrawasih Bay took their tribute to Tidore, they usually received a title in return. Initially these titles referred to real functions such as prince, head of a district or village headman. A flag and official dress went with each title. The Biak people, for example, later conferred similar titles on their trading friends. In this way these titles came to lose their functional associations.[22]

By 1858 the Sultan of Ternate lived in a large, untidy, half ruined stone palace. The Dutch government continued to pay him a pension. His suzerainty now only extended to the local people of Ternate and northern Halmahera. In the 1850s Dutch interests dominated the economy of Ternate. Over half of Ternate town was owned by a locally born Dutchman called Renesse van Duivenboden. He was known as the King of Ternate, which is not surprising as his possessions included land, ships and over 100 slaves. Much of his money was made by trading in plumes and natural history specimens as described in Chapter 4. When Alfred Russel Wallace travelled along the north coast of New Guinea, he went in the trading schooner *Hester Helena* which belonged to Duivenboden.[23]

Increasing Dutch presence in New Guinea from the 1850s

In 1855 C.W. Ottow and J.G. Geissler started mission work on Mansinam Island in Doreri Bay. Dutch navy vessels also began to increase the frequency of their visits. These voyages revealed how undesirable and disastrous Tidorese rule was and how it was not locally desired. The Dutch government put pressure on Tidore to stop using *hongi* fleets and their slave crews in the 1850s. In enforcing this ban the Dutch were following a worldwide trend, namely the growing abhorrence of slavery. Here we must remember that Britain passed anti-slavery laws in 1807, followed by the United States in 1808. British slaves were freed in 1838, French in 1848, Dutch in 1863 and American in 1865.[24]

Piracy and raiding declined when the Dutch began to use steamboats. In 1876 a member of Raja Jailolo's family *dano* Babo Hasan tried to re-establish the sultanate on eastern Halmahera. His movement was directed against Ternate and Tidore, but was suppressed by the crew of a Dutch steamboat in 1877.[25] The decline in piracy and *hongi* fleets saw an extension of trade along the north coast.

In the 1872 contract with Tidore it is made clear that the Sultan of Tidore only had the right of feudal tenure. Sovereignty of New Guinea rested with the Dutch East India government who could take over its management in full or in part at its own discretion.[26]

In 1875 the eastern border of the territory was marked and this extended the land area previously proclaimed in 1828. The Dutch Government Almanac of 1875 outlines the Dutch area of New Guinea as extending from Cape Bonpland (the eastern side of Humboldt Bay) at 140°47' east longitude on the north coast until 141° east longitude on the south coast, including the adjoining islands (Figure 23 bottom). This border apart from small changes became the boundary of Dutch New Guinea. Subsequently the north coast border was extended to 141° east longitude and the south coast one to 141°01' at the mouth of the Bensbach River.[27] The river was named after the plume trader who became the Resident of Ternate, J. Bensbach, at the suggestion of the Administrator of British New Guinea, Sir William MacGregor.[28]

Local leaders continued to make stands against foreign influences. On Halmahera in 1875–76 the so-called 'Prophet of Kau' led a movement against the Sultans of Ternate and Tidore. His cult attracted some 30,000 followers.[29] Likewise in 1894 a *konor* raised himself on Roon Island and terrorised the western part of Cendrawasih Bay. These activities declined as the Dutch presence increased. A Dutch government post was established in Cendrawasih Bay at Manokwari in 1898 (Figure 23 bottom).

The Tidorese throne became vacant in 1905 and the lack of a ruler diminished its autonomy. In 1907 the Dutch colonial government forced Ternate to relinquish its authority over east Sulawesi, as well as Banggai and other islands. The Dutch also forced the government of Tidore to sign away its independence in 1909.[30] In 1910 Ternate and Bacan signed agreements which invalidated all their old contracts with the Dutch, incorporating them more within the colonial state. In 1914 Sultan Usman of Ternate was banished to Java following a tax revolt in Jailolo. This led to further modifications as to the degree of autonomy Ternate was permitted within the colonial state. The next seven chapters are concerned with specific areas of New Guinea.[31]

Notes

1. van Fraassen 1981: 11–12; Wright 1958: 12.
2. Galis 1953–4: 17.
3. ibid.
4. ibid.
5. Haga 1884 cited by Galis 1953–4: 17.
6. Leupe 1875 cited by Galis 1953–4: 17.
7. Galis 1953–4: 17–8.
8. Ambergris is a waxy substance produced by the intestines of sperm whales. It is found floating in the sea or washed up on the shore. It is used in perfumes, as a fixative and formerly in cookery.
9. Forrest 1969: 106.
10. Forrest 1969: 101–2.
11. Galis 1953–4: 37.
12. Galis 1953–4: 19: Kamma 1972: 217.
13. van Fraassen 1981: 12, 20.
14. Galis 1953–4: 20; van der Veur 1966a: 8. Some of the islands cited could not be located.
15. Robide van der Aa 1879 cited by Galis 1953–4: 20.
16. van Fraassen 1981: 21–2.
17. Galis 1953–4: 21: van der Veur 1966a: 10–11; van der Veur 1966b: 2.
18. Haga 1884 cited by Galis 1953–4: 21.
19. Kops 1852.
20. Earl 1853: 86; Galis 1953–4: 22; Kops 1852: 335.
21. Dumont d'Urville 1834.
22. Earl 1853: 82–3; Kops 1852: 315.
23. Wallace 1986: 312, 314, 496.
24. Rowley 1966: 58.
25. van Fraassen 1981: 21–1.
26. Galis 1953–4: 48
27. ibid; Prescott et al 1977: 84–5: van der Veur 1966a: 64–5.
28. van der Veur 1966a: 64–5.
29. Muller 1990b: 56.
30. Tidore retained some jurisdiction in New Guinea, as further legislation had to be enacted in 1911 to ensure that areas formerly under Tidore were subjected to the 1909 bird of paradise hunting legislation (Wichmann 1917: 388; Staatsblad van Nederlandsch-Indie 1909, No. 497; Staatsblad van Nederlandsch-Indie 1911, No. 473).
31. van Fraassen 1981: 21–2.

7

Collecting and trading in
the Raja Empat Islands,
the Bird's Head and Cendrawasih Bay

Introduction

The part played by the people of the Bird's Head and the Raja Empat Islands in the Asian plume trade is covered in Chapter 3. This chapter covers early European acquisitions of bird of paradise skins as well as their subsequent interest in acquiring natural history specimens and plumes for the millinery trade. It also reports on the activities of Chinese and other traders supplying Chinese markets.

Bird of paradise skins

Local leaders in the Moluccas and New Guinea presented preserved birds of paradise to important people. The first Europeans to reach the Spice Islands in 1522 received gifts of Lesser Bird of Paradise from the Sultan of Bacan. This practice was to continue. For instance, in 1775 Thomas Forrest was given birds of paradise by three Papuan headmen, when they came out to his vessel off the Aiou (Ayu) islands northeast of Waigeo. Forrest was told that these particular skins had been obtained from the mainland of New Guinea.[1] Europeans in return began to offer trade goods for bird of paradise skins; see Figure 24. As the number of European visitors increased and their natural history and millinery interests and demands grew, more became known about the best places to acquire the skins of birds of paradise.

   G.E. Rumphius, the Dutch scholar who lived on Ambon from 1653 until his death in 1702, records the sources of the trade skins he obtained on Ambon in the seventeenth century. He was told that the Greater Bird of Paradise came from the Aru Islands, the Lesser from Misool and Salawati, the King from the Papuan and Aru Islands, the Glossy-mantled Manucode from Misool, the Arfak Astrapia from Sergile (the Sorong area of the Bird's Head), the Black Sicklebill from Sergile and the rare Twelve-wired Bird of Paradise from the Papuan Islands and possibly Sergile.[2] He also learnt that the plumes were traded for small metal axes and poor quality cloth.

In view of what we now know about the distribution of these species, Salawati was clearly a trade centre for the Lesser Bird of Paradise, presumably obtained from the mainland; likewise the Sorong area was a trade centre for the Arfak Astrapia and Black Sicklebill which are only found in the Arfak Mountains and in the Arfak and Tamrau Mountains respectively. Rumphius also reports that he acquired the Glossy-mantled Manucode and the rare Twelve-wired Bird of Paradise through Tidore, which suggests that these plumes were in demand there at this time.

When the French naturalist Pierre Sonnerat was on Gebe Island in 1772 he was presented with skins of the Western Parotia and Crinkle-collared Manucode by the Raja of Salawati and the Raja of Patani, an east coast Halmahera village. We now know that the Western Parotia skin would have come from the Tamrau Range of the Bird's Head.[3]

Chinese, Ternatian and other traders

In 1775 Chinese traders from Ternate, Tidore and Ambon were the only traders allowed by the Dutch East India Company to trade on the north coast of New Guinea, as they could be trusted not to trade in nutmegs. These traders wore Dutch colours and had passes issued by the Sultan of Tidore. This trade restriction was not lifted until the Dutch East India Company was disbanded in 1799.

Figure 24: This scene of Doreri Bay in 1827 shows two activities. In the background a man is trading bird of paradise skins with a Frenchman. In the foreground two men are forging metal tools whilst another operates the bellows.

Source: Dumont d'Urville 1834 drawn by M. de Sainson.

The Chinese sought massoy obtained from Warapine (Waropen) on the east coast of Cendrawasih Bay. This massoy bark was not a coastal product but came from inland forests. Inland groups harvested the massoy bark and traded it to the coastal Waropen[4] for metal implements and cloth. In 1775 one picul (60.5 kilograms) of massoy was worth 30 dollars in Java. The Chinese also traded in slaves, ambergris, trepang, turtle shell, pearls, black and red lories and birds of paradise. In return they provided iron tools, chopping knives, axes, blue and red cloth, beads, plates and bowls.[5] This trade probably led to Kurudu Island at the eastern end of Japen becoming an important trading centre.

The presence of Chinese ceramics in the Kumamba Islands (Figure 42) in 1616[6] suggests that Chinese traders have a long history of trade on the coastline extending from Waropen to the Kumamba Islands. This is not surprising as Chinese porcelain dating to the thirteenth and fourteenth centuries has been found in Sulawesi and the Talaud Islands,[7] and some from the fifteenth century in Berau Bay in West New Guinea (see Chapter 8).

By the 1840s the Chinese operating in the Bird's Head and Cendrawasih Bay area had been joined by other traders. These included traders from Ternate, especially the employees of Renesse van Duivenboden, and some Bugis from Makassar. Only one European was involved. He was Captain Deighton, an Englishman, who was a longterm resident of the Moluccas.

Ternatian traders made annual visits by schooner to the shores of Berau and Bintuni Bays. This region produced large quantities of wild nutmegs. They usually returned with a full cargo of nutmegs, but this was not achieved without risk. In the late 1850s traders were still attacked on this coast.

Trading centres

In the 1850s Samati (Semeter), the largest village on Salawati Island, was the main trading centre at the western tip of the Bird's Head (Figures 22 and 25). A Bugis trader was in permanent residence there. Traders were attracted not only by the rich turtle, pearl shell and trepang resources of the surrounding and nearby shores, but also by the great number and variety of birds of paradise to be obtained from the Cendrawasih Peninsula. Most of the trading praus and schooners which visited the western tip of New Guinea called at Salawati. Salawati villagers also supplied neighbouring groups with sago.

Few traders visited Waigeo which was sparsely populated. Waigeo villagers took their sago and pearl shell to trading centres on Salawati or Tidore. However they did provision some whaling crews and ships en route to China. When A.R. Wallace was passing through the passage between Waigeo and Batanta in March 1858, several canoes came out from both islands bringing produce for sale. They had some common shells, palm-leaf mats, coconuts and pumpkins. Wallace found them too extravagant in their demands. They were clearly accustomed to selling their trifles to the crews of whalers and China-bound ships. In Wallace's view these crews lacked discrimination and purchased items at ten times their real value.[8]

Misool did not have an established trading centre, but each year a number of Gorong and Seram Laut praus came to load sago, which they took to Ternate. It was also rich in massoy bark, trepang, turtle shell, pearls and birds of paradise. As a result of Misool's past associations with the Spice Islands, its coastal people were all Moslems and were governed by local rajas.

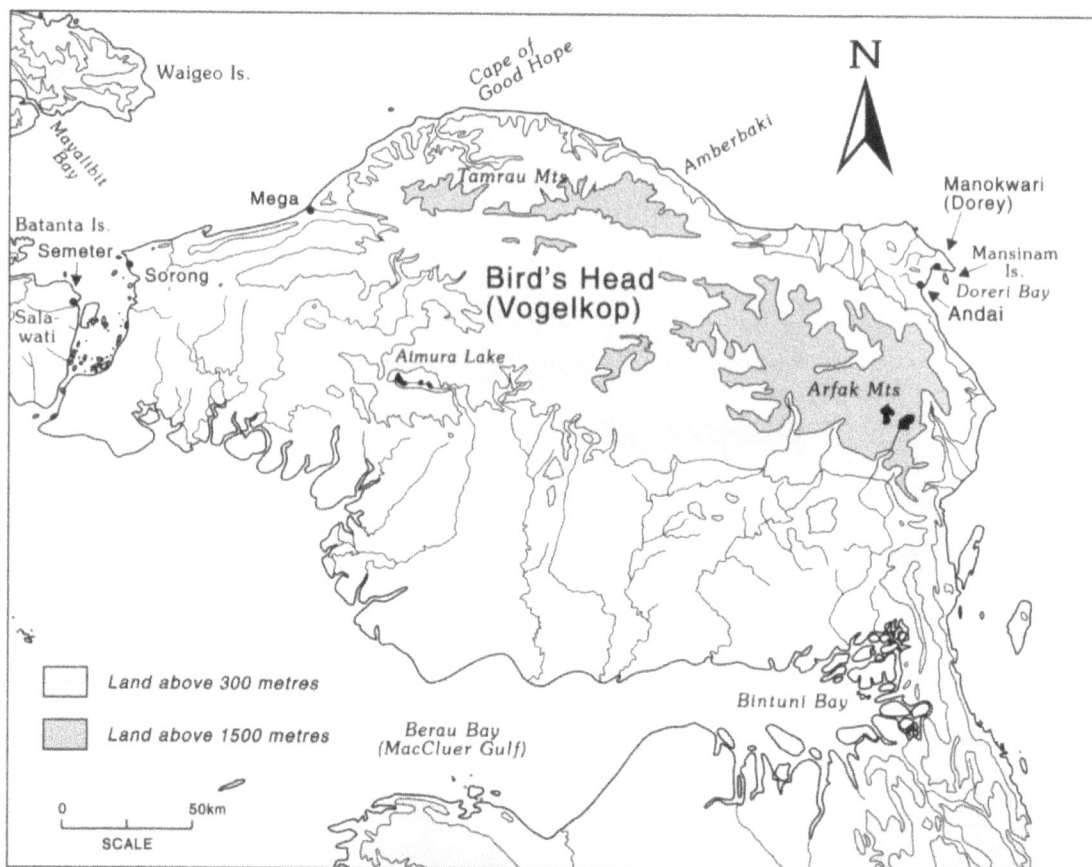

Figure 25: The Bird's Head.

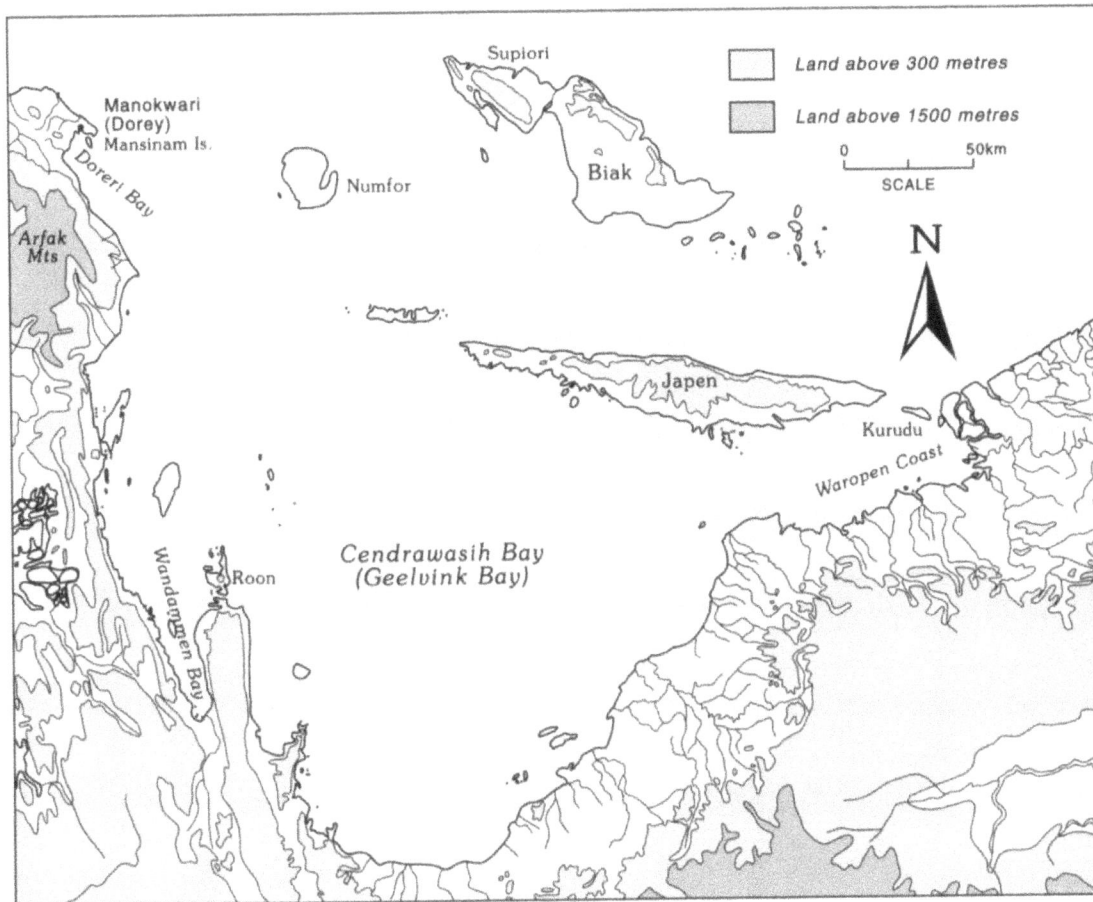

Figure 26: Cendrawasih Bay.

In the 1850s Dorey and Roon Island were the main trading centres in Cendrawasih Bay (Figure 26). Kurudu Island had formerly been an important trade centre, but this ended in the late 1840s when its people suffered repeatedly from *hongi* raids despatched by the Sultan of Tidore.[9]

By the 1850s Dorey[10] had developed into a trading centre, but Wallace[11] found its inhabitants too concerned with profits for his liking. He claims that they could not be trusted in anything where payment was concerned. They bought turtle shell, bird of paradise skins and goura (crowned pigeon) plumes from the people of Numfor, Supiori, Biak and the west end of Japen. These products were later sold to Ternatian traders when they came to Dorey.

Traders from Dorey made trading expeditions as far west as Salawati. There they exchanged their locally grown rice for sago. At Amberbaki (Figure 25), a village about 160 kilometres west of Dorey, they bought vegetables and bird of paradise skins. In addition to their coastal trade, Dorey villagers also traded with the inland Arfak Mountains people. In exchange for trade beads, knives and cloth they

Plate 22: Go Siang Kie, the leading Chinese businessman in Cendrawasih Bay in 1954, weighing massoy bark on board one of the coastal vessels which regularly call at the small ports in the bay.

Photo: Courtesy of Photo Archives Rijksmuseum voor Volkenkunde, Leiden, The Netherlands.

obtained rice, yams, bananas and breadfruit, as well as tame cockatoos and lories. The latter were then traded to Ternatian and Tidorese traders.

Captain Deighton began his annual visits to certain villages in Cendrawasih Bay in the 1820s. He was well regarded by the local people as his presence restrained the activities of Tidorese tribute collectors. All the parties concerned knew that he would report any excesses to the Dutch government. Over the years he extended the area he visited. He began visiting Roon Island in the late 1840s. In addition to massoy, Deighton sought other barks, trepang, turtle shell and mother of pearl in return for blue and red calicos, sarongs, brass wire (used to make fishhooks) and other hardware, chopping knives (*parang*), china cups and basins.[12]

Ternatian traders also went to Roon Island at the head of Wandammen Bay to load massoy. This small island became the main centre for massoy in the bay and was still active in the 1960s; see Plate 22.

Known sources of trade skins

By the second half of the nineteenth century, three coastal areas became known as the most productive outlets for birds of paradise in New Guinea. These were Sorong and Amberbaki on the Bird's Head and the area from Tanah Merah to Mount Bougainville on the north coast, see Figures 25 and 42. The latter area became known as Saprop Mani, land of birds.[13] As mentioned elsewhere, see Chapters 3 and 11, the Bird's Head and Lake Sentani area are also where most of the early bronzes have been found.

The occupants of these coastal areas obtained bird of paradise skins from inland villages. Birds of paradise, as well as massoy, nutmegs and other products, were traded by inland groups to friendly neighbours who in turn traded them to the coast. In return the inland communities received cloth and iron tools which replaced tapa cloth and stone tools. The cloth (kain timur) was keenly sought by groups in the interior on the Bird's Head and it became a central component of their ceremonies. This was the case with the Maibrat (Mejprat) people in the vicinity of Aimura Lake (Figure 25).[14]

Amberbaki was not only visited by Ternatian and Bugis traders, but also, as mentioned above, by Dorey villagers who travelled some 160 kilometres along the coast to trade there for plumes.

Sorong was where the people of Muka village on Waigeo went to obtain the bird of paradise skins they had to pay as tribute to the Sultan of Tidore. This was done by obtaining goods on credit from the Seram Laut or Bugis traders on Salawati. Then during the dry season they made a trading voyage to the Bird's Head. After some hard bargaining with the local people they obtained enough bird skins to pay their tribute as well as make a small profit for themselves.[15]

Seeking birds of paradise in their natural habitats

Prior to 1850, most traders and collectors of bird of paradise skins were happy to acquire them from coastal villagers. This meant that they did not have to deal with reputedly hostile inland tribes. Some natural history collectors such as the Leiden Museum collector H. von Rosenberg continued this practice. In 1860 he stayed with a raja on Waigeo Island at the entrance to Mayalibit Bay whilst he bought skins from the local people.[16]

In 1855 the plume merchant Duivenboden accompanied Prince Ali from Tidore on an expedition to collect birds of paradise for the feather trade. They walked from Mega village on the coast of the Bird's Head inland into the northern foothills of the Tamrau Mountains (Figure 25).[17]

Collecting specimens of birds of paradise was one of the main objectives of Alfred Russel Wallace's travels in the Aru Islands, Waigeo, New Guinea and the Moluccas from 1856–1860. His assistant, Mr Allen, also visited Misool, but this did not add to the number of species they collected during their expedition. Wallace personally collected fully plumed male specimens of the Greater Bird of Paradise (Paradisaea apoda) and the King (Cicinnurus regius) in the Aru Islands, the Lesser (Paradisaea minor) near Dorey, the Red (Paradisaea rubra) on Waigeo[18] and Wallace's Standard Wing (*Semioptera wallacei*) on Bacan. Allen also collected specimens of the Twelve-wired Bird of Paradise (*Seleucidis melanoleuca*) on Salawati and inland of Sorong.[19]

Wallace spent over three months in Dorey in 1858 from 11 April to 29 July waiting for the Ternatian schooner owned by Duivenboden to return from trading in Cendrawasih Bay. He went to Dorey because Lesson had been successful in obtaining a number of rare bird of paradise skins there in July 1824. Wallace hoped to find the source of these skins and to obtain birds that could be prepared as scientific specimens. He was surprised to find 34 years later that comparable trade skins were no longer available.[20] Wallace only acquired the Lesser, some female King Birds of Paradise and a young male Twelve-wired Bird of Paradise, whereas he understood Lesson had obtained the Arfak Astrapia, Black Sicklebill, King, Lesser, Magnificent, Superb, Western Parotia and Flame Bowerbird.[21] Wallace was unfortunate to be at Dorey when the Prince of Tidore and the Dutch Resident of Banda arrived on board the Dutch surveying steamer the *Etna*. Like Wallace they sought birds of paradise and other natural history specimens. Men were sent out in every direction, and all the bird skins, insects and animals the Dorey people had to offer were taken to the *Etna*. Wallace's trade articles proved to be poor competition for the range of items offered by the Prince, the Dutch Resident and other passengers. He could only watch in frustration whilst an amateur ornithologist on board bought two Arfak Astrapia skins from a Bugis trader.[22]

Dorey residents told Wallace that if he wanted different kinds of birds of paradise then he should go to Amberbaki on the Bird's Head, which was famous for the variety of skins one could acquire there. In an attempt to obtain specimens Wallace sent two of his best assistants and ten men from Dorey to Amberbaki for a fortnight. They were well provisioned and were instructed to buy and shoot whatever they saw. To Wallace's dismay they returned empty handed. The only skins available for purchase were common Lesser Birds of Paradise and the only species seen in the surrounding forest was one King Bird of Paradise.

His assistants were told that the variety of bird of paradise trade skins that had made Amberbaki famous were currently out of supply. They learnt that the birds were not shot in the coastal forests, but were obtained from mountain forests two or three days' walk inland over several mountain ridges. The Amberbaki people did not acquire the skins directly from the mountaineers, but from villagers living in the foothills. This meant that by the time a skin reached the coast it had already passed through two or three hands. The Amberbaki villagers then sold the skins to traders.

Wallace was sorely disappointed when his assistants returned from Amberbaki without a single specimen. His stay at Dorey had not been a pleasant one. Not only had he failed to acquire the bird of paradise specimens he sought, but one of his men had died from dysentery. In addition Wallace had suffered from ill health which was exacerbated by inadequate food supplies.[23] From subsequent travels in the Raja Empat Islands Wallace learnt that Sorong, Mega and Amberbaki were the main outlets for bird of paradise trade skins on the Bird's Head. His assistants had already visited Amberbaki without success. Sorong seemed the best location to visit next, as Wallace was told that it only took one day by foot from Sorong to reach where the birds were obtained, whereas it took three days from Mega. The area inland of Mega village was called Maas by the Biaks as this was where *maas*, the Black Sicklebill, was found. Its plumes were the most highly prized on Biak and were worn as a sign of authority.[24] Mr Allen, who had not been with Wallace at Dorey, also independently learnt of Sorong's reputation as one of the most productive outlets for bird of paradise skins on the Bird's Head. They decided that Allen should visit Sorong and journey inland to where the birds were hunted. The Dutch Resident at Ternate arranged on their behalf for the Sultan of Tidore to provide a lieutenant and two soldiers to travel with Allen to assist him in this task.

Allen found that obtaining birds of paradise at Sorong was not a simple matter. In 1860 the coastal chiefs had a monopoly on the bird of paradise trade. They obtained the prepared birds cheaply from inland communities, sold most of them to Bugis traders and paid a portion of their plumes each year as tribute to the Sultan of Tidore. The coastal chiefs did not want a European interfering in this trade, especially one who wanted to visit the inland communities who hunted the birds. They were also concerned that the number of rare birds they were acquiring should not come to the Sultan's notice, as this would cause the Sultan to raise their tribute requirements. The coastal chiefs themselves valued the common yellow Lesser Bird of Paradise. They knew this could be easily obtained at markets in Ternate, Makassar and Singapore. Why a European should go to such trouble to get other species did not make much sense to them.

When Allen arrived in Sorong and explained his intention of travelling inland to seek birds of paradise, the coastal chiefs replied that this was impossible, as no one was willing to guide him on this three to four day journey through swamps and mountains occupied by hostile tribes. Allen, however, insisted and stressed that the Sultan of Tidore expected them to assist him. Reluctantly the coastal chiefs provided him with a boat to take him as far as possible upstream. At the same time, they sent instructions to the inland villages to refuse him food so that he would be forced to return to the coast.

The coastal men landed Allen and his Tidorese assistants upstream and left them to fend for themselves. Allen asked the Tidorese lieutenant to seek out some guides and carriers. The lieutenant demanded assistance and soon found himself and his soldiers facing angry villagers armed with knives and spears. The situation was saved by Allen who managed to restore the peace by distributing some presents and displaying the knives, hatchets and beads which would be given to those who worked for him.

After travelling through rugged country for a day they came to the villages of the mountain dwellers. Allen stayed there a month. Lacking an interpreter, all communication was by sign-language and barter. Each day some village men accompanied Allen into the forest. He rewarded them with a small present every time they brought him a natural history specimen. The Twelve-wired Bird of Paradise (*Seleucidis melanoleuca*) was the only bird of paradise shot; it did not add to Wallace's species collection as Allen had already obtained a specimen of this species on Salawati.

When Allen showed the mountain people drawings of rare birds of paradise they recognised them and indicated that these birds could be obtained another two to three days' walk further inland. When told about this, Wallace remarked that the Dorey men he had sent to Amberbaki came back with the same story. Rare varieties were always another two to three days' journey away in rugged country inhabited by hostile tribes.

Wallace found it extraordinary that after five years' residence in Sulawesi, the Moluccas and New Guinea, he had acquired only half the number of bird of paradise species that Lesson had obtained in a few weeks in Doreri Bay in 1824. Only the common trade species were readily available during Wallace's visit. He also notes that the Prince of Tidore had to be satisfied with a few common Lesser Birds of Paradise when he visited Amberbaki as no rare species were available. Indeed it was said that none had been obtained there that year, despite the fact that 5–6 species had been procured there in the past.[25] Wallace attributed this scarcity of rare species to the instructions the villagers were under to supply rare species to the Sultan of Tidore as tribute. He also thought that coastal villagers were themselves discouraging such trade by refusing to buy rare species from the mountain traders and seeking only the more profitable common species.[26] The activities of traders such as Duivenboden and their willingness to pay more for good specimens may also explain the scarcity of rare species during the time of Wallace's residence in the region.

The plume boom

Less than ten years after Wallace left New Guinea, there was a rapid rise in bird of paradise skin exports; see Table 7.

Table 7: Value of bird of paradise exports from New Guinea to Ternate 1865–1869.

Value of bird of paradise exports

Year	Guilders/florins	£
1865	200	17
1867	100	8
1869	1,680	140

Source: Rosenberg 1875 cited by Whittaker et al 1975: 209. Pounds estimated on 1840 rate. (In 1840 a guilder was worth 1 shilling and 8 pence sterling. Translator's note in Kolff 1840: 34).

From 1875 to 1885 the plume merchant, A.A. Bruijn, sent teams of collectors to the western Papuan Islands and western New Guinea to hunt birds of paradise in their natural habitats for sale as scientific specimens and millinery plumes. His collectors were instructed to make a special effort to locate and obtain unknown species.[27]

In 1883 W.H. Woelders reports that there are now thirty Ternatian bird hunters operating out of Andai (Figure 25). He also notes that they are paying twelve times the price paid for carriers 10–12 years ago.[28]

In 1895 Manokwari became a government station. The export figures available for February 1905 (Table 8) indicate that, as in Kaiser Wilhelmsland, bird skins were the main export from the north coast of Dutch New Guinea.

Table 8: Export figures for Manokwari in February 1905

	Florins	£
Bird skins	10,000	1,000
Damar (4,000 kg)	7,700	770
Massoy bark (5,400 kg)	1,950	195
Copra (6,900 kg)	950	95
Trepang (500 kg)	185	18
Pearl shell (600 kg)	115	12
Total	20,900	2,090

Source: Wichmann 1917: 387. Pounds estimated on 1918 rate.
(In 1918, 30–35 guilders or florins was equivalent to 3 pounds sterling. Historical Section of the Foreign Office, London 1920: 27).

There is no doubt that an astounding number of bird of paradise skins were exported from the Bird's Head, mainly by Ternatian and Chinese traders, until the Dutch prohibited such trade in this part of Dutch New Guinea in 1924.

Notes

1. Forrest 1969: 83.
2. Stresemann 1954: 274–5.
3. Stresemann 1954: 276.
4. Held 1957: 351.
5. Forrest 1969: 87, 106.
6. Dumont d'Urville 1853 (2) cited by Riesenfeld 1951: 76.
7. Bellwood 1980: 69: Bulbeck 1986–7: 46.
8. Wallace 1986: 497.
9. Kops 1852: 335.
10. Dorey is the collective name of three small adjacent villages (Kouave, Raoudi and Monoukouari/ Manokwari) on the shore of Doreri Bay (Raffray 1878 cited by Whittaker et al 1975: 238).
11. Wallace 1860: 173–4.
12. Kops 1852: 325; Earl 1853: 78–79.
13. Cheesman 1949: 25, 126.
14. By the 1950s the Dutch administration considered the Maibrat preoccupation with obtaining cloth to be detrimental to agricultural development and the establishment of permanent settlements. In 1954 they began abolishing its use by confiscating large quantities (Elmberg 1968: 22).
15. Wallace 1986: 533.
16. Cheesman 1940: 211, 213.
17. Gilliard 1969: 424 citing Mayr and de Schauensee 1939: 101.
18. Whilst on Waigeo, Wallace observed an unusual method of trapping the Red Bird of Paradise by means of a noose. This technique was used only by eight to ten men from Bessir village. The birds were attracted to step into the noose by the red fruit of an Arum (Wallace 1986: 537).
19. Wallace 1986: 574.
20. Wallace 1860:175.
21. Wallace 1862a: 154–5.
22. Wallace 1862a: 155: 1986: 507.
23. Wallace 1862a: 155.
24. Cheesman 1949: 126–7.
25. Wallace 1986: 510.
26. Wallace 1862a: 159.
27. Gilliard 1969: 418, 421
28. Wichmann 1917: 390.

8

The massoy, trepang and plume trade of Onin, Kowiai and Mimika (Southwest New Guinea)

Introduction

The presence of massoy trees attracted traders to the Onin peninsula (Figure 27) during the spice and aromatic woods trade cycle. As massoy stocks diminished, traders began to move progressively southeastwards seeking unexploited stands. In the seventeenth century the Dutch made a number of unsuccessful attempts to participate in this trade. Interest in massoy and bird of paradise skins continued when the trade emphasis changed to supplying marine products to China. At this time the Seram Laut dominated trade on the southwest coast. Attempts by the Sultan of Tidore to extend his influence over New Guinea in the 1850s did much to destabilise the Kowiai coast. Trading by the Seram Laut went into decline when the Dutch began establishing administrative posts on the southwest coast late last century.

The early massoy trade

Southwest New Guinea is renowned as a source of massoy, an aromatic bark, widely valued in the Indonesian archipelago, especially on Java where it does not grow. The bark of the massoy tree (*Cryptocarya massoy*) yields a volatile oil comparable to cinnamon. Massoy has a sharp taste, strong pleasant smell and gives a warm feeling when applied to the skin. In Southeast Asia massoy has many uses. It is used in medicines, cosmetics, perfumes, as a food flavour and in dye fixing. In some areas a solution of massoy oil and water used to be applied to the skin to ward off the spirit of a slain enemy.[1] In herbal medicines it is taken as a tonic as well as used to treat stomach and intestinal problems, to prevent cramp during pregnancy and to assist recovery after childbirth. On Java a watery pulp made from ground massoy, cinnamon, cloves and sandalwood is smeared on the skin. This gives a pleasant warm feeling as well as an agreeable smell. Ground massoy is widely used in curries and other dishes. It is also used as a dye fixative by the Javanese batik industry.[2]

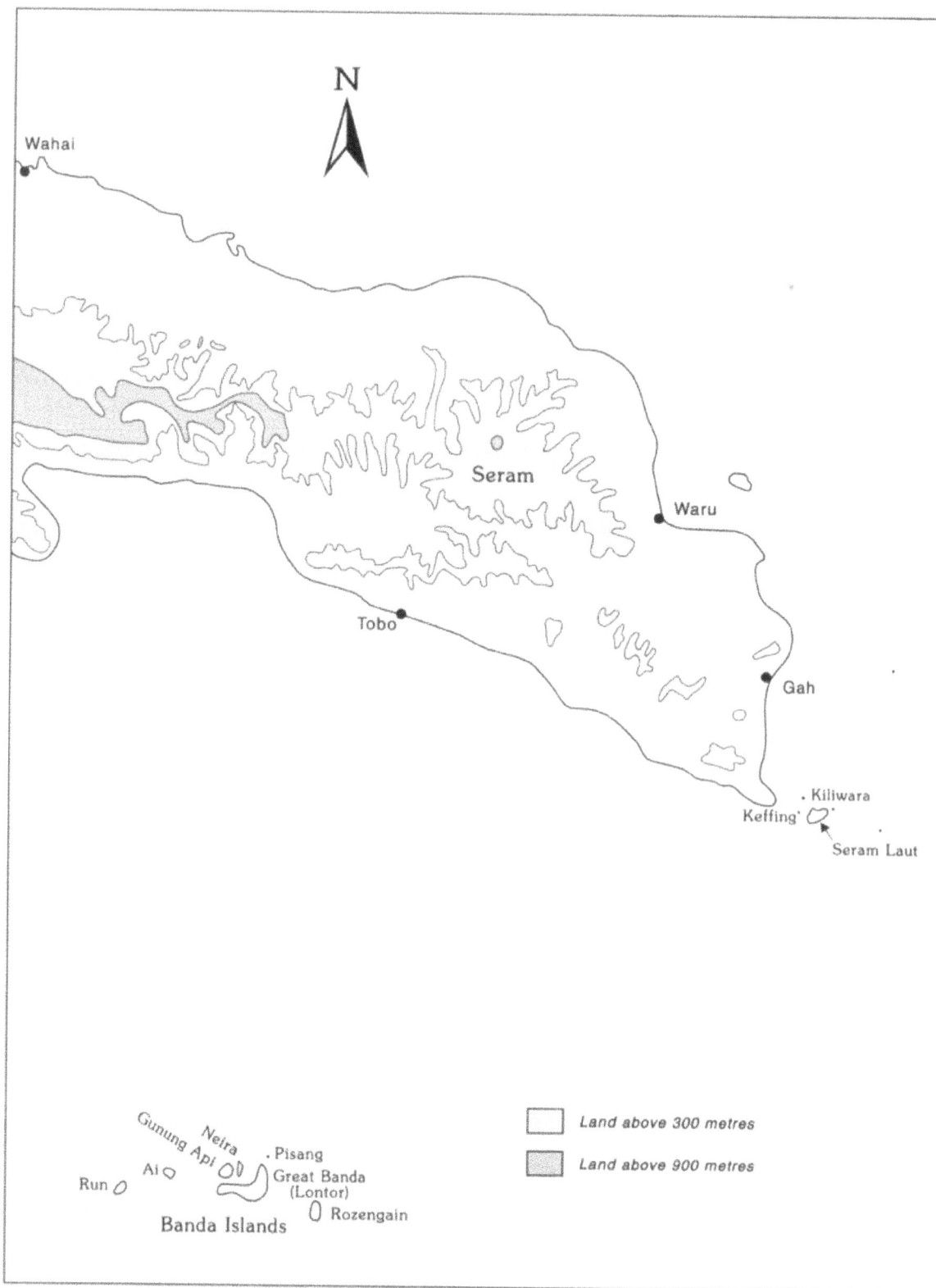

N

Wahai

Seram

Waru

Tobo

Gah

. Kiliwara

Keffing·

Seram Laut

Land above 300 metres

Land above 900 metres

Gunung Api   Neira   . Pisang

Ai   Great Banda
(Lontor)

Run

O Rozengain

Banda Islands

Figure 27: The Banda Islands, eastern Seram, the Seram Laut Islands and Onin.

The optimal conditions for massoy trees exist in foothill rainforest between 400 and 1,000 metres above sea level. The massoy tree has no buttress, a straight bole and grows to a maximum height of 25 metres. The bark is harvested by cutting a circular incision at the base of the tree by a bushknife or axe as low as possible. Other incisions are made at regular intervals up the trunk and along the larger branches. The bark is then peeled off the sapwood in as continuous a strip as possible. Freshly cut bark is easily removed, but it becomes more difficult to do so if left for several days.

After harvesting the massoy bark has to be dried. The way the bark is dried has a direct effect on the quality of the harvest. It is essential that the bark is dried without mould, fungi or rot infestations. The bark is placed in the sun innerside upwards and has to be protected from any rain.

Harvesting massoy bark kills the tree. Attempts by the Forest Products Research Centre in Papua New Guinea to take off partial strips were unsuccessful as the exposed trunk gave access to termites which ruined the tree. Sustained yields in an area are only possible if natural regeneration is encouraged.[3]

Early records indicate that Javanese traders were visiting southwest New Guinea in the fourteenth century, as Onin is mentioned in the ancient Javanese poem the *Negarakertagama* which dates from 1365 AD.[4] By the fifteenth century Chinese traders were participating in this trade. South Chinese trade pottery from this period occurs in the Risatot burial site on Arguni Island on the north coast of Onin[5] (Plate 23 and Figure 28).

Plate 23: Chinese plates from the Risatot burial site on Arguni Island in Berau Bay.
Source: Roder 1959. Reproduced by permission of the Frobenius Institute, Frankfurt (Main).

The Sultan of Bacan, who claimed Onin as part of his territory in 1512, would have played a role in the massoy trade which was dominated by Javanese and Chinese traders. This all changed when Banda was sacked by the Dutch in 1621 (see Chapter 2). Following this sacking Banda ceased to be an important entrepôt for Asian traders. Apart from disrupting their trading operations the Dutch discouraged them from visiting the Spice Islands.

The Bandanese who escaped to the Seram Laut Islands (Figure 27) during the destruction of Banda were probably responsible for stimulating an interest amongst the Seram Laut in supplying Asian markets. With Bandanese expertise these islanders were able to extend their trading activities. In this way the Seram Laut Islands became an important trade centre for massoy and other products.

Before the arrival of the Bandanese migrants, the Seram Laut were part of a well-established inter-island trade network. Schouten learnt in 1602 that the Seram Laut traded over a vast area. He was told that they went as far as Papou (Papua, i.e., the Raja Empat group), New Guinea, Beura (Burn) and Tymar (Timor).[6]

The Dutch stopped the trading activities of the Seram Laut in the Aru Islands in 1645, but this did not restrict them from trading in areas where the Dutch had no trade interests. The volume of their trade between 1621–1800 rivalled that carried out by the Dutch in this part of the East Indies.[7]

After the sacking of Banda, the Seram Laut provided products from New Guinea to trade centres at Bali, Pasir (southeast Kalimantan) and east Java. They smuggled spices when they could obtain them and traded massoy, turtle shell, pearls, birds of paradise skins, damar, ambergris, Papuan slaves and from about 1750 trepang. Most of the smuggled spices went to China and India. The Seramese were well aware of the value of spices and their rebellions against the Dutch were largely inspired by talk about a free spice trade. In return for their produce they obtained rice, guns, cloth, pottery and utensils. Bugis and other traders also illicitly met these traders at Seram.[8] Denied access to the Aru Islands by the Dutch in 1645, the Seram Laut apparently extended their activities to the Trans Fly coast of Torres Strait (see Chapter 9).

The Dutch East India Company also began to take an interest in the southwest coast of New Guinea when they realised that the Seram Laut were clearly carrying out a profitable trade there. They observed that traders from Seram Laut, including Gorong, traded on the Onin coast and further south. The trade consisted of textiles, beads, etc., in return for captured slaves and massoy. These traders established their own trade monopoly (*sosolot*) in certain areas by making agreements and intermarrying with the local people.[9] The existence of these agreements explains why the Dutch East India Company was never successful in establishing trading ventures on this coast.

In 1623 the Governor of Amboina (Ambon) sent Jan Carstensz with the yachts *Pera* and *Arnhem* to investigate how the Dutch could gain control of the massoy trade on the southwest coast of New Guinea. This investigation ceased when the captain of the *Arnhem* was killed on the Mimika coast near Mupuruka (Figure 29). In 1636 Gerit Pool made a second attempt to take over the massoy trade. He was also instructed to investigate the brown (smithing) coal reported by Seram Laut traders at Lakahia (Figure 27). Pool was killed soon after his two ships reached Namatote. His successor continued on to the east Mimika coast, but did not go ashore.

After 1650 there were a number of generally unsuccessful Dutch attempts to purchase slaves on the Onin coast. During one of these trips in 1663 Nicolass Vinck sailed the *Garnaal* and *Walingen* into Berau and Bintuni Bays (Figure 27), but failed to find a passage. Before these ships found their way out their crews had several fights with the local people.

Despite these set-backs, and the fact that the price of massoy had begun to decline, the Dutch East India Company decided to persevere in its efforts to take over the massoy trade. Observations that the Seram Laut were still profitably trading on the Onin coast encouraged them in this endeavour. Johannes Keyts was sent to try again. In 1678 he visited the Onin and Kowiai areas. Keyts distributed Dutch East India Company flags with great solemnity during this voyage. Trade contracts were made on the Onin coast at Fatagar and Karas. They also visited Sebakor Bay, Sanggala Bay, Adi Island, Cape Bitjanu (?Bitsjari Bay) and Namatote Island (Figure 28).

In the Kowiai area Keyts made a trade contract with the Namatote islanders for massoy and other products, as well as smithing coal from the then uninhabited island of Lakahia. The Seram Laut soon put an end to this agreement by turning the people of Namatote against the Dutch. In an ensuing incident six of Keyt's men were killed. Following these deaths the Dutch East India Company's interest in the massoy trade came to an end.

After Keyts the only regular trips to western New Guinea were made by Dutch planters on Banda. These voyages were risky undertakings and Gorong islanders in particular resented their competition. Many of the planters lost their lives as a result of sickness, bad weather and inter-village fights.[10]

The Seram Laut massoy trade

The Dutch scholar George Eberhard Rumphius documented that Seramese traders went to the coastline south of Berau Bay in 1684. Most of these traders came from the Seram Laut Islands, including Gorong, situated at the eastern tip of Seram. They called the western part of the New Guinea coast they visited Papua Onin and the eastern part Papua Kowiai.[11]

Rumphius collected a considerable amount of information about where and how massoy bark was obtained in the late seventeenth century. The trees were known to grow on the alkaline soils of the coastal mountains as far east as the Omba (Opa) River. It took 2 to 3 days to walk from the coast to where they grew. In addition to massoy, slaves were also obtained in this area and traded.[12]

Recorded observations indicate that massoy bark was gathered in Onin with no concern for sustained harvesting; any massoy tree found was chopped down and its bark peeled off; young trees were not excluded. This caused the massoy trade to be relocated as local supplies were exhausted. By the first half of the seventeenth century the main source of supply had moved south from Onin to the Karas Islands (Figure 28). These islanders assisted traders who settled in their islands to obtain massoy from the mainland between Gunung Baik and Arguni Bay. By 1670 the centre of trade had shifted eastwards again, this time to Namatote Island on the Kowiai coast. In addition to Namatote, other islands, namely Mawara, Aiduma, Kaju Merah and Lakahia became trading centres and some traders settled on them.

Rumphius describes the nature of the contact between the traders and the people of the Kowiai coast. The latter obtained poor quality swords and hacking knives from the traders to use in the far-off mountains to gather enough massoy bark to load one or two boats, that is 60 to 100 piculs of bark (a picul is 60.5 kilograms). When they returned to the beach they piled the bark in heaps as high as a sword. The Kowiai leader then indicated by sign language what they wanted in return for the bark. The Seram Laut traders were far from generous and gave as little as they could. In addition to the poor quality swords and hacking knives, they also gave cloth. Black sugar and rice had already been given in advance to make the Kowiai willing to go and gather the massoy.[13]

Seram Laut traders continued to expand their operations on the southwest coast until the Sultan of Tidore instigated *hongi* raids in 1850. These punitive raids discouraged trading and had a devastating impact.

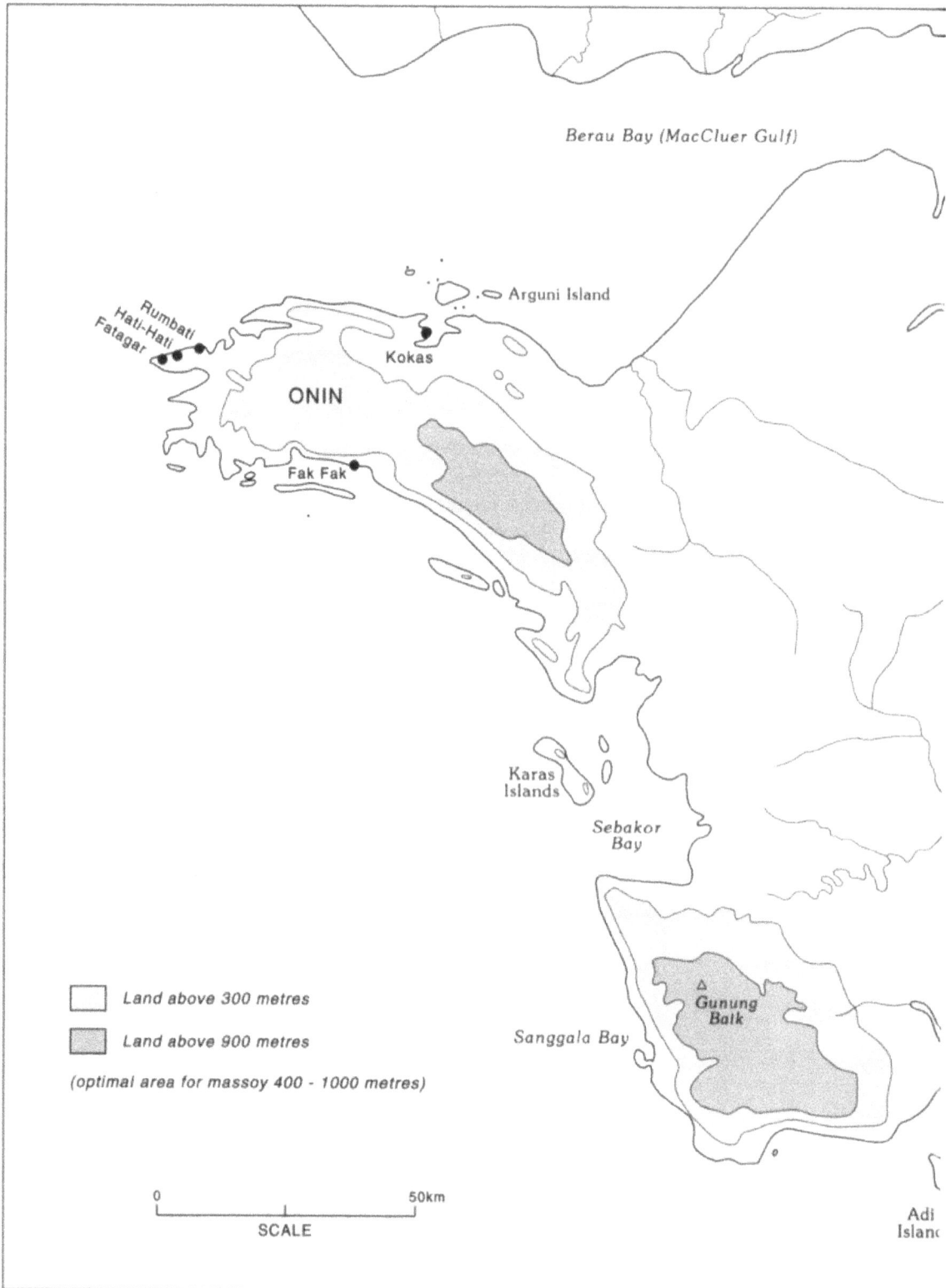

Figure 28: The Onin and Kowiai areas of southwest New Guinea.

Bintuni Bay

Roon
Island

Cendrawasih Bay
(Geelvink Bay)

N

Wandammen
Mountains

Arguni Bay

rau Bay

Jamur Lake

Kaimana
Cape Bitjamu
Bitsjari Bay
Namatote
Island
Cape Aiwa
Mawara Island

Lobo

KOWIAI

Triton Bay

Aiduma
Island

Kaju Merah
Island

Etna Bay
Lakahia
Island

Omba R.

Urama R.

Fort Du Bus and Dutch interest in New Guinea

Political upheavals in Europe from 1795–1814 resulted in alternating Dutch and British control of the East Indies (see Chapter 6). After this experience, both the Dutch and English recognised that a successful entrepôt in eastern Indonesia would be a profitable venture. The Dutch were prompted to proclaim their interest in New Guinea after the British established a settlement on Melville Island in northern Australia in 1824.

As mentioned in Chapter 6, in 1828 Dutch soldiers were landed near Lobo in Triton Bay (Figure 28) and established Fort Du Bus on the swampy shore of a sheltered inlet. From this fort on 24 August 1828 the Dutch proclaimed all the land on the south coast of New Guinea as far as 141° east longitude (a few kilometres west of the current south coast border between PNG and West Papua) and northwards as far as the Cape of Good Hope on the Bird's Head. During the next eight difficult years over 100 personnel stationed at this fort died. It was clearly a project gone wrong. The Dutch decided to demolish the fort in 1836 and relocated the soldiers who had been garrisoned there to Wahai, a small port on the north coast of Seram which at that time was frequently visited by English and American whalers.[14]

The Seram Laut traders

The main trade centre in the Seram Laut Islands off eastern Seram in 1860 was Kiliwara (Figure 27). This small island, which is some 45 metres across and little more than a metre high, had excellent ground water and good anchorages in both monsoons. When Wallace visited Kiliwara in 1860, it was the main Bugis trade centre for New Guinea. Bugis who traded in New Guinea called there to refit for their home voyage as well as sort and dry their cargoes. In New Guinea they had obtained trepang, massoy bark, wild nutmegs, turtle shell, pearls and bird of paradise skins.

Gorong and other Seram Laut traders also brought their trade produce from New Guinea to Kiliwara and obtained cloth, sago cakes and opium in exchange. The opium was smoked by the Gorong and also by chiefs and wealthy men on Misool and Waigeo, who had been introduced to opium by the Gorong. Villagers from the mainland of Seram provided Kiliwara and the other islands with sago. Rice from Bali and Makassar was also available at a reasonable price. Bugis arrived at Kiliwara from Singapore in their lumbering praus bringing produce from China and Southeast Asia and cloth from Lancashire and Massachusetts. Schooners also came from Bali to buy Papuan slaves.

142

Every year Gorong traders visited the southwest coast of New Guinea from Utanata (Figure 29) in the south to Salawati in the north. They also travelled to the Aru, Kei, Tanimbar and Banda Islands (Figure 2) as well as the islands of Ambon, Waigeo, Misool, Tidore and Ternate. All their praus were made by Kei Islanders. Their chief trade interests were massoy bark and trepang, followed by wild nutmegs, turtle shell, bird of paradise skins and pearls. They sold these to the Bugis traders at Kiliwara or Aru; few Gorong took their produce westwards themselves.[15]

The traders appointed raja where they operated, and these rajas in turn appointed their own representatives as a means of extending and maintaining their sphere of influence. These representatives were given the title of *kapitan, orang tua, major, hakim,* etc., by the raja who appointed them. In line with this practice the Raja of Namatote appointed trading agents, whom he called rajas, at Aiduma and Lakahia in 1828 and at irregular intervals collected taxes from these representatives. The taxes consisted of cups, bowls, copper rings and cloth.[16]

Seram Laut traders had begun trading as far east as Utanata before 1828. They built temporary houses to stay in during their annual visit. The traders sometimes took local dignitaries on visits to Seram. Modera describes the appearance of a chief living at the mouth of the Utanata River who was invited aboard the Triton in 1828. He wore a loose Malayan coat and a handkerchief tied round his head. Modera also reports that the Uta (Utanata) people were good-natured and did not steal articles left unattended on shore. They also traded papaya and oranges as well as other produce.[17]

When villagers promised to supply traders with a certain quantity of forest and/or marine products, the traders gave them goods on credit. In the majority of cases the promised products were supplied in the agreed time. Usually this was several months, the time required to gather the products, but sometimes the traders had to wait many years; in some cases promises were never fulfilled. Those villagers who failed to keep a promise hid in the mountains when the traders they had dealings with came back seeking their goods. In May 1874 Miklouho-Maclay met the *anakoda* of a prau from Makassar near Namatote Island. He had been waiting six years for products he had been promised.[18]

During his second visit to the Onin coast in 1828 Kolff observed that every year the Onin coast was visited by two to three traders from the Seram Laut Islands. They stayed in houses built for them at established trading stations. Among the goods they brought to Onin were elephant tusks and large porcelain dishes.[19]

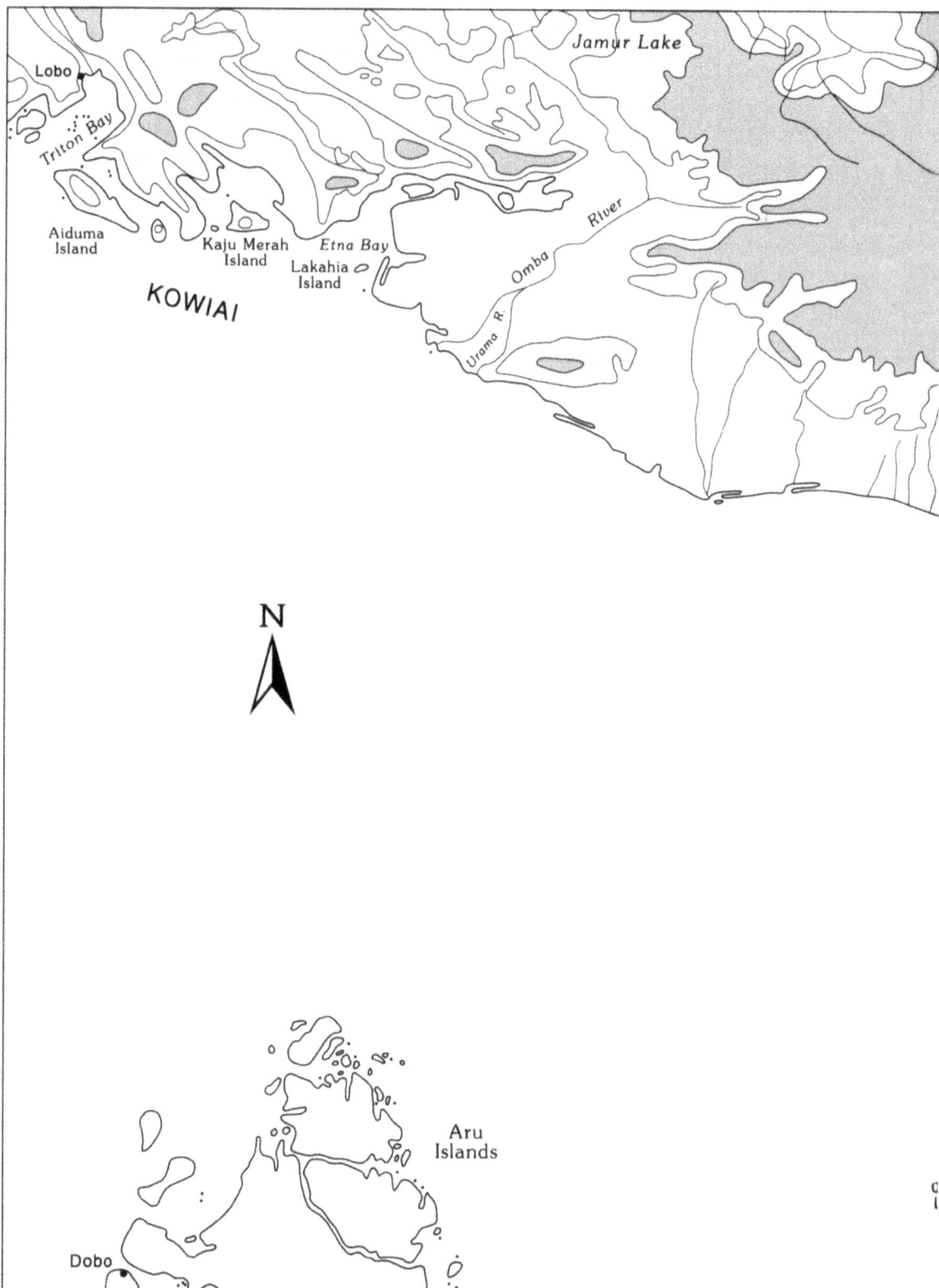

Figure 29: The Kowiai and Mimika coasts of southwest New Guinea.

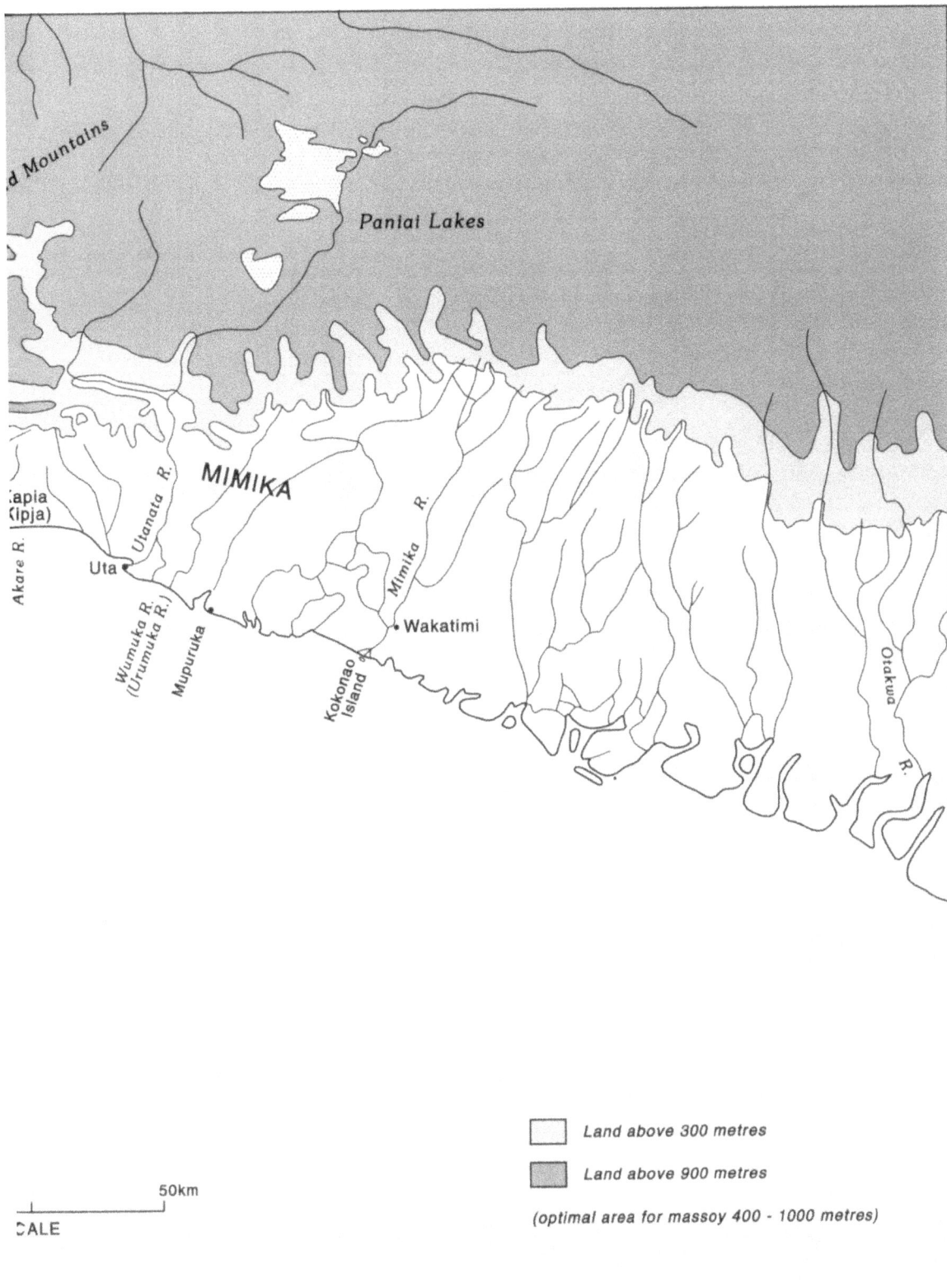

Land above 300 metres

Land above 900 metres

(optimal area for massoy 400 - 1000 metres)

50km

SCALE

The Seram Laut traders working in the Triton Bay area in 1828 usually stayed 4 to 5 months. They sought massoy and other barks (belishary, rosamala) which were used in Bali and Java as medicine and cosmetics. They also obtained nutmegs, dye woods, edible bird's nest, bird of paradise skins, live cockatoos, lories and crowned pigeons.[20]

Contact with the Seram Laut led to some Moslem converts. A Moslem missionary was resident at Triton Bay in 1826. He and other notables lived in Malay-style houses and dressed in Malay fashion. Two years later an abandoned Malay-style house was all that remained following a raid from the Karas Islands.[21]

The impact of the Sultan of Tidore

In 1850 the Sultan of Tidore, with Dutch encouragement, began to assert his authority over a greater area of Dutch New Guinea. He did this by issuing levies, which included the procurement of a certain number of slaves. If these levies were not met, punitive *hongi* expeditions were made to ensure that all future demands would be.

The Onin people were subject to Tidorese *hongi* expeditions, but seem to have fared better in the last half of the nineteenth century than those along the Kowiai coast. The *hongi* fleets avoided the Karas Islands and other places frequented by traders. In 1874 a *hongi* expedition made on behalf of the Sultan of Tidore was led by Sebiar, the Raja of Rumasol on Misool Island. He imposed heavy taxes on villages such as HatiHati and Rumbati on the Onin Coast (Figure 28). Rumbati had to supply 15 slaves of both sexes or their value equivalent in massoy, nutmeg, turtle shell and other goods.[22]

Hongi expeditions were viewed with considerable dread by traders. Although their own vessels were rarely if ever attacked, the news that a *hongi* flotilla was out drove the coastal people into hiding and all hopes of trade during the season were put to an end.[23]

In the 1850s only small quantities of massoy bark and wild nutmegs were available from the Onin coast, although it produced the usual turtle shell and trepang. There were a few Moslem villages along the coast, but these were subject to constant attacks from interior groups. The Gorong were the only traders who regularly visited Onin. They suffered frequent attacks which often resulted in fatalities. These incidents sometimes occurred when the local people were not satisfied with the trade transactions taking place.[24]

The Sultan of Tidore's efforts to extend his influence over New Guinea destablised the Kowiai coast. In 1850 'Prince' Ali[25] of Tidore raided Lakahia Island and levelled all the huts and the few coconuts to the ground. About a hundred Papuans were enslaved during this attack.

The terrified survivors fled and settled on the mainland. The island still appeared to be deserted in 1852. When Miklouho-Maclay visited the area in 1874, the survivors recalled with terror the devastation perpetrated by this *hongi*.[26]

The Sultan of Tidore's 1850 raid had a major impact on the Kowiai region. It not only caused a deterioration in relations between coastal communities, but also problems between coastal and inland communities. Confrontations between these groups were also exacerbated by the increased fatalities resulting from the gunpowder, lead and guns now readily available as trade goods.

The deteriorating situation on the Kowiai coast also affected Seram Laut trading ventures. When Wallace was in a village on Gorong in May 1860, two praus from this island were attacked on the Kowiai coast. They had been bargaining for trepang in broad daylight. The incident was not a chance encounter, as the traders had established themselves ashore and had anchored their praus in a small river nearby. The fourteen men on shore who were trading were killed. The six men remaining on the two praus were able to escape in one prau and bring the news. Once known, shrieks and lamentations were heard throughout the village as almost every house had either lost a relative or a slave. Scarcely a year passed without some lives being lost. About 50 Gorong traders lost their lives on the Kowiai Coast in 1856.[27]

The Onin coast was still being visited in the 1870s by Bugis traders in their *paduakan* and by the inhabitants of the Seram Laut Islands in their smaller praus.[28] They traded for massoy, wild nutmegs, trepang, turtle shell, mother-of-pearl and pearls. Some slaving still existed.

When Miklouho-Maclay visited the Kowiai coast in 1874, he found that traders avoided this coast. When asked for an explanation as to why they had ceased visiting the Kowiai coast, they claimed that it was no longer worthwhile going there as they were usually assaulted and their praus plundered.[29] The lives of the local people were also disrupted. Miklouho-Maclay observed the nomadic life they lived. He describes how they constantly moved from bay to bay in their small praus –

The traces of destroyed and deserted settlements scattered in various places as well as the abandoned plantations show that the Papuan can lead a settled life. Papuans often told me of their desire to have a permanent dwelling-place, and they even demonstrated this in deed, settling near my cabin at Aiwa [Figure 28] from the very moment I built it and even cultivating plantations, assuming that it would be safer for them in my proximity.

I can state myself that the fear of sudden raids was quite justified, for during my short sojourn of approximately two months on the Papua Kowiai Coast there were three devastating raids. The first of these raids was led by the inhabitants of Kamrau Bay against the Papuans of Kayu Mera Island, only a few of whom managed to escape. Most of them were killed or taken prisoner. When I visited Kayu Mera Island in March 1874, I did not find a single person there. Those who had managed to escape with their lives, fled into the mountains.

The second raid was directed against the inhabitants of Aiduma who settled near my cabin at Aiwa. The wife of the radya [raja] of Aiduma was speared to death, and his six-year-old daughter was cut into pieces with a *parang*; many women and several men were wounded; two girls and one man were taken prisoner. That was the time when my hut was looted by the plunderers, who pillaged almost all my things and provisions. The plunders and murders were perpetrated by the mountain dwellers of Bicaru [Bitsjari] Bay and the inhabitants of Namatote and Mawara.

The third raid was undertaken by the mountain people of Kamaka, called the *wuousirau*, allies of the defeated inhabitants of Aiduma; they attacked the mountain dwellers of Bicaru Bay and the men of Namatote to avenge the death of the radya [raja] of Aiduma's wife and daughter. The outcome of this raid remained unknown to me, but, as punishment for the plunder of my house, I took the captain, or chief, of the Archipelago of Mawara prisoner, wishing to hand him over to the resident of Amboina (Ambon).[30]

Miklouho-Maclay was so perturbed by the plight of the people on the Kowiai coast in 1874 that he wrote to the Governor-General of the Dutch East Indies offering to spend a year pacifying the area. He proposed to do this by founding a settlement with the assistance of several dozen Javanese soldiers and a gunboat. For his own services he sought no remuneration from the Dutch Government. His offer was rejected by the Governor-General on the grounds that the Dutch had no intention of extending their colonies.[31]

When the marine paddle steamer *Soerabaja* visited Etna Bay in 1876, the Raja of Lakahia was found living on the shore of this bay. He spoke Seramese and some words of Malay and had visited Seram, Banda and Makassar.[32]

The fighting on this coast was not over. At the end of the nineteenth century the Etna Bay people were attacked by people from the upper Omba (Opa) River and Jamur Lake (Figure 28). They had obtained guns from Ternatian bird hunters who had presumably entered their area from Cendrawasih Bay. When the inland people came to make peace in 1903, they were attacked in turn. The Etna Bay people then fled to the lower reaches of the Urama near Buru southeast of Etna Bay. There the Raja of Lakahia and 11 others were killed and 10 women and children were captured.

These and other incidents resulted in a marked decline of the Etna Bay population. Observers on the *Soerabaja* estimated in 1876 that about 300 people lived there in four settlements. By 1900 the population living in Etna Bay at Urama village was only 100. A further decline occurred as a result of alcohol abuse and the 1918–9 influenza epidemic.[33] Such a history does not allow the decline in the Etna Bay population to be primarily attributed to attacks by inland communities moving to the coast.[34] *Hongi* expeditions, influenza and alcohol abuse were also significant factors in this decline.

An administrative post was established at Fakfak (Figure 28) in 1898.[35] The presence of Seram Laut traders and their Islamic influence declined with the coming of the Dutch administration. They were replaced by increasing numbers of Chinese traders and Christian missionaries. Bird of paradise hunters remained active in the region. In 1913 it is reported that traders in Fakfak and Kokas (Figure 28) bought 8,000 skins worth £40,000.[36]

Mimika Coast

As mentioned above, Seram Laut traders were trading as far east as Utanata (Figure 29) by the mid 1820s. The Raja of Namatote appointed a raja at Kapia (Kipja) for the area east of Lakahia in 1850. In addition to Seram Laut traders, traders from the Aru Islands visited the Mimika coast.

Some Mimika have a legend about their first contact with foreign traders. It tells how two fishermen got off course and finally ended up in the Aru Islands and how the Aru Islanders took the fishermen home. In retrospect, it seems likely that these Aru Islanders seized this incident as an opportunity to establish trading ties with the Mimika.

For the Aru Islanders it was an opportunity to gain access to unexploited resources which they could obtain at low cost. The Mimika were delighted to see the trade goods (tobacco, choppers and sarongs) the Aru men brought. The Aru selected one Mimika man to be the chief (*kepala*) and he was given a paper (*surat*).[37] Before the Aru men travelled inland to gather massoy bark, they made a part payment of some choppers. On their return they bartered more choppers and sarongs to complete the payment for the massoy bark.[38] Curiously the Aru men gathered their own massoy bark, unlike the Seram Laut reported above.

According to P. Drabbe, who was a missionary, the Mimika never learnt Malay. Instead the traders learnt a certain number of words from Kamoro (the language spoken by the Mimika) and only used Malay words for newly introduced and previously unknown objects. The Mimika incorporated these words into their own language, in a form suited to it, and avoided the intricate verbal conjugations of Malay.[39] This would explain why the explorer A.F.R. Wollaston, who was a member of the 1910 expedition, found Malay no use as a means of talking with the Mimika.[40]

Seram Laut traders along the with the Raja of Namatote and his assistants kept control of the trade and contact between the Kowiai and foreigners until 1898. By appointing officials they established the non-traditional role of the raja. This person was appointed because the traders wanted someone through whom they could give orders. Some of these rajas became quite powerful. For example, the Raja of Kapia (Kipja) once controlled the entire Taija district, which included the people living along the Poraoka, Kipja, Maparpe, Akare and Wumuka Rivers.[41]

When a Dutch administrative post was opened at Fakfak on the Onin coast in 1898, Seram Laut traders and the Raja of Namatote had to reduce their slave and weapon trade in the Kowiai area. The Raja of Namatote counteracted this by strengthening his influence at Kapia in west Mimika.

The arrival of Chinese traders in about 1915, as well as the Dutch administration and the Roman Catholic Mission, brought an end to the presence of the Seram Laut and their Islamic influence amongst the Mimika. The Chinese traders sought sandalwood, damar, massoy and sago. They came every month bringing cloth, axes, knives, tobacco and betel nut (pinang). Some Arguni Bay people (Figure 28) came to the Mimika area to work for the Chinese traders, married locally and stayed on. Bird of paradise hunters also came to Mimika. The activities of Chinese traders resulted in the Dutch establishing a government post some hours up the Mimika river near Wakatimi in 1926. It was soon transferred to Kokonao at the delta mouth.[42]

By the time they came under government control imported goods such as Chinese dishes and gongs had become important bridewealth items amongst the western Mimika.[43] Some crops such as papaya, sweet potatoes, cassava, cucumbers and pumpkins were probably introduced by Seram Laut traders.[44] The traders may also have taught the Mimika how to make toddy from the Segero palm which thrives in the upriver areas.[45]

Notes

1. Muller 1990b: 66.
2. Zieck 1973: 14.
3. Zieck 1973: 15, 17.

4. Rouffaer 1915 cited by Galis 1953–4: 6; O'Hare 1986.

5. Roder 1959.

6. Galis 1953–4: 12.

7. Lerissa 1981 cited by Ellen 1987: 46.

8. Wright 1958: 6–7.

9. Galis 1953–4: 16.

10. Galis 1953–4: 13-4; Pouwer 1955: 215–8.

11. The eastern boundary of the Kowiai area changed over time. Initially it extended no further than the Omba (Opa) River (Figure 28). By 1828 it had been extended along the coast as far east as Utanata (Figure 29) (Pouwer 1955: 218). Except for those along the Mimika River, the people along this coast initially adopted the name Kowiai or Koviai (Drabbe 1947–8: 157–8), but in post World War II literature the people who occupy the swampy lowlands from Etna Bay in the west to the Otokwa River in the east are generally referred to as the Mimika or Kamoro speakers (Figure 29). Before the late 1920s they lived in semi-permanent settlements from where they made regular trips to sago areas and gardens, as well as fishing grounds located at river mouths downstream. A cycle of large and small feasts were associated with these movements. Their eastern neighbours are the Asmat, who are related to the Mimika (Pouwer 1970: 24–5; Kooijman 1966: 54).

12. Pouwer 1955: 215.

13. Pouwer 1955: 215–6.

14. Earl 1853: 56; Galis 1953–4: 21.

15. Wallace 1986: 380–1.

16. Pouwer 1955: 216, 218.

17. Earl 1853: 43, 49, 52.

18. Miklouho-Maclay 1982: 441.

19. Earl 1853: 59–60.

20. Earl 1853: 58.

21. Earl 1853: 55, 57–58.

22. Miklouho-Maclay 1982: 443.

23. Earl 1853: 54

24. Wallace 1986: 379.

25. Pouwer (1955: 218) refers to this Prince by the name Ali; Miklouho-Maclay (1982: 443) calls him Amir.

26. Miklouho-Maclay 1982: 443.

27. Wallace 1986: 378–9.

28. Miklouho-Maclay 1982: 439.

29. Miklouho-Maclay 1875: 1982: 439.

30. Miklouho-Maclay 1982: 440–1.

31. Miklouho-Maclay 1982: 444–5.

32. Pouwer 1955: 219.

33. Pouwer 1955: 219–20.

34. see van Baal et al 1984: 25.

35. Galis 1953–4: 27.

36. Historical Section of the Foreign Office, London 1920: 26.

37. *Kepala* and *surat* are both Malay words.
38. Drabbe 1947–8: 256–7.
39. Drabbe 1947–8: 158.
40. Wollaston 1912: 102.
41. Drabbe 1947–8: 257.
42. Pouwer 1955: 224, 230–1.
43. Trenkenschuh 1970: 124.
44. Pouwer 1955: 43.
45. Trenkenschuh 1970: 129.

9

Trade with the Aru Islands and Trans Fly Coast of New Guinea

Introduction

When the Portuguese arrived in eastern Indonesia at the beginning of the sixteenth century the Seram Laut were not involved in collecting or carrying products for Asian markets.[1] When the Dutch captured and destroyed Banda in 1621, some Bandanese fled and settled in the Seram Laut Islands. These Bandanese settlers encouraged the Seram Laut to supply Asian markets. From this time on the Seram Laut sought goods for these markets as well as continued their traditional trade. For the next 20 years Seram Laut traders, including those from Gorong Island, were making regular trading expeditions to the Aru Islands.

Dutch vessels first visited the Aru Islands in 1636 and soon returned to carry out trade. By 1645 the Dutch East India Company had effectively closed these islands to other traders, including those from the Seram Laut Islands. They did this by inducing several local chiefs to give exclusive trade rights to the Company who in turn allocated these rights to the Dutch residents of the Banda Islands. At first, damar, pearls, turtle shell and bird of paradise skins were the main exports from the Aru Islands.[2] Trepang did not become a major trade good until the 1720s.[3]

The Dutch consolidated their position by building a fort on Wokam Island (Figure 35) and establishing missions. In the early 1700s neat little stone churches with their construction dates inscribed over their doors were built in all the main villages in the western Aru Islands.[4] These Dutch missionaries in the Aru Islands carried out the first mission activity in New Guinea and its offshore islands. Their work predates the Woodlark Island mission in what is now Papua New Guinea in 1847 and the Mansinam Island mission in Doreri Bay in Dutch New Guinea (now West Papua) in 1855.

When trepang became a profitable trade item in the 1720s the Dutch traders from the Banda Islands sought this product in the Aru

Islands. The market was soon dominated by A. J. van Steenbergen, a resident of Banda, who had seven trading vessels. Smaller traders were unable to compete with his operation and his crews usually obtained most of the lucrative, and less bulky, black trepang. There was no profit in the plentiful, easily prepared white variety.[5]

Also available in the Aru Islands were long nutmegs, which were generally considered inferior to the round ones from Banda. Although previously sought by the Seram Laut and other traders, the Aru nutmegs were of little interest to the Dutch traders from Banda, the home of cultivated nutmegs. The Dutch also rejected the Aru nutmegs because most were worm-ridden and had been gathered before they were ripe.[6]

As a result of the exclusive trade rights given to Dutch traders from Banda by the Dutch East India Company, the Aru and Kei islanders were prohibited from supplying sago to Banda, because the Bandanese were required, in the interests of Dutch trade in the archipelago, to live on Javanese rice. When this proved unviable, steps were taken to revive the traditional Aru and Kei sago trade.[7]

Prior to 1645 when the Dutch East India Company gained a trade monopoly in the Aru Islands, Seram Laut traders were making regular trading expeditions to these islands. When the Seram Laut found that they were denied access to the Aru Islands, they sought alternative sources. It is proposed here that this is when the Seram Laut traders extended their trading sphere eastwards to the New Guinea coastline adjacent to Torres Strait. They subsequently withdrew from this coastline and reestablished their trade with Aru when the Dutch withdrew from the Dutch East Indies during the Napoleonic wars. The period of proposed Seramese influence on the Trans Fly coast of New Guinea thus dates from 1645 until the 1790s when the Dutch lost control of the East Indies.

When the British gained control of the East Indies during the Napoleonic wars, they took little interest in the Aru Islands. They just gave the Dutch businessmen from Banda time to collect their debts before destroying the fort on Wokam Island and removing the garrison.[8]

The treaty agreements signed in Europe in 1814 allowed the Dutch to regain control of the East Indies. When they returned, they abandoned the monopolistic practices of the disbanded Dutch East India Company which had restricted inter-island trading. This allowed the Seram Laut to resume trade with the Aru Islanders and, as a result, cease their trade with the distant Trans Fly coast of New Guinea.

There are enough tantalising indications of Seram Laut contact with the Trans Fly coast from about 1645 until 1790 to warrant serious oral testimony studies in the Seram Laut Islands and the Trans Fly coast of New Guinea. Archaeological surveys of sites dating to this period in this part of New Guinea should also be rewarding, but may not be possible because access to some of the known sites is restricted to initiated men. However, this restriction may change.

Indications of Seram Laut contact with the Trans Fly region from about 1645 until 1790

There are linguistic indications of contact between the Seram Laut Islands and the people of the Trans Fly region. It is only on the eastern tip of Seram and in the Seram Laut Islands that a knife is called *turika*, *tari* or other variants of this name.[9] The use of comparable words to ask for iron by Torres Strait Islanders in 1792 indicates that they were then familiar with such names for knives. The parts of western New Guinea visited by Seram Laut traders before extensive European contact still use similar words for knives. They are known as *turi* in areas such as Lobo in Triton Bay, Namatote Island off Triton Bay and Wuaussirau in Etna Bay. At Onin a knife is known as *tani*, see Table 9 and Figure 28.

In 1792 Captains Bligh and Portlock of the *Providence* and *Assistant*, and crew member Matthew Flinders, observed that Erub and Damut Islanders in the eastern part of Torres Strait were demanding iron from passing ships. Flinders visited the area again in 1802 and experienced the same demands.[10] The names for iron being used by these islanders were *toore-tooree*, *tureeke* or *toorik*. Other early nineteenth century visitors also report that iron was commonly called *turik* or *tulik*. Table 9 and Figure 30 indicate where these names and their variants are used in Torres Strait and the New Guinea mainland.

The Gizra, Agób and Idi people of the Trans Fly claim that they possessed metal implements long before the London Missionary Society established a mission on Dauan Island in 1871.[11,12] While it is possible that many of these implements were obtained as trade items from trepangers or pearlers who began working in Torres Strait in the 1830s and 1860s respectively,[13] this does not explain how Torres Strait Islanders were demanding iron as early as 1792.

The Seramese names for iron include *mamóle* and other cognates. *Mammoosee* and *malil* are other words used to refer to iron by the Gizra of the Trans Fly and the Mabuiag and Erub Islanders of Torres Strait. They may also have a Seramese origin.[14]

The proposed activities of Seram Laut traders in the Trans Fly region from 1645 until 1790, along with local trade routes, would also explain how glass beads dating to this period came to be present in archaeological sites found upriver of Kikori in the Gulf of Papua. The best dated of these finds is a bead identified as having been manufactured at Murano in Italy between 1650–1750. It was excavated from archaeological deposits which have a general date of

1630–1770 at Kulupuari, an old village site on the banks of the Kikori River, some 16 kilometres upriver from Kikori.[15]

The presence of these beads at Kulupuari is not so surprising when it is known that this site is situated on the main trade route by which pearl shells from Torres Strait were traded inland to the highlands. The route was from Torres Strait to the Papuan Gulf, thence up the Kikori River, taking an eastern tributary called the Sirebi, over the slopes of Mount Murray to Samberighi, on to the Erave area of the Southern Highlands, and thence to the Wahgi valley of the Western Highlands (Figure 34).[16]

Table 9: Words for knife and iron used in eastern Seram, the Seram Laut Islands, the Torres Strait Islands and New Guinea.

word	Seram and NW New Guinea	Torres Strait Islands	Trans Fly and adjacent mainland areas
toerik	Warn, Seram		
toolick		Erub & Mer Is.	
toore -toore		Erub Is.	
toori		Massid Is.	
toorik		E. Torres Strait Islands	
toorree		Damut, Erub & Mer Islands	
tuka	Gah, Seram		
tulik		Erub & M er Is. E. Torres Strait Islands	
tuni	Onin		
tureeke		E. Torres Strait Islands	
turi	Seram, Namatote Is., Lobo, Etna Bay	Bine	
turika	Seram	Saibai Island	Buji, Mawatta, Kiwai
turikata			Dabu
turiko			Mabudauan, Tureture, Mawatta
turito	Keffing Island Seram Laut Islands		
turuko			Tirio (lower bank of Fly River), Sisiami (Bamu River)

Notes:

1. Marind-anim (Tugeri) knew the word *turik*, but it meant woman. They therefore had their own word *wokerike*, see Haddon (1912 (4): 129).

2. The Malay and Javanese words for knife and iron are *pisau* and *busi* respectively for Malay and *lading* and *wusi* for Javanese (Wallace 1986: 616).

3. Stokes (1846) reports meeting Torres Strait Islanders on Restoration Island, on the eastern coast of Cape York Peninsula, in June 1841 who kept asking for *toolic* (Moore 1978: 323).

4. The word for knife throughout the Lake Murray-Middle Fly area is *suki*. This is also the origin of the group name Suki. Suki could be a cognate of the Seram Laut words (Mark Busse personal communication 1991).

Sources:
Flinders 1814 (1): xxii, xxiv; Flinders 1814 (2): 109; Hughes 1977: 24; Jukes 1847 (1): 133; Laba in Contribution 2; Ray in Wollaston 1912: 332–333; Stokhof 1982a: 62; Wallace 1986: 616.

Impact of the Seram Laut traders

More than three decades before the Seram Laut trade commenced, Torres passed through Torres Strait in 1606 and reported no local interest in knives or iron. It is proposed here that the Seram Laut traders who came from 1645 to 1790 sought damar from the people of the Trans Fly. Their interest in the south coast of New Guinea, rather than the Torres Strait Islands or northern Australia, would explain why Cook and Banks found no indication of Seram Laut activity or knowledge of metal at Cape York in 1766.[17]

Trepang, which gave rise to a subsequent eastern Indonesian interest in the northern Australian coastline, from Wellesley Island in the Gulf of Carpentaria to Melville Island, as well as the Kimberley Coast, did not become an important trade good until the 1720s,[18] some 70 years before the Seram Laut interest in the Trans Fly lowlands ceased. Although there is a time overlap, there is no indication that Asian trepang collectors were ever active in Torres Strait. Certainly no sites comparable to the Makassarese sites found in northern Australia were discovered during an archaeological survey of the Torres Strait Islands.[19] In the seventeenth century damar was an important Indonesian trade good, as it was the main means of illumination used throughout the archipelago. In fact the word damar means torch in Malay. Torches were made by placing pounded resin in palm leaf tubes. The use of damar for lighting continued until mineral oil became available. Other uses of damar included coating and sealing pottery.[20]

The resins used originated from the bark of *Agathis* species (kauri pine/Manila copal) or the sapwood of dipterocarps, especially *Vatica papuana*.[21] The distribution of *Vatica papuana* trees in southwest Papua New Guinea is shown in Figure 31.

The Seram Laut contact provides an historical origin for the Sido-Hido hero traditions of southwest Papua. Roy Wagner examines these and related traditions in Contribution 1 of this volume.

The Trans Fly people claim that they had books before the arrival of Europeans (see Billai Laba in Contribution 2 of this volume). This could be explained by the Indonesian trade practice of giving documents to appointed headmen in the main villages where they traded. For instance, P. Drabbe[22] reports that amongst the Mimika these were called *surat*, a Malay word meaning letter. These *surat* may have served the same

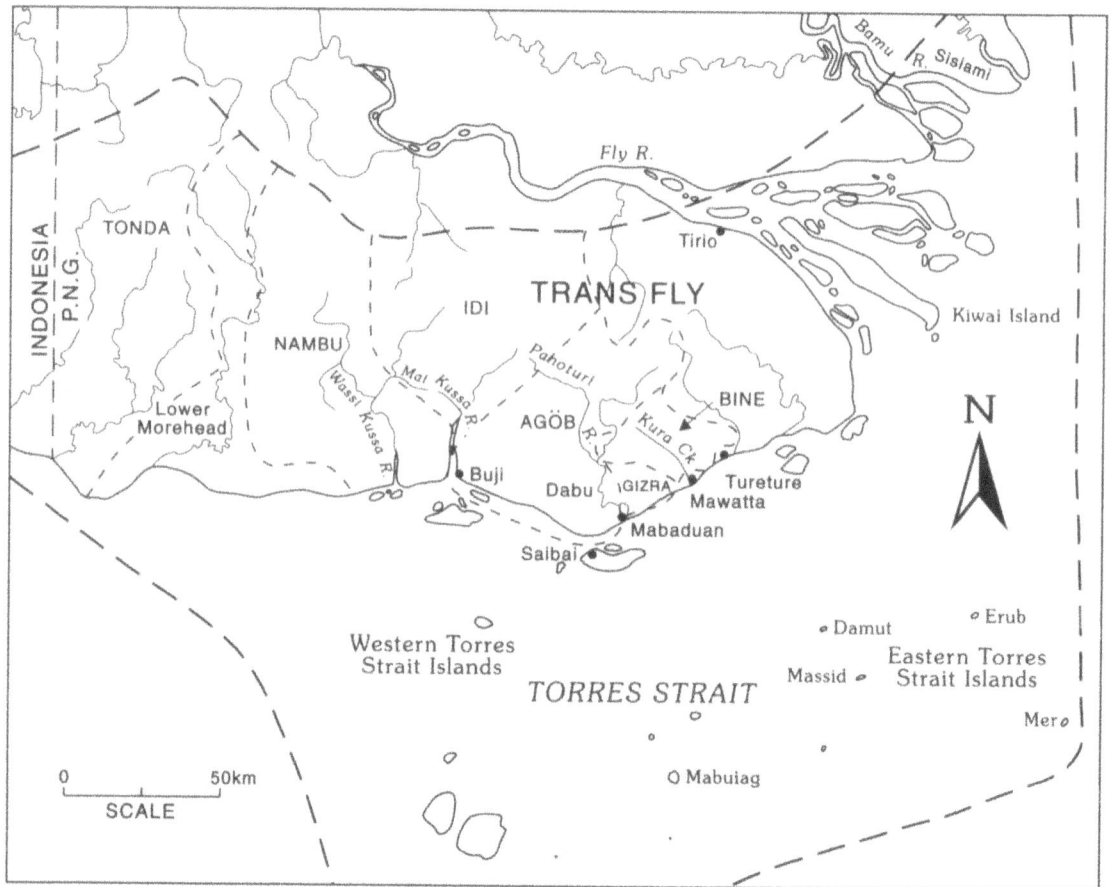

Figure 30: Where *turik, tulik, tuni* and other variants are used or known as words for knife and iron in Torres Strait and the Trans Fly.

function as the village books used during the Australian administration of Papua New Guinea. The traders could have recorded useful information, including the local people who were trustworthy and those who had failed to fulfil agreed contracts made with the traders.

The people living in the Wassi Kussa River mouth area as far east as Kura Creek (Figure 30) claim that their ancestors had books (*buk*) which had not been obtained from Europeans. Here it should be noted that *buku* is the Malay word for book. These books are reputed to have been held at Basir Puerk, near Mabudauan at the mouth of the Pahoturi River, and other depositories (see Billai Laba in Contribution 2).

The *buk* held at Basir Puerk near Mabudauan has not survived. This is not surprising. Who could have preserved them under the conditions that the Gizra, Agob, Idi and other mainland people faced at the time of European contact? At that time their main concern was to

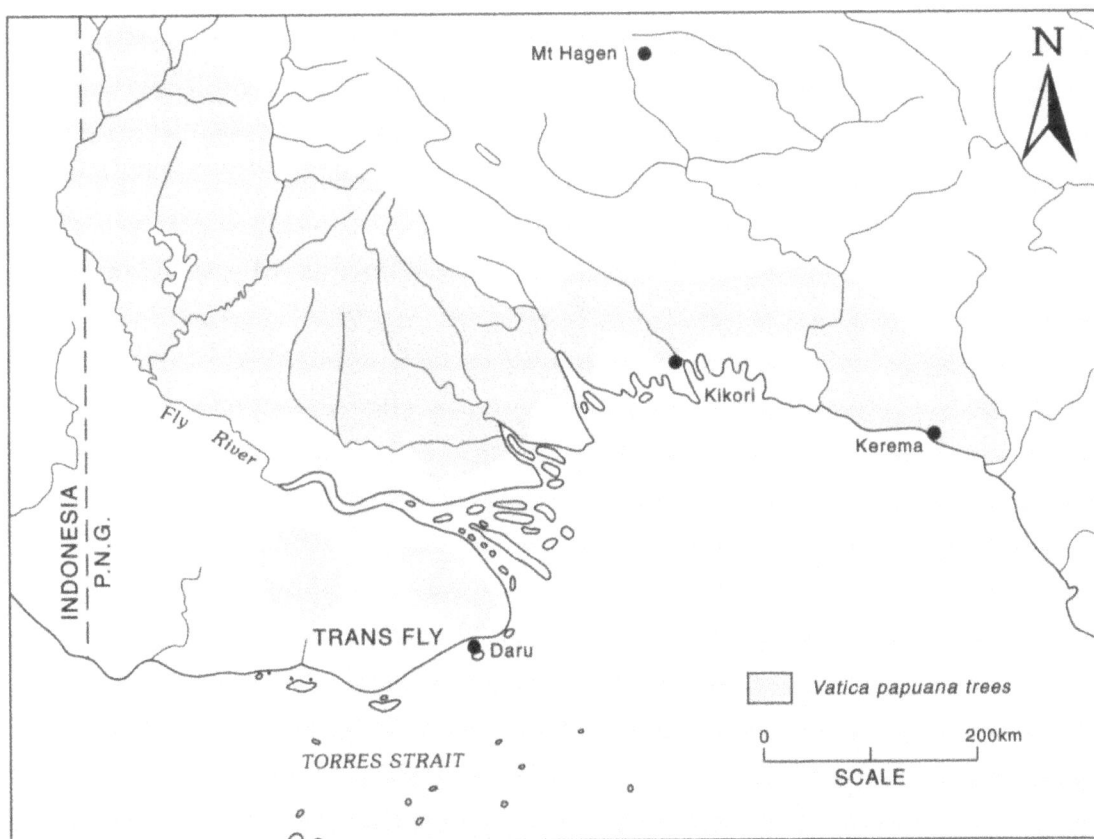

Figure 31: The distribution of *Vatica papuana* trees in southwest Papua New Guinea.
Source: Zieck 1975, 1978.

avoid being found and killed by the Tugeri (Marind-anim) raiders. The coastal stretch had been abandoned and people were hiding inland. The first European visitors to the mainland saw more of the Tugeri raiders than the traditional inhabitants of the area. This explains why the government initially thought the unoccupied land at Mabudauan had no local owner.[23]

In the early 1890s, Sir William MacGregor visited an inland Dabu (Gizra) camp where one group was living in hiding from the Tugeri. He found some 200 people living in four temporary shelters.[24] These were made of tree bark which was tied onto a framework of curved wooden poles. The continuous use of temporary shelters would not have ensured the preservation of any sacred possessions.

Knowledge about pre-European metal, the *buk* and the remains of boats located at the headwaters of the Mai Kussa and Pahoturi River is considered sacred lore by the Gizra, Agob and Idi people of the Trans Fly (Figure 63). The planks, chain and anchor of a boat located on the banks of a creek flowing into the Mai Kussa are probably not those of an Indonesian prau, but rather the remains of Captain Strachan's vessel abandoned during an attack by the Tugeri in 1884.[25] The local inhabitants were probably mystified as to how it appeared during their absence and it is not surprising that the remains are locally referred to as Noah's Ark. A similar mysticism has built up around the *buk* and these are often called Bibles.

Plate 24: A resin torch illuminating a Kamula dancer wearing Raggiana plumes at Wasapepa village in Western Province.
Photo: Courtesy of A.L. Crawford.

Contact with the Seram Laut would have led to the introduction of new crops, such as tobacco and sweet potatoes, as well as new technologies. The use of damar (tree resin) to make light and a new tool for working sago pith are examples of technological changes which were probably introduced by this contact. Plate 24 shows a resin torch being used by a Kamula dancer at Wasapea village in Western Province. Figure 32 shows examples of the special tool used to scrape sago pith which is found in Borneo, the Moluccas and the western part of New Guinea. Figure 33 indicates where this tool is used in New Guinea.

Tobacco is an American plant introduced by the Portuguese to the Moluccas. Tobacco seeds and the practice of smoking were taken from the Moluccas to New Guinea through contacts resulting from tribute payments or trade. In the Raja Empat Islands, Onin, Kowiai and Mimika areas of West Papua most of the words used for tobacco are clearly derived from *tambaku*, *tambako* or *tabako*.

In southwest Papua New Guinea the names used for tobacco appear to be derived from *sukuba*, see Table 10 and Figure 34. *Sukuba* and its variants seem to be derived from the word tobacco, with the replacement of t by s and interchangeable b's, p's, g's and k's. There is a set of words derived from *sukuba* between the mouth of the Fly and the international border, and then a distribution of related words in the languages spoken in the Strickland River, Palmer River and Ok Tedi areas to the north.[26]

Tobacco was probably introduced to the Torres Strait Islands and adjacent New Guinea mainland when the area was visited by Seram Laut traders from 1645 to the 1790s. The earliest observation of tobacco being used in this area was in the Torres Strait Islands in 1836.[27]

Table 10: List of names for tobacco derived from *sukuba* used in southwest Papua New Guinea and Torres Strait.

(Place names are given in lowercase, languages in capitals)

name	location/language
choka	Cape York, Australia
kuku	ELEMA; KOIARI; KOITA; MOTU; Purari Delta
sakaba	Dabu, AGÖB
sakoba	GOGODALA
sakop	Yende, AGÖB; Eastern Torres Straits Islands, MIRIAM
sakopa	Domori, KIWAI; GOGODALA; Tagota, SUKI; TIRIO; WABUDA KIWAI
sakpa	AGÖB; IDI; TONDA

name	location/language
sakup	Jibu, GIDRA
sakupa	Buji, AGÖB; KIWAI
sauk	Bolivip, FAIWOL
saukabata	Strickland River
sekupe	Palmer River
sikube	Anmat, Ok Tedi; AWIN
sikupa	Eastern Torres Straits Islands, MIRIAM
sogob	Eastern Torres Straits Islands, MIRIAM
soguba	KIWAI
sok	Ok Tedi; Star Mountains
sokoba	Moie (? Goi), NAMBU; Suki Creek, SUKI
sokop	Yende, AGÖB
sokopa	Dorro, IDI; Kibuli, AGOB; Eastern Torres Straits Islands, MIRIAM
soga	Lake Kutubu; lower Waga River
sogu	Lake Kutubu; lower Waga River
soku	Samberighi
suguba	GIDRA; Kunini, BINE; GIZRA; Saibai, MABUIAG; Western Torres Straits Islands, MABUIAG; KIWAI; Tureture, SOUTHERN KIWA;
sugub	Western Torres Straits Islands, MABUIAG
suk	Star Mountains
sukoba	Suki Creek, SUKI
suku	BAMU KIWAI; Foraba district, upper Purari; Goaribari Island; Mount Murray; Omati River; Paibuna River; Sisiame, BAMU KIWAI; Umaida Turama River; upper Kikori River
sukub	Eastern Torres Straits Islands, MIRIAM; Western Torres Straits Islands, MABUIAG
sukuba	above Everill Junction; Daudai, GIDRA; Karigara, IDI; KIWAI; Kunini, BINE; Mawatta, SOUTHERN KIWAI; Saibai, MABUIAG; Semariji, TONDA; Eastern Torres Straits Islands, MIRIAM; Western Torres Straits Islands, MABUIAG
sukufa	GOGODALA; NAMBU
sukup	GOGODALA
sukupa	Dibolug, Wassi Kussa R., NAMBU; Warubi, IDI
sukuva	Keriaki, NAMBU

Sources: Laba in Contribution 2; Riesenfeld 1951.

Figure 32: A special tool is used in Borneo, the Moluccas and the western part of New Guinea to scrape sago pith. In the eastern part of New Guinea wood-working tools are used for both sago scraping and wood working. Examples from Seram, New Guinea and its offshore islands are shown here.
A. South Seram, collected before 1889.
B. Aru Islands, collected before 1913.
C. Waira village, Kikori area, PNG.
Sources: Höpfner 1977: Plate 10; Rhoads 1980: Plate 111–9). Drawings by Anton Gideon.

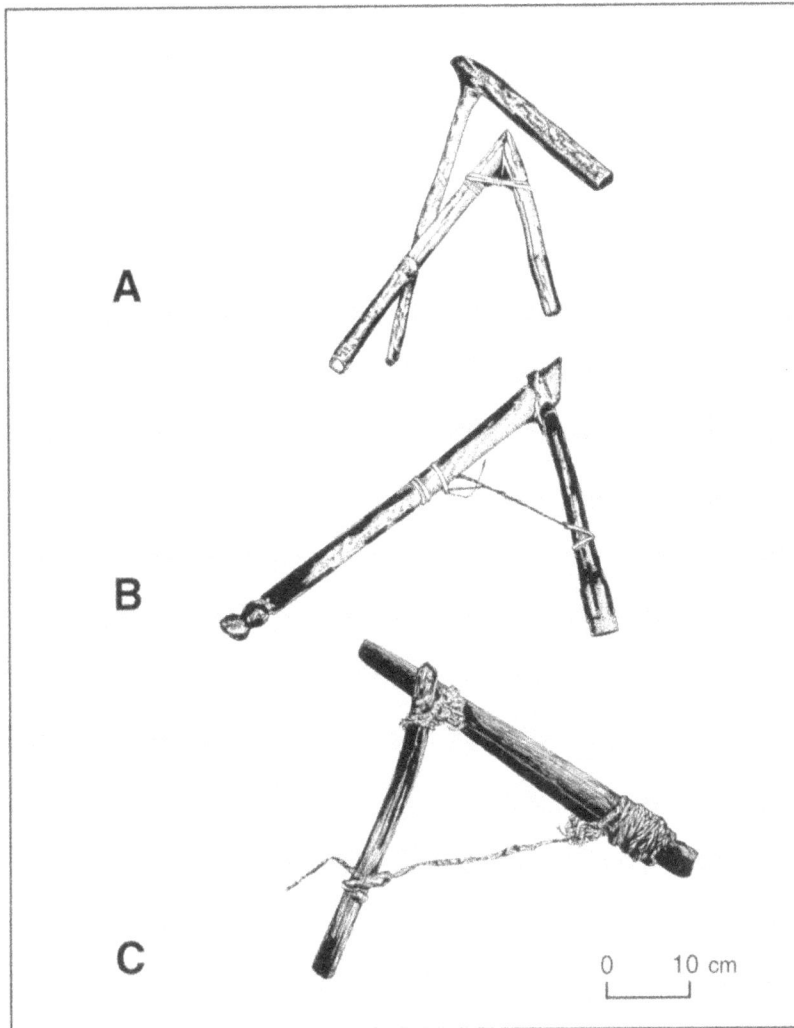

Figure 33: Where the special sago pith-scraping tool is used in New Guinea.
Source: Crosby 1976. Reproduction courtesy of Archaeology in Oceania.

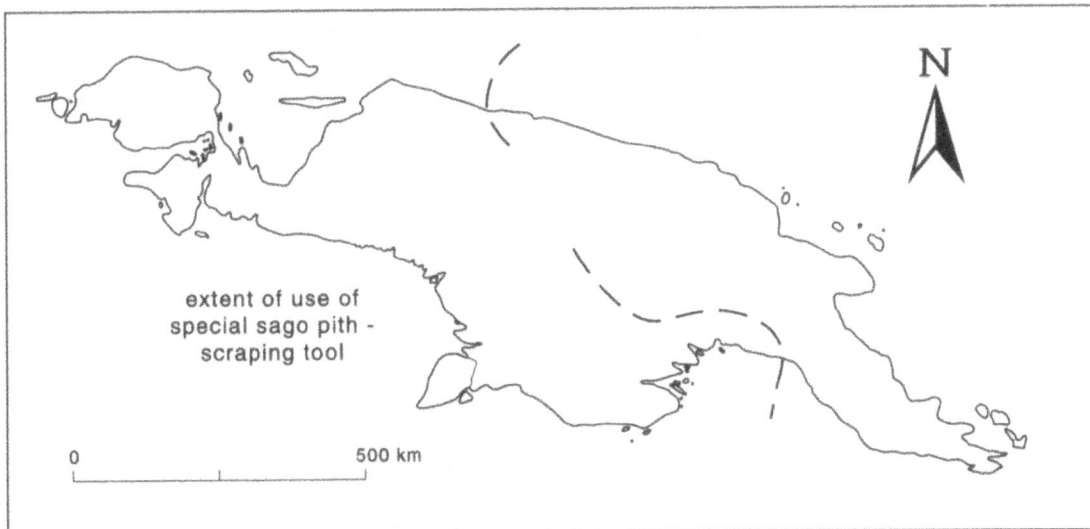

East of the Fly River mouth the name *sukuba* becomes shortened to *suku*. The distribution of this name suggests that tobacco was traded up tributaries of the Kikori River to Samberighi and Lake Kutubu in the Southern Highlands. In the Papuan Gulf, coastal villagers probably gave gifts of tobacco to the Motu of the Port Moresby area to take back on their return *hiri* (trading voyages). This would explain the distribution of tobacco and the name *kuku* (derived from *suku* with an interchange of s to t then k) as far east as Suau.[28]

Figure 34: The distribution of names for tobacco derived from *sukuba, sokoba* and *sakob* in southwestern Papua New Guinea and Torres Strait.

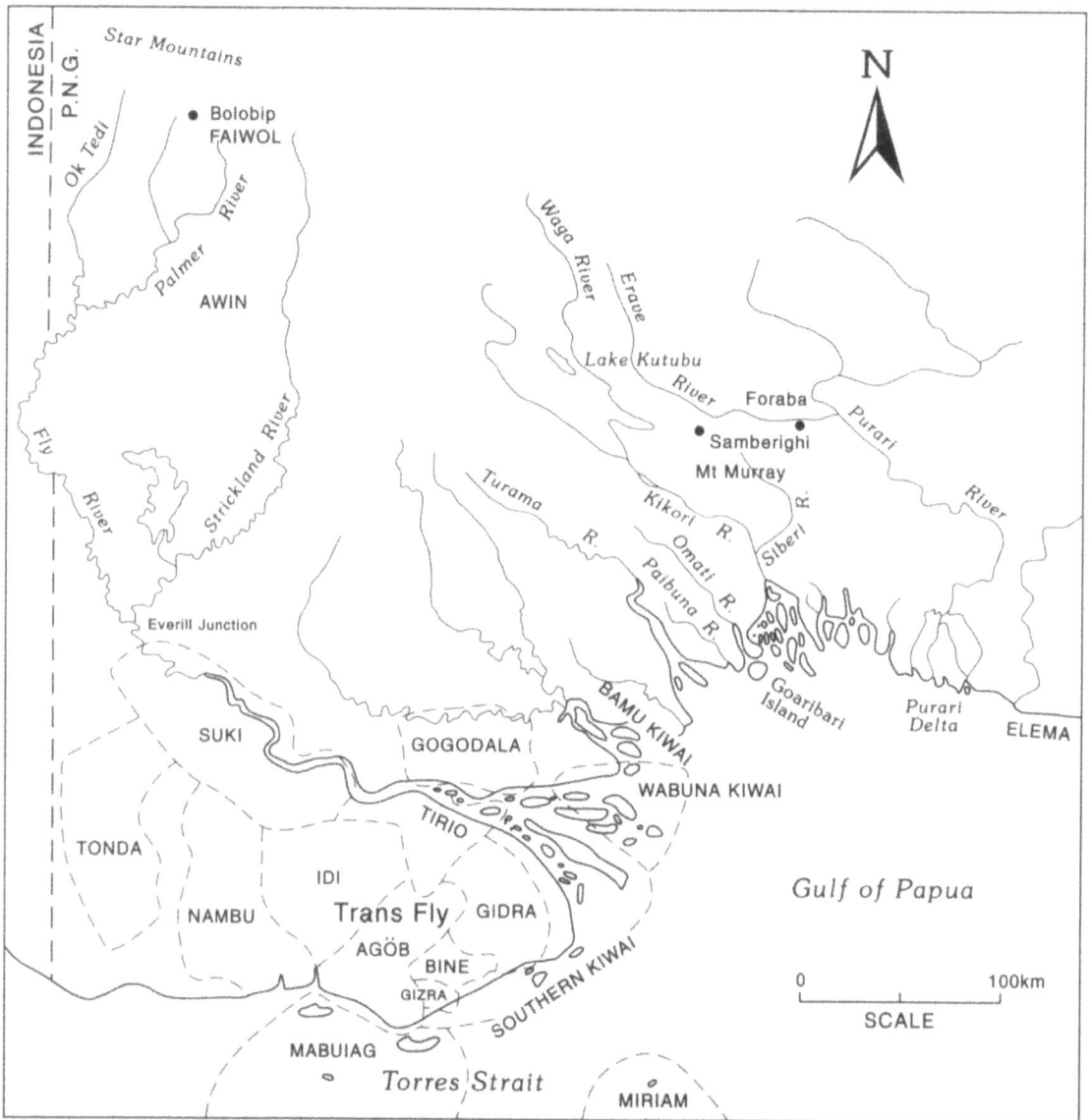

In addition to tobacco, it is likely that sweet potatoes were introduced to southern New Guinea at this time. During the seventeenth century these tubers became a popular food in the Moluccas.[29] Tom Dutton[30] has produced a fascinating set of related words not only spoken on the Bird's Head but also in the area inland from Kikori to the Southern Highlands; see Table 11. In view of the ensuing impact that this high-yielding crop had on highland societies, the possibility of this as a route of introduction deserves further study.

Table 11: Set of names for sweet potato used in the Bird's Head and region inland from the Kikori area in Papua New Guinea

(Place names are given in lowercase, languages in capitals)

name	location/language
West Papua	
sesiayuro	Iria, W. Kamarau Bay
sersiabura	Asienara, W. Kamarau Bay
sie	Iha, E. Bintuni Bay
sibu	Iha, E. Bintuni Bay
sijapido	Inanwatan, W. Bintuni Bay
siäp	Borai, NW. Cendrawasih Bay
Papua New Guinea	
siyofulu	SAMO, EAST STRICKLAND
siyafuu	KUBO, EAST STRICKLAND
siyobulu	TOMU, EAST STRICKLAND
siyabul	HONIBO, EAST STRICKLAND
siapuru/siabulu	BIAMI, BOSAVI
siapuru/siabulu	KALULI, BOSAVI
siapuru/siabulu	KASUA, BOSAVI
siapuru/siabulu	FASU, WEST KUTUBU
siyabulu	BIAMI, BOSAVI
siapuri	BAIAPI
supuru	FASU, WEST KUTUBU
tia	SAU, WEST CENTRAL
dia	POLOPA, TEBERAN
diani	Barika, TURAMA

Source: Dutton 1973: 439.

Dobo, Aru Islands

When the Dutch regained the East Indies from the British in 1814 the monopolistic trade practices of the disbanded Dutch East India Company were abandoned. Dobo (Dobbo) on the small island of Warmar in the Aru Islands (Figure 35) quickly became the largest trading centre in the New Guinea region. By the 1830s traders mainly from Seram Laut and Makassar were carrying out a profitable trade there. The low prices of their goods excluded Dutch competition.[31] Alfred Russel Wallace visited Dobo in 1857.[32] His observations provide an interesting account of the trading activities taking place at this time.

For part of each year Dobo was a flourishing trading settlement with a population of some 500 people; see Figure 36. The Indonesian traders came once a year. They arrived in January with the west monsoon and departed in July with the east monsoon. In 1857 there were about 100 small praus, mostly from Gorong, but also some from Seram and Kei. In addition there were 15 large praus from Makassar, a few Chinese traders and one Dutchman. Wallace travelled from Dobo to Makassar by prau; the journey of more than 1,600 kilometres took nine and a half days.[33]

Dobo was established on a sandspit at the entrance to a channel. Its three rows of houses were exposed to healthy sea breezes. Instead of establishing a house, some traders preferred to live on their boats or camp on the beach. The traders anchored their praus on the sheltered side of the sandspit. Some pulled their praus up on the beach. There they were safe from worm damage and could be prepared for the homeward journey. Apart from trading at Dobo, the traders also sent small vessels to trade on the eastern side of the Aru Islands.[34]

Some 20 people died at Dobo in 1857. Among the traders there was a Moslem priest who superintended the funerals and called the faithful to prayer at a small mosque on Friday. The Chinese showed their superior wealth by erecting granite tombstones, imported from Singapore, for their dead.[35]

Some traders married Aru Island women. Wallace[36] reports that men from Makassar, Java and Ambon had each married an Aru wife and that a few traders had decided to become permanent residents.

Traders who used houses either built a new house or repaired their old one.[37] Once the traders were established, the inhabitants of the Aru Islands brought their wares. These were displayed at each house. They brought bundles of smoked trepang, dried shark's fins, pearl shells, turtle shell, edible bird's nest, pearls, ornamental woods, timber and birds of paradise. All these products had been collected throughout the Aru Islands during the preceding six months. The trepang and pearl shell provided the bulk of the Aru exports. Damar was no longer a major export. Some foodstuffs such as fish, turtle and vegetables were

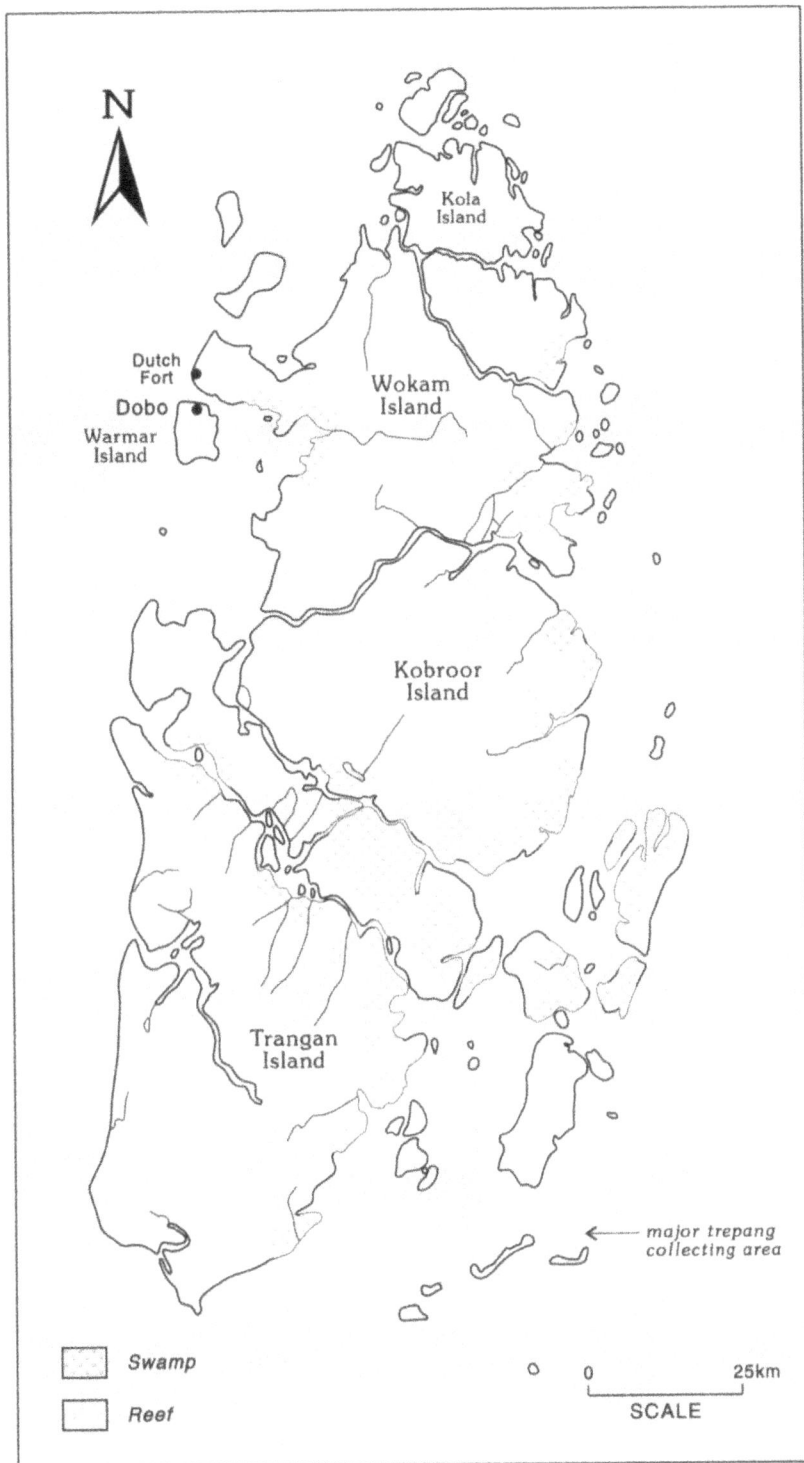

Figure 35: The Aru Islands.

Figure 36: Dobo on Warmar Island in the Aru Islands during the height of the trading season in 1857.

Source: Wallace 1986 (first published 1869).

also traded. The Greater Bird of Paradise (*Paradisaea apoda*) and the King Bird of Paradise (*Cicinnurus regius*) were the first birds of paradise described by natural historians. The Greater Bird of Paradise skins would have come from the Aru Islands (see Figures 15 and 16). There was also some transshipment of products obtained in New Guinea by Seram Laut traders through Dobo. In this way Wallace obtained skins of the Lesser Bird of Paradise in the Aru Islands.[38]

In return the Aru Islanders desired German knives,[39] choppers, swords, muskets, gunpowder, tobacco, gambier,[40] plates, basins, crockery, cutlery, handkerchiefs, sarongs, cloth from Sulawesi, white English calico, American unbleached cottons, arack, gongs, small brass cannons and elephant tusks. If the particular item desired was not forthcoming, the Aru Islander would move on to display his wares at the next house. Some stores contained tea, coffee, sugar, wine, biscuits, and the like for the supply of the traders, and others were full of fancy goods, china ornaments, mirrors, razors, umbrellas, pipes and purses with which to take the fancy of the wealthier Aru.[41] Some 3,000 boxes each containing 15 half-gallon bottles of arack, comparable in strength to West Indian rum, were consumed annually in the Aru Islands.[42]

The availability of these imported goods led to socioeconomic changes. For instance, by 1826 bridewealth payments in the Aru Islands always included imported gongs, elephant tusks, crockery and cloth, plus other items, and this was still the case when Wallace was there in 1857.[43]

That year the bulk of the exports from the Aru Islands went out on 15 Makassarese praus. The cargo of one of these was worth about £1,000, whereas other small praus from Seram, Gorong and Kei together took goods worth about £3,000. The total exports from Dobo in 1857 were some £18,000.[44] Some of the pearls, mother-of-pearl shell and turtle shell ultimately reached Europe, whereas the trepang and edible bird's nest were solely destined for China.[45]

This trade attracted pirates. In February 1857 Wallace[46] reports that a prau arrived at Dobo which had been attacked. One man on board had been wounded. Everyone was alarmed. The Aru Islanders feared attacks on their villages and the capture of their women and children as slaves. The Indonesian traders were concerned that their small praus trading on the eastern side of the islands would be plundered. Although the pirates were not expected to attack Dobo, sentries were posted and fires were lit on the beach to guard against a surprise night attack.

The pirates were said to be from Soolo (Sulu)[47] and had some Bugis amongst them. The Indonesian traders were justified in their fears, as the pirates on this occasion did plunder some of the small praus trading on the eastern side of the Aru Islands. A crewman of one of these praus was killed. Pirates had last visited the Aru Islands eleven years previously.

In 1857 Dutch influence was minimal in eastern Indonesia. Makassar was guarded by a 42-gun Dutch frigate but this vessel, together with a small war steamer and 3 or 4 tiny cutters, was insufficient to deter piracy in the region.[48] The Aru Islands only received a visit from a commissioner based in Ambon about once a year. He toured the islands, hearing complaints, settling disputes and taking prisoner any serious offenders.[49]

Bird of paradise hunting and trade on the Aru Islands

Each year the Aru Islanders killed large numbers of fully plumed adult males of the Greater Bird of Paradise (*Paradisaea apoda*) and traded them at Dobo. Some of these skins were taken home by Europeans as curiosities, making this species the second bird of paradise to be taken to Europe. The first was the Lesser Bird of Paradise obtained by the Spanish in the Moluccas in 1521. The trade skins of the Greater Bird of Paradise described by Linnaeus lacked feet, hence his tongue-in-cheek name, *Paradisaea apoda*, 'the footless bird of paradise'.

Although J.O. Helwig and Herbert de Jager[50] had described the courtship behaviour of the Greater Bird of Paradise and the hunting methods of the Aru Islanders in the seventeenth century, their work was not widely known. Wallace was the first naturalist to observe and make known the courtship behaviour of this bird.[51]

Wallace was disappointed that the Greater Bird of Paradise was not in full plumage when he was in the Aru Islands for six weeks (March to May) in 1857. The trade skins he was offered were clearly last year's rejects; Wallace was dismayed that fresh skins were not available as those remaining from last year were all dirty and poorly preserved.[52] The islanders told him that the birds would be at their best from September to October.[53] Although he dearly wanted to observe and obtain specimens when the birds were in full plumage, Wallace was unable to delay his departure as the last prau returned in July. To be present in September to October would require him to spend a full year in the Aru Islands.

The Greater Bird of Paradise did start to display whilst Wallace was there, so he was able to observe their display and the hunting methods of the Aru Islanders on Kobru (Kobroor) Island; see Figure 37. The male birds congregated and displayed at favoured trees. The same trees were used for generations. The islanders used bows and arrows to shoot the birds from hides in the tree tops. Some hunters used arrows which had large blunt conical caps which killed the birds without damaging their plumes and skins;[54] others preferred pointed arrows. When the birds fell to the ground, they were collected by a boy who accompanied the hunters.[55]

When O. Beccari, an Italian naturalist who was collecting birds of paradise, visited Dobo from February to July in 1873, he obtained only seven specimens of the Greater Bird of Paradise in full plumage. All of these had been prepared in the local way, which smoked and deformed the specimens. Beccari wanted freshly killed birds which he could prepare as natural history specimens. He was dismayed to observe that many of the skins offered were in various stages of moulting and that a high price was paid for each skin. The Makassarese traders were then paying 15 half-gallon, square bottles of arack (an actual case of arack), worth 16 to 18 shillings, for each skin. He was told that at least 3,000 bird of paradise skins had been exported from Dobo in 1873.[56,57]

By the turn of the century Dobo was no longer a great market place; pearling was now the main activity. However, the export of bird of paradise skins continued and Sir William Ingram, the founder and first editor of the *Illustrated London News*, became so concerned about the extinction of the Greater Bird of Paradise that he set about establishing a colony of 44 of these birds on Little Tobago Island in the West Indies in 1909. The birds survived and in 1958 there were about 35 birds on the island.[58]

Figure 37: Aru Islanders shooting the Greater Bird of Paradise (*Paradisea apoda*) in 1857.

Source: Wallace 1986 (first published 1869).

Notes

1. Meilink-Roelofsz 1962: 100.
2. Earl 1840: x.
3. Macknight 1986: 69.
4. Earl 1853: 110; Kolff 1840: 180, 189.
5. Wright 1958: 18–20.
6. ibid.
7. Meilink-Roelofsz 1962: 219, 222; Ellen 1979: 69.
8. Wright 1958: 45.
9. Stokhof 1980, 1981, 1982a: 62, 1982b.
10. Flinders 1814 (1) xxii, xxiv; Flinders 1814 (2): 109.
11. See Billai Laba's Contribution 2 in this volume.
12. The first London Missionary Society teachers were established on Darnley (Masig) and Dauan Islands in 1871–2 (Whittaker et al. 1975: 347).
13. Haddon 1912 (1): 15: Hughes 1977: 32; Macknight 1976: 40; Yonge 1930: 165–7.
14. Wallace 1986: 616; Billai Laba in Contribution 2 this volume; Flinders 1814 (2): 109.
15. Rhoads 1984.
16. Crittenden 1982; Hughes 1977.
17. Beaglehole 1962 cited by Hughes 1977: 21.
18. Macknight 1986: 69.
19. Vanderwal 1973.
20. Ellen and Glover 1974: 357, 375.
21. Jack Zieck personal communication 1979.
22. Drabbe 1947–8: 256–7.
23. Later the Mowatta (Mawatta, Kiwai) claimed the land, but when the Dabu(lai) (Gizra) tribe was discovered, they declared themselves to be the real owners. Both groups were brought to Mabudauan and the government ended their claims (MacGregor 1892: 42). However, recent events indicate that the Gizra are still dissatisfied with the outcome (Mark Busse personal communication 1990).
24. MacGregor 1892: 43.
25. Strachan 1888: 47.
26. The *sukuba* set was noted by Tom Dutton in 1974 when preparing a manuscript on tobacco in New Guinea. He remarks (Dutton n.d.) that the most satisfactory explanation of this set would require contact between Indonesians and the Trans Fly, something hitherto undocumented.
27. Brockett 1936 cited by Riesenfeld 1951: 80.
28. Riesenfeld 1951.
29. Ellen 1987: 38.
30. Dutton 1973: 439.
31. Kolff 1840: 155, 196; Brumund 1853.
32. Wallace 1986: 432–6, 442–3.

33. Wallace 1986: 485–6.

34. Wallace 1862b: 131; 1986: 476.

35. Wallace 1986: 483.

36. Wallace 1986: 454.

37. In 1826 the traders had new houses built each year. This was necessary as the old ones were burnt at the end of each season by the Aru Islanders so that they would be paid to build new ones the following year (Kolff 1840: 197).

38. Wallace 1857: 415.

39. One German knife was worth 3 half-pence (Wallace 1986: 433).

40. Gambier is a yellowish catechu obtained from a woody vine, *Uncaria gambir*, and is used for chewing with betel nut or tanning and dyeing.

41. Wallace 1986: 435, 442.

42. Wallace 1986: 485.

43. Kolff 1840: 162; Wallace 1986: 485.

44. Wallace 1986: 485.

45. Wallace 1986: 409.

46. Wallace 1986: 440–2.

47. Wallace (1862a: 154) states they were from Magindano. This was a general term for such raiders used by the Sulawesi (Warren 1981: 160–1). Their presence upset Wallace's plans as it meant that no one ventured far from home until they were sure the raiders had left. This situation required Wallace to spend two months in Dobo without seeing a bird of paradise.

48. Wallace 1986: 219, 455.

49. Wallace 1986: 444.

50. Stresemann 1954: 273.

51. Gilliard 1969: 216; Stresemann 1954: 281.

52. Wallace 1986: 435.

53. In the Mapi River area of West Papua (Figure 38), the male Greater Bird of Paradise moults at this time (Rumbiak 1984: 8).

54. The use of blunt-ended arrows, which stun rather than pierce the flesh, remains a widespread way of shooting birds of paradise in New Guinea (see e.g. Barth 1975: 40).

55. Wallace 1857: 413–4; 1986: 446–7.

56. Whittaker et al 1975: 232.

57. In the 1850s Wallace reports that village-prepared trade skins fell in value from two dollars to six pence (see Chapter 5). Subsequently these skins must have regained some of their former value, as in 1873 Makassarese traders, presumably supplying Asian markets, were willing to pay 16–18 shillings per skin.

58. Gilliard 1969: 401, 413.

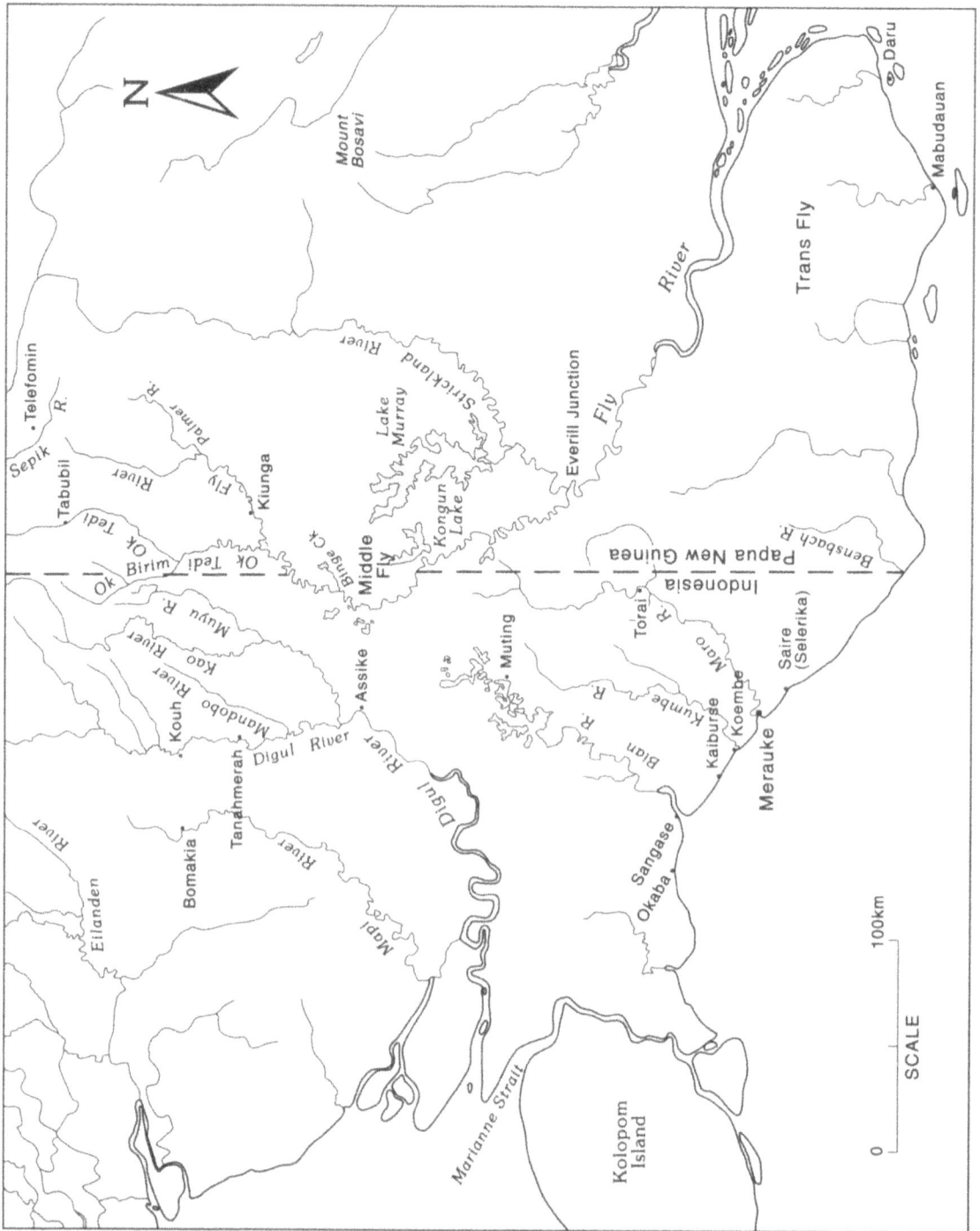

Figure 38: The Merauke region.

174

10

Copra, birds and profits in the Merauke region

The establishment of Merauke

The Merauke coast of New Guinea (Figure 38) was not brought under effective government control until early last century. The Dutch were prompted to take action after the administration of British New Guinea[1] made an official complaint in 1891 about the frequent raids being made across the border by the Marind-anim (Tugeri).[2] To show their good intentions the Dutch established a station at Selerika (Sarire) on 7 December 1892. This was the second Dutch Station to be established in New Guinea; the first was, as mentioned above, Fort Du Bus at Lobo in Triton Bay in 1828. The Selerika Fort was located close to the border and was manned by 2 Europeans, 10 Indonesian soldiers and 10 convicts. A few days after its establishment one soldier was already dead and 10 wounded; the station was then quickly withdrawn.[3]

During the 1890s the Dutch were unable to halt the Marind-anim raids across the border. The Administrator of British New Guinea, Sir William MacGregor, actually led an attack which routed a Marind-anim raiding party on 'Papuan' soil in June 1896. Despite this confrontation further Marind-anim raids were made in 1900 and 1902.

It was not until the Dutch established a garrison with 100 troops at Merauke in mid February 1902 that the Marind-anim began to be effectively discouraged from raiding.[4] Relations then began to be established between the Marind-anim and the Dutch (Plate 25). The superiority of Dutch weapons would have been clearly demonstrated when 2,000 Marind-anim failed in an attempt to take Merauke in 1902.[5]

Marind-anim raiders travelled remarkable distances by canoe and on foot. Figure 39 gives some idea of the extent of their journeys. Although coastal raids into British New Guinea ceased soon after the establishment of Merauke in 1902, inland raids were still being made to the Digul as late as 1912.[6]

During the early years of contact, strangers who ventured too far from Merauke risked their lives. A.E. Pratt, an English naturalist interested in collecting birds near Merauke, visited the station two months after it had opened. After assessing the local situation he departed at the first opportunity ten days later. The evident hostility of the Marindanim was enough to discourage any thoughts he had of bird collecting.[7]

Other individuals decided to stay. An Englishman named Montague was the first missionary to live among the Marind-anim in 1896, but the first mission station was not established until 1905. A number of Chinese and Indonesian traders as well as run-away convict labourers also ventured out from Merauke. Many were killed by the Marind-anim.[8]

By 1905 the situation had improved sufficiently for the Dutch to withdraw their garrison. In 1907 a police post, later an administrative post, was established at Okaba, some 90 kilometres west of Merauke. This post may have been established after a Chinese trader based at Kaiburse had been killed by Sangase villagers from further west. They took the trader's four Marind-anim assistants to their village. To avoid being beheaded like their employer these four assistants decided to discard their clothes and abandon their foreign habits.[9]

Plate 25: Establishing relations between the Marind-anim and the Dutch in Merauke in 1902.

Source: Courtesy of Fotobureau, Koninklijk Instituut voor de Tropen, Amsterdam.

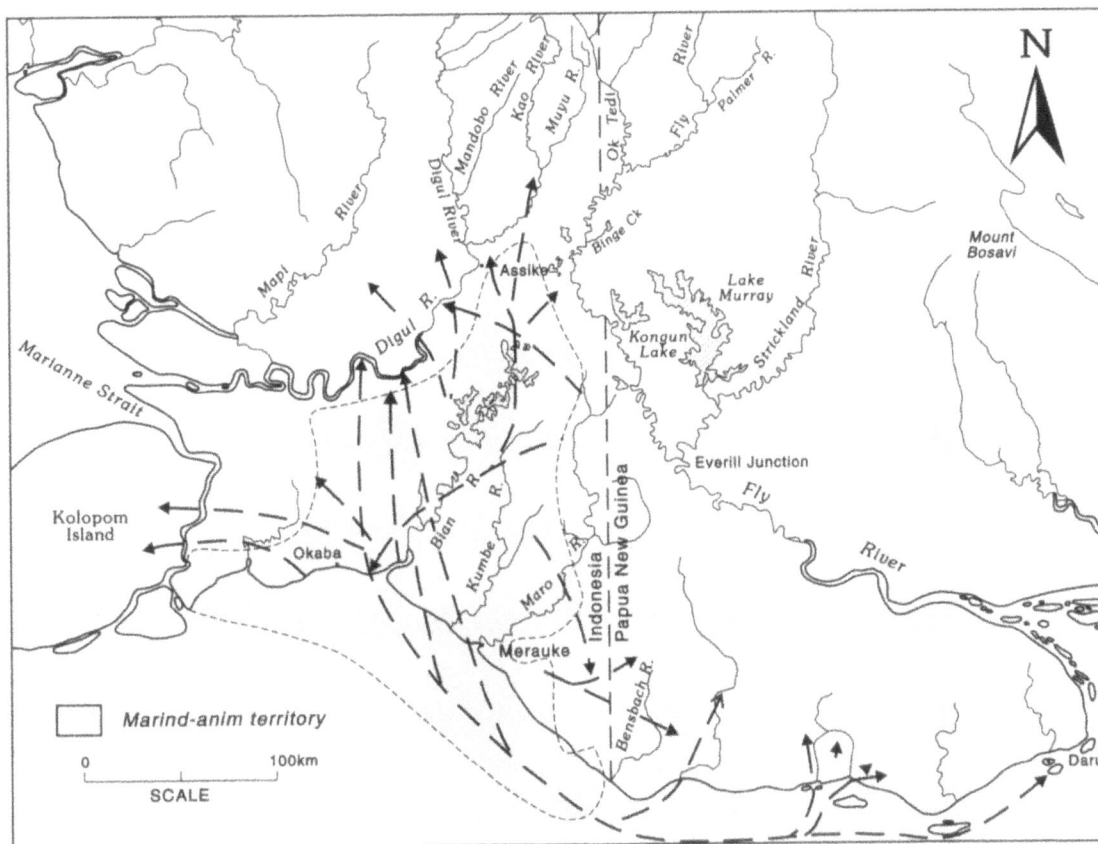

Figure 39: The raiding routes of the Marind-anim.

Despite such incidents, Chinese and Indonesian traders continued to live among the Marind-anim. One of these was Kure Kiong Sioe, a man with Chinese and Indonesian parents. He married a Marind-anim woman, learnt her language and was initiated. His knowledge of the *mayo* initiation ceremonies was subsequently recorded and in later years he worked as a government interpreter.[10] This interaction and contact with plume traders and hunters probably explains how *sambi* and variants of this word (all being variants of *sambut*, a Malay greeting) became common in the Middle Fly region.[11]

After 1907 Dutch military patrols expanded the area under Dutch influence and considerable efforts were made to explore the hinterland accessible by the Digul, as well as the shorter rivers east and west of Merauke.[12] This exploration was undertaken in the belief that by opening up the territory economic development would be promoted. Anyone able to establish a business was encouraged by the government, as the maintenance of Merauke and, to a lesser extent Fakfak and Manokwari, was a considerable burden on the financial resources of the Dutch East Indies.[13]

The Merauke Trading Company was established in 1903.[14] By 1910 there were fourteen Europeans or part-Europeans employed by the government, two European traders and about twelve Chinese

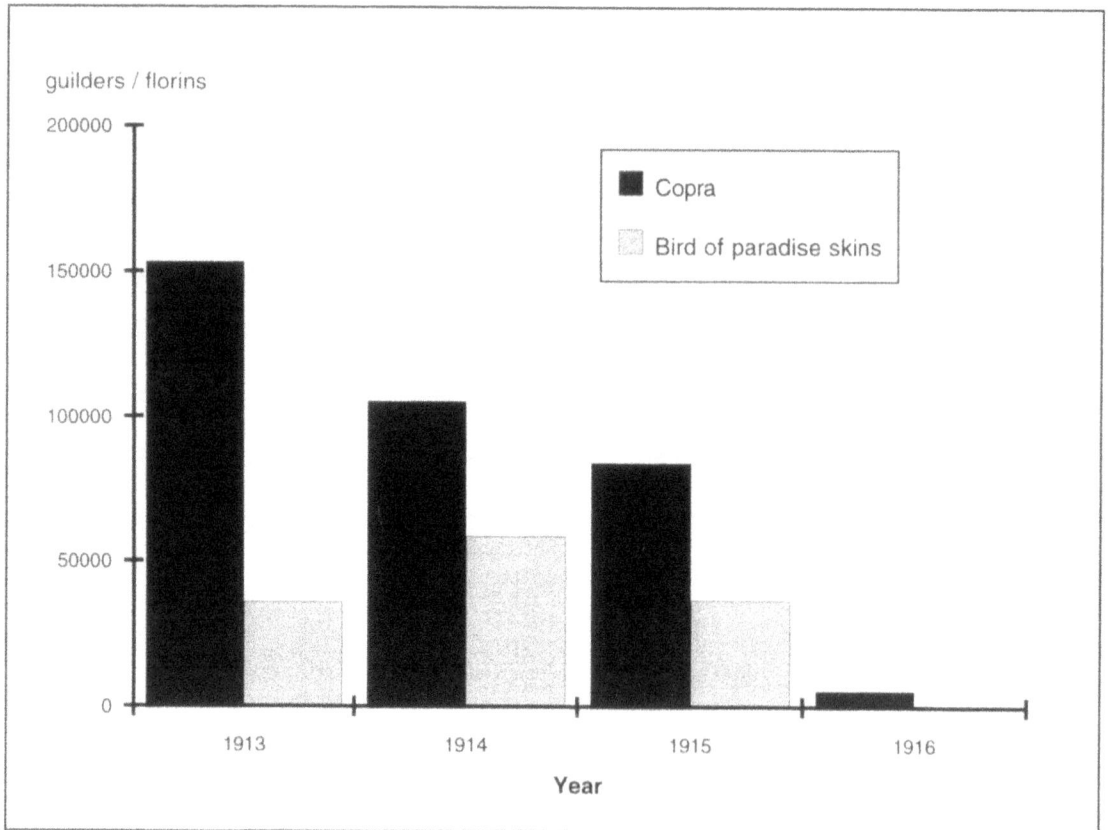

guilders / florins

Figure 40: The value of copra and bird of paradise exports out of Merauke from 1913–16. (In 1918, 30–35 guilders or florins was equivalent to 3 pounds sterling).

Source: Based on Historical Section of the Foreign Office, London 1920: 27.

traders at Merauke. The Marind-anim had traditionally kept large stands of coconuts for symbolic and religious reasons.[15] In 1902 they had hundreds of thousands of coconuts. This made copra trading a profitable venture, a development not possible on the north coasts of Dutch New Guinea and mainland German New Guinea (see Chapter 12). Trade copra quickly became the principal export from Merauke; see Figure 40. Lacking coconuts to trade, the people inland of the Marind-anim were given their first tenuous experience of the vagaries of world trade systems through their contact with bird hunters.

The plume hunters and traders

Most of the bird of paradise skins exported by traders from Merauke prior to the 1908 plume boom were obtained from local (Kaiakaia)[16] hunters who brought them to the coast (Plate 26).[17] This changed when the European and American markets began paying higher prices for

Plate 26: Marind-anim man with Greater Bird of Paradise skins.

Source: Nielsen 1930.

plumes during the European plume boom. It soon became apparent that local hunters could only shoot a small number of the potential stock of birds with their bows and arrows. A hunter with a gun could make large profits. One visitor to the area commented:

Everyone who could obtain a rifle and supplies, moved as quickly as possible into the interior, before the rumour of the price rise could penetrate that far. [During the early years of the boom it was possible] ... to purchase a bird of paradise or the right to shoot one from the local inhabitants for a box of matches or a few large nails.[18]

In exchange for items worth a few shillings at the most, hunters obtained bird of paradise skins worth more than two pounds each. Large profits were made as prices continued to rise.[19]

More and more people were drawn to Merauke by the prospects of making their fortune from birds of paradise. They were attracted by the prospect of obtaining substantial profits with relatively little outlay in a short period of time. Europeans, especially Australians, Indonesians from Ambon, Kei and Timor and Japanese and Chinese came to take part in the hunt.[20] The Chinese specialised in providing the hunters who lacked business capital with rifles and provisions.

Motor boats were obtained from as far afield as Singapore and Brisbane. All types and brands appeared. As long as they could float and travel some distance they were put into use. One hunter made himself a cheap and easily managed craft by fitting an old Ford motor in a large dinghy. This motley collection of motor boats allowed an ever increasing number of hunters to penetrate deep into the interior.

Each boat contained at least five men. They carried enough supplies for approximately four months. These included provisions, weapons, ammunition and a good supply of large and small knives, axes, pickaxes and other iron implements, tobacco and strings of beads to exchange with the Kaja-Kaja's for birds of paradise. The boats, in spite of their limited space, had to serve as a base for the hunters throughout the trip.[21]

Plume hunters were usually accompanied by locals who acted as guides and interpreters. For example, the Bian River people took hunters to the Fly River, whereas the Muyu acted as guides eastwards to the Ok Tedi and beyond (Figure 38). In both cases the guides were going into areas where related languages were spoken and where they had either recently established friendly contacts or had traditional trade ties. However, some hunters seem to have taken New Guineans from other areas along as marksmen. Both the Chinese and European hunting parties observed by W.F. Alder, an American adventurer, had marksmen from the Port Moresby area.

Alder provides a fascinating description of his encounter with two Chinese plume hunters and their party. This probably took place in a coastal village west of the mouth of the Bian River.[22] Alder and his companions were waiting for a copra boat to come along the coast (Plates 27 and 28). Their boat, the *Nautilus*, had been wrecked in the vicinity. While they were waiting, two Chinese hunters and their party of Moresby men stopped at the village. The hunters were tired after making their way to the coast. After a rest, they planned to travel along the coast to Merauke, where they would sell the bird of paradise skins they had taken. Alder describes the incident as follows:

The Chinese are of the typical trader class and appear prosperous, for their watch-chains are very heavy and pure gold – not the red gold we know, but the twenty-two-karat metal of the Orient.

Their advent causes a stir in the *kampong* [village], for the moment the dogs give warning of the approach of strangers the natives all dive into the shacks, to peer furtively through the crevices until assured the visitors mean them no harm. The Chinese enter the *kampong* boldly and, espying our camp, come to greet us immediately; and as the Chinaman is always hail fellow well met, we invite the men in and give them a cup of tea ...

Plate 27: Chinese trader collecting copra along the Merauke coast.

Source: Alder 1922.

Plate 28: Prayers on the Chinese trade boat were accompanied by gong beats.

Source: Adler 1922.

They seem much surprised to find two white men here and question us regarding the purpose of our visit, thinking at first, doubtless, that we are on the same errand as they. They cannot comprehend how we two Americans can find recreation and amusement in coming to this Godforsaken spot, putting up with untold hardship and inconvenience merely to meet and study the lives of the Kia Kia ... The Chinese is first, last, and always a business man and bends all his energies towards succeeding in his business. The Moresby boys immediately take up their abode with ... the crew of the *Nautilus*, who are camped near the *kampong*, and we make the Chinese comfortable in a spare tent, where they spread their mats and prepare to stay a day or two to rest.

They have been successful in their hunting and have nearly 60 codies, or 1,200 skins, though they have been in the interior only since last May. The skins, well preserved in arsenic, are done up in parcels. There is a small fortune in the proceeds of their season's hunting and they are most happy at their success, though they of course do not boast of it ...

In the course of the evening our visitors tell us in perfect Malay – they speak only a word of two of English – of the manner of hunting their beautiful quarry. The habits of the birds are most interesting. They also tell us something which is news to us. We had supposed that the restrictions placed upon the importation of the skins into America[23] were due to the possibility of the species becoming extinct, but the hunters tell us that is not the case. They say that only the male birds in full plumage are taken and that the bird never attains his fullest plumage until after the second bird-mating season. This being the case, it would seem that there is no danger of extinction, and the Chinese seemed to think that the ruling was unjust.

The method of hunting the birds is odd and requires much patience. When the locality they frequent is located, a search is made for the dancing-tree. This is usually an immense bare-limbed tree that towers above the surrounding jungle. When such a tree is found it is watched for several mornings to see if the birds come to it, and if this is the case, a blind is constructed well up in its branches where the hunters can hide from the sight of the birds but are within easy bow-shot of them. Two bowmen will ascend to this masking shelter, two or three hours before dawn, and lie in wait for the birds that they know will come with the first rays of the rising sun.

The trees surrounding the large one fill with female birds, come to witness the dancing of the males who strut and dance on the bare branches of the large tree. The hunters lie in wait in their blind until the tree is literally filled with the gorgeous male birds.

The birds become so engrossed in their strutting and vain showing-off to the females that the hunters are able to shoot them down one by one with the blunt arrows used for this purpose. The large round ends of the arrows merely stun the birds, which fall to the ground and are picked up by the men below.

Frequently the hunters are able to kill two thirds of the birds before the others take alarm and fly away. The skins, as they are gathered, are washed in arsenic soap and packed away in bundles of twenty. The washing shrinks a skin so that the true proportions of the bird are lost: the head is large in relation to the rest of the body, but with the removal of the skull it shrinks to such an extent that it seems to be exceedingly small.

The skin is taken for the gorgeous plumes which spring from the side of the bird and are best seen on the live bird when he is strutting or in flight. It is a matter of interest that the nests of the birds, and consequently their eggs, are never[24] found, and large prices have been offered for a specimen of each. Among the hunters there seems to be a general belief that only one bird is reared at a time, though this is only conjecture.

On the morrow the hunters gather some surf-fish as a welcome change in their diet and, after smoking these a little and drying them after the Chinese fashion, depart on the last long leg of their trip to Merauke. We tell them in response to their invitation to accompany them that we are quite content here and will await the coming of the next trading Malay [Indonesian] who happens along.[25]

The administration of Dutch New Guinea imposed a hunting season in response to the demands of conservationists. According to J.W. Schoorl,[26] a former government officer, this extended from April to September.[27] This did not inconvenience plume hunters as they were not interested in hunting beyond this season for two reasons. First of all, there was little point as the birds were not in plumage. Secondly, life would have been even more unpleasant. From about May to October the steady southeast trade wind brings fairly dry and cool air. This gradually dries up the flooded swamplands which are inundated during January to April by the heavy squalls of the northwest monsoon.[28] Only government patrols tended to venture out in the northwest monsoon.

Many individuals came and braved the inhospitable countryside and virtually unknown inhabitants for the quick profits that could be gained from plumes. The occupation of plume hunter attracted some tough characters. Many got on well with the locals, but others had few moral scruples and antagonised them, and some died in pay-back killings.

A.K. Nielsen, a Danish visitor to the Merauke area in the late 1920s, makes the following comments about the relations that existed between the plume hunters and the local people. His statement on this topic is extracted in full as it catches some of the atmosphere of the period:

Plume hunting was a life filled with exhaustion and danger. Despite the presence of the daily glowing tropical sun, the nightly mosquitoes, ant swarms and the deadly tropical diseases lying in wait in the swampland, the greatest danger remained in the battle with the locals, who saw every stranger who penetrated into their hunting grounds as an enemy ... The bird hunters themselves were rough fellows who did not have much conscience when it came to collecting birds of paradise. Some barely knew the traditions nor the way the locals reasoned, others did not take these into account at all. In their eyes the jungle was a no-man's-land where anyone could shoot where he visited.

Under Kaja-Kaja law, each bird, animal and tree in the jungle which had any value belonged to the tribe or to the village. Any stranger, whether he be white or from another tribe, who did not respect these rights had to be prepared to be treated as an enemy.

Most important of all were the birds of paradise and the specific trees to which they returned every year. These trees were tabooed. The hunters could only obtain the right to shoot the birds in these trees by either a friendly agreement or by the payment of a given amount per bird to the tribe who collectively owned the hunting area. Many a bloody tragedy occurred between the locals and bird hunters because these unwritten laws of the jungle were not respected ...

When bird hunters subsequently contact Kaja-Kaja belonging to tribes who had been involved in [killing bird of paradise hunters], there was a merciless revenge. The arm of Dutch authority was too weak and did not extend far enough to exert any meaningful control in these isolated, unexplored regions. It was the bird hunters or the Kaja-Kaja's, depending on which group was the strongest, who judged and punished when a crime was committed.[29]

Local accounts of relations between villagers and hunters are generally negative in the Middle Fly. Two such accounts come from members of the Wamek and Sanggizi tribes of the Boazi speakers of the Middle Fly. The Wamek relate an incident which involved their parents and grandparents, and European hunters near the headwaters of Kongun Lake (Figure 38). Being unfamiliar with Europeans, they mistook them for ghosts on the basis of their light skins, beards and long hair, and fled in horror. The disconcerted Europeans responded by indiscriminately shooting at them, and as a result a number of men, women and children were killed. Those that survived never forgot this incident and presumably initiated their own indiscriminate retaliations against plume hunters. This probably explains why most Wamek accounts of bird of paradise hunters end with hunters shooting and killing at least one Wamek.[30]

In another incident a man from the Sanggizi tribe saw some Indonesian bird hunters pass by his bush fowl hide. He quickly returned to his village on an island in the middle of Kai Lagoon (Figure 38) to alert his people. Soon afterwards five Indonesian hunters and a man from a Marind-anim village near Merauke arrived on the shore of the lagoon and indicated that they wanted to make friendly contact. The Sanggizi took the hunters to their village. The hunters then showed the villagers how guns worked and asked if they wanted knives, axes and food. They were then offered gifts of trade goods. The Sanggizi accepted some trade tobacco, found salt and sugar to their taste, but being unused to the texture of rice and biscuits found them unpalatable. It was then explained that the hunters wanted to exchange these goods for birds of paradise. Concerned that the hunters might shoot all the birds of paradise on their land the Sanggizi decided to kill the hunters. Only the Merauke man managed to escape.[31]

By contrast the Muyu, Yonggom, Ningerum and Awin who live further inland generally speak more positively of their relations with bird hunters (see Muyu and Ok Tedi case studies below).

Some insights into the attitudes of those Europeans who chose to become plume hunters and traders is provided by the statements of a European plume trader called Reache. He entertained his drinking companions in Merauke with tales about his exploits as a bird of paradise trader. His account went as follows:

You fellows know, I guess, what I'm here for. It's paradise. Not the country, no! The country is hell and no mistake, but the birds – that is what I go after, and get, too. I outfitted in Moresby[32] and when I got my hunters together and plenty of petrol for the launch I headed for the upper [Digul]. It's way up in the interior where we get the best birds. It's bad country up there … The governor warned me that I was taking my life in my hands, but I don't know any one else's hands I'd rather have it in, so I went inside. My crew of hunters was as ripe a gang of cut-throats as one would wish to see and they tried cutting a few *didoes* among themselves, but after I'd knocked a couple cold they took to behaving and I let things go at that.

You want a gang like that for hard going. They're necessary. The only way to keep them happy is to give them plenty of work or, what they like best, plenty of scrapping. Then they haven't time to brood over differences of opinion amongst themselves. I loaded up a couple of bushels of [baler] shells [which the men wore as pubic coverings] … Well, I use those shells for currency. One first-class shell which costs me about 10 cents Dutch money buys a bird of paradise skin that is worth 1200 guilders a cody, that is, 20 skins – or, as it figures out in real money, 40 dollars [worth of skins]. It's a fair margin of profit …

Well, … we went inside – I, seven shooters, and some other Moresby boys for packers. Soon we had all the shooting and trading we wanted. Everything went all right for a time and there was no trouble with the natives. I gave them one nice shiny shell for one prime skin and they were as pleased as possible.

Some Chinese hunters were also operating in the vicinity. They were attacked and killed after they came into conflict with the local people. After this incident one of Reache's crew members took exception to a villager dressed in Chinese trousers trying to sell him bird of paradise skins. He killed the villager and this led to a fight from which only Reache and his launch-operator survived.[33]

In the Mapi (Mappi) River area (Figure 38), the Jaqaj indicated to J.H.M.C. Boelaars[34] many places deep in the interior where bird hunters had been killed. The most famous incident was on the Dutch and Papuan border and involved two Australians called Dreschler and Bell. The investigation of this incident by a joint Australian and Dutch patrol towards the end of 1920 is described in the Middle Fly section below.

Plume hunters and traders were speculators. They clearly profited during the plume boom, but they became victims of their own greed when prices plunged downwards. The recorded comments of the old Irish bird hunter, who settled at Merauke after plume hunting became illegal in most of Dutch New Guinea in 1924, clearly illustrate this point:

After many dangers the exhausted hunters returned to Merauke with their precious booty. There they had to face the surprise and emotion each time of learning what price their birds of paradise would fetch. No one could predict what variations would occur on the world market. The Irishman had experienced all the possible vagaries of the market. He told me of the exciting days when the prices increased from week to week. The hunters obtained £5 for one bird which cost them one knife, worth a shilling, and the same birds were later offered for £15–20 in the fashion magazines of London and Paris. In that year some 25,000 birds of paradise were exported from Merauke. They had a value of 2–2,500,000 kronen.

He also experienced the shock of learning that World War I had broken out. This news was brought to Merauke by mail boat [see Plate 29]. In those days there was still no radio station on New Guinea. The people there were totally isolated from world news. Even as the ship was sailing into the harbour, buyers were still bidding £78 for each set of birds; the Chinese who ruled the market asked £80. As soon as the news of the outbreak of war reached those on land, hunters could not get more than £1 for 20 birds. Many bird traders were ruined in just a few minutes. Large fortunes melted away like snow in the sun.[35]

Plate 29: Mail boat coming into Merauke before World War I. On shore there would be anxious speculation over the current price of bird of paradise skins and last-minute transactions.
Photo: Courtesy of Photo Archives, Rijksmuseum voor Volkenkunde, Leiden, The Netherlands.

The plume boom began in 1908 and continued until the outbreak of World War I in August 1914. It resumed again after the war. After hunting resumed, the Dutch administration made a number of punitive expeditions against groups who had killed plume hunters working in their areas. To monitor the activities of plume hunters and to gain more control over local groups two new government stations were established: Torai on the upper Maro (Merauke) River in 1918 and Assike on the Digul in 1919 (Figure 38). Assike was strategically located 290 kilometres up the Digul River, just south of where the Kao River forks northeastwards.[36]

When Leo Austen, a patrol officer from Papua, visited Assike in 1922 he reported that there were houses for Keyzer, the officer-in-charge, and Veelenturf, the police master. The barracks, gaol and quarters for seamen and others were made of local materials. In addition to van Grunungen, the European merchant established at Assike, there were several Chinese stores. To Austen's amazement these contained everything one could want for sale, and at prices cheaper than could be found at either Daru or Port Moresby. A steamer came up the Digul to Assike once a month from Merauke to bring passengers and supplies and to take out plumes.[37]

The vast area within which the plume hunters operated made it an impossible task to oversee their activities. However, it appears that Keyzer, the officer-in-charge at Assike, did record the proposed routes of hunting expeditions in his area.[38] Some hunters also sent him details of their progress. He went out on patrols up-river, not only to the Muyu area but also to the country of the upper Digul to the west. South of Assike he was familiar with the rivers, countryside and people almost down to Merauke.

Keyzer had been instructed to prevent clashes and to punish any acts of violence. His superior was a long way from Assike at Taul in the Kei Islands.[39] He was probably unaware that Keyzer was affected by 'bird of paradise fever'. It is said that Keyzer earned some 500,000 kronen in one year alone. This income suggests that his surveillance patrols were used as an opportunity to shoot birds of paradise.[40] No wonder Leo Austen,[41] the patrol officer from Papua, commented that most of the plume hunters entering Papua were probably the Dutch police themselves. Despite the fortune Keyzer made from plumes, he never left Assike. At the end of 1922 he died from swamp fever and was buried in the graveyard there. His companions include 40 police soldiers who also died from swamp fever.[42] Assike was closed after Keyzer's death and Torai was closed in 1924.

By the late 1920s there was no market for bird of paradise plumes. Merauke like Hollandia (Jayapura) had become a sleepy settlement.

Nielsen personally observed the aftermath of the plume boom in Merauke.

These days no one is interested in birds of paradise, consequently Merauke is now peaceful and quiet. In the tin trunks of the Chinese buyers lie thousands of birds that cannot be sold, they are preserved by means of camphor, awaiting better days. In the primeval forest, the male birds are now able to dance undisturbed and show off their feathered glory.

The knives and axes the Kaja-Kaja's obtained for their birds have long become blunt and the tobacco has all been smoked. Both have disappeared, the same is true of the millions in currency which had flooded into the country, thanks to the golden, feathered glory. The bird hunters have gone. Many died here, the rest have been attracted to new regions in search of luck. None of them became rich, despite their exertions, the danger, and the fortunes which passed through their hands.[43]

The species hunted and where they were sought

During the European plume boom, the Merauke and Mimika areas[44] became new sources of the Greater Bird of Paradise (*Paradisaea apoda*). In the 1920s the Raggiana Bird of Paradise was scarce in Dutch New Guinea, but was common over the border in Papua.[45] Today in the Middle Fly this species is only found in the ridge forests north of Kongun Lake and Lake Murray (Figure 38).[46] Although plume hunting was prohibited in Papua in 1908, this did not daunt plume hunters seeking Raggiana from entering the upper and middle reaches of the Fly River system. Like their counterparts who crossed into German New Guinea from Hollandia without hunting permits, these hunters were able to break existing laws by operating in inland areas far beyond any government surveillance.

Before 1909–1910, the Raggiana Bird of Paradise was rarely seen at European plume markets. It then became quite common,[47] presumably because of exports from Merauke, as well as German New Guinea, which later became the Mandated Territory of New Guinea. In 1920 an export ordinance was passed in the Mandated Territory which restricted the export of plumes and by 1922 they were illegal exports. This meant that from 1920 the border area of Papua became the only source of Raggiana, and explains why the chance of acquiring some red Raggiana plumes tempted a group of Chinese and Ambonese traders to stop at the Kaiakaia camp (Figure 41). There they found evidence that some European plume hunters might have been murdered.[48] This was the beginning of the Dreschler and Bell case described below.

In their search for plumes, hunters travelled to the lower foothills of the central mountain chain. At times they crossed watersheds and

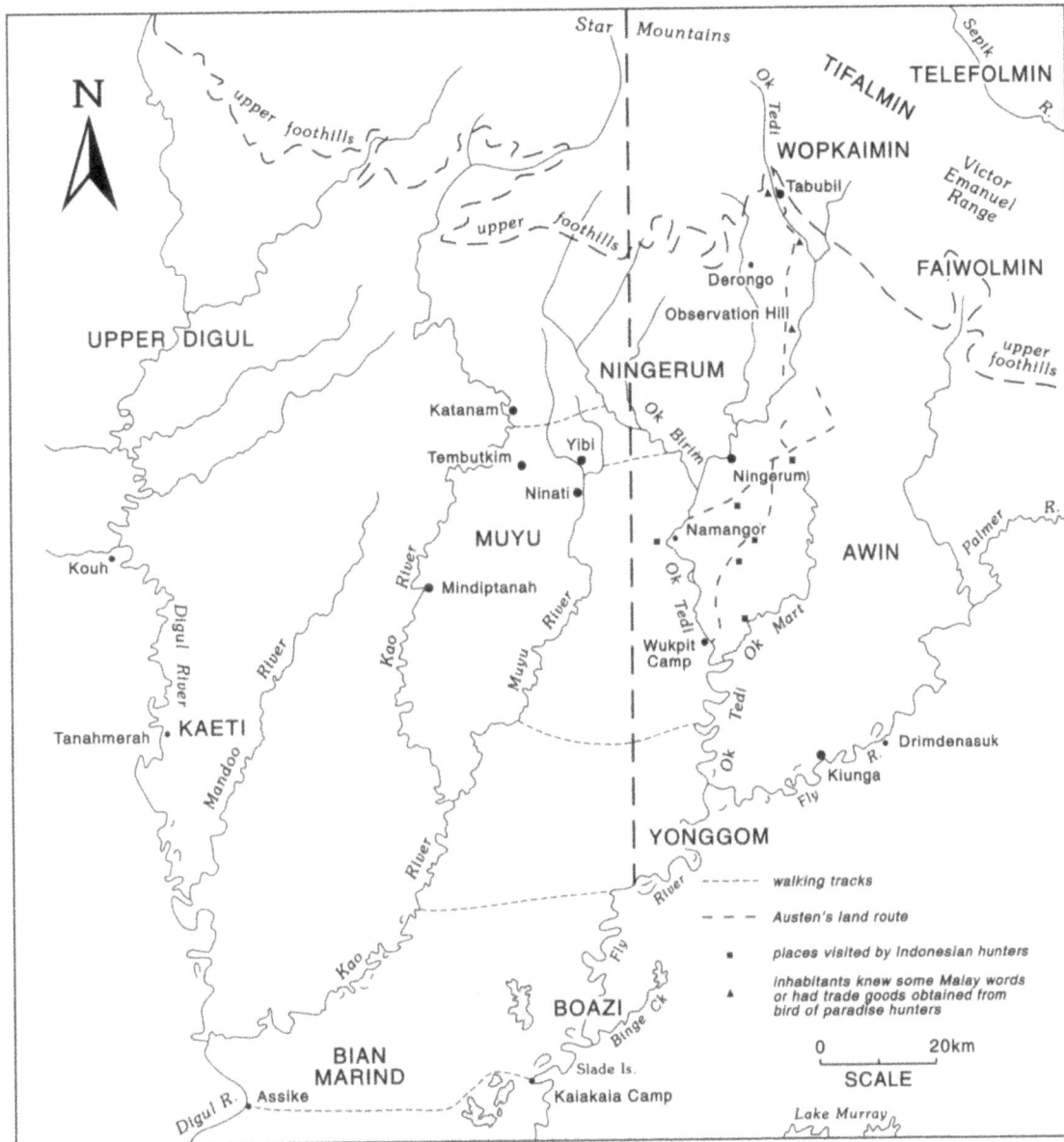

Figure 41: The upper reaches of the Fly and Digul River systems showing the tracks used by bird of paradise hunters. Also shown are indications of Indonesian hunters observed by Leo Austen along the Ok Tedi.

continued their expeditions by local canoes. They are known to have travelled up the many branches of the upper Digul. Of these the Muyu tributary was one of their favoured areas. From there they visited the country drained by the Ok Tedi and returned to Merauke via the Fly, upper Maro and Bian Rivers (Figure 38).

In their travels to and from Merauke plume hunters often travelled on similar routes to those taken previously by Marind-anim raiders,[49] for example, via the Bian River and then overland to Assike or the Fly River. Another important route from Merauke was along the coast to Okaba, then overland to the Digul. This was presumably the route taken by the Chinese hunters and their Motuan assistants described by W.F. Alder, cited above. When returning after working far inland, many hunters without motor boats followed this route. They floated down the Digul River on rafts and landed directly north of Okaba. They walked to Okaba and then along the coast to Koembe. From Koembe they travelled by motor boat to Merauke.[50, 51]

Three regional studies

The Muyu, Middle Fly and Ok Tedi areas are each discussed below. The studies cover what is known in each case about the activities of plume hunters, the local reception they received and their impact on the local people.

The Muyu

The Muyu live in undulating forest-covered country. Their area became one of the main sources of plumes in the Merauke region during the European plume boom. According to the Muyu, the first foreigners just came up and returned down the Kao River (Figure 41) in a house placed on top of a boat. Some time afterwards, plume hunters came seeking birds of paradise. Government records reveal that the first military patrol up the Kao River was in 1909, whereas plume hunters only began working the area in 1914. Some hunters went to the upper Muyu River in small motor boats.

Some of the first plume hunters to enter the Muyu area received a hostile barrage of arrows. This was mainly because the Muyu thought they were spirits. When the Muyu realised that they were dealing with real people, who could provide them with useful items, their attitudes changed. Friendly relations were then established by gifts of tobacco and other goods.

The Muyu assisted the plume hunters when it became known that these people were after birds of paradise. In exchange for plumes and the rights to shoot the birds, the Muyu received axes, chopping knives and clothing. Some Muyu men became guides and interpreters

190

and accompanied the hunters on trips throughout the Muyu area and beyond. For example, some crossed into Papua and went east of the Ok Tedi.

Those who learnt how to use guns also helped with hunting. This cooperation was further encouraged by the Dutch regulation which required hunters to employ local assistants. The hunters were also expected by law to pay the owner of the land where a display tree was located before any birds were shot.

The Muyu soon found that there were good and bad hunters. They claim they never killed a plume hunter unless he did something wrong. Food thefts seem to have been the main offence. Two Indonesians and their Muyu guide were killed and eaten at Tembutkim because they had stolen food from an associated settlement; but later another Indonesian and other Muyu avenged their deaths. The Australian who climbed Bombin Mountain in the upper foothills was probably also killed for stealing food. For their part, the Muyu never hesitated to steal the possessions of plume hunters if they had the opportunity. They also used plume hunters to kill their personal enemies. For example, a Yibi man apparently persuaded a hunter to shoot a Katanam man who had murdered his father.

Plume hunters introduced the Muyu to the Malay language and foreign goods and also made them aware of places beyond their borders. Some of them trusted these strangers enough to go with them to other areas. Those who went to Merauke learnt about the foreigner's world by seeing it for themselves. When Muyu youths arrived at Merauke wharf, the police usually took them away from the plume hunters and put them in mission school. In this way they not only came to know about schools and towns, but also something about the behaviour of different foreigners. When they returned home, these youths told stories about their observations and adventures, which made others who had not travelled also aware of the outside world. Later many men who had gained outside experience in their youth became village headmen or their assistants.

When the plume trade ceased in the Muyu area in 1926, the Muyu found themselves without a source of foreign goods. The plume hunters came no more. They began to look for new sources of supply. Some Muyu went to the government post at Tanah Merah which was established in 1926 (Figures 38 and 41). There they either sold their produce or worked for officials or internees at the adjacent Boven Digul internment camp. Others moved south towards Muting (Figure 38) where there were Chinese traders. A government station was opened at Muting in 1924 and a mission in 1930.[52]

The Middle Fly

When Sir William MacGregor returned from his December 1889 to February 1890 expedition up the Fly, he recommended that future government patrols should be made in the months of June or July. This would allow information about the conditions during the southeast season to be recorded, and since this was the time the birds were in full plumage, some could be collected for scientific purposes.[53] Unfortunately this suggestion was ignored. Throughout the period when bird of paradise plumes were sought for European plume markets, no Papuan government patrols were made when the birds were in full plumage; see Table 12. Thus there are no first hand historical documents which describe the activities of plume hunters in the Fly region of Papua. The only recorded information on the activities of plume hunters on the Middle Fly resulted from the joint Australian and Dutch investigation of the alleged murder of two plume hunters in the area.[54]

Table 12: Official and scientific expeditions to the middle and upper Fly from 1875 to 1926

expedition leader	date	purpose of trip
L.M. D'Albertis	1875	exploration
L.M. D'Albertis	1876	exploration
Captain Everill	1885	exploration
Sir William MacGregor	1889 Dec 26–1890 Feb 4	exploration
Baker & Burrows	1913	exploration
J.H.P. Murray	1914 Mar 27–1914 Apr 18	exploration
Captain Frank Hurley	1914	exploration
Sir Rupert Clarke	1914	exploration
A.P. Lyons & Leo Austen	1920 Oct 24–1920 Dec 16	investigate alleged murders
Leo Austen	1922 Jan 12–1922 Apr 5	investigate alleged murders
Leo Austen	1922 Oct 16–1922 Nov 14	investigate alleged murders

Sources

Based on Austen 1923a, 1925; D'Albertis 1880; Everill 1888; Goode 1977; Hurley 1924; Lyons 1922; MacGregor 1889–1890; Murray 1914; personal communication Michael Quinnell 1983, see footnote 54.

When the Dutch came they discouraged raiding. This allowed Chinese traders to become established at Torai and in the Muting area (Figure 38). The Bian Marind then found it to their advantage to make peace with the Boazi of the Middle Fly (Figure 41).[55] A major factor behind this peace treaty was probably the presence of the highly desired Raggiana Bird of Paradise in the forests on the ridges north of Lake Murray in the Middle Fly. The red plumes of this species would have commanded a high value with the Chinese trade store owners at Muting. From this time on Chinese and other plume hunters with Bian Marind guides would have been entering this area via the upper Bian.

An increasing familiarity with traders and hunters probably explains why on two occasions men on the banks of the Fly River made the motion of cutting or chopping when they saw J.H.P. Murray's expedition going up the Fly in April 1914. One incident was some 15 kilometres north of where the Fly extends the international border westwards and the other was some 45 kilometres upriver from Everill Junction (Figure 38).[56]

By early 1914 the interests and activities of plume hunters were widely known. The trade goods they brought with them were also appreciated. In 1913 an overland journey was made by a Dutch military patrol from the Kao to the Fly at the northern end of where it bulges west at the international border (Figure 38). On their way to the Fly a trade axe was left at a settlement where the people were very apprehensive of their presence. When the same patrol passed through the settlement on their return, one man offered them a bird of paradise headdress, with the apparent intention of exchanging it.[57]

When trade goods were left at base camps and appeared to be abandoned, the chance was not wasted. When Murray in 1913 visited the base camp established the year before by Baker and Burrows near Everill Junction, he found that tomahawks and other goods had been stolen. The only item not stolen was the stick tobacco.[58] The case had been opened but the contents were presumably considered inferior to the local product.

After the First World War, bird hunters from Dutch territory were keen to hunt the Raggiana Bird of Paradise found across the border in Papua. This was illegal, but profitable. There were a number of ways to reach the Fly. For instance, it was possible to go overland and via channels and small lakes from the Bian River (Figure 38). This took two days.[59] Alternatively they could go overland from Assike, the Kao River or the Muyu River. These routes took a great deal longer. The shortest walk was from the upper Muyu to the Ok Birim, a tributary of the Ok Tedi which flows into the Fly (Figure 41).

Some bird of paradise hunters lost their lives, but we know little about these incidents. Those killed include Europeans such as Penrode and a number of Indonesians. A Timorese hunter was killed in the Ok Tedi (Alice River) in 1920.[60] Some of the bodies that were recovered were buried at Merauke.[61] Other hunters were lucky enough to escape. This was the good fortune of a party of Chinese hunters who were attacked in the headwaters area of the Maro (Merauke), Bian and Kumbe Rivers (Figure 38).[62]

In late 1920 some Chinese and Ambonese plume traders reported to the Dutch authorities that some Europeans had probably been murdered on the Australian side of the Fly at its most westerly extension into Dutch territory. A joint Dutch and Australian patrol was then made to investigate the alleged murder of two Europeans called Dreschler and Bell and the rest of their party.

The Chinese and Ambonese plume traders had reached the Fly by a creek accessible overland from the headwaters of the Bian River (Figure 38). Their Bian guides had obtained two canoes which they used to travel down a stream which in half an hour brought them to the Fly. The Chinese claimed they thought they were on a branch of the Bian.[63] However, the Papuan Resident Magistrate A.P. Lyons clearly understood their strange loss of geographic sense. The Chinese could not admit to knowing their true whereabouts, as this would make them guilty of illegally collecting and shooting birds in Papua.

Kaiakaia Camp was the name the patrol gave to a burnt-down village on the most westerly bend of the Fly River (Figure 41). The village had extended for about 800 metres along the river's edge and was divided into two parts. These were separated by a scrub-covered area. They not only found the remains of traditional-style buildings but also a house with certain European features. These included two slab bunks and a fireplace which had forked supports for hanging billycans by means of a horizontal bar. Nearby were tins and bottles, a rough baking dish made from a kerosene can and the remains of a newspaper called the *American Exporter*. In another part of the village they found a human jaw with two metal-filled teeth,[64] brass caps from a Remington repeater, Winchester shot cartridges, an old tin, a cardboard cartridge box, a broken leather sheath for a knife and steel, and a broken glass bottle. The whole village appeared as if it had been wantonly ransacked and burnt. In the lagoon behind the village they found four canoes which had been damaged beyond repair by cuts from steel axes.[65]

The village had not been destroyed when the Chinese and Ambonese traders had stopped at the settlement after being offered Raggiana plumes. However they had fled once they had seen a human jaw which had teeth with metal fillings, shirts bearing Bell's name and

194

had obtained a book. The writing inside this book was later identified as Bell's.[66]

Another camp was found several kilometres from the Kaiakaia Camp at the southern end of the lagoon on the Dutch side of the Fly. Two cognac bottles of the brand drunk by Dreschler and other indications of European habitation were found. Leo Austen, now Assistant Resident Magistrate at Daru, found further items on a subsequent patrol made in 1922. These finds were made at a new settlement which was abandoned when his patrol approached. Austen called the settlement Bamboo Creek, now probably known as Binge Creek,[67] see Figures 38 and 41. There he found Bell's pocket-book, several photographs, a 300 guilder note, a sock, an enamel pannikin, a reel of cotton and two or three empty bottles.[68]

It is possible that other plume hunters attacked and ransacked the village when they discovered that Dreschler and Bell had been killed. Another house with certain European features was found a short distance further up the Fly in 1920. It was located near a sago swamp on the west bank not far from Slade Island. There were two rough bunks and a fireplace with forked sticks and the walls had rifle-fire loop holes. No tins or bottles were found.[69]

Unfortunately the local story is not known. In retrospect it is strange that the Dutch did not take a Bian Marind or Marind speaker on the joint expedition made to investigate the deaths of Dreschler, Bell and other members of their plume-hunting party. The Dutch officials had apparently assumed that the Ok Tedi people were responsible, as they had recently killed a Timorese hunter.

The Sydney Morning Herald[70] provides further information about Dreschler and Bell. Dreschler was a well-known trader. He was 30 years old, married, with a home in Melbourne. Bell was 26 and had run a store in Port Moresby until the outbreak of the First World War. He then returned to Sydney to enlist. Bell served in France with the Light Trench Mortar Brigade where he was awarded the Distinguished Service Medal, gained a lieutenancy and then joined the First Artilleiy Brigade. He returned to Australia in August 1919 and sailed with Dreschler for New Guinea in March 1920. Bell was to have returned to Sydney in October that year to be married.

Bell and Dreschler were apparently part of a larger party, most of whom returned to Merauke, leaving Bell and Dreschler to go further inland with eight New Guinean assistants. These ten men presumably perished at Kaiakaia Camp. The larger party of nineteen New Guineans was led by Rosenhain. He was related to the firm of Rosenhain and Company based in Sydney, which had an agency in Surabaya and trading stations in Dutch New Guinea.

The Ok Tedi

During the joint Australian–Dutch patrol the Australians learnt from a Dutch interpreter from Muyu (Muiu) River that a supposedly large population lived in the vicinity of the Ok Tedi. Leo Austen's subsequent patrols were concerned with checking this claim. People from villages located on the west bank of the lower Ok Tedi told Austen that Indonesian plume traders came to their area each year. These foreigners not only shot on their land, but they also crossed over to the east bank in their search for plumes. Later in his patrol, Austen observed a number of plume hunters' camp sites in Awin (Aekyom) territory east of the Ok Tedi. These shelters had been built at different points along the main walking tracks; see Figure 41.[71] According to present-day Awin informants, the hunters usually built temporary shelters in the vicinity of the Awin garden hamlets and stayed for a day or two to trade for plumes.[72] On the night of the 26th of February 1922, Austen's patrol spent the night in one of these abandoned camps.

Plume hunters also ventured up and east of the Ok Mart. When sighting Austen's patrol, the people on the lower reaches of this river had assumed that these foreigners were also going upriver to shoot birds.[73] Present-day Awin claim that the hunters penetrated as far north as the vicinity of Tmansawenai village on the upper Fly near the foothills of the Victor Emanuel Range. Further south they went as far east as the present-day location of Drimdemesuk village which is south of the Fly-Elevala junction.[74] This suggests that few hunters crossed to the eastern banks of the upper Fly River.

When the Yonggom-speaking Or villagers heard gunshots, some went to Austen's camp at Wukpit expecting to find plume hunters. The Awin seen by the patrol were very timid and all their villages were deserted. From this Austen concluded that they had recently had trouble with plume hunters. Another explanation might be that plume hunters had only recently expanded their activities across the Ok Tedi in search of cheaper plumes. The villagers also told Austen through interpreters that the plume hunters did not pay them enough. Since the Muyu had trade relations with the Awin,[75] they were probably aware that they were receiving far less payment than the people further west. It was the practice of plume traders to keep their payments as low as possible.

Austen observed that the Awin had received knives, tomahawks and trade beads from the plume hunters. There was also a northward movement of trade goods from the south. A Yonggom (Iongom) man from Namangor village joined Austen's patrol as an interpreter. He took along a metal axe that he wished to trade with the Ningerum.[76] A northern Ningerum settlement is shown in Plate 30.

Plate 30: Derongo, a Ningerum settlement, in 1966.

Photo: Courtesy of H. Bell. PNG National Museum Files.

The Ningerum Austen met near and north of his Observation Hill, see Figure 41, had some trade items and a limited knowledge of certain Malay words. They had metal axes, as cuts made by iron axes as well as stone axes were seen along the track. They were terribly keen to obtain *kapak*, which is the Malay word for axe, but were not interested in knives until it was demonstrated how they could cut wood. They then immediately recognised these implements as *karanang*, the Malay word for large knife. Presumably they had heard about these from the Muyu or other Ningerum. but had never seen them. Austen certainly doubted whether they had seen an Indonesian. Although they knew some Malay words, the errors they made seemed to suggest that they had learned the words by hearsay.

Austen's observations in the upper Ok Tedi suggest that no hunters had actually ventured into that area and that trade goods were only beginning to reach these people. The people in the hamlet he visited near the Moyansil suspension bridge across the Ok Tedi some 5 kilometres southeast of Tabubil had only one iron axe (*kapak*). It had

197

reached them via their trade links with the southwest and they claimed that they were the only people in the vicinity who possessed one. They had never seen knives and did not know the word *karanang* (knife). When given a knife, a man used the back rather than the sharp side of the knife to cut taro.[77] Further up the Ok Tedi, Austen met a man who had never seen an iron axe before but strangely knew "many words of the trade language,[78] but mixed them up so much that it was difficult to get what he was driving at."[79] Perhaps when he was on a trading expedition to the Muyu area, he had heard Indonesian traders talking to the Muyu or had been told some words by his Muyu trade partners.

In the mountain foothills Austen experienced the problems plume hunters would have faced in their search for high-altitude bird of paradise species. North of Observation Hill he arranged to purchase some taros and bananas from the local people. From Austen's point of view he paid a high price and only gained enough to give his 32 man patrol one meal.[80] The local people were keen to acquire more axes and knives but were not in a position to provide any more food. It would seem that they had none to spare.[81] The upper range of most bird of paradise hunting expeditions was probably the northern extent of where sago was the main staple. It was probably their mainstay, as it would have been impossible for them to have carried enough provisions. This would also explain why the hunters' house was located near a sago swamp near Slade Island. It may also help to explain the deaths of Dreschler and Bell if they were working sago without permission.

Trade goods obtained from plume hunters were traded on beyond their area of activity. Some were probably traded via the Faiwolmin, others may have been taken back by Tifalmin or perhaps even Telefolmin trading expeditions. When Keyzer was in the upper Muyu area in the early 1920s, he met a party of traders who had come from the headwaters of the Sepik some four days' walk away. This was probably how a Telefolmin man, observed by Ivan Champion, had acquired two large white beads to wear in his beard.[82]

Plume hunters and venereal disease

In an attempt to eradicate venereal disease, bird hunting was prohibited in the South New Guinea Subdistrict, specifically the Marind-anim area, from October 1922.[83] Hunting was allowed to continue in the Digul and Muyu areas. This was part of the effort the Dutch authorities made to control this disease amongst the Marind-anim. Such steps were thought necessary as the Marind-anim were experiencing a sharp drop in their birth rate.[84]

After October 1922 a man could only obtain a bird hunting licence to work in the Muyu or Digul areas if he agreed to submit himself for a medical examination. He was then allowed to leave Merauke for his chosen hunting locality. This was done in order to minimise the risk of venereal disease being spread by plume hunters.[85]

Border crossing by plume hunters

At the time of the Dreschler-Bell investigation, there was presumably an agreement that the Papuan administration would not press charges if the Chinese and Ambonese hunters who reported the incident guided the Australian and Dutch authorities to the scene of the crime. A certain degree of confusion as to the location of the border did not help matters.

Despite the cartographic work done during the Dutch military patrols, there was still in the early 1920s considerable confusion about the position of the border between Dutch New Guinea and Papua in different localities. For instance, in 1922 the Dutch thought the headwaters of the Muyu were in Papua and passed on to the Papuan administration, for approval, the request of Penrose and Jackson for permission to go there in search of minerals. Permission was granted.[86] In reality the area was in Dutch territory.

Austen makes no comment in his report published in 1925 on the likelihood that Dreschler, Bell and the rest of their party were hunting in Papua, nor does he make any recommendations about stopping illegal border crossings by plume hunters. However, the Australians must have voiced their objections to the Dutch administration, as the Muyu area was closed to plume hunters in 1926. By then there was little protest from plume hunters as the prices paid for plumes had fallen and the boom was over. The Digul area was closed two years later.[87]

Notes

1. From November 1884 to September 1888, British New Guinea was a British Protectorate. It became a British colony from 1888 until September 1906, when the Australian government assumed responsibility for the area and renamed it Papua (Joyce 1972: 115–6).

2. The suffix anim in the name Marind-anim means men. The Marind-anim were called Tugeri by the people of southwest Papua (van Baal 1966: 10, 23).

3. Galis 1953–4: 26.

4. van Baal 1966: 23–4; Galis 1953–4: 27; Joyce 1971: 139–41; Wollaston 1912: 223.

5. Galis 1953–4: 41.

6. van Baal 1966: 707.
7. Pratt 1906: 43–4.
8. Galis 1953–4: 41.
9. van Baal 1966: 691.
10. van Baal 1966: 497.
11. Champion 1966: 4, 18, 101.
12. Militaire exploratie 1920.
13. Schoorl 1957: 129.
14. Galis 1953–4: 41.
15. van Baal 1966: 544; 659–60.
16. Kaiakaia (Kajakaja; Kaiyakaiya) is the Marind-anim word for peace. On meeting a European they would usually say this greeting. The Dutch adopted it as a name for the local population and later also used the term to refer to a native in other parts of Dutch New Guinea (Meek 1913: 209; Thomson 1953: 6; Schoorl 1957: 131).
17. Nielsen 1930: 217.
18. Nielsen 1930: 218.
19. Nielsen (1930: 228) reports hunters bought birds worth £5 for one-shilling knives; Reache quoted by Alder (1922: 21) says for 10 cents Dutch currency he got 40 dollars worth of skins. Note there is a misprint in Alder's text which reads that each skin was worth $40. This was never the case even in London; see Table 5. In 1917 birds fetched the Chinese traders and hunters 50 florins (Schoorl 1957: 131) or just less than £2 each.
20. The Timorese and Japanese were probably indentured labourers who had completed their contracts as divers in the Torres Strait pearl beds. They had been brought by the Dutch from Japan and the Dutch East Indies (see e.g. Singe 1979: 172). The Ambonese would have come on Dutch government ships from the administrative centre at Ambon. The Catholic mission at Merauke was founded by missionaries from Toeal in the Kei Islands (Wollaston 1912: 225, 257). Contact between these two missions probably explains why Kei islanders were at Merauke.
21. Nielsen 1930: 219–20.
22. W.F. Alder does not provide a map of his travels, but the few geographic features he gives suggest that they sailed west of Merauke. The Bian would have been the large river they passed, before being shipwrecked near a deserted Jesuit mission building probably in the vicinity of Okaba. Alder claims he was shipwrecked 300 miles (483 km) from Merauke (Alder 1922: 74). This is too great a distance, as it would either place him on the mangrove shoreline of Kolopom Island or in the other direction well inside Papua. The copra trading schooner which picked his party up and took them back to Merauke would not have been frequenting either the Papuan or the Kolopom coast.
23. This probably refers to the United States Federal Tariff Act of 1913 which imposed import restrictions on plumage; see Chapter 5.
24. Eggs of birds of paradise are rarely rather than never found.
25. Alder 1922: 167–72.
26. Schoorl 1957: 276.
27. Neilsen (1930: 218) however claims that the season was from May to September, rather than from April.

28. van Baal 1966: 16–17.

29. Nielsen 1930: 220–1.

30. Busse 1987: 140.

31. Busse 1987: 140-2.

32. As his party was provisioned in Port Moresby, this probably suggests that the incident took place before Assike was established on the Digul in 1919.

33. Alder 1922: 19–25. See also footnote 18.

34. Boelaars 1958: 155.

35. Nielsen 1930: 227–8.

36. Galis 1953-4: 42; Wirz 1922: 11.

37. Lyons 1922: 118, 121; Austen 1923a: 124–5.

38. These records were probably the responsibility of the clerk at Assike. They would contain much information about the movements of plume-hunters. For instance, Keyzer received a letter on the 11th of August 1920 from the ill-fated Dreschler who was then in the Muyu area (Lyons 1922: 118). It is hoped that these records still exist and might one day be found in Dutch government archives.

39. Boelaars 1981: 5.

40. Nielsen 1930: 224.

41. Austen 1925: 36.

42. Nielsen 1930: 224.

43. Nielsen 1930: 228–9.

44. The intervening Asmat area, from the Otakwa River to the mouth of the Digul (Figures 29 and 38), was avoided by plume hunters because of the known hostility of the Asmat towards foreigners (Pratt 1911: 47). Between 1904 and 1913, several Dutch military patrols penetrated the Asmat region, but they were more concerned with gaining access to the enticing snow-covered peaks of the central mountain range than pacifying the local people (Gerbrands 1967a). However it is possible that plume hunters entered the area after World War I. During World War II, Thomson (1953: 3) may have encountered Asmat familiar with the interests of Indonesian bird hunters. A government post had been established at Agats just before World War II in 1938. The post was established because the Mimika complained that they were being attacked by the Asmat. It was closed soon after the war broke out and was not re-established until 1955. The region was then opened up to outsiders and as a consequence Asmat carvings became known throughout the world (Gerbrands 1967a; 1967b).

45. Lyons 1922: 121.

46. Mark Busse personal communication 1992.

47. Downham 1911: 43.

48. Lyons 1922: 114.

49. J. Verschueren, who was a mission worker amongst the Marind-anim, travelled on one of the raiding tracks of the upper Bian in 1953. He was taken from Womod River in the Auyu area down to Mutung. Crossing the Digul by canoe, they entered a small southern tributary. When they had arrived near the springs, the canoes were put away in the brushwood. From there they went on foot through the forest and after four hours' walk emerged on the bank of a swamp, where after some searching, the guides found a canoe which had been hidden there. Boarding the canoe, they went to Manggis, the southernmost of all the

upper Bian villages. The path they had followed was a typical *kui-kai*, a straight, rather broad, cleared passage through the forest, with on either end a hiding place for canoes. If necessary, new canoes would be made on the spot (van Baal 1966: 705).

50. Schoorl 1957: 129–35; Schoorl 1967; Schoorl 1993: 147–53.

51. One advantage of this route was that it avoided the strong tidal currents at the mouth of the Digul and in the Marianne Strait (Figure 38) (van Baal 1966: 707).

52. Schoorl 1957: 133.

53. MacGregor 1889–90: 64.

54. Sir Rupert Clarke who travelled up the Fly into the Awin area in 1914 may have kept a diary, but to date such a document has not been located. His ethnographic collection is held at the Queensland Museum in Brisbane. Since he arrived in Port Moresby in early May from Australia and was consigning his collection for shipment from Port Moresby in January, he would have been in the Fly during the plume-hunting season (Michael Quinnell personal communication 1983).

55. van Baal 1966: 706.

56. Murray 1914: 22, 24.

57. Schoorl 1957: 129–135, 278–9; 1967: 170–1.

58. Murray 1914: 24.

59. Lyons n.d.

60. Lyons 1922: 117; Nielsen 1930: 225.

61. Nielsen 1930: 227.

62. Lyons 1922: 123.

63. Lyons n.d.; 1922: 113.

64. A Sydney dentist identified the gold filling in one of the teeth and confirmed that the jaw belonged to one of the Australians (Nielsen 1930: 225).

65. Lyons 1922: 114–5.

66. Lyons 1922: 118.

67. Mark Busse personal communication 1984.

68. Austen 1923a: 124, 132.

69. Lyons 1922: 116.

70. Anon 1920.

71. Austen 1923a, 1923b, 1925.

72. Depew n.d.

73. Austen 1923a: 131.

74. Depew n.d.

75. Austen actually met some Muyu at the Awin village of Gwembip (Austen 1923a: 128). Schoorl (1957: 11) also confirms that the Muyu knew about and traded with the Awin.

76. Austen 1925: 27–8.

77. Austen 1925: 32, 34.

78. Austen (1925: 36) lists words from the trade language found in the Ok Tedi area.

79. Austen 1925: 33.

80. Hunters primarily concerned with obtaining rare natural history specimens rather than millinery plumes would have travelled in a small group. The fact that some collectors were able to obtain some high-altitude species which have a restricted distribution indicates that Indonesian hunters did visit such regions in other parts of Dutch New Guinea.

81. They would have faced the dilemma of whether to obtain tools to improve their future livelihood at the risk of illness and possibly death because of inadequate supplies.

82. Lyons 1922: 118; Champion 1966: 172.

83. Schoorl 1957: 131.

84. van Baal 1966: 25–6.

85. Lyons 1922: 118.

86. Austen 1923a: 140.

87. Schoorl 1957: 131; Schoorl 1967: 171.

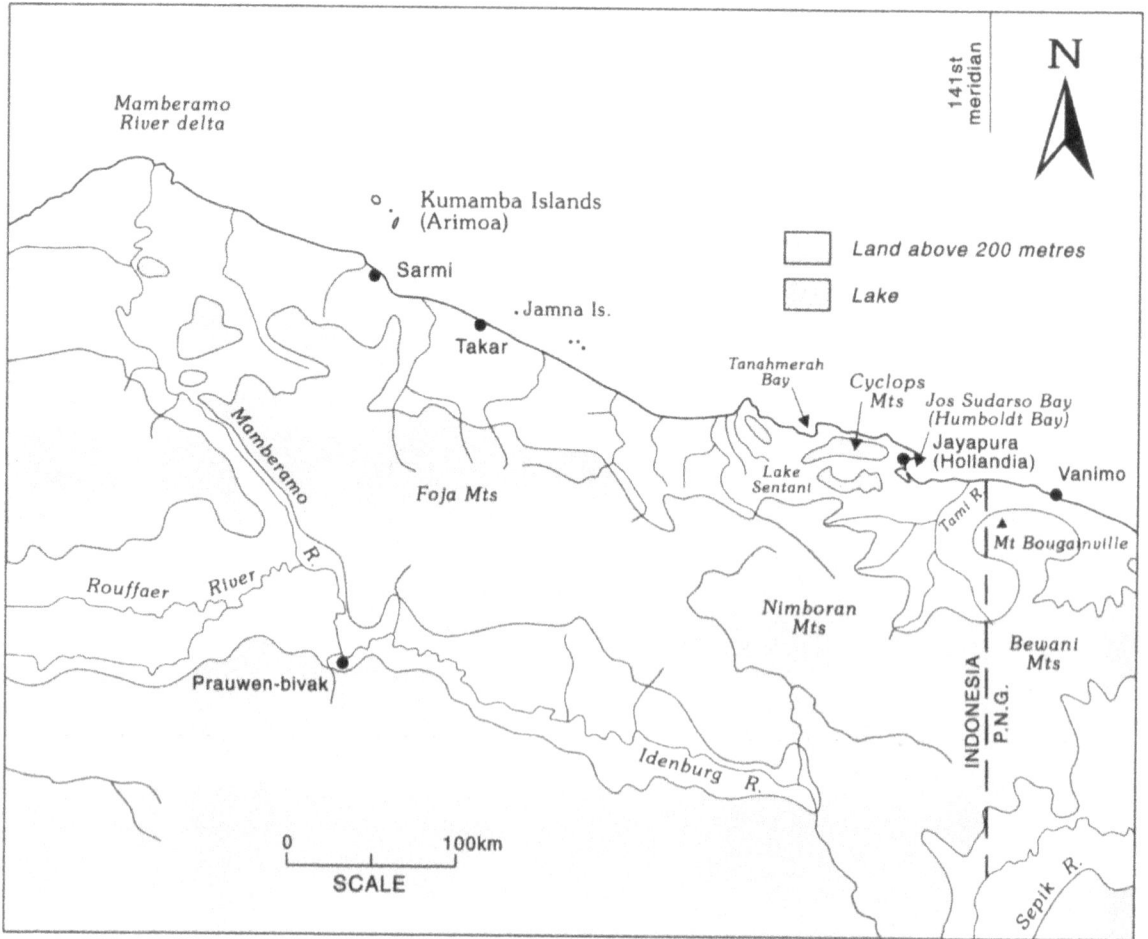

Figure 42: The north coast of New Guinea from the Mamberamo River delta to the border with Papua New Guinea.

11

Bronzes and plume hunting in the Jayapura (Hollandia) region

Asian plume trade

Although there were links within mainland New Guinea 5,000 years ago, as shown by the distribution of stone mortars and pestles, archaeology has not revealed any with Southeast Asia. Even within New Guinea it is curious that so few mortars and pestles have been found in what is now West Papua (Figure 9), but the existence of interaction along the north coast of New Guinea is confirmed by the find of a stemmed obsidian artifact at Biak in Cendrawasih Bay. It is made from obsidian that originated from Manus in Papua New Guinea.[1]

Three thousand years later the north coast gains archaeological prominence again. This time because of the large number of prehistoric bronze artifacts that have been reported at Lake Sentani inland of Jayapura (Figures 42 and 43).[2] These artifacts date from just before 2,000 years ago until about 250 AD. During this period Asians are known to have keenly sought beautiful bird plumes. The occurrence of these artifacts at Lake Sentani is not so surprising, when it is known that Hollandia (now Jayapura), was a famous export port for bird of paradise plumes on the north coast of New Guinea during the late nineteenth and early twentieth centuries.

Some of the bronze artifacts were dug up by villagers in places where sacred objects used to be buried, others were held as heirlooms in men's houses. While many bronzes are now in museums, some still remain in village ownership, such as the collection held at Kwadeware (Figure 43), and can be viewed by interested individuals after paying a viewing fee. The main finds are illustrated in Figures 44 and 45 and Plate 31.

As mentioned in Chapter 3 some of the Sentani bronzes are comparable to those found elsewhere in Indonesia, whereas others are unique to West Papua. The latter include three ceremonial axe forms, namely a, c and d illustrated in Figure 44 and the spearheads from Kwadeware (Figure 45: c and f).

When George Agogino[3] investigated two Bronze Age archaeological sites on the north side of Lake Sentani during World War II he found the bronzes to be associated with glass beads. This suggests that many of the antique glass beads,[4] earrings and bracelets found in the Jayapura region could have a comparable antiquity to the bronzes. These glass artifacts (Plate 32) have also become traditional valuables for the people of the Vanimo region, who continue to obtain them from Jayapura. In the Vanimo region in 1980 a single blue bead was worth K100, whereas bracelets were valued at K400 to K700 each.[5] Observations of similar artifacts were made before 1656 at Biak and on Seram. They were so highly valued in the eastern Indonesian archipelago that Dutch traders requested that green glass bracelets be manufactured in the Netherlands in the eighteenth century (Plate 32B). The Dutch replicas were not a success.[6]

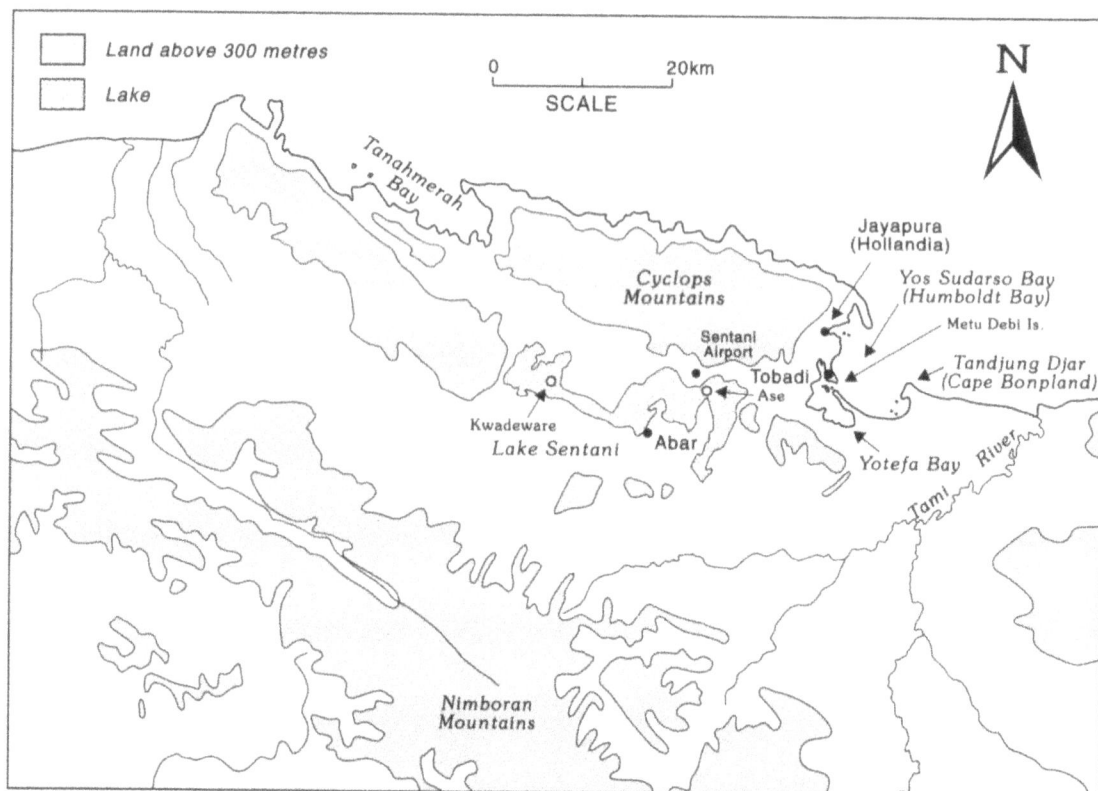

Figure 43: The Jayapura region.

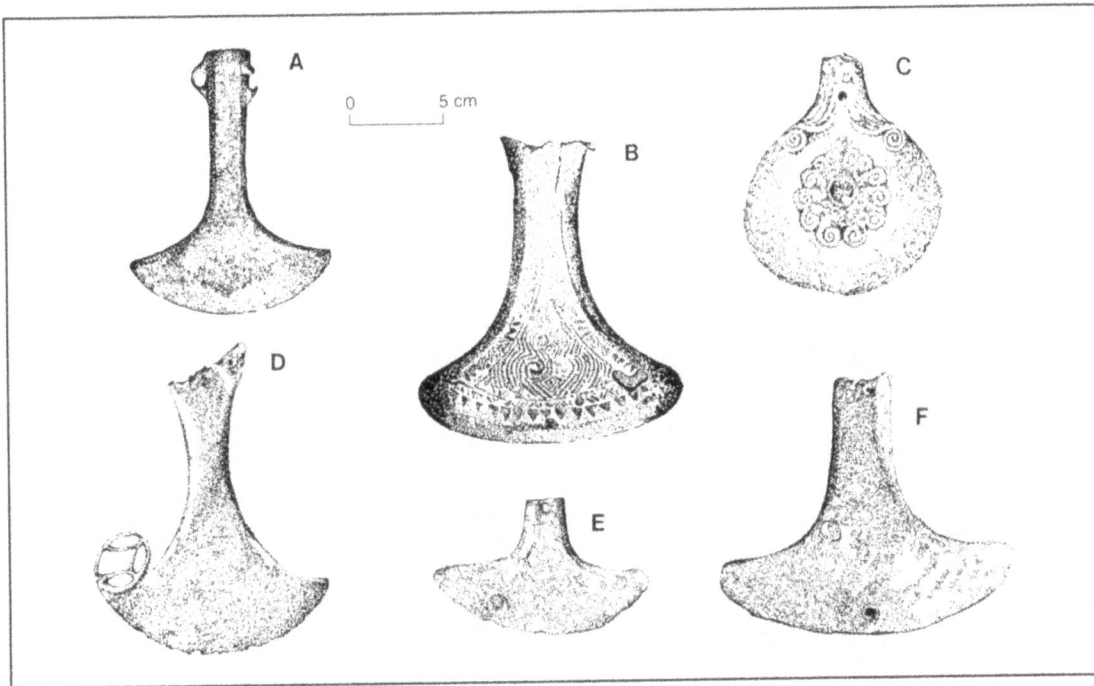

Figure 44: Some of the bronze axes found at Lake Sentani **A.** axe from Kwadeware **B.** ceremonial axe from Ase **C.** ceremonial axe from Abar **D.** ceremonial axe from Ase **E.** axe from Kwadeware **F.** axe from Kwadeware.
Sources: de Bruyn 1959; de Bruyn 1962; van der Sande 1907; Soejono 1963. Drawings by Anton Gideon.

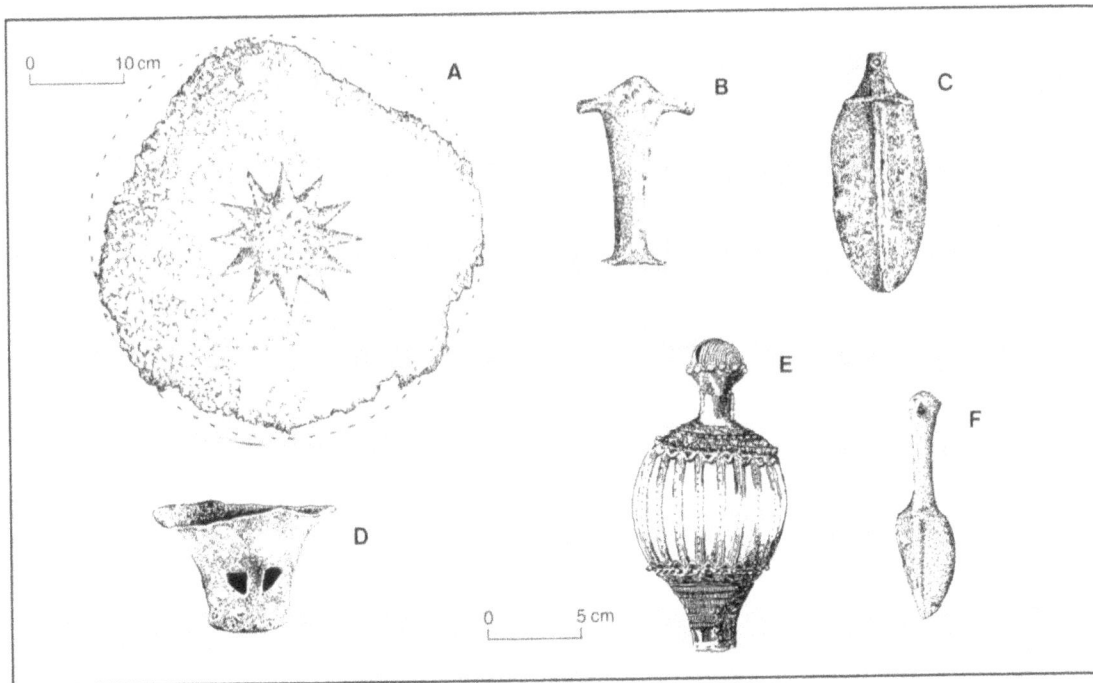

Figure 45: Some of the bronze artifacts other than axes found at Lake Sentani and the Bird's Head. (larger scale only applies to the drum top). **A.** drum top from Aimura Lake **B.** dagger handle from Kwadeware **C.** spearhead from Kwadeware **D.** lamp from Kwadeware **E.** bell from Ase **F.** spearhead from Kwadeware.
Sources: de Bruyn 1959; de Bruyn 1962; van de Sande 1907; Soejono 1963. Drawings by Anton Gideon.

Plate 31: Bronze bell and ceremonial axes from Lake Sentani villages, Jayapura region (for scale see Figures 44 and 45).
A. bell from Ase **B.** ceremonial axe from Abar **C & D.** ceremonial axes from Ase.
Photos: Courtesy Rijksmuseum voor Volkenkunde, Leiden, The Netherlands.

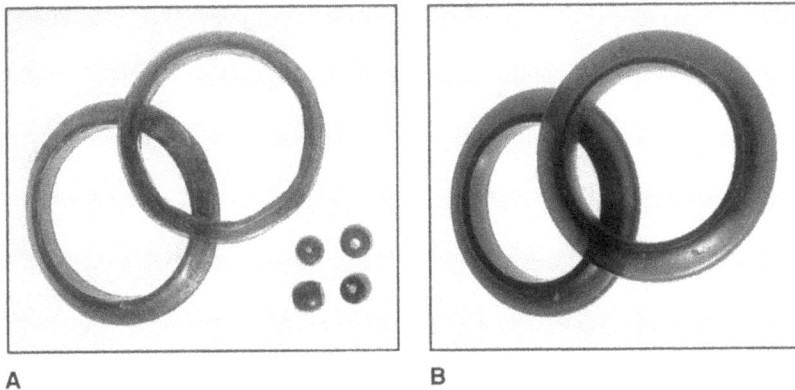

Plate 32: Prehistoric and historic glass bracelets and beads from the north coast of New Guinea.
A. The prehistoric bracelets are from Ase and the beads from Tobadi. Width of rings 8 and 10 centimetres. The Vanimo people have similar artifacts. Today these artifacts are prohibited exports from Papua New Guinea.
B. Glass bracelets manufactured in the Netherlands in the eighteenth century. Width of each bracelet 10cm.

Photos: By Rocky Roe for PNG National Museum.

Other cultural practices of the people in the Jayapura and Vanimo regions may date back to 250 AD and before. For instance, they use a special implement to cook and eat sago. These were also traditionally used on Seram and in the Moluccas (Figure 46).[7] Many of the Vanimo implements look like tied chopsticks. The small ones (*heai*) are used to eat stirred sago (Plate 33), whereas larger tongs are called *heai pilo*. The latter are used to get the sago out of big saucepans. Mothers with newborn babies use these tongs for all food consumption, as they cannot touch food by hand for a period of about three months after giving birth. The tongs are made from palm stem.[8]

The withdrawal of Asian interest from the Jayapura region and the Bird's Head occurred with the downturn in the Asian plume trade about 300 AD. There was then a long hiatus before traders again brought metal implements to the Jayapura region.[9]

Plate 33: Frances Deklin from Wanimo village demonstrates how *heai* (tongs) are used to eat stirred sago.
Photo: By Pou Toivita for PNG National Museum.

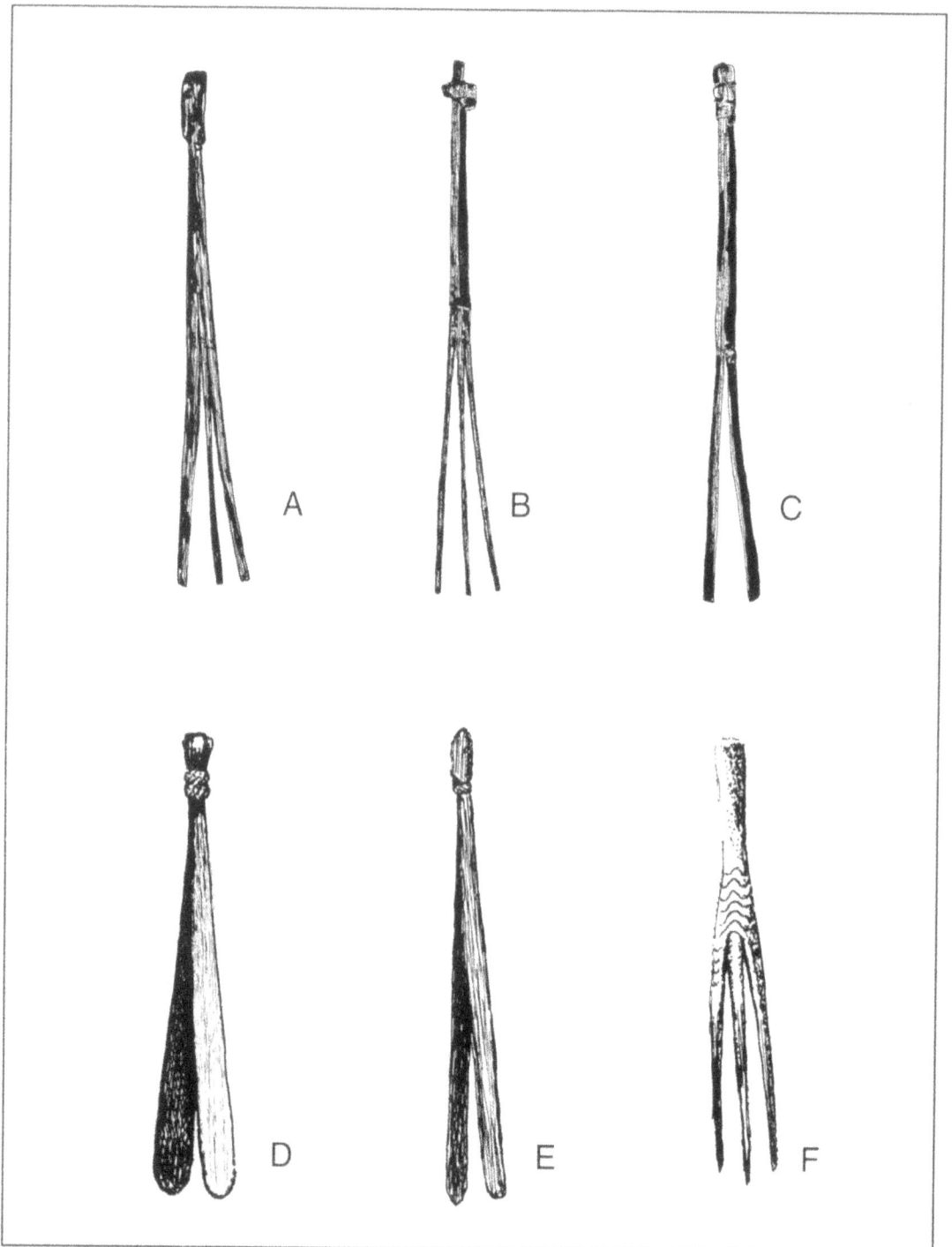

Figure 46: Tongs and forks used in the Moluccas and Jayapura region.
A. Moluccas **B.** Moluccas **C.** Moluccas **D.** Humboldt Bay **E.** Lake Sentani **F.** Ase, Lake Sentani Similar tongs to D and E are used in the Vanimo region of Papua New Guinea. A–C are 26–27 centimetres and D–F about 22 centimetres in length.
Sources: Avé 1977; van der Sande 1907.

Subsequent foreign trade on the north coast of New Guinea

The presence of Chinese ceramics in the Kumamba Islands in 1616 and T. Forrest's observation that Chinese traders were visiting the Waropen coast for massoy in 1775 suggest a history of Chinese trade along the coastline from Waropen to the Kumamba Islands (Figures 26 and 42). These Chinese traders may have been responsible for introducing tobacco, as tobacco was offered by Kumamba (Arimoa) Islanders to the crew of Schouten's ship in 1616. They also had Chinese porcelain in their canoes.[10] Coastal trade would have led to the distribution of tobacco seeds and explains the chain of related words for tobacco found from Amberbaki on the Bird's Head to just west of the Sepik River mouth,[11] see Figure 47.

Until the Tidorese *hongi* raids, the Kumamba Islanders had a long record of welcoming visitors. Abel Tasman in 1642 reports obtaining 6,000 coconuts and 100 bags of bananas in exchange for knives made from hoop iron on Jamna Island in 1642.[12] Likewise, in 1840 E. Belcher reports that Jamna Islanders in the Kumamba group were interested in trading coconuts for hoop iron and beads. Curiously, although the Jamna Islanders wore bird of paradise plumes in 1840, they did not offer them as trade goods.[13]

In 1848 the Sultan of Tidore began asserting his authority over New Guinea. *Hongi* raids on this coast had the same devastating impact as in the Kowiai area (see Chapter 8). When B.G.F. de Kops visited Kurudu Island off the Waropen coast (Figure 26) in 1849, he learnt that the *Singaji* from Gebe, who was appointed by and answered to the Sultan of Tidore, had recently ransacked the island and seized 200 men as slaves. Kops also reports that this same *Singaji* claimed that his *hongi* fleets had already been to Kurudu six times.[14]

The coastline east of Kurudu was also subjected to Tidorese *hongi* attacks. In 1848 a fleet was sent by the Sultan of Tidore to subjugate the mainland near the Kumamba Islands (Figure 42). It appears they were expected, as their crews were attacked and they were compelled to retreat with six dead and many wounded.[15] Retaliation by Tidore probably took place.

The chief objective of the voyage of the *Circe* in 1849 and an accompanying Tidorese *hongi* fleet was to assess the potential of Humboldt Bay (now Yos-Sudarso Bay) for settlement and to mark the north coast as far east as the 141st meridian for the Sultan of Tidore (Figure 42).[16] The *Circe* became separated from the *hongi* fleet and had to return to Ambon without landing at Humboldt Bay because of strong southeast winds and a lee current.

On the north coast west of Humboldt Bay but east of the Kumamba Islands, Kops reports in 1849 that some men came out in canoes to the *Circe* with bundles of bows and arrows, bird beaks, leaves and empty coconuts. For the bows and arrows they received some empty bottles and beads. What they really wanted were knives, but their trade items were considered useless by those on the *Circe*.[17]

Early in 1852 a garrison was established at Humboldt Bay consisting of a party of *burghers*, or native militia from Ternate.[18] This garrison must have been short-lived as there is no further mention of their activities. Their presence probably antagonised the local people and made them less receptive to visitors, as the Prince of Tidore and Resident of Banda who visited Humboldt Bay in 1858 onboard the *Etna*, a Dutch war steamer, initially received a hostile reception. The local people indicated that they would fire their arrows if any attempt was made to land, but after the Captain threw some presents ashore, they permitted those who wished to do so to go ashore. Fruits and vegetables were provided for the visitors and they were free to wander around. As the Dorey interpreter was unable to communicate with the people, all communication was by sign language.[19]

The Tidorese raids which occurred in the 1840s clearly had a devastating impact on the Kumamba Islands and nearby coast. There is no doubt that the belligerent response it brought about slowed the extension of foreign trade along this coast. Even in the 1870s most visitors avoided the Kuramba Islands and the nearby mainland coast. Those traders that did try to make contact received a hostile reception. This was the case in the early 1870s with Captain Deighton who was highly respected in Cendrawasih Bay.[20]

When the steamship *Dossoon* visited Humboldt Bay in October 1875, the people were keen to trade but had little to offer. All they had was some smoked fish and unripe fruit.[21] Traders and bird of paradise hunters did not become active in the area until the early 1880s and the first trade store was established in the 1890s. When the missionary G.L. Bink visited Lake Sentani in 1893, he found that the people there still did not have metal and used stone tools and shells for woodworking.[22] This quickly changed. By 1903 iron was widely available, but some village men at Lake Sentani continued to make stone axes.[23]

Bird of paradise collectors and hunters

The first bird of paradise collectors to work in the Jayapura region were probably participants of the 1858 Dutch border expedition. Rosenberg, a German naturalist and draughtsman, was a member of the survey team who sailed on the *Etna* in 1858. He took two assistants with him. They were delegated the task of shooting and skinning birds. Rosenberg also purchased a few rare skins from the local people.[24]

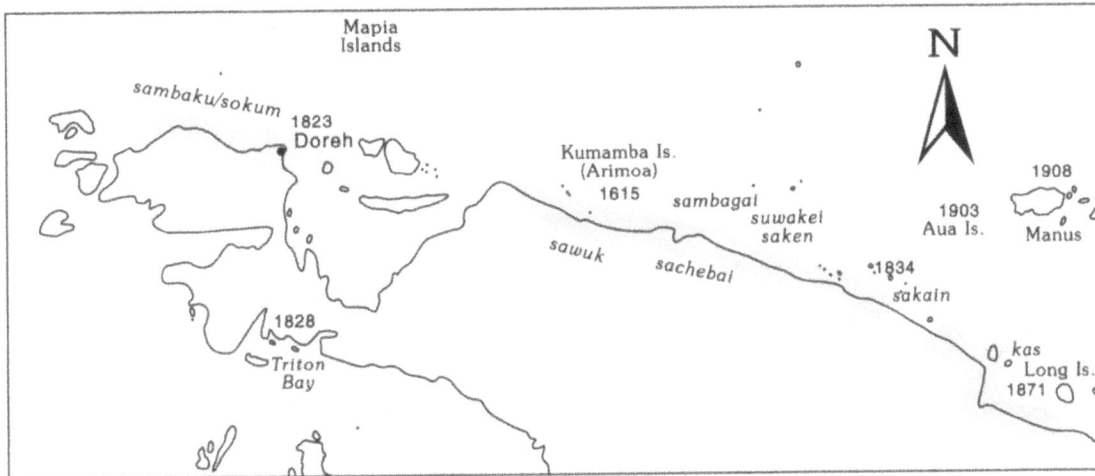

Figure 47: The distribution of cognate names for tobacco and the earliest reports of its presence on the north coast of West Papua and Papua New Guinea.

Source: Based on Riesenfeld 1951.

Although bird of paradise collecting had begun in the Jayapura region in 1858, Ternatian hunters were not active on this part of the north coast and its immediate hinterland until the 1880s. This was when Cape Djar (Cape Bonpland) became known as Cape Saprop Mani (land of birds) (Figure 43).[25] In the 1890s a number of Chinese, Ternatians and Tidorese established a trading station on Metu Debi Island at the entrance between Yotefa Bay and Humboldt Bay (Figure 43). Bird of paradise hunting and trading was their main source of income. A European trader, J.M. Dumas, also established a trading post on this island. Their activities not only supplied the plume trade but also scientific specimens for European museums.[26]

Apart from establishing coastal bases Ternatian bird hunters began to venture inland. The sale of three specimens of the Golden-Fronted Bowerbird (*Amblyornis flavifrons*) to the British zoologist Lord Rothschild in 1895 indicates that Ternatian hunters had penetrated inland to the Foja Mountains by the early 1890s (Figure 42). These trade skins made the species known to the scientific world in 1895, but it remained a mystery until recently as to where in New Guinea the Indonesian bird hunters had obtained this bird. It was not until 1981 that the natural habitat of the species was discovered in the Foja Mountains.[27]

Hollandia was established in 1909–10 as the base camp for the expedition which had the task of determining the boundary between Dutch and German New Guinea. Its leader condemned the Hollandia (Jayapura) region as being unhealthy when one member of the expedition died and others became ill with malaria, beriberi and sleeping sickness. The people of the Humboldt Bay region also became renowned for killing bird hunters. Scarcely a month passed during the boom years when there was not some conflict between the local people and bird hunters.

This reputation played a part in discouraging European traders and planters. Even in the 1930s Chinese traders owned and ran most of the trade stores at Hollandia and other centres on the north coast of Dutch New Guinea. Their success owed much to their ability to obtain a wide range of cheap goods from China and Japan and have lower overheads than any Dutchman could achieve. These Chinese traders were not discouraged by the Dutch colonial government as they made a considerable contribution to the colonial revenue by means of the taxes and import and export duties they paid.[28]

In 1900 bird of paradise skins were worth about 15–20 guilders (about 1 pound 10 shillings to £2) and goura pigeons 2 guilders. Hunters brought the skins to traders who exchanged them for goods.[29] Prior to 1907 two Chinese traders are reported to have exported 12,000 birds every three months.[30] Chinese businessmen in Hollandia also advanced large sums of money to Ternatian (Plate 34) and Tidorese bird hunters. In 1911, for instance, some 60 hunters owed traders the sum of 20,000 guilders.[31]

These hunters covered large areas in their search for plumes. They travelled over the border into German New Guinea (see Chapter 12), and also covered vast distances in Dutch New Guinea. For instance, H.J. Lam, a Dutch naturalist, was impressed by a party of two Chinese and nineteen New Guinean bird hunters who visited his camp at Prauwen-bivak (Figure 42) during his 1920 expedition (Plate 35). They had travelled overland from Hollandia to the headwaters of the Idenburg River, living off the land, in order to hunt birds of paradise and goura pigeons. Near the coast they had been able to obtain food from villages through which they passed, but in uninhabited areas they had to live off the land. Each day part of their group either made sago, fished or hunted for food, whilst the others hunted birds of paradise and goura pigeons. Travelling in this way they reached the banks of the Idenburg in just over 70 days. There they made four praus and after seven days reached Prauwen-bivak. The hunters stayed with Lam's party for some time while they sought birds nearby.[32]

Hollandia was the main centre on the north coast of Dutch New Guinea for trading in bird of paradise skins (Plate 36). When the Australians occupied German New Guinea during the First World War, some German planters crossed the border and settled in Hollandia in Dutch New Guinea. One of these Germans was Herr Stuber. He continued his plume-hunting trade,[33] whereas other Germans either established coconut plantations near Hollandia and Sarmi (Figure 42) or became active in the copal (tree resin) industry.[34]

Plate 34: Rassip and Marinki, bird hunters from Ternate.

Plate 35: Some of the nineteen New Guineans employed by two Chinese bird hunters who visited Prauwen-bivak on the lower Idenburg River in 1920. To reach Prauwen-bivak they had travelled for 70 days overland and 7 days by river since leaving Hollandia.

Both photos: Courtesy of Fotobureau, Koninklijk Instituut voor de Tropen, Amsterdam.

Plate 36: Lesser Bird of Paradise skins hanging in front of a trade store, probably in Hollandia.

Photo: Courtesy of Fotobureau, Koninklijk Instituut voor de Tropen, Amsterdam.

When the plume trade was prohibited in the Mandated Territory of New Guinea in 1922, bird skins continued to be smuggled across the border into Dutch New Guinea and exported from Hollandia. In 1924 bird of paradise trading was prohibited in much of Dutch New Guinea,[35] but was allowed to continue in the Hollandia area until 1931.[36] Even so the boom was over.

As described in Chapter 5, the passing of the Plumage (Prohibition) Bill in 1921 by the United Kingdom played a major role in the trade's decline. It meant that Britain had now joined the United States and Australia in banning the importation of birds of paradise. The demand for plumes by the European fashion market slumped. Although the Asian market remained, it could not absorb the large numbers of bird skins previously destined for European markets. This allowed fully plumed male birds of paradise to be seen displaying on the outskirts of Hollandia in 1929.[37] When bird of paradise hunting was prohibited in the Hollandia area in 1931, most hunters left.

In the 1930s Evelyn Cheesman found Hollandia to be a small village, most of the inhabitants being Indonesian or Chinese. A few old Indonesian down-and-outers, who not so long ago had been making fortunes as bird hunters, still remained. The large number of Chinese stores in the small settlement were another indication of the past boom.[38] These Chinese traders continued to import all sorts of foreign goods, including rice, textiles, metalware, fuel and beads.[39]

When bird hunting was prohibited, the main products exported from Hollandia became massoy bark at 100 guilders (ca £9) a pikul (60.5 kilograms), *lawang* bark at 60–70 guilders a pikul, trepang at 100 guilders per pikul, trochus shell at 50 cents each, mother of pearl shell at 25 cents each and, after 1930, coffee and cotton in small quantities.[40]

The Dutch Controller at Hollandia in the 1930s was responsible to the Assistant Resident based at Manokwari, who in turn reported to the Resident at Ambon. The Dutch had made a good road from Humboldt Bay to Tanah Merah Bay (Figure 43). Villagers near this road were taxed, but the Dutch had no control at that time over inland groups. Cheesman was surprised to find how few planters were established in the vicinity of Hollandia. Most plantations were run by local men with foreign fathers. Of the seven European planters, three were Germans who had crossed the border after the First World War.[41]

Notes

1. Torrence and Swadling 2008; Torrence, R., Swadling, P., Kononenko, N., Ambrose, W., Rath, P. and Glascock, M.D. 2009.

2. Bintarti 1985; de Bruyn 1959; de Bruyn 1962; Galis 1956; Galis 1964; van der Sande 1907; Soejono 1963; Tichelman 1963.

3. Agogino 1979, 1986. These references were kindly brought to my attention by Chris Ballard.

4. Other beads are recognised as having recently come into circulation.

5. Frances Deklin personal communication 1980.

6. van der Sande 1907: 224.

7. van der Sande 1907: 7; Ave 1977: 24.

8. Tony Deklin personal communication 1979.

9. The lack of regular trade between eastern Indonesia and the Madang coastline suggests that the sixteenth century Malay *kris* (dagger), reputedly dug up on Long Island in association with a human skull (Egloff and Specht 1982: 444), may have reached Long Island as an heirloom or curio on board a European ship.

10. Dumont d'Urville 1853 cited by Riesenfeld 1951: 76.

11. The use of tobacco was not known in the 1890s on Wuvulu or Aua, nor on any of the other Manus islands (Riesenfeld 1951: 72–3). On the Madang coast the name *kas* and its derivatives (*kash*, *kast*) are dominant. When Miklouho-Maclay went to the Rai coast in 1871 people were cultivating and smoking tobacco. The old men said that their fathers had obtained tobacco seeds and had adopted the practice of smoking from the west. Miklouho-Maclay observed that smoking and cultivating tobacco was not known to some

villagers living in the inland mountains when he was resident on the Rai Coast (Riesenfeld 1951).

12. Forrest 1969: ix.
13. Belcher 1843 cited by Hughes 1977: 28.
14. Kops 1852: 338.
15. Kops 1852: 323.
16. Kops 1852: 323, 348.
17. Kops 1852: 342.
18. Earl 1853: 91.
19. Wallace 1986: 511.
20. van der Crab 1879 cited by Whittaker et al 1975: 237.
21. van der Crab 1879 cited by Whittaker et al 1975: 237–8.
22. Kooijman 1959: 16.
23. van der Sande 1907: 174–5.
24. Wallace 1986: 508.
25. Cheesman 1949: 25, 126: Prescott et al 1977: 84.
26. Galis 1955: 14; Gilliard 1969: 430–1.
27. Aschenbach 1982; Diamond 1982a, 1982b.
28. Cheesman 1938a: 24–6, 35.
29. Galis 1955: 210–1.
30. Goodfellow 1907 cited by Buckland 1909: 161 (in German New Guinea colonial documents)
31. Galis 1955: 211.
32. Lam 1945: 65.
33. Cheesman 1938a: 30.
34. van der Veur 1972: 281.
35. Schultze-Westrum 1969: 300.
36. Cheesman 1938a: 40–4.
37. E. Mayr cited by Mary LeCroy personal communication 1991.
38. Cheesman 1938a: 36
39. Galis 1955: 210.
40. Galis 1955: 211.
41. Cheesman 1938b: 25.

12

Plumes fund economic development in Kaiser Wilhelmsland

Indonesian presence

Indonesian and Chinese traders from Ternate began to trade eastwards along the north coast in the latter half of the nineteenth century.[1] By the early 1880s they were active as far east as the Tarawai and Walis Islands off the Sepik coast of northern New Guinea (Figure 48). Some Sepiks travelled to the Moluccas with these traders. Richard Parkinson reports in 1900 that he met three Tarawai Islanders who had been to Ternate, when he visited Tarawai and Walis.[2] As a result of this contact certain Malay words such as *tuan* (master) and *kiappa*[3] (coconut) became known on the Sepik coast.

The people on Kairiru Island in the East Sepik claim that iron tools were first introduced to their island by a Chinese trader living on Tarawai Island. Their forbears exchanged taro and bananas for axes and knives with this trader, whom they called Ternate.[4] This trader probably visited the volcanic island of Kairiru for food, whilst his commercial interest was centred on the trepang and green snails found off the coral islands of Tarawai and Walis.

The German New Guinea Company did not initially see these Indonesian and Chinese traders as a threat to their economic interests. At first its directors were more concerned with establishing large plantations than engaging in barter trade with New Guineans. This policy changed in 1897. By then the Company directors had come to realise that crops such as cocoa, coffee and tobacco were not viable plantation crops on the north coast of New Guinea. The Company then began to establish coconut plantations and to engage in barter trade with New Guineans. The first Company trading posts were established in 1897 and it soon became apparent that greater profits would be made if they did not have to compete with Indonesian and Chinese traders operating out of Dutch New Guinea. In 1904 Governor Hahl of German New Guinea sought

Dutch assistance to prohibit the entry of Indonesian and Chinese bird of paradise hunters from Hollandia and Ternate on the basis that they were causing unrest in German New Guinea. By the end of the decade Indonesian and Chinese hunters operating out of Dutch New Guinea had ceased plying their praus along the coast of German New Guinea. Some however continued to operate in the vicinity of the border.[5, 6]

The border crossing prohibition was successful on the coast, but not inland where it could not be enforced. The Dutch agreed that certain measures should be taken to control illegal inland boundary crossings, but little was achieved as there was no active supervision on the German side.[7]

Indonesian hunters and traders usually returned to the same areas year after year. They tended to stay in one locality for a while, perhaps a month, and traded goods such as beads, tobacco, knives and cloth for bird skins hunted by the local people. In 1910 Leonhard Schultz-Jena observed Indonesian bird hunters providing local men with guns to shoot birds for them.[8] Some hunted birds themselves. The good relationship these hunters seem to have had with many inland groups suggests that they paid villagers for the right to hunt on their land. Indonesian hunters in the Amanab area used muzzle loading muskets. The old men relate that if the hunters ran out of shot they used pebbles and powder instead.[9] The people in the Waina-Sowanda area south of Imonda also describe flintlock muskets.[10]

When the Indonesian hunters and traders penetrated the interior, they kept to certain defined trade routes, which, although no more than bush tracks, were recognised by local groups as lawful thoroughfares for Indonesian bird hunters and the New Guineans employed by them. As long as they were traders, they passed through the most aggressive tribes without fear, for their lives were sacred while they remained on these tracks.[11]

At Krisa village, some 20 kilometres inland from Vanimo in the West Sepik, an old man told Evelyn Cheesman[12] in the 1930s, through an interpreter, about the Indonesian bird hunters and traders who had come to his village.

He was delighted to talk about the traders who came no more, only his generation remembers them. They were trading of course in paradise birds. One man came every year and stopped for a month at a time, while the villagers hunted birds for him and he paid in beads, knives, cloth, cowrie shells, tobacco – things that would cost a few shillings. I learnt that this was a regular trade route leading inland, and this same trader went beyond the Bewani Mountains. I asked whether the villagers liked the traders. The old man beamed, there was no doubt about his feelings: "*Abidi wai-ai!*" (traders good), he repeated several times. The old trading road crossed the plain to the Bewani Mountains and beyond them to country inhabited by the Bendi tribe ...[13]

The high market prices resulting from the European plume boom after 1908 would have encouraged Indonesian hunters and traders to expand their operations further into the sparsely populated interior of what is now the West Sepik (Sandaun) province. The hunters were attracted by the large numbers of birds of paradise that could be found there.[14]

Many Indonesian bird hunters got on well with the local people. One recorded exception concerns a complaint made by Wanimo villagers to Governor Hahl about bird hunters who supported one village against another during a local dispute.[15]

Sepiks employed by Indonesian hunters sometimes kept some of the birds shot on hunting expeditions. On one occasion, a Wanimo youth working for two Indonesian hunters in the Osima and Bewani areas of the West Sepik managed to keep the best of his catch. He was one of five youths employed by these hunters. They had been told to use their catapults and try and shoot 24 birds each before coming back to camp. This youth shot only 11 birds and four of these were fine specimens. After hiding the best in the bark of a tree, he returned to the camp and gave the Indonesians the other seven birds. He then got leave to visit a relative in a nearby village. The four birds were given to the relative living in this village to prepare and keep safe until he could return to collect them. The skins were later used in his niece's marriage ceremony.[16]

The first Australian patrol officers to enter the Amanab-Lumi area were surprised to learn that they were not the first foreign visitors to these parts. In the 1920s to early 1930s Australian government patrols in the Vanimo hinterland crossed the tracks of Indonesian hunters from over the border.[17]

As we have seen in Chapter 11, Hollandia in Humboldt Bay was one of the main centres in Dutch New Guinea exporting bird of paradise skins. It also became an outlet for plumes smuggled out of the Mandated Territory of New Guinea, as from 1920 all plume exports were restricted and registered. They were finally prohibited early in 1922. In 1921 the Australian patrol officer based at Aitape had his carriers help the Vanimo patrol officer carry certain boxes, which had to be kept dry, some 25 kilometres from Aitape to Arop. Twelve months later the Aitape officer learnt that he had assisted in carrying 300 contraband bird of paradise skins destined for Hollandia.[18] The Vanimo officer involved was dismissed.[19]

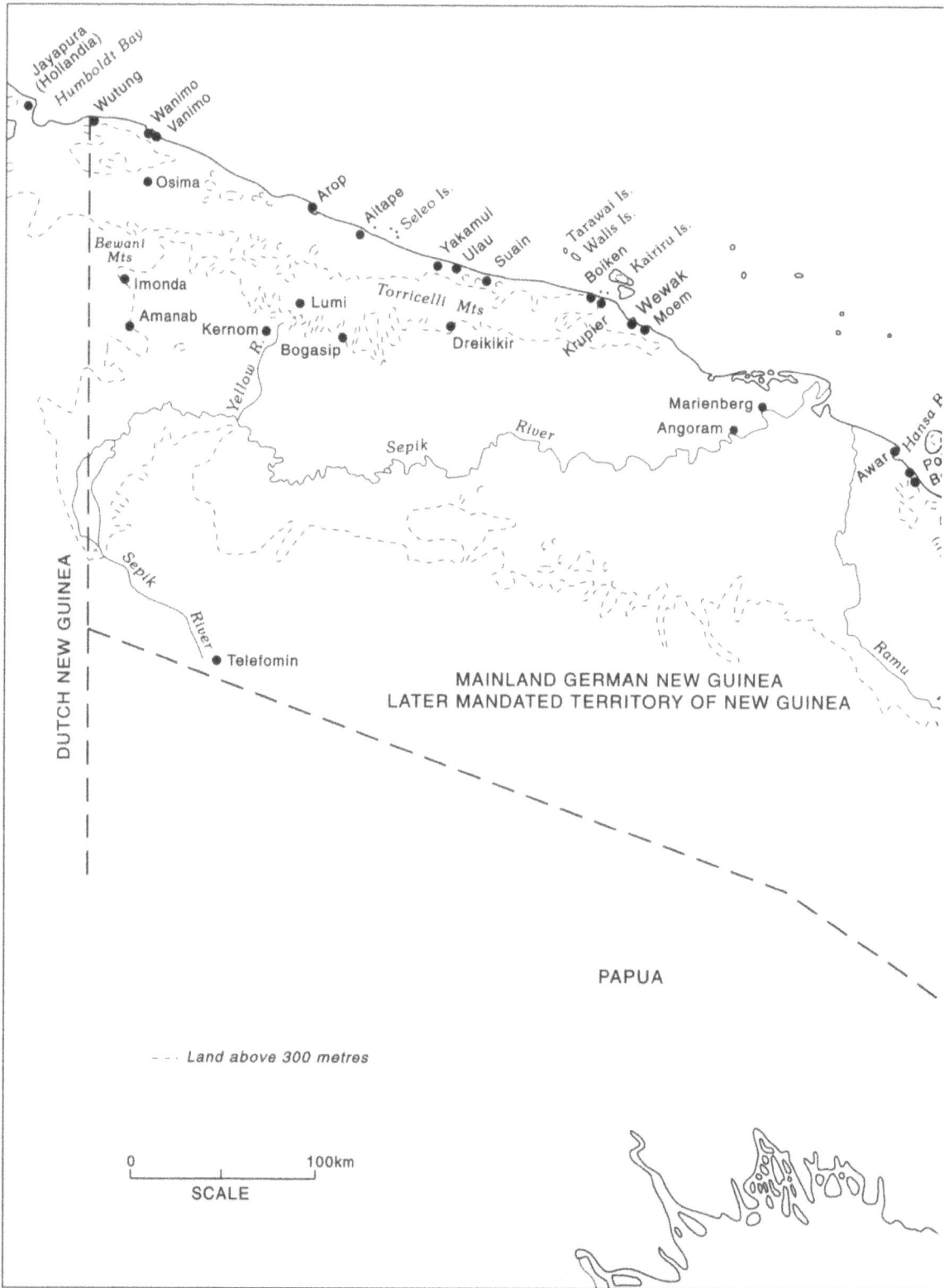

Figure 48: Mainland German New Guinea (Kaiser Wilhelmsland), later the Mandated Territory of New Guinea.

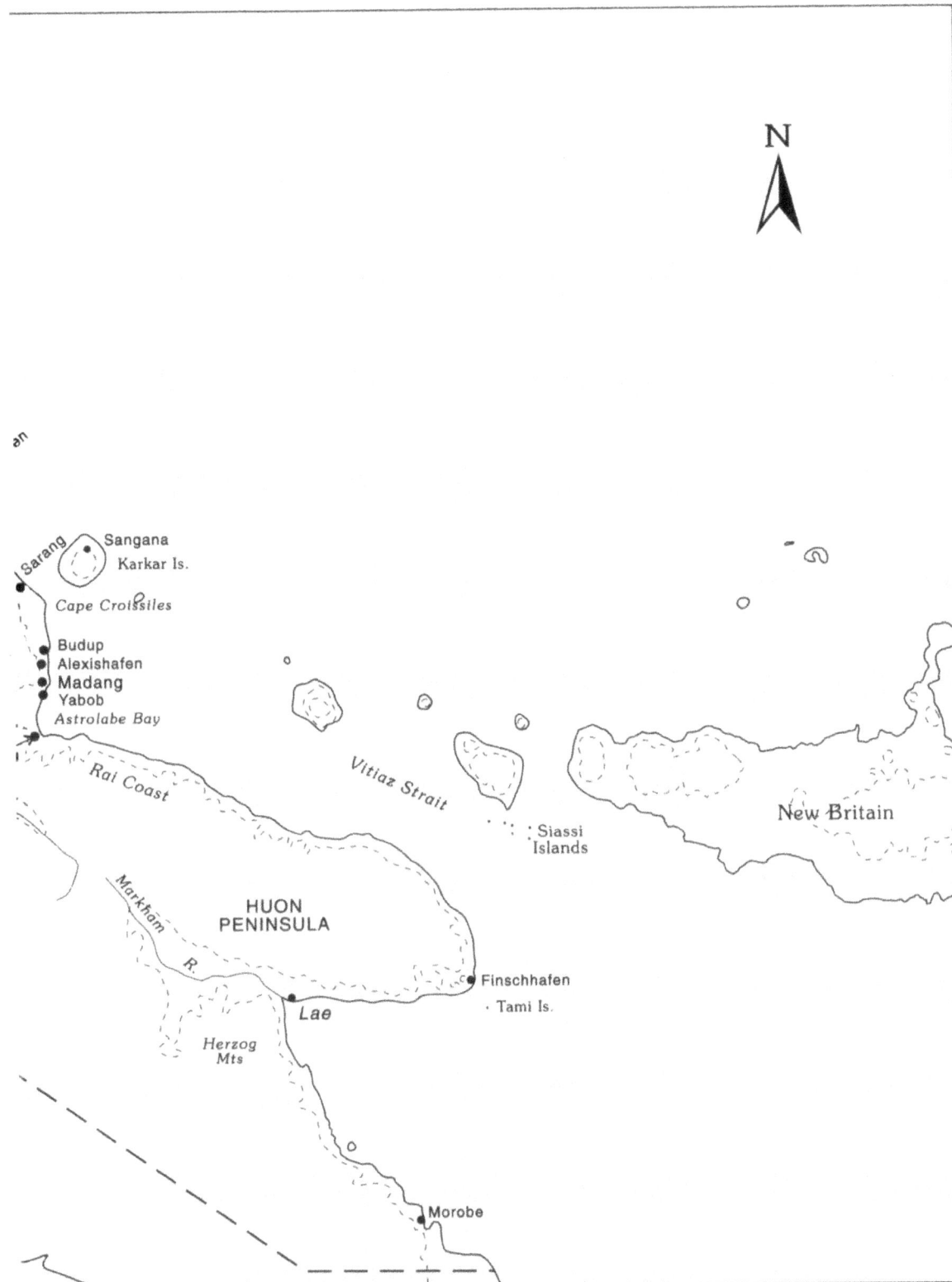

N

Sangana
Karkar Is.
Sarang
Cape Croissiles

Budup
Alexishafen
Madang
Yabob
Astrolabe Bay

Rai Coast

Vitiaz Strait

: Siassi
Islands

New Britain

Markham
R.

**HUON
PENINSULA**

*Herzog
Mts*

Finschhafen
· Tami Is.

Lae

Morobe

E.D. Robinson in 1934–5 reports in his patrol report[20] that while at Kernom (Kernam) on the Yellow River, he learnt through his corporal, who was able to talk to a local in pidgin Malay, that two Indonesians and a party of New Guineans had been in the vicinity shooting birds of paradise about five months previously. Although contraband hunting continued, the amount of trade going through Hollandia quickly declined once commercial hunting was prohibited in much of Dutch New Guinea in 1924,[21] though hunting was allowed to continue in the Hollandia region until 1931.[22] Once European markets were closed, Asian demands continued. The Indonesian hunters reported by Robinson would have been supplying this old market which still continues in Indonesia in the 1990s.

German presence

By the middle of the nineteenth century, Britain, France, the Netherlands, Portugal and Spain had raised their flags and established settlements on most of the islands of Southeast Asia and the Pacific. They colonised all the islands that gave the appearance of having an economic potential. New Guinea was largely ignored. Some enthusiastic mariners had claimed it for their homelands,[23] but no nation was willing to bring any of these claims into reality by maintaining an interest on the island.

Although the Dutch did annex the western half of New Guinea in 1828, they did not colonise their claim. At that time the Dutch were not interested in New Guinea's resources; they merely wanted to keep other countries from the eastern flanks of the Dutch East Indies. They avoided the problem of administrating an unprofitable colony by championing the rights of the Sultan of Tidore to be the overlord over their annexed territory (see Chapter 6).

In the early 1880s, the president of one of the largest private banks in Berlin, Adolph von Hansemann, began to promote New Guinea to his countrymen as a profitable investment area. He was so convinced of its potential that he established a group of German financiers to acquire land on the New Guinea mainland in 1884. On behalf of this group Otto Finsch and Captain Dallman travelled to New Guinea and acquired land rights from the local inhabitants in 1884–5. When the required land rights had been obtained, the German financiers persuaded their government to claim northeast New Guinea as a colony. This took place in 1884. In the same year Britain was persuaded to annex territory in New Guinea on behalf of the Australian colonies. These claims led to the division of eastern New Guinea into two parts in 1885, the northern becoming German, the southern British.[24] In 1895 the southern border was adjusted to the natural boundary of the Bensbach River mouth between Dutch and British New Guinea (Figure 38).[25]

The German Chancellor, Count Otto von Bismarck, was willing to acquire new colonies,[26] but was reluctant to invest large sums of government money in their administration. This problem was overcome by making chartered companies, which were modelled on the former East India Companies, responsible for the administration of new colonies. For undertaking this responsibility these companies received economic concessions from their home government. In 1885 the German financiers obtained a charter from Bismarck to establish the New Guinea Company (Neu Guinea Kompagnie). This charter allowed the New Guinea Company to administer and acquire land in German New Guinea, but the German government reserved the rights over foreign relations and justice.[27]

Von Hansemann and his associate directors thought northeast New Guinea was a fertile land where they could quickly establish successful cocoa, coffee and tobacco plantations. In less than two years after obtaining its charter the New Guinea Company had spent two and a half million marks (about £125,000) on shipping, staff and supplies in German New Guinea. Unsuitable soils and climate, as well as disease, labour and shipping problems brought about these high costs. By 1890 scientific surveys funded by the Company had established that there appeared to be no rich faunal, floral or mineral resources available for exploitation. Nevertheless the Company persevered and established four tobacco plantations near Stephansort (Bogadjim) in Astrolabe Bay in 1892. Javanese and Chinese labourers were recruited from Java and Singapore to work in these plantations (Plate 37). Although the tobacco leaf sold well in European markets, the plantations were not a financial success.

By 1897 the tobacco, cocoa and coffee ventures were acknowledged failures. From this time the German New Guinea Company concentrated on trading for village copra and establishing coconut plantations. Six trading stations were established. One was on Seleo Island off Aitape. Herr Lücker was the manager, assisted by Diack. They traded in copra, trepang, turtle shell and pearl shell. Five other trading stations manned by Chinese or Indonesians were established on the mainland and neighbouring islands. The Chinese and Indonesians running these trading posts did not receive regular wages. At first they were only repaid the cost of the products they purchased and given provisions. They received a profit margin once they had sold the goods allocated to them.[28]

In 1898 Lücker established a trading station at Arop on the eastern side of the Sissano Lagoon. It was staffed by an Indonesian trader called Kromo, two Chinese and four New Guinean assistants.[29] Apart from trading in the limited supplies of trade copra, the staff of this trading station, as well as others further east along the Aitape coast, investigated the inland mountains for birds of paradise.

In 1897 the Company began to establish coconut plantations at Berlinhafen near Aitape and on the Gazelle Peninsula of New Britain in the Bismarck Archipelago.[30] In 1898 the Company's exports were worth 115,400 marks (£5,770). This was a poor return on a total investment of eleven million marks (£550,000) over 14 years. Financial difficulties led the imperial government to relieve the New Guinea Company of its administrative responsibilities in 1899.

Plate 37: Three Indonesian women employed on one of the New Guinea Company's tobacco plantations at Stephansort (Bogadjim) in the Madang area in 1897.
Photo: By Lajo Biro, courtesy of the Ethnographical Museum, Budapest, Hungary.

Starting in 1899, the German government made annual compensatory payments of 400,000 marks to the Company in return for it relinquishing its administrative control over German New Guinea. Although no longer administrating the colony, the Company continued to dominate its economy. In 1914 one-third of all German planters and traders worked for the Company and it owned half the alienated land in the colony. Its plantations were located in New Ireland, the Duke of York Islands and New Britain (Gazelle Peninsula and Witu Islands) in the Bismarck Archipelago and the north coast of mainland New Guinea. By 1914 in terms of its capital value it was the largest plantation company in any German colony.[31]

The impact of early European contact in German New Guinea

Most people in mainland German New Guinea had experienced little direct contact with Europeans prior to annexation, but a number of local interactions had occurred. Artifacts and historical records indicate that these involved European sailors at Budup in Madang, Dutch sailors at Arop in West Sepik and a Russian scientist on the Rai Coast of what is now the Madang Province. The Budup incident became incorporated in the Kilibob and Manup origin myth of the Madang coast.[32]

The villagers living in the vicinity of the tobacco plantations established at Stephansort (Bogadjim) in Astrolabe Bay and those in contact with the trading stations established on the Sepik coast seem to have borne the brunt of the demoralisation that emerged in their societies when faced with the different technology and world view of the Germans. In 1891–3, when the tobacco plantations were being established, the Hungarian natural history and artifact collector Samuel Fenichel was able to collect cult objects for the Hungarian National Museum. A few years later in 1897, another Hungarian, Lajos Biro, was only able to collect everyday utensils, as cult objects no longer existed in Astrolabe Bay.[33]

Similar changes occurred on the Sepik coast. The German ethnographer Richard Parkinson first visited what is now the Wewak-Aitape coast in 1893. He was astonished and dismayed to find on a subsequent visit in 1898–9 that it was now difficult to acquire artifacts which had been easy to acquire only five years earlier. However, the presence of European traders and the Catholic Mission had brought one change which was to the ethnographer's advantage. No longer was sign language the only means of communication. It was now possible to communicate with the local people through interpreters who had worked for the traders or the mission.[34]

Copra

By the 1850s a market had developed for coconut oil in Europe. In the 1870s it was replaced by a growing demand for copra.[35] When the Lever Brothers discovered that copra could be used instead of tallow in soap manufacturing in 1885, not only was Sunlight soap born, but also the parent firm of Unilever. This new demand for copra led to increased trading for village copra and subsequently to the establishment of coconut plantations in many parts of the world.

Coconuts grow well in New Guinea. Despite an antiquity of the palm of over 5,000 years on the north coast, culturally induced scarcities were the norm on this coast and in other parts of New Guinea in the 1880s.[36] With the exception of the Aitape area, villages on the north coast of German New Guinea did not have large stands of village coconuts. They were rare and highly valued.[37] The Siassi and Tami islanders of Vitiaz Strait and the Huon Gulf were observed to grow more coconuts than the people on the mainland, but in order to maintain their monopoly, the Tami broke the nuts before trading them. This induced scarcity seems typical of the north coast. Ber, an elder of Yabob village near Madang who was born in 1904, could remember when Rai Coast villages had very small stands of coconuts.[38]

In other parts of New Guinea villagers had large stands of coconuts. They were able to supply copra to barter traders. This was the case in the New Guinea Islands villages, especially those in East New Britain and New Ireland. The availability of village copra led to the establishment of trading posts. The first trading post to be established in what is now Papua New Guinea was in the Duke of York Islands in East New Britain in 1872.[39]

In the New Guinea Islands, trade copra was the usual source of funds by which plantations were established. By contrast Kaiser Wilhelmsland (mainland New Guinea) settlers were unable to raise capital in this way. The growing demand for bird of paradise plumes in Europe which became a boom industry in 1908 provided an alternative source of income.

Bird hunting before the plume boom

Before 1908 birds of paradise were shot in German New Guinea, as in British and Dutch New Guinea, to supply both natural history collectors and the growing plume market. There was probably an upsurge in this activity when Carl Hunstein joined the New Guinea Company in 1885. He had previously worked in British New Guinea as a bird collector and continued to do so in German New Guinea (see Chapter 4).

Most of the reports of bird hunting in German New Guinea before the plume boom of 1908 concern either the New Guinea Company's first administrative centre at Finschhafen, the tobacco plantations established near Stephansort (Bogadjim) in Astrolabe Bay in 1891–2 or scientific expeditions.

From the beginning the German administration took steps to protect the birds from extinction. For instance, on the 18th of July 1887 the administrator introduced a police regulation that prohibited the hunting of either moulting male or female birds of paradise in the Finschhafen district.[40]

In 1891, some seven years after the annexation of Kaiser Wilhelmsland, an ordinance was passed requiring bird of paradise hunters to have a licence.

Apart from controlling the use of firearms by non-Europeans, this legislation was considered overdue at the time as many New Guinea Company staff were not obtaining permission before using their company's boats and employees to hunt the birds.[41] By 1891 there were two full-time European bird hunters, German brothers by the name of Geissler, working in the Astrolabe Bay and Huon Peninsula area of Kaiser Wilhelmsland (Figure 48). They spent long periods out hunting, but were not considered to be making a profit.

By mid 1892, fourteen individuals had applied for three-month licences and paid the fee of 20 marks. Only two individuals, Geissler and Grubauer, had paid 100 marks for six-month licences. The introduction of licences had the effect of encouraging more hunting than previously, as holders attempted to recoup the cost of their licences and make a profit from their activity. This increase in hunting from 1891–2 was especially noticeable in the Astrolabe Bay area.[42] As mentioned above, this was when the tobacco plantations were established near Stephansort.

The plume boom of 1908

There was little further growth in the number of licences after 1891 until the bird of paradise plume boom of 1908. In 1891 bird of paradise skins fetched 8–12 marks (about 7–11 shillings) in German New Guinea. After 1908 they were worth three to four times as much. This price rise encouraged more hunting. This is evident from the revenue the administration obtained from hunting licences. In 1891 it was 480 marks; just prior to the plume boom of 1908 it became 600 marks. By 1909 the administration of German New Guinea was receiving 20,000 marks in revenue from licences.[43]

The impact of the European plume boom was felt in both German New Guinea and Papua by late 1908. While the Papuan administration took steps to prohibit the commercial hunting of these birds, the German administration was allocating exported bird of paradise skins a separate entry within the colony's statistics. Until 1909 the number of bird of paradise skins exported had been insufficient to warrant such recognition; they had just been grouped with other small-scale income earners,[44] see Table 13 and Figure 49.

Table 13: The number of bird of paradise skins exported from German New Guinea and the Mandated Territory of New Guinea between 1909–22 and their value.

Year	Number exported	Value (in marks)	Value (in pounds)[a]	Export Duty (in marks)
1909–10	3,200	65,000	2,979	4,400
1910–11	5,706	171,000	7,838	11,412
1911–12	8,779	278,000	12,742	43,900
1912–13	9,837	449,260	20,591	49,190
1913–14	16,691	1,096,961	50,277	83,455
Commencement of World War I				
1914–15				
1915–16			98	
1916–17			125	
1917–18				
1918–19			100	
1919–20			34,133	
1920–21			5,812	
1921–22			2027	

Notes:
1. The New Guinea (Rabaul) Gazette (1916: 44) gives the conversion rate of one German mark to 11 English or Australian pence. For those not familiar with pounds, shillings and pence, there were 20 shillings in a pound, and 12 pence in a shilling.
2. The period from 1915–22 includes other feathers.

Sources: Sack and Clark (1979: 315, 316, 330, 331, 348, 368).
Sack and Clark (1980: 156).
Government Gazette, Territory of New Guinea 1913–14, Appendix A.
Government Gazettes, Territory of New Guinea 1916–22. (There are some discrepancies in the figures given in the 1914–21 and 1921–2 reports to the League of Nations in the New Guinea Government Gazettes).

From the beginning Governor Hahl proposed that the plume boom should be managed in such a way that the birds were harvested and not depleted, with the profits contributing to the cost of developing and administering German New Guinea. His management policy was to harvest the birds without exterminating them, until fashions changed. The value of plumes would then decline on the world market, hunting would cease and the birds would be able to recolonize depleted areas.

Over the years the legislation controlling commercial bird of paradise hunting in Kaiser Wilhelmsland was amended and new regulations and requirements introduced. This legislation was concerned with hunting licences, export duties, closed seasons and conservation areas.

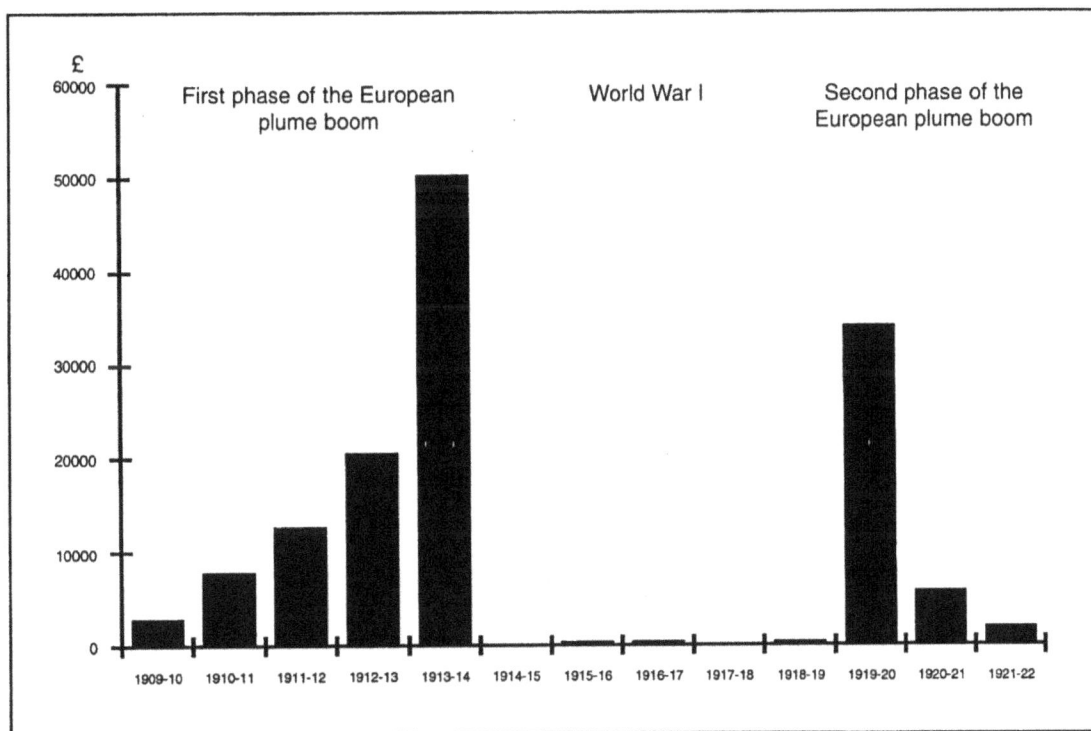

Figure 49: The value of bird of paradise skins exported from German New Guinea and the Mandated Territory of New Guinea from 1909–22.

Notes:

1. The period 1914–22 includes other feathers.

2. Inflation does not play a part in explaining the large increase from 1909-1914, as prices remained stable in Germany between 1890–1916. For instance, a domestic letter cost the same price (10 pfenning or 10 parts of a mark) to post throughout this period (J. Tschauder personal communication 1991).

Source: Based on Table 13.

Measures taken by the German administration to ensure the survival of birds of paradise in German New Guinea

1. Licensees had to invest their profits in development projects within the colony

After 1908, a hunting licence was only issued by district officers to those who agreed to invest the profits they made in development projects within the colony.[45] Once the 'plume fever' started, the cost of an annual hunting licence rose in accordance with the world price for plumes. A licensee could shoot any number of birds. However, if requested to do so, he was obliged to give a report at the end of each year which detailed how many assistant hunters and carriers he employed, where he hunted and how many birds had been shot according to species and what was the sum total of his profit.[46]

Table 14 details the changing cost of licences and the conditions imposed on the licensees.

Table 14: Summary of the main bird-hunting licence legislation in German New Guinea.

11 Nov. 1891	Ordinance regarding hunting birds of paradise. Licence now required, fee 20 marks. Fine for hunting without a licence, 1,000 marks or one month in gaol.
27 Dec. 1892	Ordinance regarding hunting birds of paradise. Licence must indicate number of assistants employed and area where hunting. Fee for one year is 100 marks, or a short term licence is 20 marks.
13 March 1907	Ordinance of 1892 amended, increasing licence fees: • One year, 160 marks • Six months, 90 marks • Three months, 50 marks
18 March 1911	Ordinance. Licences now issued at district office at Friedrich Wilhelmshafen (Madang) and sub-district offices at Eitape (Aitape) and Morobe. The content of this licence is given in Figure 50. Licences for non-indigenous people (e.g. Chinese) require them to hunt in a stipulated area; they cannot employ New Guinean hunters, unlike Europeans. The licence holder has to personally supervise his assistant hunters or authorise another European to supervise them on his behalf. To have more than two New Guinean hunters the licence holder has to be both a resident and businessman in German New Guinea, for example running a tradestore or establishing a plantation.

Fees are now as follows:

months	number of Melanesian hunters	cost in marks
3	1 or none	20
3	2	125
6	1 or none	150
6	2	200
12	1 or none	200
12	2	300

There was a limit of six New Guinean hunters for any one venture.

1913 Ordinance

From this date, for security reasons, New Guinean hunters are only allowed to use muzzle-loaders and are not allowed to hunt in the immediate neighbourhood of their own villages.

Licences are now required for all birds with decorative plumage with trade value.

Licence fees are now as follows:

number of New Guinean hunters	cost in marks
1 or none	200
2	300
3	400

Hunters are required to provide on request the following information: number of assistants, number of muzzle and breech-loaders used, number of permanent workers (carriers), area(s) where hunted, number of birds shot according to species and profit made.

Sources: Ordinances of 1891, 1892, 1907, 1911 and 1913.

The content of the bird of paradise hunting licence as issued on the 18th of March 1911 is given in Figure 50:

Licence to hunt birds of paradise

Day .... Month............... Year ....

The bearer of this licence

.... has herewith permission to hunt birds of paradise from .... until .... in Kaiser Wilhelmsland in the .... District.

The hunting may be done
a. by the bearer himself
b. by Melanesian hunters whose names appear on this licence

....

This licence is only valid in the hands of the persons named on it.

In case of abuse it can be withdrawn by the Authorities without having to give the reasons for the withdrawal, and without any claim to a refund of fees paid for it.

The further employment of native hunters can be forbidden.

If the holder of a licence changes to another district the district authorities there shall have to be informed by producing a copy of this licence. Whilst hunting the holder of this licence has to be able to produce it on demand by the authorities, likewise a Melanesian assistant must produce on demand his special licence as issued for Melanesian assistants.

The Imperial District Office...

Figure 50: Text of licence to hunt birds of paradise.
Source: Hahl 1911.

2. Export Duty

The German New Guinea government not only obtained revenue from bird hunting by charging licence fees; they also imposed an export duty (Table 15). It was first introduced for bird of paradise skins on 10 June 1908 and was increased to 2 marks per skin in 1910.[47] The rate varied according to species and increased in accordance with the world prices for skins. In 1911 the export duty on recognised commercial skins rose from 2 to 5 marks as a means of raising more revenue for the administration, rather than increasing licence fees.[48] In November 1912 the Colonial Office in Berlin requested that the export duty be raised from 5 to 20 marks.[49] Governor Hahl[50] thought this unreasonable and complained unsuccessfully about the extent of the requested rise. In 1914 it became 20 marks.[51]

Table 15: Summary of the export duties on bird of paradise skins in German New Guinea.

1908 10 June	introduced on bird of paradise skins (rate not stipulated)
1910 21 Sept.	raised to 2 marks per skin
1911	raised to 5 marks per skin
1914	raised to 20 marks per skin

A different rate was charged for rarer species shot by natural history collectors, as it was thought that if a higher duty was imposed on rare species, it would make them less attractive to commercial hunters.

The market demand for new types of plumes and the increasing prices being offered saw goura (crowned) pigeon feathers listed for the first time as an export commodity in 1911–12[52] and cassowary and egret feathers were mentioned for the first time in 1913–14.[53] Export duties were also levied on these species. In October 1913 the export duty on goura pigeons was increased from half a mark to 5 marks.[54] Whilst goura pigeons first appear in official statistics for German New Guinea from 1911–12, they had been exported from Dutch New Guinea for some time as they are mentioned in fashion magazines from the 1890s.[55]

Although some bird of paradise skins may have been smuggled across the border into Dutch New Guinea to avoid paying customs duty, the bulk of the skins shot in German New Guinea were shipped to either Singapore or Hong Kong by the North German Lloyd Line, and thence to their overseas markets. The service from Singapore visited

Friedrich Wilhelmshafen (Madang) or Stephansort (Bogadjim) four times a year.[56]

3. Closed seasons

The administration of German New Guinea also declared closed seasons as an additional way of protecting the birds; see Table 16. In 1911 a closed season was declared from the 1st of February to the 30th of April. During this time it was illegal to hunt birds of paradise.[57] In 1912–13 the hunting season was made even shorter, and hunting was made illegal between the 1st of November and the 15th of May.[58] In December 1913 the same closed season was declared for goura pigeons and cassowaries as for birds of paradise.[59]

These closed seasons were declared in an attempt to satisfy the conservationists; they had little impact on hunting practices, as most of the favoured birds were not in full plumage during the closed period. From late 1912 the Colonial Office considered a proposal to ban bird of paradise hunting for eighteen months beginning the 1 April 1914.[60] A closed season of this duration was then demanded by the Colonial Office. The German Ornithological Society did not think this was long enough and suggested a ten-year ban. This request was rejected by the German Colonial Committee for the Protection and Commercial Use of Birds, as it considered the eighteen-month ban met the immediate demands of the Society.[61] It was finally decided to enforce a one year ban from the 1st of April 1914. On the 28th of June 1914 the assassination of Archduke Franz-Ferdinand set in train a series of events in Europe leading to the outbreak of the First World War in August. By September 1914 German New Guinea had been occupied by Australian Forces, whose record in regard to bird of paradise hunting and conservation will be described below.

Table 16: Summary of the closed seasons for birds of paradise, goura pigeons and cassowaries in German New Guinea.

February 1 - April 30 (3 months) declared 18 March 1911 for birds of paradise

November 1 - May 15 (6½ months) declared 1913 (also goura pigeons and cassowaries)

Total ban from 1 April 1914 for 18 months is proposed for consideration in late 1912; a one-year ban was imposed from 1 April 1914

These closed seasons, as in Dutch New Guinea, centred on those months when the birds were not in full plumage and hunting would not have been profitable. Nevertheless there were some in German New

Guinea who considered a closed season of six and a half months as having a crippling effect on development. In their view this placed the owners of many small ventures in a difficult position, as even in 1913 there was still little trade copra available on the north coast.[62]

4. Conservation areas

In 1910 consideration was given to establishing reserves for rare and uncommon species to prevent their extinction, but this was not considered a priority as hunters were only operating in the coastal regions of Kaiser Wilhelmsland.[63] This it was believed left the birds free to retreat into the inaccessible mountains of the coastal hinterland.[64] This misconception was abandoned as more information about the distribution and habitats of different species became available.

There was also a demand for further protective measures from various outside agencies. In line with the international nature protection movement of the period, the creation of nature reserves in German colonies followed a resolution of the Plenary Session of the German Colonial Society at Stuttgart on 9 June 1911. It was proposed that in these reserves flora and fauna would be preserved and protected as in Yellowstone Park. The overall aim was to preserve the designated areas in their untouched condition for generations to come.[65] In 1912 the governor of German New Guinea declared three areas as wildlife protection areas;[66] see Table 17 and Figure 51.

Table 17: Wildlife protection areas (National Parks) in Kaiser Wilhelmsland

In 1912 three areas were declared out of bounds to bird of paradise hunters (Sack and Clark 1979: 366).

Closed Area 1	protected the Yellow Bird of Paradise (Lesser Bird of Paradise, *Paradisaea minor*). It was well known that this area was heavily hunted by Indonesian hunters.
Closed Area 2	protected the Yellow Bird of Paradise (Lesser Bird of Paradise, *Paradisaea minor*) and White Bird of Paradise (Emperor Bird of Paradise, *Paradisaea guilielmi*).
Closed Area 3	protected the habitat of the Blue (*Paradisaea rudolphi*) and Raggiana (*Paradisaea raggiana*) Birds of Paradise.

Source: (Hahl 1913a: 190–3).

It was recognised that the areas set aside as wildlife protection areas in German New Guinea had to be chosen in such a way that their existence would not interfere with current economic interests nor jeopardise the colony's future development. Doubt was expressed

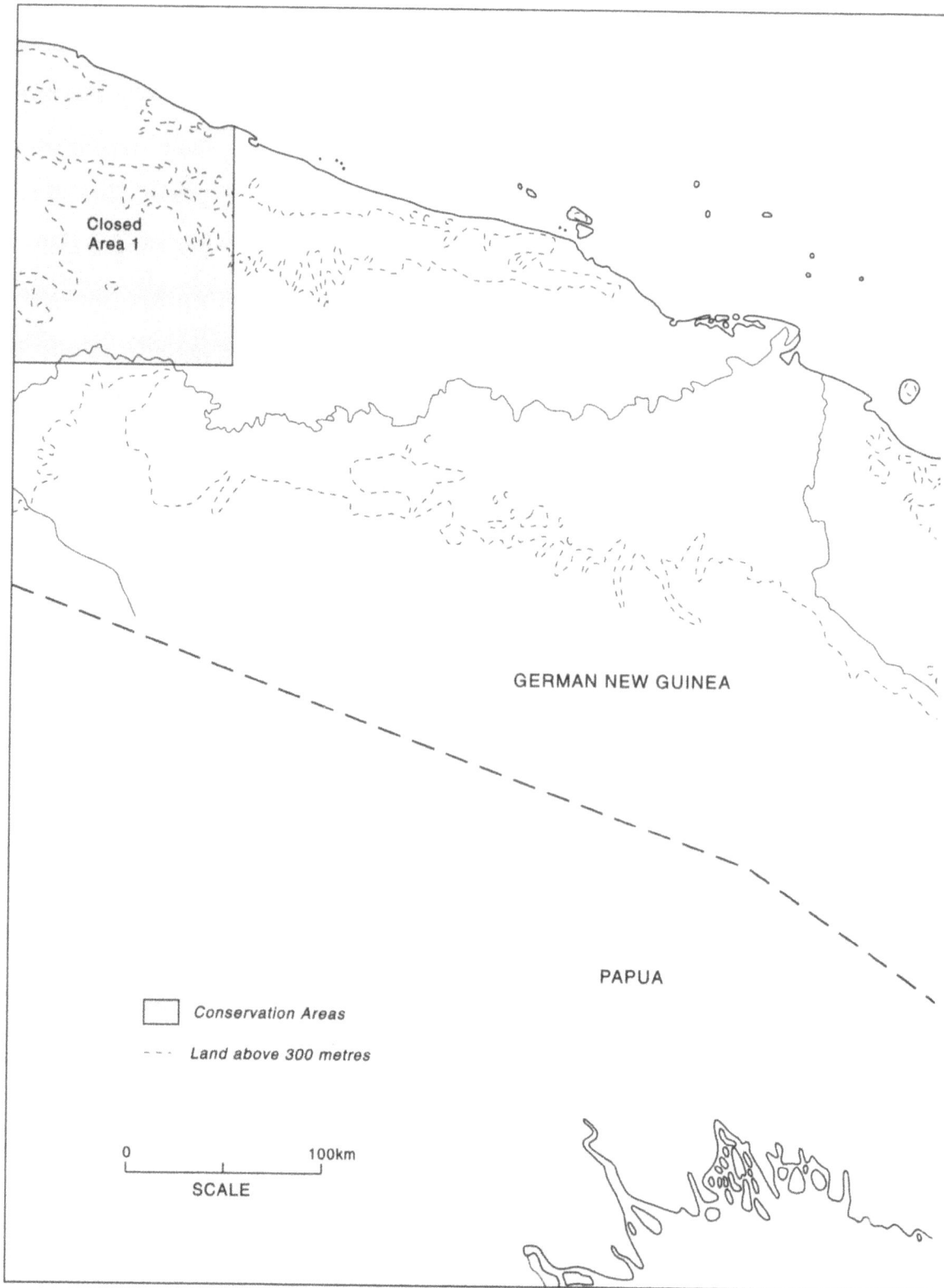

Figure 51: The conservation areas declared in Kaiser Wilhelmsland in 1912.

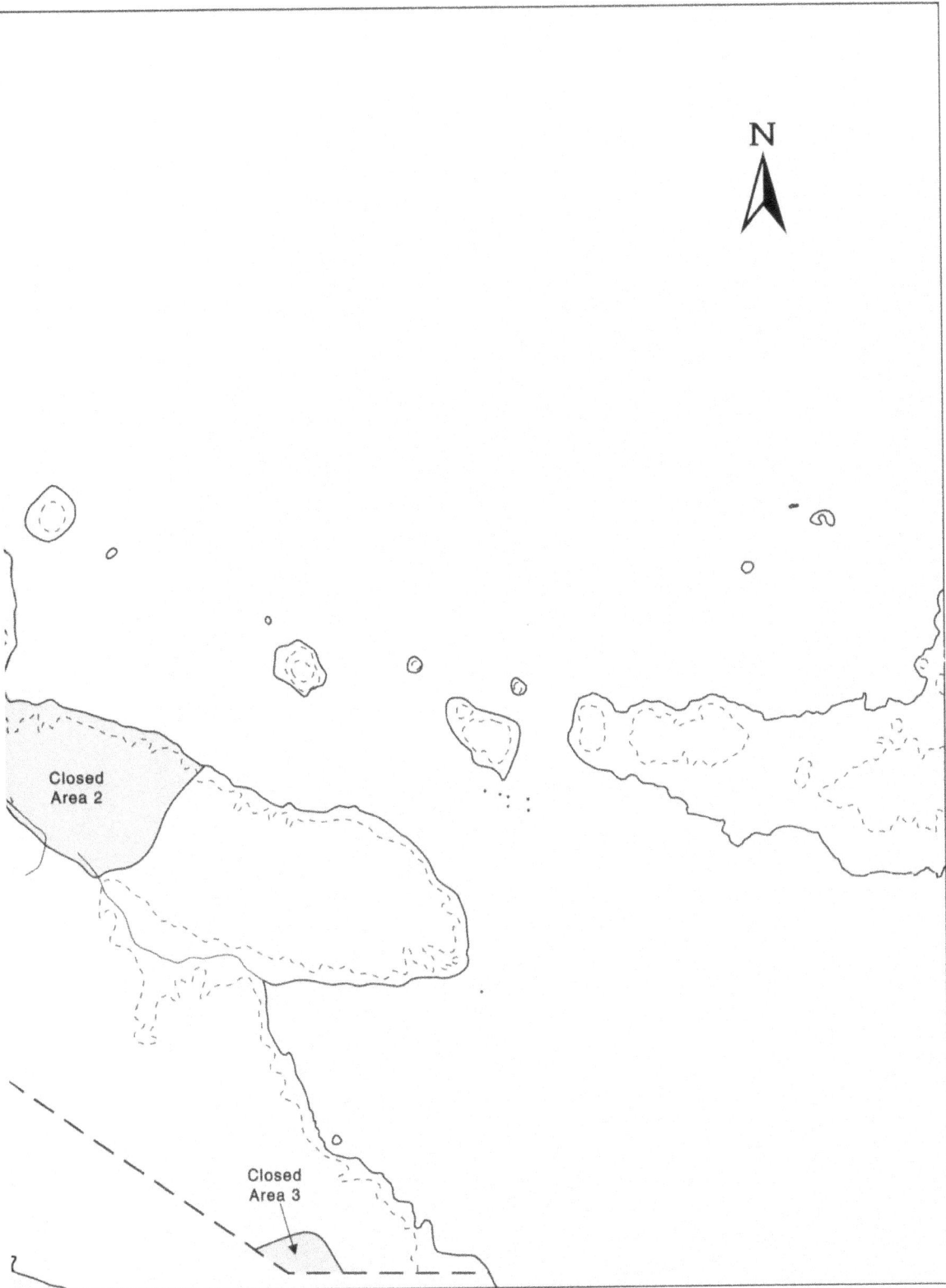

Closed
Area 2

Closed
Area 3

about the administration's ability to declare nature reserves in perpetuity when little was known about the resources of the areas concerned. There seemed little advantage in declaring an area protected if it was later allowed to be exploited because rich resources were subsequently found to be present.[67]

The main bird of paradise species hunted in German New Guinea for the European plume trade were the Lesser Bird of Paradise, the Raggiana Bird of Paradise, Augusta Victoria, a subspecies of the latter, and the Emperor Bird of Paradise. Their gregarious display habits meant that the hunters could find large numbers of these birds together and get good returns for their time. Sometimes a hunter would find a dozen birds displaying together in a cluster of trees. Less important were the Blue, King and Magnificent Birds of Paradise and Stephanie's Astrapia. These species are more difficult to hunt as they generally display alone.[68]

Skilled hunters learnt the habits of the birds they sought. Thomas Gilliard[69] describes the technique used by Adolph Batze to hunt the King Bird of Paradise in the Markham River forests. Walking through the forest Batze would make a short, medium-strength, ascending whistle, followed by a rapid series of shorter, lower notes, every half a kilometre. He would then stop and listen. Batze's call seemed to agitate King Birds of Paradise as any bird in the vicinity would invariably respond from his tall forest tree.

The natural distributions of the main species hunted in German New Guinea for the European plume trade are shown in Figure 52. The Lesser Bird of Paradise was obtained from an area extending from the Upper Ramu Valley in the east to the Dutch border in the west. Raggiana, including the Augusta Victoria subspecies, would have been shot in the Markham Valley, the southeast part of the Huon Peninsula and around Morobe Station. Most of the Blue Birds of Paradise were shot in the mountains behind Morobe, and others may have been taken in the mountains to the south of both the Ramu and Markham Rivers. The Emperor Bird of Paradise is restricted to the hills and mountains of the Huon Peninsula. The King is common in coastal lowlands and the Magnificent is found on lower mountain slopes. Most of the Stephanie's Astrapia would have been shot in the mountains inland of Salamaua.

An examination of the locations of the three protection areas (Figure 51) suggests that they were chosen partly to protect the birds, but also to provide legislation against Indonesian plume hunters. Prior to 1912 area 1 was mainly visited by Indonesian bird of paradise hunters illegally crossing over from Dutch New Guinea, rather than hunters operating from within German New Guinea. The presence of these Indonesian hunters irritated the German administration, but they had insufficient resources to monitor and stop their illegal border crossings. Occasionally German patrols would catch Indonesian plume hunters operating across the border. One incident occurred near the border in 1912, the two men caught were set adrift in their canoe. When it was washed ashore sometime later at Wutung (Figure 48), it was evident that they had died from starvation.[70]

Area 2 is now known to be a marginal area for both the Lesser and Emperor Birds of Paradise which it was declared to protect. The Lesser is only found in the western and the Emperor only in the eastern parts of Area 2. Protecting species in marginal areas where they are vulnerable to overhunting is a good conservation strategy.[71]

Area 3 protected the Blue and Raggiana Birds of Paradise inland of Morobe Station. This too was probably a good conservation strategy.

Anyone caught hunting in these reserves faced a month in jail or a 1,000 mark fine. This measure was taken to ensure that all species would survive the period of commercial hunting. The official view of the administration in German New Guinea was that the danger would be over once fashions changed and the value of plumes subsequently declined on the world market.

Size of hunting parties and employment of assistant hunters and traders

In 1910 the Hernsheim Company in Hamburg requested permission to establish a large hunting company in German New Guinea. This company had been founded in 1872 when the Hernsheim brothers became the first copra traders in the New Guinea Islands. Despite the company's long history in German New Guinea, the Hernsheim proposal was turned down by the administration.

The proposal outlined an efficient hunting venture that would shoot large numbers of birds and thus be extremely profitable. The company wanted to employ 10 New Guinean hunters who together would shoot some 1,000 birds each year. W.J. Hahn of Hatzfeldthafen Plantation was to supervise operations.[72] It was estimated that this would earn the administration 2,000 marks from licences and 2,000 marks from export duty. Governor Hahl rejected their application as he believed that large-scale ventures would soon exterminate the birds from the areas where they were allowed to operate. For this reason all entrepreneurs were restricted to a limited number of hunters.

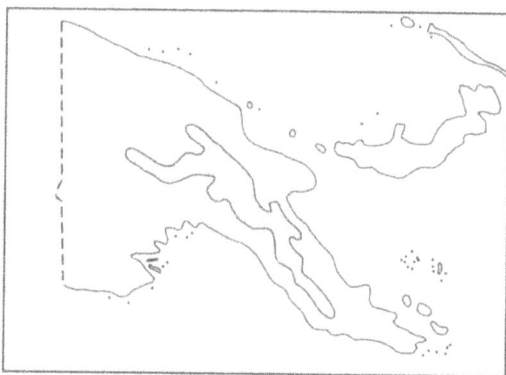

Blue Bird of Paradise

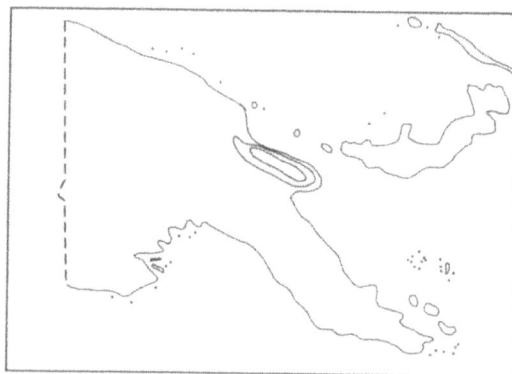

Emperor Bird of Paradise

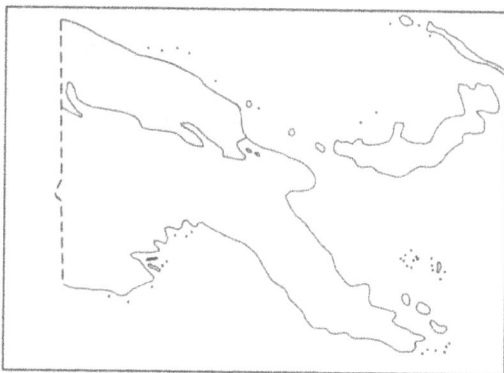

Lesser Bird of Paradise

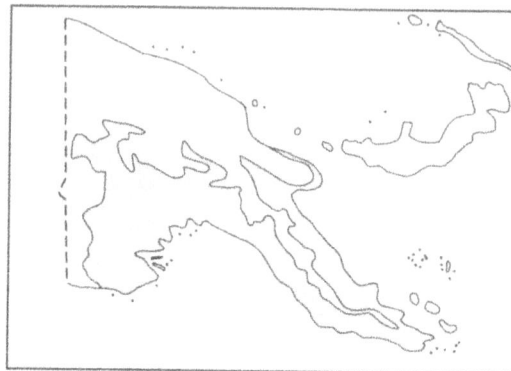

Raggiana Bird of Paradise

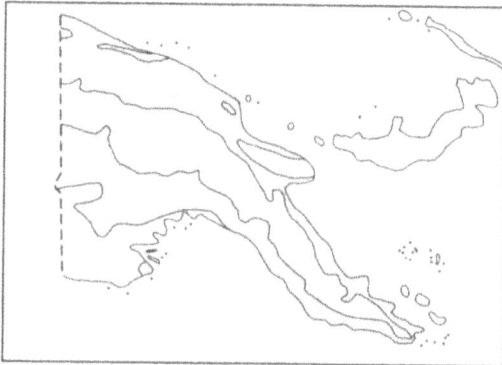

King Bird of Paradise

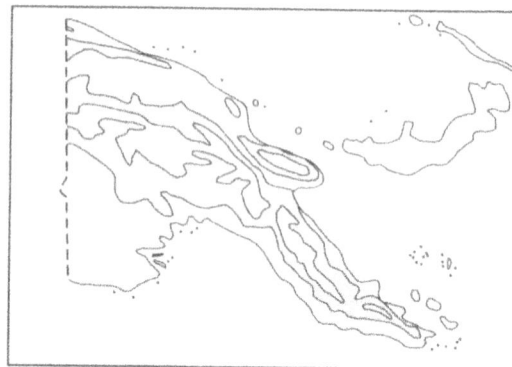

Magnificent Bird of Paradise

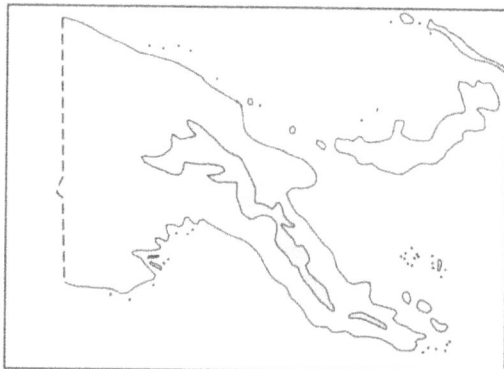

Stephanie's Astrapia

Figure 52: The natural distribution of the Blue, Emperor, King, Lesser, Magnificent and Raggiana Birds of Paradise and Stephanie's Astrapia. **Source:** Based on Coates 1990. Beehler 1993.

The administration expressed concern about the size of New Guinean bird hunting parties for a second reason. This was the detrimental impact they could have if they joined with coastal communities and bullied little-contacted inland communities. Apart from control of group size, New Guinean hunters were also restricted to using muzzle-loaders which were suitable for hunting birds of paradise, but less effective for shooting people than bullet-firing guns.[73] The main guns used for bird hunting were either 12, 16 or 410 gauge shotguns.[74] In order to prevent pay-back killings by hunters in their home areas, they were not permitted to hunt in the vicinity of their own villages.

It became a requirement in 1911 that the employment of more than one assistant was only possible if his employer took up residence in Kaiser Wilhelmsland and became engaged in establishing a plantation or some other business.[75]

Bird of paradise hunting assistants were New Guineans, Indonesians or Chinese in the employ of Europeans. Each year when the hunting season began, small columns of men could often be seen leaving coastal settlements for inland areas to hunt birds of paradise usually under the leadership of Europeans.[76] Plates 38 and 39 show New Guinean hunters after their return from successful hunting trips.

Indonesians and Chinese, initially from Singapore and later from Hong Kong, were recruited by the Germans to work in German New Guinea. The Indonesians willingly came and successfully worked as hunters, traders and plantation labourers, but they returned home after they had saved a few hundred marks. The Germans were unable to persuade them, or others they brought in as plantation labourers, to settle down and cultivate the land.[77]

In the early 1970s, the old people in the Dreikikir area of the Torricelli Mountains could still remember when the first Indonesian and Chinese hunters and traders came into their area (Figure 48). These hunter/traders worked out of the trading posts established on the coast at Yakamul, Ulau and Suain. They followed the north-flowing rivers inland. Eye-witness accounts suggest that when the Indonesians and Chinese first went inland they were not prepared for long expeditions and did not expect to find large populations lying behind the coastal mountains.[78] Most of the Indonesians and Chinese were accompanied by coastal men. Their parties were guided by men from the Torricelli Mountain villages who could speak the Kombio and Wam dialects spoken in the villages they visited. Once contact was made, they usually returned to the same villages and traded goods such as knives, beads, paint, cloth and salt for skins.[79] This contact rather than intrusion from the border probably explains how people in the Yellow River area became more proficient in Malay than people further west.[80]

Plate 38: A New Guinean bird of paradise hunter in German New Guinea with his gun and catch, which includes Lesser Birds of Paradise and pigeons. The latter would be for eating.

Source: Gash and Whittaker 1975, from M. von Hein Collection, Sydney.

Some hunters and traders penetrated to villages south of Lumi. When E. W. Oakley, then assistant district officer, was attempting with a surveyor to find a vehicle road route from the Sepik River to Aitape in this area in 1932, their camp was rushed by an armed party of fifty men. Two Vanimo constables recognised a few Malay pidgin words and soon found they had encountered people who had formerly been in touch with Indonesian plume traders. These traders had lived at Yerimi hamlet and Tabatinka village for some months, whilst engaged in bird hunting.[81] Alan Marshall[82] similarly reports the former presence of Indonesian traders in the Lumi area and notes that further west people could still speak a few words of pidgin Malay. At Bogasip village in 1935 people brought bird of paradise plumes to Marshall's party eager to trade. The plumes were mainly those of the Lesser Bird of Paradise (*Paradisaea minor*).

Interaction between hunters and local communities

The slaughtering of beautiful birds was only one of the unpleasant aspects of the plume trade. Many people also suffered as a result of this activity and we can assume that new diseases were introduced. Concern about the impact of bird of paradise hunters on inland communities was expressed both by the authors of newspaper articles, for example Schillings 1912,[83] and government officials, for example Ebert 1912.[84] They were especially concerned about those people uncontacted by the administration who had no means of voicing their complaints. Apart from having their birds and other game shot, their gardens were probably also raided. Commander Ebert of the *Cormoran*, who in 1912 was making an official political and military report on German New Guinea, stressed the need to recognise local practices. He understood that hill-country people regarded everything that flew and walked around in their forests as their property. To hunt birds of paradise in the forests without the consent of the local land owners had to be seen as a serious breach of their rights. Some bird of paradise hunters took this into account and paid the people who owned the bush where they were hunting. This was evidently the practice of the Chinese and Indonesians visiting the Lumi area. Those who did not pay were frequently attacked as this was the hill-country people's reaction to unwelcome strangers intruding into their territory.

Unlike most Indonesian and Chinese hunter/traders working in the Sepik area, some European hunters such as Alfred Mikulicz came into conflict with the local people. In August 1912, Mikulicz and two other Europeans were hunting with their assistants down the right bank of the Ramu, eight to ten days' walk from Alexishafen. Mikulicz had seven men with him and on this expedition they had already been involved in four fights. After setting up camp, he rested there with his cook boy whilst the others went hunting birds of paradise. The camp was attacked by the local people and he was speared to death. The cook boy raised the alarm, but by the time the other hunting groups arrived at the camp, there was no sign of Mikulicz or the local people.[85]

A number of Europeans, Indonesians and New Guineans hunting birds of paradise in inland regions were attacked in German New Guinea. Those on record are listed below:

Table 18: Plume hunters attacked whilst shooting in German New Guinea.

year	who and where
1907–8	Indonesian hunter was killed in Hatzfeldthafen area and his firearms seized. Germans made a punitive expedition.
1908–9	Umlauft and New Guinean assistant were shot at with arrows while in Rai Coast mountains. Escaped without injury.
1909–10	European hunter was killed by Wamba people in hinterland of Herzog Range on the right bank of the Markham River. Punitive expedition killed 40 people and burnt several villages.
1912 June	Peterson had been a medical assistant for the New Guinea Company for about a year, when he decided to go bird of paradise hunting. He was killed inland of Madang. A punitive expedition from 21–26 June arrested the main culprits, killed five men and burnt Bemari village. Police were left to carry out further punitive measures.
1912 July	Three Chinese and ten New Guinean assistants employed by the Hansa Bay planter Gramms were killed by Kagam tribes inland of Hansa Bay. A punitive expedition was made.
1912 August	Alfred Miculicz before becoming an independent bird of paradise hunter had been a planter in the employ of the German New Guinea Company. He was killed on the right bank of the upper Ramu eight to ten days' walk from Alexishafen. Miculicz was one of a group of three European hunters and their assistants who had been involved in four fights with inland communities.
mid 1913	Two Europeans were attacked in the hinterland of Laden. Shot at with arrows whilst bathing in a stream. Rifle fire made the attackers flee.
1913 July	Indonesian and two New Guinean assistants were killed in hinterland of Sarang. Their rifles were voluntarily sent to the coast and given to government officers.

Sources: Anon 1912d: 139; Ebert 1912; Preuss 1912: 123; Sack and Clark 1979: 277, 292, 322, 354; Sack and Clark 1980: 9–10; Schillings 1912.

While some hunters were killed, others were lucky enough to escape. The German administration stressed that it was not possible, in terms of the cost and personnel required, to punish all the groups involved in these incidents. Bird hunters and gold prospectors were therefore requested to restrict their activities to areas where there was some guarantee for their personal safety. It was advised that they should not venture beyond those areas where the local people recognised German authority.[86]

Plate 39: New Guinean bird of paradise hunters in German New Guinea with guns and Lesser Birds of Paradise they have shot.
Source: Lyng 1919.

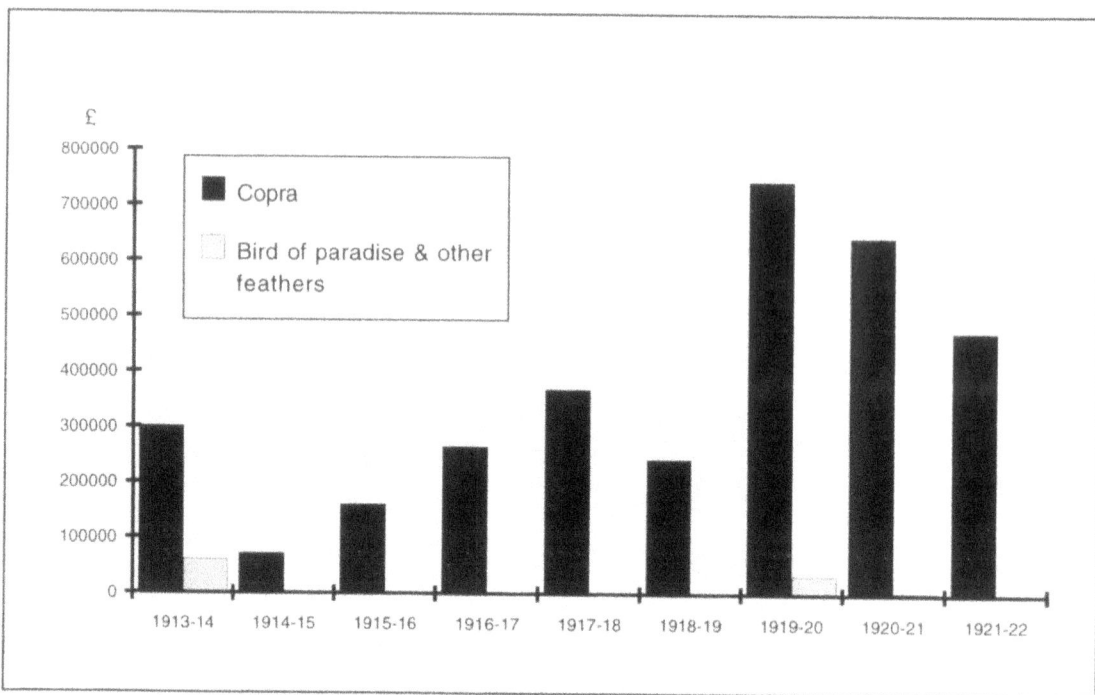

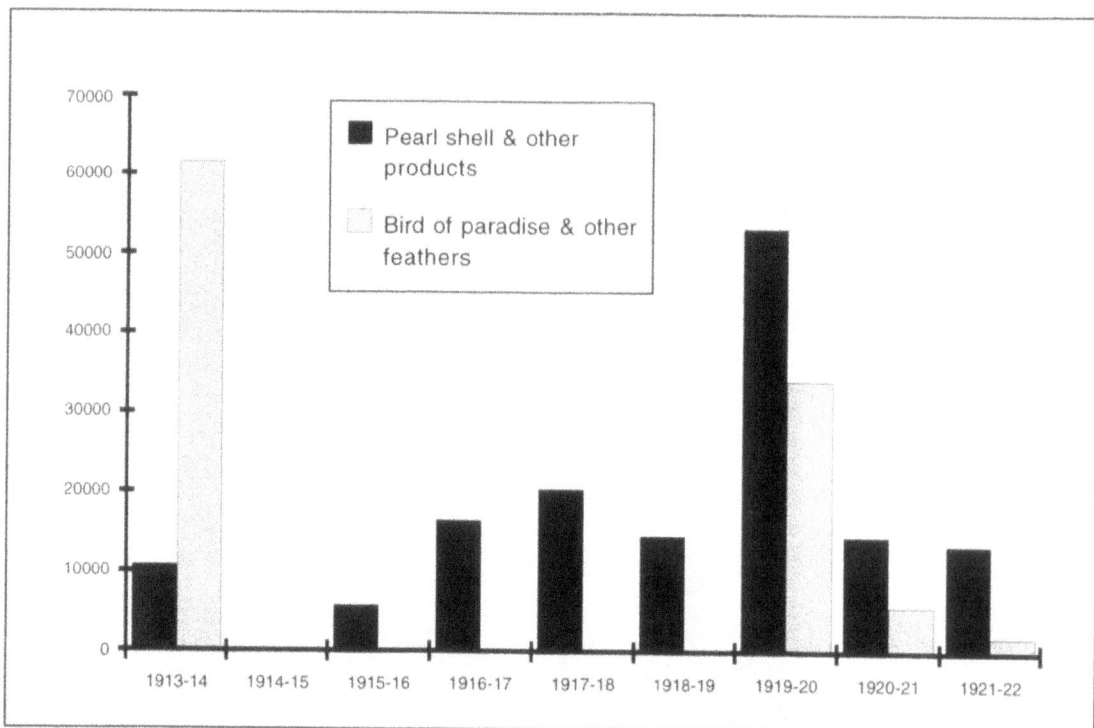

Implications of German legislation for Melanesian villagers

When studying a draft of a new ordinance in 1912, Busse, the Privy Counsellor at the Colonial Office in Berlin, raised the issue that the draft did not consider independent hunting by New Guineans. He wanted to know whether they should be required to obtain a licence and pay the required fee in order to hunt cassowaries.[87] This was probably recognised as an unenforceable piece of legislation, as the matter was not given any further attention.

Role in development

Figure 53: The value of copra and birds of paradise (and other feathers) exported from German New Guinea and the Mandated Territory of New Guinea from 1913–1922.

Source: New Guinea Annual Reports 1914–1922.

The two main exports from German New Guinea in 1910 were trade copra and bird of paradise skins. Village production remained dominant as only some 20 per cent of the copra exported was produced on plantations.[88] Copra yielded the highest returns. In 1910–11, 9,244 tonnes of copra earned 3,039,000 marks, whereas skins only brought in 171,000 marks.[89] This was the case for the colony as a whole (see Figures 53 and 54), but bird of paradise plumes were the main revenue earner for Kaiser Wilhelmsland. This discrepancy between the export earnings of the New Guinea mainland and the New Guinea Islands made Rabaul the financial capital of German New Guinea. By 1909 it had also become the administrative capital as well.

Plume "fever"

Many features of bird of paradise hunting were like prospecting. This similarity was not missed by the administration of German New Guinea who likened bird of paradise hunting to a small-scale gold fever, with all its associated bad aspects and unpleasant incidents, in their 1911–2 report.[90]

Many prospectors took up bird hunting after unsuccessful prospecting expeditions. This was the case with the three experienced Australian prospectors who were unsuccessful in their search for gold in the upper Markham River area.[91] Other men probably combined both activities, and some may have kept their eyes open for stands of wild rubber. In a few cases hunters reported interesting finds. An Indonesian hunter based at a coastal trading station reported oil-bearing deposits near Eitape (Aitape) in 1913.[92]

The investment by hunters in plantations

Figure 54: The value of birds of paradise (and other feathers) and pearl shell (and other marine products) exported from German New Guinea and the Mandated Territory of New Guinea from 1913–1922.

Source: New Guinea Annual Reports 1914–1922.

According to Paul Preuss,[93] a director of the New Guinea Company, the majority of planters in German New Guinea were former company employees. Many took the opportunity provided by the rising plume prices to establish their own plantations. Settlers usually worked in pairs or groups of three when plume revenue was used to fund new plantations. One would work their jointly purchased plantation, whereas the other partner(s) hunted birds of paradise. The income derived from the sale of the bird skins paid for its development. This practice was encouraged by the administration, as all licensed hunters were required to clear land and plant about 50 hectares of coconuts each year.

Many planters only survived the seven or more years they had to wait, between the planting and harvesting of their first paying crop of copra, because of the ready cash they got from bird hunting. Their palms did not begin bearing fruit until after 6–7 years of growth and reached full bearing only after 10–12 years.[94]

One of the pioneer planters who got his start through bird hunting was Adolph Batze of Lae. Accompanied by his father and two brothers, he reached New Guinea from Germany in 1906. Each hunting season the four Batzes went hunting and each man brought in between 200 to 700 birds. On a good day Adolph Batze claims he got 50–60 Augusta Victoria (a subspecies of Raggiana) and several King Birds of Paradise. While in the field, they skinned the birds and treated the skins with arsenical soap.[95] The average price paid per bird in 1910–11 was 35–40 marks but in 1911–12 it fell to 30–35 marks.[96]

In the two years prior to 1 January 1913, thirteen plantations with 20 owners were established in Kaiser Wilhelmsland. These enterprises covered a total of 4,850 hectares and brought under cultivation some 1,138 hectares (Table 19). By the end of 1913, it was envisaged that another 1,000 hectares would be brought under cultivation.[97]

The plantations ranged in size from small enterprises to large holdings, but their continued existence and development was dependent on bird of paradise skin sales. Without an income from bird of paradise hunting these small independent enterprises did not have sufficient capital to stay afloat, nor were they sufficiently developed to obtain loans or mortgages. The standard of living on these north coast plantations was based on a shoe-string budget, but thanks to bird of paradise hunting they kept going with the expectation that once their coconuts started yielding they would be able to achieve a comfortable standard of living. The option of selling out to big wealthy firms was not attractive, nor in the view of the plantation owners was it in the interests of the colony for a number of reasons. Firstly, unlike the large companies, they were not transitory workers. Owner-planters had a long-term commitment to their plantation and were thus concerned about the well-being of German New Guinea. Secondly, like missionaries, they promoted development as they were dependent on neighbouring villages and for this reason also cultivated friendly relations with them. Thirdly, unlike large companies, they could not afford to recruit staff from distant places, but were dependent on local workers whom they trained. Finally, they obtained food from neighbouring villages in return for trade goods. By supplying villagers with iron tools, clothing, and the like, the villagers obtained improved living conditions.

Table 19: Planter settlers in 1913 who had established plantations in the last two years and were dependent on income from bird of paradise hunting to finance their plantations. (This list consists of those who signed the petition against the proposed legislation to prohibit bird of paradise hunting.)

area	owners(s)	plantation size in hectares	hectares planted	number of coconut palms	number of employees
Eitape (Aitape)	Bechner	150	30	3,000	33
Eitape (Aitape)	Piper	200	90	12,600	50
Boiken	Brinkmann	150	100	10,000	62
Moem	Peuker	500	100	10,000[a]	46
Awar	Gramms	500	250	30,000[b]	80
Hatzfeldthafen	Hahn, W.J.	500	100	10,000	75
Sarang	Stiller	150	30	3,900[c]	30
Sarang	Kempt and Sturm	1,000	30	-	60
Sangana (Karkar Is.)	Andexer and Merseburger	200	83	5,100[d]	103
Alexishafen	Penn	500	-	-[e]	-
not stated	Glasemann and Kempter	400	120	10,000	93
not stated	Ahr and Gathen	400	20	2,000	60
not stated	Meiro Company	200	175	5,000[f]	112

Other crops
a. some rice had also been planted
b. 3.5 hectares with 1,400 ficus trees
c. hemp and bananas
d. 12,600 Hevea (rubber) trees
e. some rice was planted in 1913
f. 200 hectares with 45,000 coffee trees

Source: Hahl 1913a: 208.

The owner-planters believed that the administration should be able to benefit from the plume boom, but its fees should not be so large as to deprive them of a reasonable return for their efforts. The introduction of the 20 mark export duty was more than they could bear. To obtain profitable returns with such a duty level, a market value of 50 marks per skin was required. This price was rarely obtained at that time. In their view the introduction of a 20 mark export fee as well as an increased licence fee would be ruinous.[98]

Conservation demands

In Germany there were frequent calls to prohibit the hunting of birds of paradise in German New Guinea. When Governor Hahl was there in 1910, he gained first hand experience of the widespread protests against bird of paradise hunting organised by the Association of Friends concerned with the Protection of Nature, Animals and Birds.[99]

Those opposing the ban were adamant that not only would it ruin certain planters, but it would also weaken the economy. Their argument was that further taxes would have to be imposed to cover the deficit previously met by hunters' licence fees and the taxes imposed on exported plumes.

By 1911 the conservation call was gaining momentum in Germany. Many articles appeared in German newspapers dealing with New Guinea in general and birds of paradise in particular.[100]

For a while it was thought that the birds were free to retreat into the inaccessible mountains of the coastal hinterland,[101] as hunters were only operating in the coastal regions of Kaiser Wilhelmsland.[102] In a newspaper article dated the 29th of September 1911, Professor Richard Neuhauss,[103] an anthropologist, pointed out that this was a totally misguided view which would have tragic consequences. He explained that coastal areas are the natural habitat of many of the species being hunted, consequently they cannot be expected to save themselves by retreating into the mountains. Neuhauss called on the government to prevent the extinction of birds of paradise by prohibiting their commercial hunting.

The German public reacted in different ways. Some were concerned about the birds, whereas others used the issue for political ends. Those interested in the birds fell into three main camps. These consisted of those who proposed a complete ban on hunting, those who would permit some hunting but demanded greater protection, and finally those who wanted to put the birds into reserves where they could be bred in captivity. In contrast members of the Social Democrat party used the issue to criticise Germany's colonial activities.[104]

There was considerable discussion about breeding birds of paradise in captivity in the same way as pheasants were bred in Europe and ostriches in southwest Africa.[105] The administration of German New Guinea declined to be involved in investigating this idea, but agreed to help finance such an enterprise if it was shown to be viable and profitable.[106]

Several specialists were drawn into this debate. Professor Heck, Director of the Berlin Zoological Gardens, considered that more could be achieved by making rules and laws about bird of paradise hunting than by breeding them in reserves or in captivity. Birds kept in his zoo had not bred. He also mentioned the conservation measure of releasing birds of paradise on Little Tobago in the West Indies;[107] see also Chapters 5 and 9.

Further information was also sought. J. Bürgers, the zoologist and medical doctor of the Empress Augusta (Sepik) River Expedition was asked to observe as much as possible about the habits, habitats and numbers of birds of paradise in the Sepik.[108] He did not restrict his activities to birds of paradise, but made a general collection which has become a landmark in New Guinea ornithology. He collected some 3,100 specimens of 240 bird species, mainly from the Middle and Upper Sepik.[109]

By 1912 there was a strong call for a complete ban on the hunting of all species of decorative birds. A large number of articles appeared in newspapers and periodicals protesting against the slaughter of birds of paradise and a resolution was tabled in the German Parliament.[110] It was proposed that a ban should be introduced on the 1st of April 1914. If this was enforced, the administration of German New Guinea would have to cease being dependent on the proceeds from hunting and exporting of bird of paradise skins as a reliable source of public revenue. When faced with finding the predicted 40,000 marks shortfall for the 1914 budget, the Colonial Ministry requested that the opinion of the German Financial Minister be sought before going ahead with the proposed ban.[111]

It was the view of the German New Guinea administration that a total ban on the hunting and shooting of birds of paradise could not be immediately introduced and made to work effectively for two reasons. Firstly, there were no alternative local means within Kaiser Wilhelmsland of raising the shortfall in government revenue as there was insufficient trade copra and little pearl shell, apart from the green snail shell obtained from Tarawai and Walis Islands (Figure 48). Secondly, the plantation enterprises established so far would only be economically viable once their palms started yielding copra, but this was not yet the case and they would be subject to considerable losses if there was a total ban on hunting. The governor was requested to determine when a complete ban could be proclaimed without harming established economic interests.[112]

Berlin was keen to introduce a complete ban as from 1 April 1914 which would expire in May 1915. In preparation for such a ban the administration of German New Guinea was instructed to exclude expected bird of paradise revenues from the 1914 budget. They were also instructed to inform intending settlers and plantation owners of Kaiser Wilhelmsland that they could no longer expect to finance their enterprises from bird of paradise hunting.[113]

Over the years the administration of German New Guinea had taken considerable measures to protect the birds and at the same time avert a hunting prohibition. They had licensed hunting, declared three special reserves, prohibited hunting for six and a half months each year and levied high taxes on rare species. When the Secretary of the Colonial Office instructed Hahl to raise fourfold the export duty on plumes, he responded by saying that this rise was less acceptable than a complete ban on hunting.[114] In 1913–14 Hahl planned to restrict hunting to those involved in the economic development of Kaiser Wilhelmsland, namely the planters and those engaged in activities such as prospecting which opened up hitherto uncontacted areas. He intended to issue only 20–30 licences and had declared three closed conservation areas. These measures in his view would adequately protect the birds of paradise from extinction.[115]

Most staff of the German Colonial Office in Berlin saw the hunting and exporting of bird of paradise skins from German New Guinea as a short-term source of private and public revenue that could now be discontinued.[116] The Secretary, Dr. Solf, personally supported the banning of bird of paradise hunting. His views and particularly his address to the German Agricultural Society resulted in congratulory letters from a number of conservation organisations.[117]

By 1913 the conservationists were adamant that the measures proposed by the administration of German New Guinea were inadequate to ensure the survival of birds of paradise. Nature lovers in Germany wanted nothing less than a total ban on bird of paradise hunting. The Association for the Protection of Birds petitioned the Kaiser of Germany and the King of Prussia on the 21st of February 1913 to press for a ban on the shooting of birds of paradise so that the decimated birds would have a chance to recover.[118] The German Colonial Office in Berlin was keen to enforce a complete ban, comparable to that in force in British New Guinea, but was hesitant to do so as they envisaged more hunters would infiltrate from Dutch New Guinea.[119] The Kaiser believed that the rise in export dues did not improve the situation and that the only solution was a complete ban on the shooting of birds of paradise. He requested that such a ban be enforced immediately without waiting for the Dutch to introduce comparable legislation for Dutch New Guinea.[120] The Secretary for the Colonial Office carried out these instructions and advised the Governor of German New Guinea to impose a complete ban for one year. During this period district officers were to review the situation by surveying what was known about the habits and breeding seasons of the birds so that this information could be used to ensure that the birds were saved from extinction.[121]

Australian administration

Australian occupying forces took over German New Guinea in September 1914. Until a peace treaty was signed and the future sovereignty of German New Guinea determined, international law did not allow the Australians to change existing legislation except in cases of military necessity.[122] The German law in force permitted licensed hunters to shoot birds of paradise in the Mandated Territory of New Guinea from May 1915.

In German times there had been some smuggling of bird of paradise skins across the border into Dutch New Guinea during the hunting ban and this continued after the Australians took over in 1914. The Australians found it difficult to control the coastal movement of Germans into Dutch New Guinea. This led to a standing patrol being established at Vanimo to prevent German citizens from making contact with enemy agents in Dutch New Guinea.[123] The Australians suspected that uncensored letters were being smuggled to Hollandia by coastal schooners involved in the illegal trafficking of bird of paradise skins.[124]

Apart from possible espionage during smuggling activities, the Australians monitored bird of paradise hunting because it meant that certain civilians possessed firearms. The military administration took steps to control the possession of these weapons. Each owner was required to obtain a licence from the senior military officer in his district.[125]

The military administration did not interfere with the hunting licences in force nor did they take steps to seize the large quantity of plumes stored for export. Although it had been illegal from 1913 to import bird of paradise skins into Australia,[126] the Australian military administration imposed no restrictions on their export to other countries. However, since bird of paradise hunting was prohibited in neighbouring Papua, it was widely recognised that the Commonwealth government would eventually take steps to discourage and prohibit the export of plumes from former German New Guinea.[127]

These steps began in 1915. In August of that year, any persons possessing more than 3 bird of paradise skins, 12 goura pigeon crests or 6 heron (egret) sprays were required to register their collections.[128] Customs duty was imposed on bird plumes in 1916; see Table 20.

Table 20: Customs duty imposed on bird plumes in New Guinea in 1916.

species	rate
birds of paradise (portions and feathers of one bird)	£1 each
goura pigeon (portions and feathers of one bird)	5 shillings each
cassowary feathers	12 shillings 6 pence per lb
heron (egret) feathers	£25 per lb

Source: Customs Duties Ordinance of New Guinea (Rabaul) Gazette, 15 May 1916: 47.

After the end of the First World War in November 1918 the plume trade resumed. During this period the export value of bird of paradise skins fell behind not only copra but also pearl shell and other marine products; see Figures 53 and 54.

The question which is not easily answered is how many of the bird of paradise skins and other feathers exported from the Mandated Territory of New Guinea were skins brought out of storage after the war (as happened in Merauke) or were from birds hunted at the time. Many were probably recently acquired as the months with the highest exports (May–June in 1919–20 and August in 1921–22) fall in the hunting period for birds of paradise.

The plantations which had been established during the German colonial period were expropriated by the Australian Expropriation Board as part of the international policy adopted by the victors of World War I of making Germany pay reparations. It also reflected the antagonism felt by Australians towards Germans. This had begun when the Germans annexed northeast New Guinea and had increased during the war.[129]

The president of the Australian Expropriation Board who made decisions about expropriations in New Guinea was Walter Lucas, a representative of Burns Philp Company, one of the largest Australian trading companies operating in the Pacific. In retrospect the plantation settlers in Kaiser Wilhelmsland were poorly treated. During the war the settlers had continued to develop and expand their plantations, never envisaging, even with Germany's defeat, that they would be dispossessed. By the end of the war these plantations were viable commercial enterprises, but their developers were never compensated for their efforts.[130]

In 1920 an export ordinance was passed. Any individual, firm or company who possessed plumes they wished to export had to register them with the Department of Trade and Customs in Rabaul. These plumes had to have been acquired before the end of February 1920 and exported before early March 1921.[131] The closing date was later extended to the end of December.[132] On the 1st of January 1922 bird of paradise skins were a prohibited export from the Mandated Territory of New Guinea as former German New Guinea had now become.[133] In order to prevent bird of paradise skins from being smuggled into Dutch New Guinea, the administration reestablished an office at Vanimo. It had been withdrawn during the war. A district officer was based there until after 1931, when plume hunting became illegal throughout Dutch New Guinea. It was not until 1936 that Wewak was made the main government station on the Sepik coast.[134]

Special licences were only granted in the Mandated Territory of New Guinea, as in Papua, to the duly accredited agents of a government, a museum, zoological or acclimatization society, or other scientific institution. Legislation passed in 1922 allowed such agents to either shoot or capture and subsequently export birds of paradise, goura pigeons and white herons under permits restricting the numbers collected.[135]

Notes

1. This was how the first Chinese came to Papua New Guinea. Other Chinese were brought by the German administration to work as labourers, initially from Singapore, but later from Hong Kong (Wu: 1977: 1047; Hahl 1980: 145).

2. Parkinson 1979: 40.

3. A variant spelling of *kelapa*, the Malay word for coconut.

4. Kachau, Saulep and Pinjong 1980: 18.

5. Hahl 1980: 109–10; 120. This means that itinerant traders and hunters from Dutch New Guinea were not welcome in German New Guinea, whereas Indonesians who came either to work as hunters or traders, or to settle, were encouraged. They willingly came to work for German employers as hunters and traders, but returned to Dutch New Guinea after they had saved a few hundred marks. None wished to settle and cultivate the land (Hahl 1980: 144).

6. A similar restriction led to the end of the Makassarese trepang industry on the north coast of Australia in 1906. From that date trepang collecting licences were only issued to locally owned boats (Macknight 1971–2: 284).

7. Hahl 1980: 110.

8. Seiler 1985: 147.

9. Molnar-Bagley 1982: 25.

10. Gell 1975: 2.

11. Cheesman 1960: 27–8.

12. This remarkable woman made many expeditions to the Pacific collecting insects for the British Museum and other museums from 1923–54. Overall she spent some six years in New Guinea (Huie 1990).

13. Cheesman 1941: 184–5; also in 1949: 270–1.
14. Mackenzie 1934: 313.
15. Hahl 1980: 109, 120.
16. Deklin 1979: 33.
17. Robinson 1934–5.
18. Gilliard 1969: 26–7; Townsend 1968: 63–6.
19. Bryant Allen personal communication 1991.
20. Robinson 1934–5.
21. Schultze-Westrum 1969: 300.
22. Cheesman 1938a: 42.
23. Although slow to be colonised, New Guinea has not lacked in flag raising. The first instance was as early as 1545 when New Guinea was claimed for Spain when de Retes landed just east of the Mamberamo River mouth in what is now West Papua (Figure 42).
24. see Whittaker et al 1975: 459.
25. van der Veur 1972: 277.
26. In 1884–6 Germany took possession of Kaiser Wilhelmsland (northeast mainland New Guinea), the Bismarck Archipelago, the Solomon Islands and islands in Micronesia (Hahl 1980: 6). The Bismarck Archipelago was included as German traders and labour recruiters had been active, with other nationalities, in the Duke of York Islands and the Gazelle Peninsula of New Britain for almost a decade.
27. Jacobs 1972: 486.
28. Jacobs 1972: 486–7; Sack and Clark 1979: 133–4: May 1989: 114.
29. Sack and Clark 1979: 143.
30. Jacobs 1972: 487.
31. Jacobs 1972: 486–90: 496–7.
32. Budup is on the northern shore of Sek Harbour some 15 kilometres north along the coast from Madang. Local traditions and recovered artifacts indicate that European sailors probably repaired a beached vessel there. In the 1920s one old man recounted that when his father was a boy, he had seen a sailing ship at Budup. This would have been in about the 1830s. It had been damaged and was dragged ashore and repaired in the very same hole as Kilibob, a major mythological hero, is said to have built his ship. Local residents report that planks, hammers and a chain were once present at this site. Father Kirsch, the missionary at Sek, and Franz Moeder obtained some ship's fittings, four steel daggers and two bronze statues at this location and from surrounding villages. The daggers had carved horn handles and rusty blades. The two bronze statues were carved in considerable detail with breast and leg plates, a helmet with horns and each figure held a sword. Each statue was mounted on a decorated black ivory base. They were considered to be Portuguese artifacts. The artifacts were kept in the Sek school for many years before Father Hirsch packed them up and sent them to a museum in Europe (Mennis 1979: 92–5). Their current whereabouts are unknown to PNG National Museum staff.

A bronze cannon was thrown overboard from a Dutch sailing boat in the vicinity of Arop village west of Aitape to enable it to float free of a sandbar. The Catholic mission acquired the cannon and sent it to Marienberg, a large mission station on the lower Sepik. The initials VOC are marked on the cannon, signifying the Vereenigde Oostindische Compagnie/Dutch East India

Company. The canon is listed as File No. 272 in the National Cultural Property File at the PNG National Museum.

The Russian scientist Miklouho-Maclay (Maklai) lived on the Rai Coast of what is now the Madang province in September 1871 to December 1872, June 1876 to November 1877 and March 1883 (Miklouho-Maclay 1982).

A silver bracelet of recent Indian origin, with an attachment holding a Greek coin made between 344 and 334 B.C., has been found just inland of Wewak beach (Borrell 1990). I suspect this bracelet was probably lost by one of the Indian soldiers captured by the Japanese in Malaysia or Hong Kong and brought to work for them in the East Sepik, especially from But to Wewak (see Melnnes 1992: 227).

33. Bodrogi 1953: 91–2; Molnar-Bagley 1993: 17–18, 53.

34. Parkinson 1979: 35–6.

35. Brookfield with Hart 1971: 136.

36. The coconut fragments recovered from the Aitape skull site (Hossfeld 1965) and from the Dongan site (Swadling et al. 1991) indicate that coconuts have been present on this coast for at least 5,800 years, but the historical evidence suggests that the people resident on the north coast have restricted its availability.

The relative scarcity of coconuts may explain why coconut cream and taro pudding was a traditionally important food on the north coast. See Swadling (1981: 52) for a photo of this pudding being prepared in the Madang area.

Wallace (1986: 462) reports that coconuts were also a luxury in the Aru Islands in the 1850s. There people were reluctant to plant a nut which would take 12 years to bear. Any planted nut had to be watched night and day to prevent it from being dug up and eaten.

Ishige (1980: 340) also reports that coconut oil and cream have only recently become common in daily meals amongst the Galela of northern Halmahera. Traditionally coconuts were not planted as a cash crop and some families lacked even a single palm for household use.

The lack of coconuts on the north coast of Dutch New Guinea, also meant that like Kaiser Wilhelmsland, its economy was initially dependent on plume hunting (Wichmann 1917: 389).

However, this pattern of culturally induced scarcity was not the case along the entire north coast of New Guinea and nearby regions. As already mentioned in Chapter 11, at Jama (Jamna) Island off Takar village on the north coast of West Papua (Figure 42), Abel Tasman reports obtaining 6,000 coconuts and 100 bags of bananas by barter in 1642 for knives made by his sailors from metal hoops (Forrest 1969: ix).

37. Otto Finsch observed this in 1885, see Wiltgen 1971: 331; Reina 1858 cited by Lilley 1986: 63.

38. Mennis 1981: 14; Mary Mennis personal communication 1993.

39. Oliver 1961: 237.

40. Peter Sack personal communication 1991.

41. Ordinance 1891; Rose 1891.

42. Rose 1892.

43. Hahl 1910a; Rose 1892; Sack and Clark 1979; 330.

44. Sack and Clark 1979: 315.

45. Hahl 1980: 114.

46. Preuss 1912: 133; Mackenzie 1934: 313–4.
47. Ordinance 1911; Neuhauss 1911.
48. Sack and Clark 1979: 323.
49. Solf 1912c.
50. Hahl 1912
51. Mackenzie 1934: 314.
52. Sack and Clark 1979: 348.
53. Sack and Clark 1980: 156.
54. Sack and Clark 1980: 12.
55. Doughty 1975: 22.
56. Gilliard 1969: 25; Jacobs 1972: 497.
57. Ordinance 1911.
58. Sack and Clark 1979: 366.
59. Sack and Clark 1980: 12.
60. Solf 1912c; Solf 1913a
61. Vohsen et al 1913: 239.
62. Sack and Clark 1980: 90–1.
63. N.S. 1910.
64. Hahl 1910a.
65. Strauch 1912: 51.
66. Hahl 1913a: 190–1; Sack and Clark 1979: 366.
67. Strauch 1912: 51; Solf 1912b.
68. Preuss 1912: 130–1; Gilliard 1969: Beehler et al. 1986.
69. Gilliard 1969: 195.
70. Tschauder 1989d: 174. (see German Colonial documents).
71. Mary LeCroy personal communication 1991.
72. Hahl 1910b; Thiel 1910.
73. N.S. 1910.
74. Gilliard 1969: 26.
75. Ordinance 1911; Hahl 1912b.
76. Preuss 1912.
77. Hahl 1980: 144.
78. Being on reconnaissance trips, they probably wanted to travel light. West of Lumi the area behind the coastal mountains is very sparsely populated. Their expectation of finding few inhabitants is not surprising as they probably knew from personal experience, or from talk at Hollandia, that the area behind the mountains across the border in German New Guinea was very sparsely populated. However, this is not the case east of Lumi.
79. Allen 1976a: 58–9.
80. see Seiler 1985.
81. Patrol Report A 3/32–33: South Wapi extending to the Sepik River, August to October 1932 cited in Allen 1976a: 57.
82. Marshall 1937: 495, 1938: 49–50.
83. Neuhauss 1912b.

84. Ebert 1912.
85. Anon 1912d: 139; Neuhauss 1912a; Preuss 1912: 123; Sack and Clark 1979: 354.
86. Sack and Clark 1980: 104.
87. Busse 1912.
88. Jackman 1988: 37.
89. Sack and Clark 1979: 331.
90. Sack and Clark 1979: 346.
91. Sack and Clark 1980: 110.
92. Hahl 1980: 142–3.
93. Preuss 1912.
94. Cobley 1976: 308.
95. Gilliard 1969: 26.
96. Sack and Clark 1979: 330, 348.
97. Hahl 1913a.
98. Hahl 1913a.
99. Tschauder 1989a: 26.
100. Tschauder 1989b: 37.
101. Hahl 1910a.
102. N.S. 1910.
103. Neuhauss 1911.
104. Tschauder 1989c: 42.
105. Schobel 1911: 45.
106. Anon 1911a: 43.
107. Anon 1911b: 46: Anon 1913f.
108. Busse 1911:46; Hahl 1913b; Solf 1912a.
109. Gilliard 1969: 451; Mary LeCroy personal communication 1991.
110. Schillings 1912; Solf 1912a.
111. Anon 1912c.
112. Anon 1913a: Hahl 1913a.
113. Solf 1912c.
114. Hahl 1912.
115. Hahl 1913a.
116. Anon 1912a; Solf 1912c.
117. Anon 1913b; Anon 1913c; Anon 1913d; Anon 1913e; Sarasin 1913; Schillings 1913; Solf 1913b; Solf 1913d.
118. Hahnle and Neuhauss 1913.
119. Conze 1913.
120. Valentini 1913.
121. Solf 1913c; Solf 1913e; Solf 1913f; Reichenow 1913.
122. Rowley 1958: 3.
123. Cheesman 1941:180; Allen 1976b: 325.
124. Mackenzie 1934: 312–5.

125. Mackenzie 1934: 313; Gun or shooting licence 1915.

126. A proclamation prohibiting the importing of bird of paradise plumes into Australia was issued under the Commonwealth Customs Act in 1913 (Mackenzie 1934: 314).

127. Mackenzie 1934: 313–4.

128. Order requiring people in possession of the skins and plumage to declare and register the same ... 1915.

129. Nelson 1989: 29.

130. Tschauder 1989e: 211.

131. Birds of Paradise (Exportation) Ordinance 1920.

132. Birds of Paradise Exportation (Amendment) Ordinance 1921.

133. Birds and Animals Protection Ordinance 1922.

134. Allen 1976b: 325; Cheesman 1941: 179–180.

135. Birds and Animals Protection Ordinance 1922.

13

Conservationists protect Papua's birds

Natural history collectors

Natural history collectors became interested in British New Guinea[1] after the Raggiana Bird of Paradise was first reported at Orangerie Bay (Figure 55) in 1873 (see Chapter 4). Collecting natural history specimens was a profitable activity as museums and collectors paid high prices for new and rare species. Some collectors, such as Carl Hunstein, combined gold prospecting and natural history collecting. During one of his expeditions in 1884, in the mountains some 90–105 kilometres from Port Moresby at Mount Maguli in the Owen Stanley Range, Hunstein was the first European to see the Blue Bird of Paradise.[2] There was renewed interest in British New Guinea after this discovery.

Although profitable, natural history specimen collecting and exploration were risky undertakings. In 1884 there were two expeditions to Papua supported by competing Melbourne newspapers. Bird collecting was part of their activities. One of the members of the *Argus* expedition, William Denton, died of fever on the southern watershed of the Owen Stanley Ranges. Koiari villagers carried him to Berigabadi village some 24 kilometres from Sogeri (Figure 55), where he was buried.[3]

Other expeditions, especially those in high altitude areas, had tragic consequences for local assistants. In 1905 A.S. Meek went into the upper Aroa area on the southern watershed of the Wharton Range. Some of his hunters became ill with the cold and one man died. This suggests that Meek did not ensure that his hunters had clothes to cope with the cold in high altitude areas. It is therefore not surprising that his carriers deserted him on a subsequent expedition on the upper Kumusi River in 1907.[4]

Natural history collectors report that they paid villagers for permission to hunt birds on their land, or paid the villagers for the birds they brought to their camps (Plate 40). The chiefs in the Kairuku District required a fee before any birds could be shot in display trees

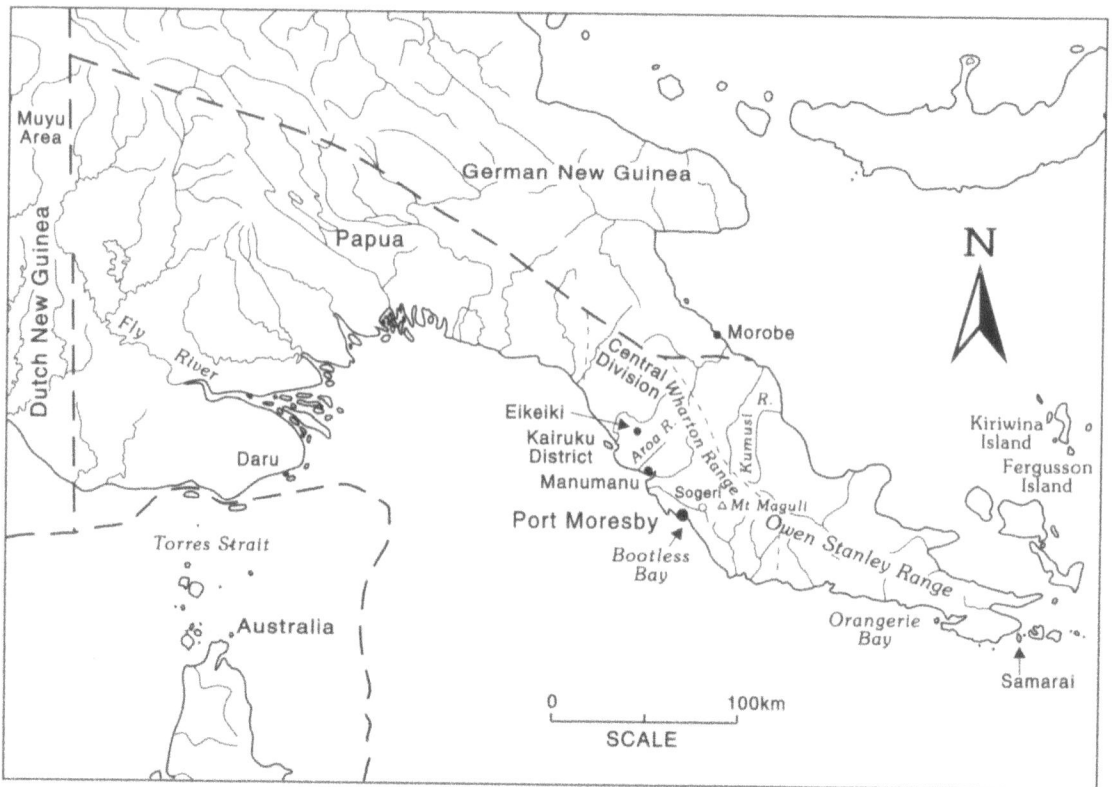

on their land. They considered the birds to be their property. As Pratt commented, this practice amounted to a local game law.[5]

In 1903, in the upper Aroa River area, A.S. Meek describes how he had as many as 150 to 200 snared birds of paradise in his camp. These birds had been captured by local villagers and brought in bound with nooses to long sticks. Meek purchased most of the birds offered to him, released the females and kept only the males for his collections. The birds had been caught by placing a loop on the bough of a tree. This loop was connected by a long twine to the hunter who concealed himself nearby. He pulled the snare as soon as a bird stepped inside the loop and in this way captured the bird.[6]

Figure 55: British New Guinea (became Papua in 1906).

Protective legislation

In line with international trends and British colonial legislation, the British and Australian administrations introduced a number of ordinances which initially controlled natural history specimen collecting and later prohibited hunting for natural history specimens and the millinery trade in Papua.

By 1894 there was sufficient concern about the number of birds being hunted in British New Guinea that legislation was introduced to protect them from extinction. The Wild Birds Protection Ordinance of 1894 was passed to protect the colony's wild birds; this legislation states:

264

Our knowledge of the birds of the Possession is as yet very far from being complete, but it is sufficiently great to make it manifest that restrictive measures are necessary in order to preserve certain kinds from speedy extinction.

It would not be possible to prepare an inclusive law that could at once embrace all the different species that may require now or hereafter to be put under protection. The Ordinance therefore provides that protection may be extended from time to time, as may be found necessary, to any species that extended knowledge and greater experience show to be in need of it.

By a Proclamation issued under this Ordinance the destruction or capture of all wild birds, except birds of prey, is prohibited on the watershed of the harbour of Port Moresby, and on the islands of Samarai and Daru. This was shown to be very necessary by the fact that the feathered fauna in the neighbourhood of Port Moresby has twice within the last six years been ruthlessly and inconsiderately slaughtered, so that for months hardly a singing bird was heard in the neighbourhood.

Plate 40: Hunters with birds acquired after a few hours hunting at Eikeiki, (Keke) near Bakoiudu in Kairuku District. These birds were obtained for a natural history collector.

Source: Pratt 1906.

The 1894 Ordinance also prohibited the collecting of two rare birds of paradise found on Fergusson and other islands in the D'Entrecasteaux group.[7] Large numbers of birds continued to be killed by collectors. Further restrictions were imposed on their activities in 1897. The British administration did not consider their occupation as an industry worthy of encouragement.

Formerly the collector had to incur danger where now he is perfectly safe. He had, some years ago, to cut his own track, to find his own way, and it was difficult to obtain native assistants. Now he generally follows up tracks cut by Government; he can employ native assistants almost anywhere; and can thus shoot down the birds of a district in a short time. Ordinance No. VI of 1897 imposes on the collector a licence of £5, and a licence of £1 for each shooting assistant. It does not appear that this licence has any effect in diminishing the number of collectors. It will soon be necessary to proceed a step further and to limit the number of birds of certain species that any collector may kill under his licence, for it would be a great mistake to suppose that birds of paradise are plentiful in the Possession. Only two species are common; some are confined to certain altitudes; others to a few small isolated spots that lie far apart. It would be easy to reduce some kinds to practical extermination, a matter that should not be left till it is too late. It may be, however, that when other forms of employment are provided the number of collectors may be less.[8]

In 1907–8 the sum of £103 was raised in revenue by issuing bird collectors' licences. Most of the licences were issued for the Central Division of Papua, raising the sum of £92, with £6 for Eastern Division and £5 for Western Division.[9]

In early 1908 Sir William Ingram sponsored Charles Horsbrugh to collect birds of paradise in Papua for the British Zoological Society. Horsbrugh based his expedition at Madiu inland of Eikeiki in the Owen Stanley Range and obtained skins and live specimens of birds of paradise and other species.[10]

According to Archibald Whitbourne, a plume hunter working from Bootless Bay near Port Moresby, the valuable Blue Bird of Paradise was difficult to obtain. It could only be found in the interior mountains and a hunter once there only rarely sighted a plumed male. This was not the case with the Raggiana Bird of Paradise. In good years a European hunter and a team of Papuans might bag 600–700 male Raggianas with their shotguns. The average market value of a Raggiana plume was one pound sterling, whereas the King Bird of Paradise obtained £20–30.[11,12]

The progressive legislation adopted in British New Guinea was not locally inspired, but a feature of British colonial legislation initiated in India. The shipment of wild bird plumes for the millinery trade from

India was prohibited in 1902. After the founding of the Society for the Preservation of the Wild Fauna of the Empire in 1903, similar laws were implemented in other British colonies (see Chapter 5).

The newly established Australian administration managed to prohibit plume hunting in Papua, despite considerable local protest, just as the demands of the European plume boom caused market values to rise higher than ever before in 1908. The Wild Birds Ordinance of the 9th of December 1908 made it illegal to capture, willfully destroy, buy, sell, or deal in the skin, feathers or plumage of birds of paradise, goura pigeons and ospreys. Only the duly accredited agent of a museum, zoological society or some other scientific institution could now obtain a permit to shoot these birds. An amendment made in 1909 also allowed the capture of these prohibited birds for purposes of acclimatisation in some other country. The 1908 Ordinance was further amended and consolidated by the Birds Protection Ordinance of 1911.[13]

Despite such legislation, plume hunting continued in western Papua. Many hunters illegally crossed the border into Papua from Dutch New Guinea and sought plumes in Papua. Their story is told in Chapter 10. It was not until 1926 that this was stopped. That year the Dutch authorities made it illegal to hunt in the Muyu area (Figures 38 and 41) and thus effectively closed the border area with Papua to plume hunters.

An assessment of current and potential exports from British New Guinea published in 1906 by the naturalist, A.E. Pratt, did not even consider bird of paradise skins worthy of mention. He considered cattle, chillies, cocoa, coffee, copra, gold, rubber, sandalwood, trepang and tobacco to be British New Guinea's potential income earners.[14] By that date a large number of gold-mining ventures had been established in Papua. Today one can only speculate as to whether the administration of Papua would have so promptly prohibited plume hunting in 1908 if at the time promising mineral prospects had not been found.

Notes

1. British New Guinea was first a Protectorate from 1884 until 1888 and then a Colony. In 1906 the Commonwealth of Australia was given full responsibility for the Territory of Papua.
2. Gilliard 1969: 250.
3. Armit 1884 cited by Whittaker et al 1975: 274; Gilliard 1969: 445.
4. Gilliard 1969: 448–9.
5. Pratt 1906: 135.
6. Meek 1913: 132, 150.
7. The Wild Birds Protection Ordinance of 1894.
8. The Bird Collectors Ordinance of 1897.
9. Papua Annual Report 1907–8: 125–7.
10. Horsbrugh 1909.
11. Gilliard 1969: 24–5.
12. By 1910 plume hunters had penetrated into the mountains behind Morobe Station in German New Guinea (Figure 48) and had found the Blue Bird of Paradise to be common there. In that year the price for the Blue Bird of Paradise fell to 30 shillings (one and a half pounds). Some specimens were even taken back alive to Europe (Gilliard 1969: 24–5; Downham 1911: 43–44).
13. The Wild Birds Ordinance of 1908, The Wild Birds Amendment Ordinance of 1909 and The Birds Protection Ordinance of 1911.
14. Pratt 1906: 335–43.

14

Trade cycles in outer Southeast Asia and their impact on New Guinea and nearby islands until 1920

Birds have provided a focus for cultural expression in eastern New Guinea for 5,000 years, since bird heads and wings decorate some of the stone mortars and pestles from highland, lowland and coastal areas (Figure 56). These finds plus other stone mortars and pestles and stemmed obsidian artifacts indicate that substantial trade connections existed in New Guinea by this date (Figure 9). Bird of paradise plumes were presumably amongst the products that were traded.

Initially trade between Asia and outer Southeast Asia was achieved by inter-island trade networks. These interlocking group or community networks allowed goods to travel remarkable distances by means of a chain of trading transactions. Early domesticates of banana and sugarcane from New Guinea were traded to Asia and beyond by 4,000 years ago. The arrival of specialist traders just before 2,000 years ago changed this situation. Trade between Asia and outer Southeast Asia then became dominated by merchants, who at first came from Asia, but later also from Europe. When the Portuguese reached outer Southeast Asia in 1512 the Bandanese were the only group in this region who were transshipping produce to Asia.

The people of New Guinea and nearby islands have long considered their land and all its faunal, floral and mineral resources to be their property. When outsiders come to collect and export local products, resource owners not only reassess the value of their resources but also the nature of their relationships with foreigners. Problems arise when rich resources are exploited and the local inhabitants believe they are not participating in the decision making and receiving what they consider to be a fair share of the profits.

Disagreements of this nature date back to the beginning of specialist interactions with foreigners more than 2,000 years ago. The bronze spearheads and a dagger found in the Jayapura region (see Figure 45), as well as the militant nature of the bronze boat miniature found in Flores (see Figure 57), indicate that the first specialist traders faced confrontations. In historical times the first uprisings against the

Portuguese in the Spice Islands occurred a little more than a decade after they had established a permanent settlement there in 1522. By 1574 the Portuguese had been driven from Ternate. The Bandanese managed to keep European merchants from establishing bases in their islands somewhat longer, only to be devastated by the Dutch in 1621 when they failed to uphold a trade agreement. This brought about the end of Banda as a regional trade entrepôt.

Dutch records for the Moluccas, which date from 1814, when they established a regular administration in these islands, document a history of constant litigation. This occurred not only between itinerant traders and local rulers, but also amongst local inhabitants as to who owned and had the right to exploit commercially valuable resources.[1]

Rebellions and litigation continue in outer Southeast Asia. In 1989 the Australian-owned copper mine on Bougainville was closed by rebels seeking to secede from Papua New Guinea. In addition to the Bougainville Revolutionary Army (BRA), there are also the West Papuan Freedom Fighters (OPM) in West Papua and the Fretilin forces in former Portuguese Timor. Arrangements for the exploitation of mineral resources in Papua New Guinea by such multinational corporations as the major oil companies and Rio Tinto Zinc (and its subsidiaries CRA and Kennecott) remain contentious.

The first cycle: plumes and specialist Asian traders

The plumes reaching Asia via inter-island trade brought bronze-using traders to New Guinea, just as spices subsequently attracted Asians and later Europeans to the Spice Islands. This Asian plume trade dates from just prior to 2,000 years ago to about 300 AD. The specialist traders were probably able to obtain the products and safe passage they sought by presenting exotic goods to local community leaders. These leaders in turn incorporated many of the goods they received into traditional exchange networks, thus establishing alliances and fostering peace within their own societies. Such exotic goods would have been keenly sought as their acquisition indicated social ascendancy, and by the same token inability to acquire them indicated failure in this regard.[2] The militant nature of the bronze miniature boat (Figure 57) found at Dobo in Flores, eastern Indonesia, as well as bronze weapons found elsewhere, suggests that some early traders were also prepared to fight if the friendly relationships established on the basis of gift-giving failed to protect them.

The appearance of large valuable bronze artifacts in eastern Indonesia can be seen as marking the arrival of outsiders seeking rare natural products. Large ornamented bronze vessels, clearly intended to impress as display items, occur from the Asian mainland to Java and

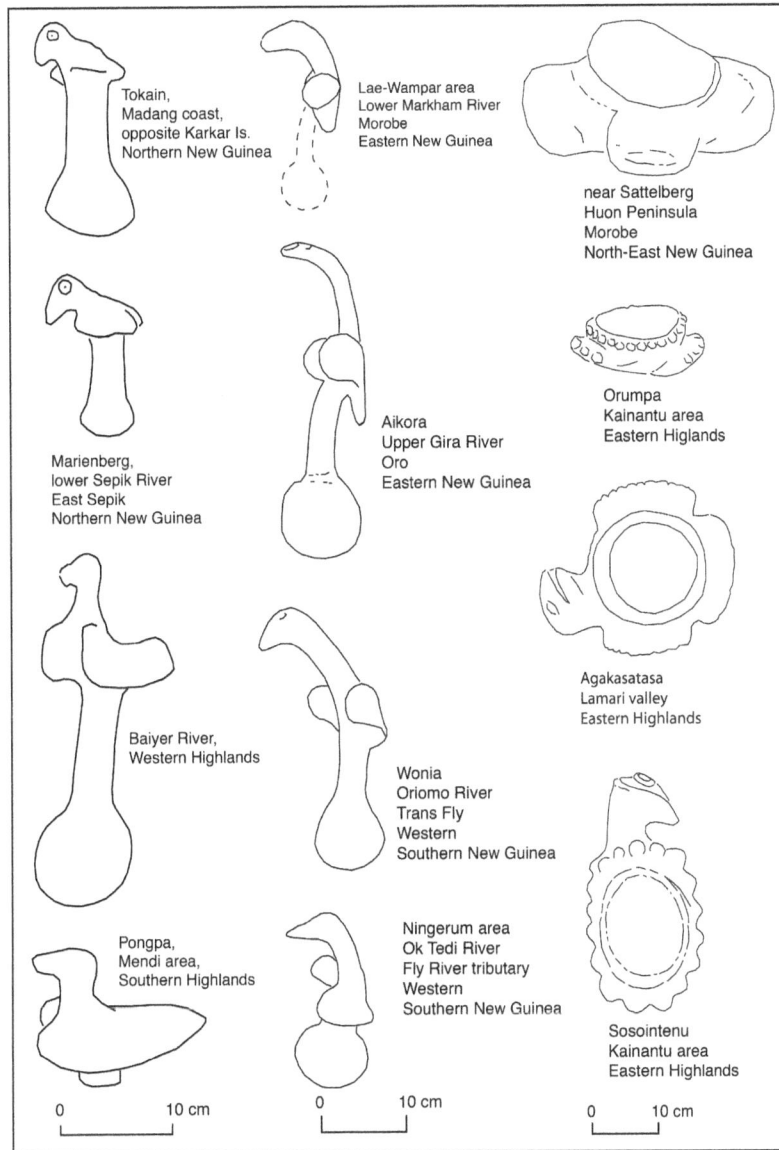

Figure 56: On left bird pestles with folded wings, in centre those with raised wings and on right bird head and wing mortars. Scales are provided for each column.

Source: Swadling database. For more information see Swadling 2005; Swadling 2017; Swadling and Hide 2005; Swadling, Wiessner and Tumu 2008; Torrence and Swadling 2008.

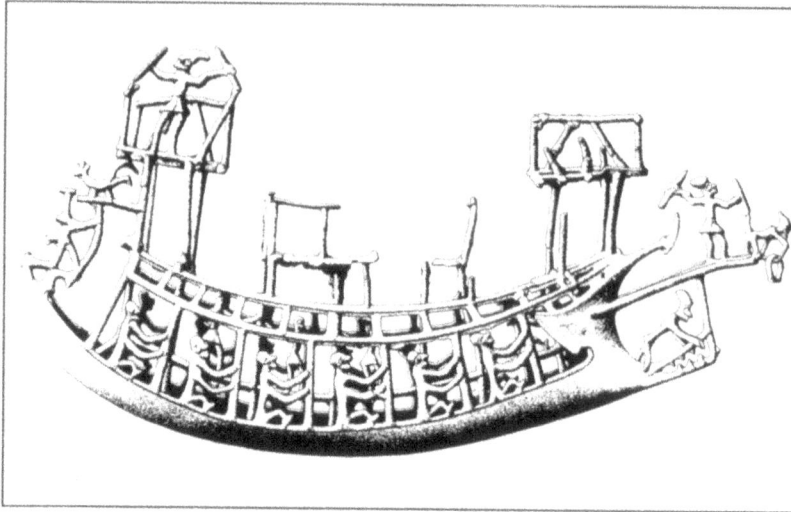

Figure 57: Bronze miniature boat found in Dobo village on Flores in eastern Indonesia. Parallels with Dong Son art suggest that it was made in the first century AD in North Vietnam. It was probably imported to Flores early in the second century AD. **Source:** Spennemann 1985a. Reproduction courtesy of the Linden-Museum, Stuttgart.

through the Sunda chain as far as New Guinea (Figure 58). In Soejono's view,[3] those found in eastern Indonesia are some of the finest examples of these bronzes. As we saw in Chapter 3, the infatuation with plumes in Asian kingdoms led to a high demand for bird of paradise skins. The trail of these large bronze artifacts to New Guinea and not the Spice Islands is the archaeological verification of this interest.

Bronze and glass artifacts themselves do not extend, with the exception of the Manus fragment, beyond the New Guinea mainland, but influences derived from contact with people using these artifacts did extend by means of local trade systems further east[4]. These influences are evident in stone skeuomorphs of bronze artifacts[5] and certain design motifs which occur in Manus, Sepik, Oro and Milne Bay Provinces and the Bismarck Archipelago within what is now Papua New Guinea.[6]

The second cycle: forest products – spices and aromatic woods

By 300 AD changing demands in Asia had led to a declining interest in plumes. Other forest products were sought instead, notably spices and aromatic woods and barks. Knowledge of their existence in eastern Indonesia would have been gained during the plume trade and it is likely that during this time there was some trade in these products. As the interest in plumes declined, the small islands off western Halmahera, as well as the Banda Islands and Timor, became important centres respectively for cloves, nutmegs and sandalwood. When these products had become the main products sought by traders, they went directly to their source and plumes then became a minor trade item, provided by local traders to these new centres (Figure 59).

Figure 58: Route of bird of paradise traders as indicated by the presence of bronze kettledrums in eastern Indonesia and other valuable bronze artifacts in New Guinea. They were active from just before 2,000 years ago to 300 AD. At the same time inter-island contact with communities in Borneo, Sulawesi and the southern Philippines led to the introduction of the practice of secondary pot burials to Western New Guinea and subsequently to eastern New Guinea and the New Guinea Islands.

The Spice Islands are located some 400 kilometres to the west of New Guinea. When the world demand for spices began to grow early in the first millennium, some Southeast Asians probably wondered whether volcanic islands rich in spices, like the Moluccas, existed at the eastern end of New Guinea. It is not known whether such investigations occurred in prehistoric times. The British did check out this possibility when they were seeking an alternative source of spices when the Moluccas were under Dutch control. That other islands rich in spices might be found at the eastern end of New Guinea was acted on when Captain John MacCluer found wild nutmegs on the west coast of New Guinea in 1791. A private expedition to the eastern end of New Guinea was financed by some merchants in Calcutta and made by Captain John Hayes. He investigated the Louisiade Archipelago but found nothing of economic interest. On his voyage back to India he decided to promote a spice growing venture on the Bird's Head. This led to the establishment of the first European settlement on New Guinea at Doreri Bay, near modern day Manokwari, on the northwest coast of West Papua.[7]

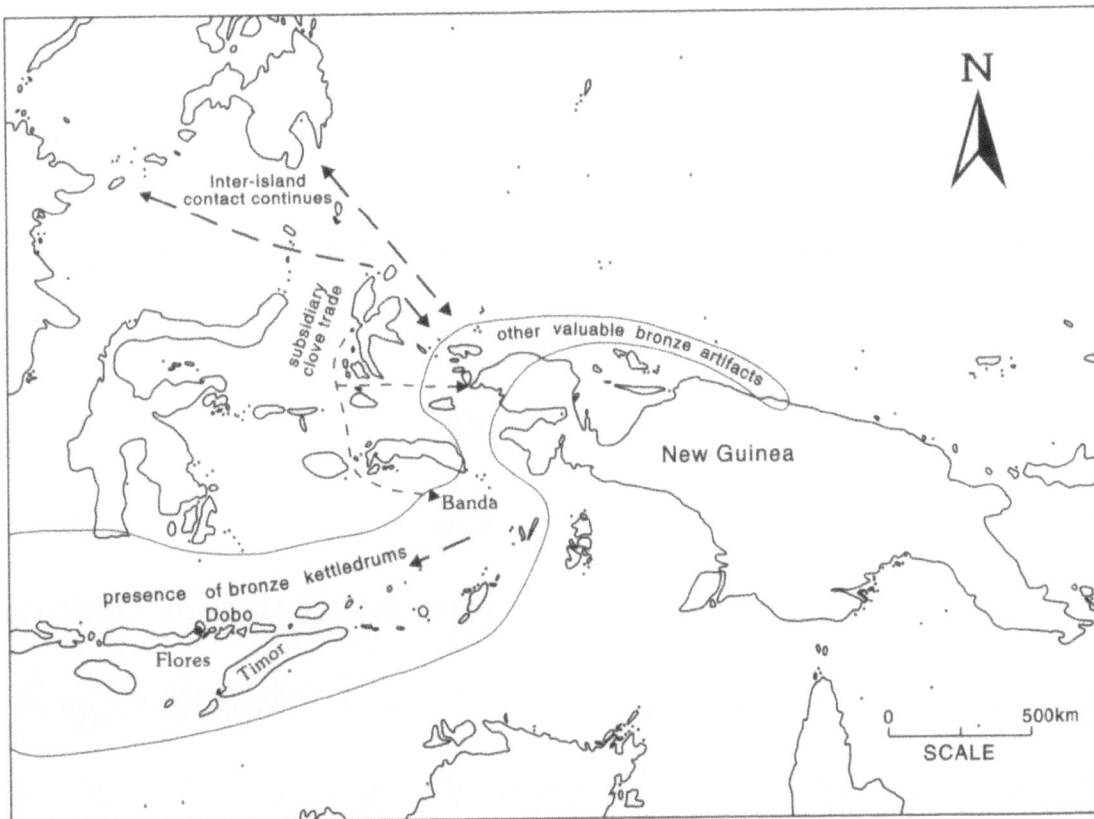

By 1400 AD the profits to be made from trading in cloves, nutmeg and mace had given rise to interlocking merchant networks which came to extend all the way from eastern Indonesia to medieval Europe. This caused a spice boom and increased trade in the Indonesian archipelago. Malay was the lingua franca of the traders in Indonesia and international contacts with the west led to Islam being spread along the trade routes. By 1500 Melaka had become the most important entrepot in Southeast Asia. Chinese, Indian, Malay, Javanese and other traders came to exchange goods there. Javanese traders supplied most of the cloves and nutmegs from the Spice Islands, as well as sandalwood from Timor.[8] The Javanese came to the Spice Islands via the Sunda Islands. Chinese traders became active in the Talaud Islands, Sulawesi and presumably the Spice Islands in the thirteenth and fourteenth centuries, reaching Onin and possibly also the Waropen coast on the New Guinea mainland in the fifteenth century (Figure 59).

As the use of spices increased in Europe, ships were launched into the unknown to seek their source. Once this was discovered,

Figure 59: Main spice trade route 300–1512 AD.

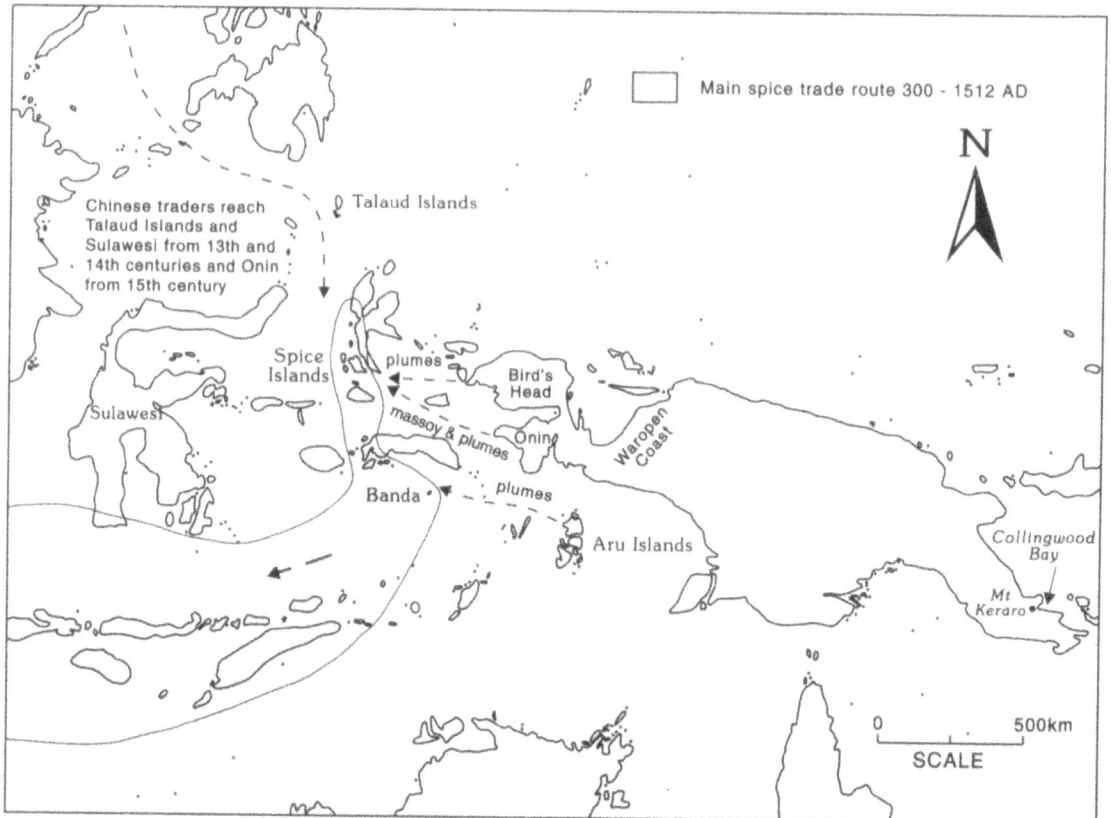

Figure 59: Main spice trade route 300–1512 AD.

mercantile powers from Europe sought to dominate the spice trade by their military might. They soon found that conquests of trading centres did not always give them the financial rewards they sought. For instance, the Portuguese took Melaka in 1511, thinking it would give them control over trading transactions in the region. They were mistaken. Instead, this Portuguese takeover led to the dispersal of trade to other parts of the archipelago. Asian merchants and traders moved into eastern Indonesia and established new trading centres, particularly Makassar in the state of Gowa in southern Sulawesi.

In eastern Indonesia Dutch intervention was far more disruptive than that imposed by the Portuguese, as the Dutch attempted to gain a full monopoly of the spice trade for themselves through their Dutch East India Company.

During the early phase of European contact, the growing world demand for spices – pepper from western Indonesia, cloves, nutmeg and mace from eastern Indonesia – not only stimulated trade in these commodities, but also led to increased production. The inhabitants of the Spice Islands and nearby islands responded to what they envisaged to be an insatiable demand by Asians and Europeans for cloves and nutmegs by planting more trees. In the long term this was not sustainable, as the world demand for these products did not continue to grow, so painful structural adjustments by producers and suppliers were required. The spice glut came in the 1630s. From 1632 the price for cloves began to decline.[9] The Dutch tried to ease the clove and nutmeg glut by not only destroying cultivated trees to reduce the supply but also by introducing trade restrictions. From 1653 the Company started paying annual subsidies to the Sultans of Ternate and Bacan, and from 1657 the Sultan of Tidore, in lieu of their foregone spice profits. By this time the trade monopoly and extirpation activities of the Dutch East India Company had seriously disrupted economic ventures in the Moluccas and it ceased to be a prosperous region.

Largely as a consequence of the trade disruptions brought about by the Dutch, the Seram Laut Islands emerged as the new trade centre in outer Southeast Asia (Figure 60). They collected massoy from the Onin and Kowiai coasts, as well as damar from the Trans Fly coast from about 1645 until 1790. A similar forest trade developed at Magindanao on Mindanao from 1621 to 1770.[10]

Following the spice price collapse, the prices for aromatic barks and woods also began to decline. By about 1670 the price for massoy had fallen[11] and by the eighteenth century the sandalwood trade was in decline.[12] The era of forest products was at a close. Changing needs, tastes and industry were impacting on world and regional trade. In the western world new products were in demand. These included

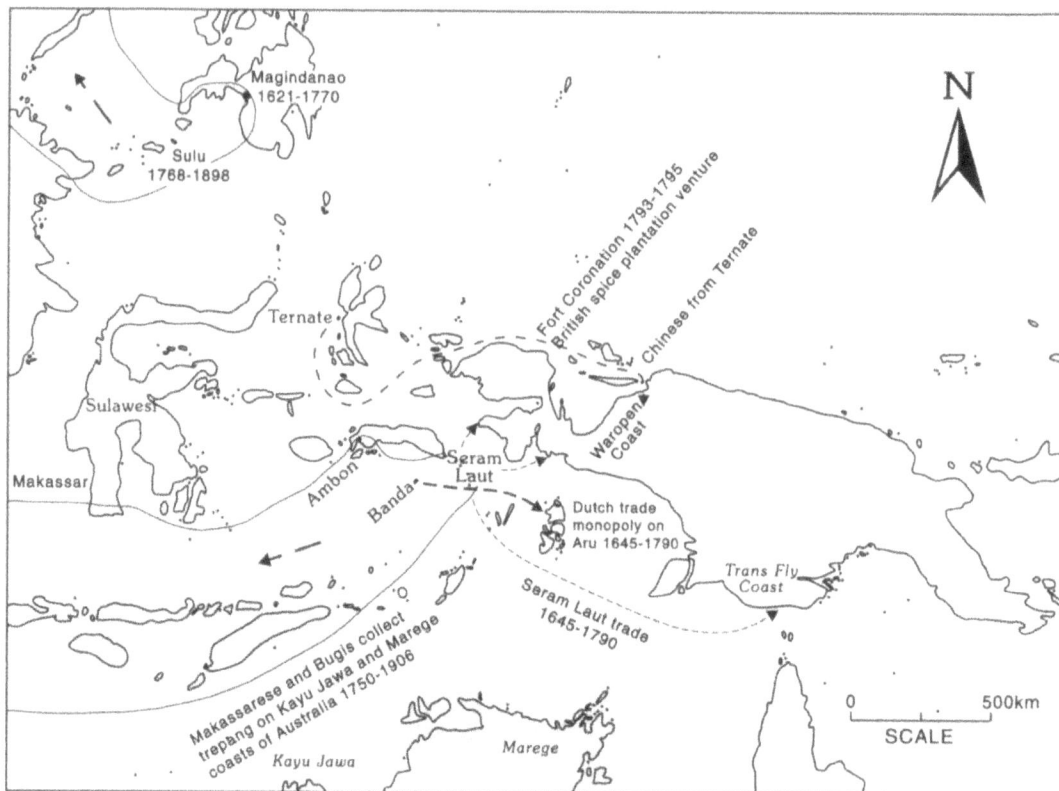

Figure 60: Following the regional trade disruptions brought about by the Dutch the Seram Laut Islands emerged as the new trade centre in far eastern Indonesia from 1621 until after 1814.

coffee, tea, sugar and tobacco, as well as minerals, in particular tin. In Southeast Asia the growing of coffee, sugar and tobacco became centred on Java, the northern Philippines and the shores of the Straits of Melaka.[13] Outer Southeast Asia no longer attracted European investment capital as its spices were produced now more cheaply elsewhere. By 1770 the Dutch East India Company faced bankruptcy.

The third cycle: marine products for China

At much the same time as the world prices for spices fell, another major change occurred which had repercussions for outer Southeast Asia. This concerned events in China. In the 1640s China was thrown into turmoil by the Manchu invasion of the southern Ming-controlled provinces. As a result of this struggle coastal towns were devastated and trade disrupted for more than 40 years. When the Manchu (Ch'ing/Qing dynasty) gained control of southern China in 1684, ports were reopened and trading links with Southeast Asia reestablished. The Chinese found that they needed new trade goods, as many of the commodities they had freely obtained forty years previously were now subject to European monopolies. They began to concentrate on marine and jungle goods, such as mother-of-pearl, bird's nests and trepang, which were easy to acquire in outer Southeast Asia as no one else used them. In this way China became the main market for goods from this region from the late seventeenth century.

The demand for these new products in China encouraged a great diaspora of Makassarese and Bugis throughout the archipelago in the late seventeenth to early eighteenth centuries. Campaigns by the ruler of the Bugis state of Bone, who was a strong ally of the Dutch, against Gowa and other neighbouring states also encouraged many Makassarese and Bugis to leave Sulawesi. They founded new settlements and trading centres throughout the archipelago at the same time as the Chinese expanded their trade there.

China's tea exports also had an impact on outer Southeast Asia. This beverage had replaced ale as the national drink in England and was in high demand. Until alternative goods acceptable to the Chinese were found, tea had to be obtained in exchange for silver. In 1740 British traders realised that by trading Indian goods, such as cotton, for marine and jungle products from outer Southeast Asia, they obtained trade goods which allowed them to acquire the tea they sought in China. British traders thus began to seek mother-of-pearl, edible bird's nest and trepang for this expanding trade. For example, the export of mother-of-pearl from Sulu increased from some 121 tons in 1760 to some 726 tons in 1835.[14]

The interchange of trade goods between India, outer Southeast Asia and China led to the need for a major entrepôt for this trade. The obvious location was somewhere in the western Indonesian archipelago. Riau, established by the Bugis, nearly became such a centre, but was destroyed by the Dutch in 1784; the harbour fees at Melaka were too expensive; and Penang was too far north. In 1819 the British founded Singapore on the edge of Dutch territory.

A number of trade centres developed to supply marine products to China (Figure 60). Sulu became such a centre and a regional power from 1768 until 1898.[15] Makassar was another centre. From about 1720 to 1906 Makassarese (Macassans) went trepang collecting on the north coast of Australia.[16] In the vicinity of New Guinea, the Seram Laut Islands and subsequently Dobo in the Aru Islands developed into important trade centres.

The trepang collectors who visited Australia were mainly Makassarese and Bugis. They sailed to northern Australia on prau which tended to be owned by Chinese merchants in Makassar. Their voyages utilised the northwest monsoon on their outward leg to Australia and the southeast trade winds on their return to Makassar. Each leg took about ten days. They collected trepang from two stretches of coastline. The main area they visited they called Marege. This extended from Bathurst Island in the west to the Wellesley Islands in the east. The second area was the Kimberley coast, which they called Kayu Jawa. In 1803 Matthew Flinders learnt that there were some 60 praus crewed by over a thousand men working in the Marege area.[17]

The annual visits by Makassarese to collect trepang on the north coast of Australia led some British investors to propose that a similar entrepôt to Singapore could be established in northern Australia to serve outer Southeast Asia. Both the Dutch and the British recognised that a successful entrepôt in the region would be a profitable venture. It would allow them to despatch large quantities of local products to foreign markets and to sell their own products to the producers. With this intention in mind, the British founded a number of settlements on the north coast of Australia, these were Fort Dundas in 1824–29 on Melville Island, Fort Wellington in 1827–29 at Raffles Bay and Port Essington in 1838–49 (Figure 61). The Dutch countered these attempts by their own settlement at Triton Bay in 1828–1836 and by proclaiming the southwestern coastline of New Guinea from the northern tip of the Bird's Head to the vicinity of the present international border on the south coast to be under Tidore's suzerainty. All the British and Dutch settlements were sorry failures. Meanwhile, the Seram Laut Islands flourished as an eastern entrepôt for goods mainly destined for China, as local traders disregarded British and Dutch efforts to control trade in the region. However, like other marine-orientated centres in Southeast Asia, the Seram Laut Islands went into decline in the late 1890s.

The fourth cycle – new European interests: copra, plumes, pearls and minerals

To counter increasing European interest, the Dutch in 1848 extended the area of New Guinea claimed to be under the control of the Sultan of Tidore to the vicinity of the current international border on the north coast of New Guinea. By 1850 traders from Ternate and Tidore were starting to trade on the Bird's Head and north coast of New Guinea, whereas Seram Laut and Bugis traders were more active in the Raja Empat Islands and south coast of New Guinea (Figure 61). In practice Tidore had no real influence in Dutch New Guinea and the Dutch increasingly assumed direct rule of the region. By the 1890s a trading post was operating in Humboldt Bay and government stations were established at Manokwari, Fakfak and Selerika. The latter was unsuccessful and was replaced by Merauke in 1902. In 1905 the legal fiction of Tidore's rule ceased when the Sultanate of Tidore lost its independence and was for the most part incorporated within the Dutch colonial state.

The resources of eastern New Guinea became known in Europe and Australia as a result of observations made by whalers and travellers using shipping routes that passed through the area (Figure 61). This led to interest in the New Guinea Islands, especially New Ireland and the Duke of York Islands as these lay on the fast ship routes from eastern Australia to Asia and Europe. These fast routes passed either north or south of New Ireland. Slower, smaller vessels took the rougher Dampier Strait, whereas Torres Strait was generally avoided until reliable maps were available to navigators after the reef surveys of Captain Blackwood in 1842–46 and Captain Owen Stanley in 1848–49.[18] In 1847 the Marists established the first mission in what is now Papua New Guinea on Woodlark Island on the basis of advice from the captain of a whaler.[19]

The increased attention paid to eastern New Guinea was part of a general European interest in undeveloped areas. For instance, the Northern Territory was annexed by South Australia in 1863 on the basis of plans for pastoral development and dreams of mineral discoveries. This affected the eastern Indonesian trepang collectors as the South Australian government soon introduced licences and

Figure 61: Whaling grounds as well as trade centres and sea routes from 1814-1850.

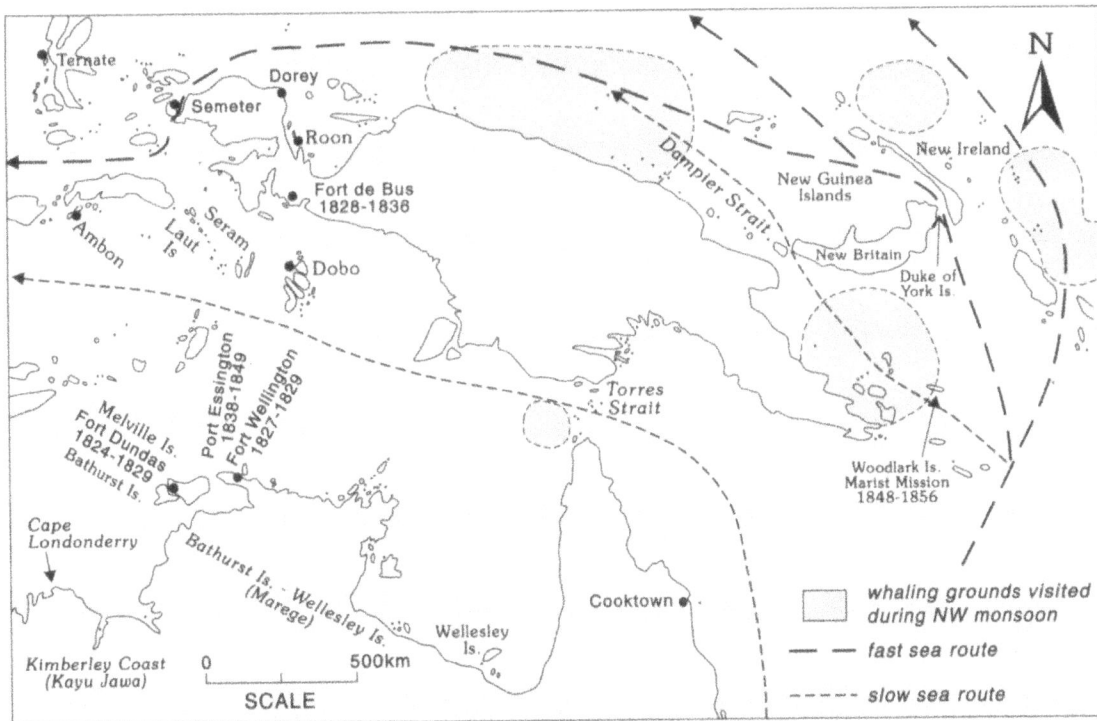

customs duty on food and other items they used. This reduced the profit margins of a declining industry and by 1902 fewer and fewer Indonesians were coming in search of trepang. The industry ceased when the South Australian government prohibited the entry of Indonesian trepang collectors into Australia in 1906.[20]

The marine resources of Torres Strait and its increasing importance for navigation attracted investors and settlers. Trepang collecting began in Torres Strait in the 1830s, a few years after the first exports from the Queensland coast in 1827.[21] In 1862 the Governor of Queensland established a coaling and refuge station on Somerset Island in Torres Strait. Pearling began in the Strait in the 1860s. By 1870 the London Missionary Society had established a base there. In 1878 the Torres Strait Islands were annexed by Queensland and a government post was established on Thursday Island.

The Duke of York Islands and nearby areas had become known to the outside world as a result of being on a major sea passage. In the 1870s copra traders became active in the Duke of Yorks and nearby areas. The Hernsheim brothers and Queen Emma were pioneers in this trade. The large number of established coconut palms in the villages of New Britain and New Ireland allowed copra trading, which in turn provided the capital to establish large plantations. This was how Rabaul quickly became the financial capital and in due course the administrative capital of German New Guinea.

By the 1870s businessmen in both Australia and Germany believed that New Guinea was a profitable area for investment. By 1884 both the British and German governments were persuaded to annex parts of eastern New Guinea, and the border which established the extent of their claims was agreed on in 1885. The main income earners in German New Guinea prior to World War I were copra in the Islands and bird of paradise skins in Kaiser Wilhelmsland. The economy of the north coast of Dutch New Guinea was also dependent on plume hunting.[22] After the war copra was the main income earner in what then became the Mandated Territory of New Guinea. In Papua mining, mainly of gold but some copper, became the main economic pursuit. A large number of projects were established before 1920 (Figure 62). They were Sudest Island (1888–98), Misima Island (1889–1942), Woodlark Island (1895–1920), Gira River (1899–1910), Yodda River (1899–1910), Milne Bay (1899–1909), Cloudy Bay (1901–07), Waria River (1906–09), upper Lakekamu (1909–20) and the Astrolabe Mineral Field at Laloki and Dubuna (1910–26).[23]

On the periphery of the Spice Islands

The success and wealth of the Spice Islands had an impact on western New Guinea, as many of the innovations and goods brought to these islands were also introduced to western New Guinea. These introductions included sociopolitical practices such as bestowing titles and paying tribute; a new religion, as some New Guineans were converted to Islam; a new language, as some New Guineans learnt trade Malay; new crops such as rice, sweet potatoes and tobacco; and new products such as metal tools, cloth, fine porcelain and metal gongs.

The early role of Melaka as the major trading centre for the Indonesian archipelago had led to the rapid spread of Malay and Islam. By the fifteenth century Malay was the dominant trade language in the Indonesian archipelago. The inhabitants of the Javanese seaports had been converted by proselytizers from Melaka and the Javanese in turn carried the faith to the Spice Islands.[24] When the Portuguese arrived there, they found that the coastal merchants, probably Javanese and Malays, were practising Moslems and that this had been the case for the last 50 to 80 years. Proselytizers from the Moluccas later introduced their faith to western New Guinea. For instance, a Moslem missionary was observed at Triton Bay in 1826.[25]

Figure 62: Mining ventures established in Papua and New Guinea prior to 1920. (Also showing colonial divisions).

In 1528 the Spaniard Alvaro Saavedra Ceron found that the people on an island called Harney in western New Guinea were already acquainted with iron tools.[26] Once familiar with metal tools, some New Guineans learnt how to forge them. In 1606 Captain Don Diego de Prado y Tovar observed New Guineans using a bellows to work harpoons and other iron implements in Triton Bay.[27] By the beginning of the nineteenth century New Guinean smiths were established at Dorey in Cendrawasih Bay, as well as at Triton Bay and most likely Berau Bay. The work of these smiths was limited to the forging or reforging of imported iron using bamboo bellows (Figure 24).[28] European visitors found that iron bars were highly desired trade goods and used them in payment for goods and services. For instance, Thomas Forrest paid Captain (kapitan) Mareca from Tomoguy Island off the west coast of Waigeo, whom he had employed as a translator on his trip to New Guinea in 1775, with iron bars.[29] Beccari and D'Albertis in 1872 also used iron bars to pay for the hire of a prau to travel from Cendrawasih Bay to Sorong.[30]

In areas receiving a constant supply of these goods, such as the Bird's Head, metal tools and cloth quickly superceded stone tools and tapa cloth. They also replaced these items in traditional trade and exchange networks.[31] The possession and display of these new artifacts, like the bronze artifacts before them, indicated their owner's ascendancy within his community.

Supplies of rice were imported by the Spice Islands from Java to feed the ruling elite. The high prices paid for rice[32] probably encouraged its local production. Rice is reported to have been grown on Motir (Moti) Island at the beginning of the sixteenth century.[33] It was being grown on Gebe in 1849.[34] In the 1850s Alfred Russel Wallace observed rice being grown on Halmahera at Galela and Gilolo, Kaioa Island and Bacan off the west coast of Halmahera, as well as Dorey in New Guinea.[35] By the late nineteenth century rice was a prestige food.[36] Although infrequent in daily meals, upland rice has become the most desired food and is a feast food at Galela on Halmahera.[37]

The Portuguese introduced the sweet potato, tobacco and other crops from South America to the Spice Islands, from where they were introduced to other parts of outer Southeast Asia. As described in Chapter 9, the Seram Laut contact with the Trans Fly coast from 1645–1790 probably led eventually to the introduction of the sweet potato into the highlands of what is now Papua New Guinea. The sweet potato had a revolutionary impact on life in the New Guinea highlands, as its high yields from poor and cold soils allowed more people to live in this region than ever before. Both the sweet potato and tobacco were quickly adopted in many parts of New Guinea.

There was also an impact on the local flora and fauna. For example, early records indicate that the massoy trade was not sustainable and had a serious impact on the local flora (see Chapter 8). The extent to which massoy trees have recovered in the heavily exploited areas of western New Guinea is not known. Fears about the overfishing of trepang in northern Australia led to the closure of an area of the Cobourg Peninsula from Cape Don to De Courcy Head from 1903–5.[38] Although there were fears of extermination, the European bird of paradise trade, which declined in the 1920s, did not have a long term impact on the local fauna of New Guinea. Today diminishing habitats and the widespread use of guns are having an impact and the survival of some species is threatened.[39]

Conclusion

Initially the goods obtained by specialist traders from New Guinea and nearby islands were only known to the rich and powerful of Asia and the Middle East. They subsequently became known in Europe and other parts of the world. All the goods obtained by specialist traders went through boom and bust cycles. For forest resources this is demonstrated by the trade histories of products such as plumes, spices, aromatic barks and damar and for marine resources by trepang and pearls. Today's commercial crops, as well as minerals and oil, are also not immune to these cycles, nor are the main forest and marine products harvested today, namely timber, mackeral, tuna and prawns. The latter range of products are very different from those sought in the 1920s, and this difference raises the question as to what will be the main natural resources of New Guinea in another 70 years time. For instance, will the rich biodiversity of this island region be providing marine or forest products for food, medication or other purposes of which today we can only dream? Or will tourists be paying large sums just to have the pleasure of ballooning over or walking through some of the world's few remaining natural wilderness areas? Time will tell.

Notes

1. Holleman 1925 cited by Ellen 1987: 51.
2. Dalton 1977 cited in Higham 1989: 186.
3. Soejono 1963
4. Likewise during the period of European contact in New Guinea, trade goods and knowledge of Europeans travelled far in advance of their actual presence (May 1989: 130).

5. For example Bulmer and Tomasetti 1970: Golson 1972.
6. For example Badner 1972.
7. Galis 1953–4: 19; Kamma 1972: 217; Roe 1966; See also Chapter 6.
8. Schrieke 1955; Meilink-Roelofsz 1962.
9. Chaudhuri 1965: 169.
10. Laarhoven 1990.
11. Galis 1953–4: 14.
12. Glover 1986: 11.
13. Steinberg 1985.
14. Urry n.d.; Warren 1990: 197.
15. Laarhoven 1990; Warren 1990.
16. Macknight 1986.
17. Macknight 1976: 27–9; Mulvaney 1989: 22–3.
18. Whittaker et al 1975: 314–16.
19. Nelson 1976: 50.
20. Macknight 1976.
21. Macknight 1976: 40.
22. Wichmann 1917: 389.
23. McKillop 1974; Nelson 1976; Waiko 1993.
24. Meilink-Roelofsz 1962: 34.
25. Earl 1853: 55.
26. Galis 1953–4: 8.
27. Stevens and Barwick 1930.
28. Kamma and Kooijman 1973.
29. Forrest 1969: 55, 88.
30. Goode 1977: 47.
31. Elmberg 1968.
32. Meilink-Roelofsz 1962: 287.
33. Meilink-Roelofsz 1962: 352, footnote 73.
34. Kops 1852: 306.
35. Wallace 1986: 323, 331, 348. 498.
36. de Clercq 1890 cited by Ellen 1979: 61.
37. Ishige 1980: 334–40.
38. Macknight 1976: 122.
39. Kwapena 1985: 154–5; Peckover 1978. Beehler (1993: 119) lists the most threatened birds of paradise as the Black Sicklebill, the Blue Bird of Paradise and the Macgregor's Bird of Paradise. Navu Kwapena (personal communication 1994) also considers that the King of Saxony Bird of Paradise should be added to this list.

Contribution 1

Mysteries of origin: early traders and heroes in the Trans-Fly

Roy Wagner

Those who are familiar with traditional Australian mythology will know of the accounts of "travelling creators," heroes or beings of the primeval era, or "dreamtime," whose exploits in creating the landscape and its inhabitants are narrated in continuing episodes from one people to the next. Allowing for cultural and linguistic differences, the identity and very often the name of the creator is retained from one region to another. Usually the "track," or route, followed by such a hero is likewise continuous from one people's "country" to the next, so that knowledgeable people can tell a visiting ethnographer where their accounts leave off and those of the next people along the track begin. The result is a common "track" that coordinates the origin traditions of diverse cultures over many hundreds of miles of terrain.

Fewer people, perhaps, are aware that similar accounts of travelling creators, and of their routes, are found on the island of New Guinea. They occur, in fact, along the south coasts of the Western and Gulf Provinces, in adjoining areas of West Papua, in southern areas of the Simbu Province, and on the Torres Strait Islands – largely in regions that lie in near proximity to Australia. During my anthropological research among the Daribi people of Mt. Karimui,[1] I was told, after considerable hesitation, several accounts of the creator Souw, and those who told me the stories were able to map out his route. But if I wished to know what had happened to Souw beyond a certain point, they added, I would have to ask the Pawaian speakers who live in the Sena River valley to the east of Mt. Karimui. I was able, subsequently, to collect accounts of the hero and his route from the Sena River Pawaians and from those of the Pio River, to the southeast of Mt. Karimui.[2] During a visit to a population of Polopa (Foraba)-Daribi speakers living on the lower Erave, an additional account, linked closely with local landscape features, came to light, recounting the hero's adventures *before* he entered the Karimui area. Most intriguing, however, was the name with which the Erave people identified their hero

– Sido, the very name associated with the hero of a very similar myth by the people of Kiwai Island in the mouth of the Fly River.

The Polopa-Daribi speakers of the lower Erave had no knowledge, at that time, of the Kiwai people or their mythic tradition, and it seems certain that no single people within the 800 kilometre range of the complex was ever aware of its total extent. Yet there is a compelling similarity of imagery and thematic content, as well as a geographic continuity of the hero's route and a linguistic cognacy in the names attributed to him, that argue powerfully for the unitary nature of the complex. Even more significant, perhaps, is the place that many of the myths occupy in the religious cosmologies of the respective cultures. Whereas they may or may not involve the creation of the earth and its landforms, as they do at Karimui, they almost invariably address crucial questions of human mortality, of fertility, and reproduction, and of how these are related to one another: how did it come about that man must die? How is death related to sexuality and human relationships? The myths are basic, epitomising articulations of these essential religious or philosophical issues, and as such they are often treated as repositories of revealed power, sacred mysteries, and secret knowledge. The Daribi withheld their accounts of Souw from Australian administration officials, missionaries, and linguistic missionaries, and disclosed them to me only after they had become certain of the nature of my work. In his book *Dema*, J. van Baal relates the amazing story of how some interior Marind-anim villagers suffered imprisonment and ritual discrediting (by showing their bullroarers to women and uninitiated children) rather than reveal their version of the myth of Sosom.[3]

Clearly there is more to a myth than a mere plot or story; on the level of the individual culture, it has a profound meaningful relationship to the people's conception of the world and of the human place within it. On a broader, intercultural level, as a complex or tradition shared, knowingly or unknowingly, by a number of cultures with different languages and cosmologies, it can tell us something about the contacts and historical affinities among those cultures. Whether we choose to identify the unifying factor with a specific event or happening, with a widespread affinity in conceptual thinking, or with some combination of these, there is more to myth than mere story on this level too.

The known extent of what have been called "Papuan Hero Tales," the tradition with which we are concerned here, is from the Marind-anim of West Papua to the southern part of the Simbu Province of Papua New Guinea, at Karimui (Figure 63). The stories, and reported travels of the hero, are more or less continuous between these points. Traditions of a travelling creator are found elsewhere beyond these

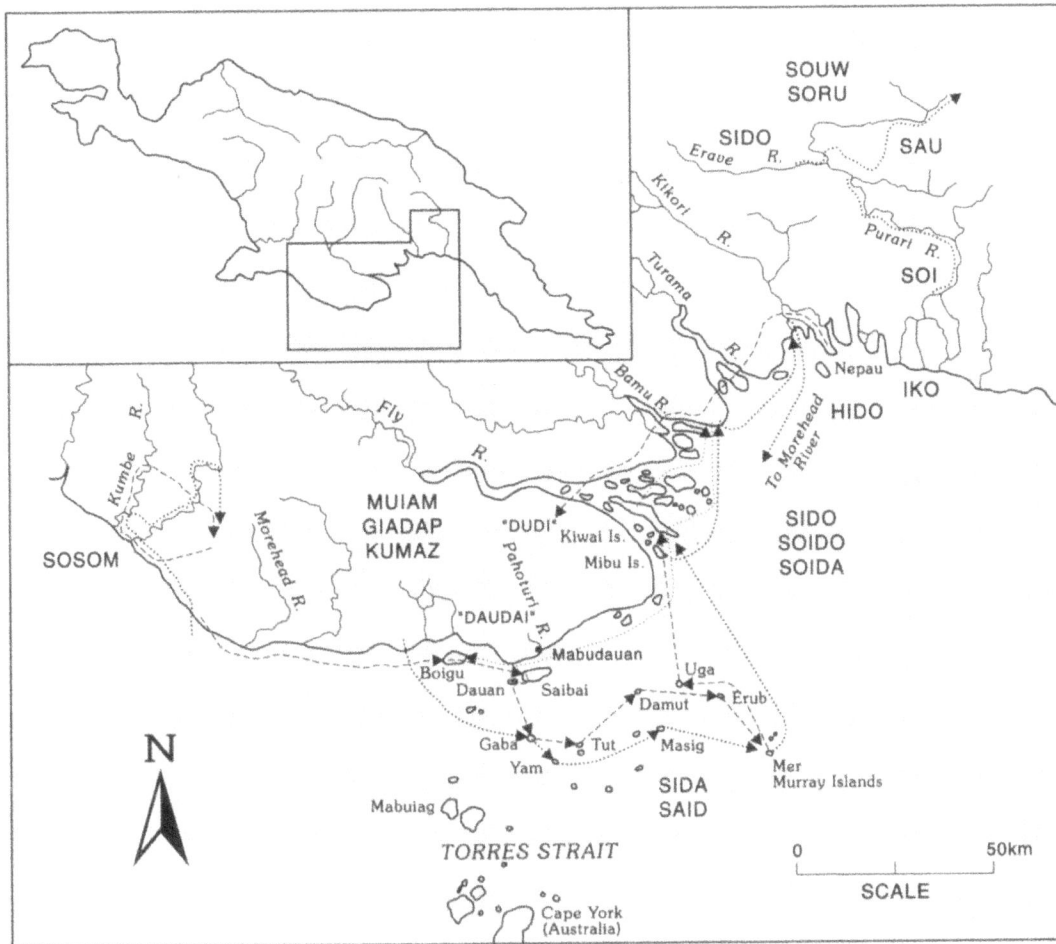

Figure 63: Routes of heroes and creators in southern New Guinea.

points, particularly in the eastern highlands of Papua New Guinea, but only within the area designated do the names and stories appear to be clearly cognate. From Torres Strait eastward and northward, the hero is said to have come from the west, initially, and moved eastward ("from Sadoa where the Togeri [Tugeri] men come from" in a Torres Strait version).[4] West of Torres Strait, however, among the Marind-anim (the so-called "Togeri men"), the tradition is that Sosom, the hero, came from the *east*, and indeed, according to van Baal, the Dema (creative spirit) Sosom is said to return yearly from the east during the east monsoon as a presence during initiation rites.[5]

The reversal in direction here suggests a centering of the tradition somewhere roughly in the Trans-Fly-Torres Strait region. It is, moreover, in this area that we find, in some cases, alternate versions of the story co-existing, and mention of certain place-names far beyond their local areas. This is not surprising, as the peoples of this region are great travellers; not only did the Marind-anim themselves conduct their famous raiding expeditions far to the east along the coast, but the Kiwai people of the

Fly estuary knew the coast intimately as canoeists, and maintained a far western settlement at Mabudauan,[6] at the mouth of the Pahoturi River, opposite Torres Strait. Adding to this the fact that Austen collected the legends of Hido, clearly variants of the Kiwai Sido story, among the Gope, a people (one of several between the mouths of the Bamu and Kikori Rivers) he identifies as being "of Kiwai extraction,"[7] it appears likely that the Kiwai and those with whom they were in immediate contact carried the tales over much of their central range.

In his monograph *The Folk-Tales of the Kiwai Papuans*, probably the most extensive collection of Melanesian mythology ever published, the Finnish ethnograpmer Gunnar Landtman[8] records the Kiwai myth of Sido in 22 episodes, most of them followed by a long list of variant, or alternative, versions. The text is followed by a section of "songs of Sido" and an Addendum of related stories from the Kiwai area and from various of the islands in and around Torres Strait.[9] Interestingly, the name of the hero varies in the accounts quoted from the *Reports of the Cambridge Anthropological Expedition to the Torres Straits* from Sida on Saibai and Mabuiag to Soida on Kiwai Island itself.[10] Landtman follows his discussion of Sido with the tale of what he considers to be an altogether different hero, Soido, "the promoter of agriculture," and provides a list of related stories.[11] He comments that the *Reports* of the Torres Straits Expedition mix together the tales of Sido and Soido under the name of *Sida, the Bestower of Vegetable Food*, and indeed, the Cambridge expedition's "Soido" tales include episodes found in Landtman's "Sido" epic.[12]

It is clear that Landtman wishes to distinguish the motif of Sido, as "the first man who died," from that of Soido as a "promoter of agriculture," and tends to regard any association of these motifs within a single story as a result of confusion or misidentification. But it is also true that the final episode (43) of Landtman's (main) Sido text, recounting Sido's adventures in Adiri ("at the extreme western border off the world"), *is virtually identical in its content with the Soido stories*. Sido, the first man who died, brings agriculture to Adiri, located far to the west, in exactly the same way (e.g. by ejaculating food plants through his large penis) as Soido, *in Landtman's own account*, brings agriculture to the Torres Strait Islands.

Whether we are dealing with a confusion of two myths here, or a diffusion of one, is less important than the implications of the issue itself for our interest. The name of the hero (Sido, Sida, Soido, Soida) is interchangeable, but the location of the Soido episode (sexual introduction of food plants) is invariably to the west of Kiwai - at Adiri or on the Torres Strait Islands. Thus the far-ranging Kiwai would appear to have incorporated two separate versions of the hero myth within their extensive mythology. One of these, the "Kiwai" version, is that of Sido, who brought death into the world. The other version, identifiable with the Torres Strait Islands, that of the sexual introduction of food production, has both been incorporated within the Sido epic, as an episode recounting the hero's adventures far to the west, and presented as a separate tale, that of Soido.

Landtman's distinction between the two versions is, nevertheless, significant in that the shift in thematic emphasis from one to the other corresponds to the reversal in the direction of the hero's route discussed above. In the Torres Strait tales collected by Rivers and Haddon,[13] and in van Baal's accounts of the Dema Sosom among the Marind-Anim,[14] the hero is a bringer of food plants and of human fertility and growth, all mediated through the agency of his large penis. To the north and east of the Trans-Fly-Torres Strait juncture, beginning with the Kiwai tale of Sido, the hero's adventures, and even his often prodigious sexuality, have the opposite implication – that of the origin of death rather than life. From Kiwai northward and eastward, across the Papuan Gulf and up the Purari watershed, this emphasis on the origin of human mortality is consistent, suggesting that the myth itself moved thence.

The implication here is that the successive regional variations of the myth were in some sense derived from, or based upon, an original model corresponding to something like the Kiwai story of Sido. Recurrence of the name "Sido" on the lower Erave River would tend to confirm this, though the name "Soi," recorded in association with a similar myth by Egloff and Kaiku on the lower Purari,[15] points rather to "Soido." There is, nevertheless, a further consideration here, one that reconstructions based on straightforward word-of-mouth transmission or diffusion might fail to take into account. This is that mortality, reproduction, and food production are powerful themes, and are likely to be central to any people's ideas and values and they relate to the interpretation of life and human action. Their origin is the origin of the human condition as this is made sense of in the symbolisations of a particular culture, and so the way in which the account of their origin is articulated will necessarily reflect the indigenous ideas and values. To the extent that these "hero tales" have been accepted as vital and secret knowledge by a range of diverse cultures, they have been diversified on the model of those cultures' differences.

Thus, for example, the hero's large penis serves as a conduit for plant domesticates and a device linking these to human sexuality in the Torres Strait stories, but is an immoderate and stealthy implement of violation in the Karimui and Purari tales. Among the Marind-anim, where the hero Sosom is associated with a boy's initiatory cult involving sodomizing practices, the story involves the severing of the long penis following its entrapment in heterosexual intercourse, leaving a remnant useful only in sodomy.[16] In effect, Sosom's enlarged penis becomes an ideologically justifying foil for non-heterosexual insemination practices.

It is through a series of such selective re-interpretations that the Kiwai conception of Sido, the son "of everyone" born of his father's connection with the earth, the "first man who died," who nevertheless arose from his grave as a light,[17] and thus seemed to Landtman's informants as being "all same Jesus Christ,"[18] undergoes a transformation into the being of which my informants at Karimui said "you call him God, we call him Souw."[19] Souw is the *to nigare bidi*, creator of the land, who cursed mankind with death, but is himself immortal. Thus in addition to the life/death inversion that we encounter in moving from Torres Strait to Kiwai, there is an additional inversion of the hero from the victim of mortality to its perpetrator. The process of reinterpretive adaptation would seem, as Lévi-Strauss might suggest, to rely heavily upon inversion.

The continuities are no less apparent for all of this. The Daribi name "Souw" is a contraction of "Sorouw," given as an alternative name for the hero. "Sorouw," also the specific for a kind of grass, seems in turn to represent a phonetic approximation of the Polopa name Sido, in that Daribi phonology tends toward a kind of "harmonising" of vowels and avoids the combination of extreme front and back vowels within a single word. Thus the sequence of names, moving from Kiwai through Gope to Polopa, and finally, Daribi, is Sido-Hido-Sido-Sorouw (Souw), by no means an unnatural or unexpected phonological transition by Melanesian standards. There are also fairly explicit similarities between the Kiwai and the Karimui peoples, including the basic longhouse frame (shared also by the Gope and Polopa); a report on blood groups among the Karimui peoples cites impressive statistical evidence to the effect that "in particular, the Kiwai have ABO, P and MNS gene frequencies strikingly similar to those of Karimui."[20]

It is as difficult, perhaps, to distinguish historical from adaptive or accidental connections in population genetics as it is in myth; we know little about gene frequencies in the populations between Karimui and the Fly River estuary, and the possibility of accidental similarities always exists between peoples with a similar general genetic makeup. In the present case, however, there is something of a progressive change, or tendency, in the construction of the plot itself as we move from Kiwai to Karimui, and this tendency complements both continuities of the myth and the hero's names, and the inversions noted above. The basic heterosexual relationship in the Kiwai Sido tale is conjugal – Sido meets his death in a conflict arising from a separation with his wife. In the Gope tale, however, Hido (or Waea) is seduced by his sister, and in his shame he embarks on a journey to the land of the dead, followed by the *sister*, Hiwabu.[21] (From this point eastward the woman, a blood relative, follows the hero, rather than vice-versa as in the Kiwai story). On the lower Erave and at Karimui the hero is shamed through his attempts to copulate with a (virgin) woman who is clearly much younger (perhaps generationally) than he is, and in all cases it is the hero's *daughter*, not involved in the sexual attempt, who sentimentally follows her departing father.[22] In the tale of Soi recorded by Egloff and Kaiku on the middle Purari, Beri, the victim of the sexual attempt, addresses Soi as "grandfather,"[23] though it is Soi's *nephew*, Hoa, who accompanies him afterwards. The sequence of transformations here is a most intriguing one: from the conjugal relationship as the moral and motivational fulcrum of the story we proceed to the sibling relationship, thence to the father-daughter bond, and finally, at least in formal terms, to that between grandfather and granddaughter. As we pass from a conception of the hero as "all same Jesus Christ" to one more nearly suggestive of Jehova, the connection between the hero and the significant female protagonist becomes more intense and, often, forbidden, and the hero's status becomes increasingly enhanced in contradistinction to an increasingly dependent woman. Whatever else might be said of this tendency, the very fact that the transition is a regular and systematic one argues for the integrity of the mythic tradition itself, and supports the likelihood of a common derivation.

Successive versions of the tale, as we move eastward, also tend to intensify the relationship between the sexual motivation of the hero's journey and the loss of human immortality. In the Kiwai story of Sido, the relationship is almost incidental: Sido is killed by Meuri, a rival lover of his wife, and his soul follows his body toward the land of the dead. Along the way, in a seemingly unconnected episode, Sido attempts to shed his old body and regain life, but he is disturbed by some boys and is thus unable to achieve rejuvenation.[24] Among the Gope, however, Hido flees to the land of the dead after being ashamed in incest with his sister, and sheds his skin en route in an effort to escape detection. Farther to the east, on the lower Erave, at Karimui, and on the lower Purari, the curse of human mortality follows directly upon the frustration and sexual anger of the hero, thus culminating the resonance between the two dialectically related themes.

Thus the eastern versions can be understood as a result of a process of condensation or distillation of the dialectical polarity in the course of the tale's transmission. This would, again, point to the possibility of an origin farther to the west, perhaps among the Kiwai. But the association of sexuality and mortality in these stories also seems to be involved with another motif that is only vaguely suggested in the Kiwai and Gope tales, and is absent from the Torres Strait and Marind-anim versions. This is the identification of the hero, in various ways, with a snake, and the association of the snake with a bird. Since the association of a bird and a snake with accounts of human origin or mortality occurs elsewhere, in Melanesia, as well as Australia, it is possible that the "eastern," or interior Gulf versions of the hero tales represent a blending together of two traditions. This would certainly not deny or controvert the evidences noted above for derivation of the tales from the west, but it does deserve consideration.

Heider reports an origin myth episode among the Dani, a large people inhabiting the Baliem Valley in the highlands of West Papua, in which a python and a bird symbolise contrasting immortal and mortal destinies; man chooses to be like to a bird, and thus foregoes the ability to rejuvenate himself by shedding his skin.[25] Among the Polopa and Daribi, the huge penis of Souw is identified by a bird as a "snake" as it becomes erect in the bush, and the bird gives its characteristic cry, thus signalling women to come and look for the reptile. (Identification of the hero with a snake is strengthened at the end of these tales when he sheds and "throws down" his skin for men to take up). Interestingly, the bird, *kaueri*, that cries out in these stories is either the same species as, or closely related to, the Black Cuckoo or Koel (*Eudynamis orientalis*)[26] the hero of a series of Australian "travelling creator" myths.

A mythic tradition as widely and diffusely ramified as this is doubtless an old one indeed. But there is a persistent strain of symbolic or ideological interpretation among the Daribi people of Mt. Karimui that corresponds to its general premises. This is a contrast between human beings and birds based on the fact that the Daribi language uses a single word, *ge*, with reference both to the pearl shells used traditionally as the major item in bridewealth and the eggs of birds (and of other creatures, including snakes). In effect, then, both human beings and birds, for instance, reproduce themselves through *ge*. But human beings do so by passing their "eggs" around from one group to another and never hatching them, while birds and reptiles retain their "pearl shells" and transform them into their young. A whole complex of Daribi origin myths relating to pearl shells, various birds, and hairless creatures generally, has been developed around this theme.[27]

Whether or not the Daribi share any sort of historical connection, via their mythology, with the Dani people of the Baliem Valley or with any aboriginal Australian peoples is difficult to determine. Such similarities may simply be based on the practice (widespread in Melanesia, and not unknown elsewhere in the world) of using radically different kinds of animals to symbolise different mortal states. It is likely, for instance, that any new origin account, or even any new factual material relating to human existence, introduced to the Daribi would have been interpreted in terms of such a contrasting symbolism, and adapted to it. In discussing Dani totemism, in fact, Heider[28] cites evidence that just such an interpretation was made of Europeans by the Dani. Dani, who symbolise themselves as "birds," often speak of Europeans as "snake people," and considered them, in many cases, to be immortal (this was still a widespread assumption among older Daribi - possibly for the same reason – in 1968).

In any case, the bird/snake/human contrast amounts virtually to an abstract cosmological principle when compared with the highly explicit details of plot and motif that can be traced in virtual contiguity from the Trans-Fly region up through Karimui on one hand, and into the Marind-anim area on the other. Moreover, all of the evidence we have reviewed here indicates the likelihood of a specific point of origin for the complex of "Papuan hero tales" somewhere in the region of the junction of the Torres Strait Island complex and the Trans-Fly.

Billai Laba's account (Contribution 2) of "Oral Traditions about Early Trade by Indonesians in Southwest Papua New Guinea" is highly significant in the context of these evidences, for it provides specific information about foreign contacts at an early period in just the area where the mythic differentiation seems to have taken place. At the very least, Laba's account offers a highly likely historical source for the continuities of the "Papuan hero tales"; beyond this, however, it furnishes an ethnohistorically strategic and plausible means for the introduction of a basically Middle-Eastern set of mythic motifs into a Melanesian region. Unless some sort of diffusion from Malayan, Indonesian, or other nearby Islamic traditions can be shown to be a likelihood, many would be tempted to ascribe these motifs and their introduction to the message of recent Christian missionising activity – a very unlikely source, considering the likely time-depth of the Papuan tales and the degree to which they have been incorporated into local religions and cosmologies.[29]

In this regard, it is most intriguing to speculate on the nature of the *buk* mentioned in Laba's discussion, and also on the school established at Waidoro and on what the content of its lessons might have been. (The suggestion that rituals and secrets of the fertility of coconuts were taught, and the school ceased operation because of a young girl's pregnancy brings the whole matter very close to the content of the Papuan hero tales themselves). It seems most probable that the *buk* amounted, as Laba suggests, to trade diaries, though the possibility that they were copies of the Koran or some other religious book should not be ruled out. Either the *buk*, or, more probably, the *siikull*, could have provided vehicles for the introduction of Islamic or other, related Middle Eastern mythic motifs.

The complex account involving a first man and woman, the original instance of sexual "knowledge," man's loss of immortality, and, very often, a snake or serpent, is widespread in the mythologies and religious traditions of the Middle East, and is part of the religious beliefs of many sects and traditions originating there. A version has been incorporated into the Book of Genesis of the Christian Bible, and is also known in Islam. The myth itself, however, seems to predate the founding of these religions. It is difficult in a cursory account to do justice to the philosophical profundity of the mythos, which involves not only man's differentiation from other creatures, but also the deep, dialectical relationship between sexuality, reproduction, and death – that reproduction implies death just as death necessitates reproduction. In my work I have found that the Melanesian tales are no less profound in this regard than the Middle Eastern ones – in some cases they seem more so.

I have been circumspect here regarding the mythic elements that might have been brought across in an Indonesian contact largely because – although this may not be generally known – any of the great old-world religions is surrounded by an extensive unofficial or semiofficial apocryphal literature. Thus it would be very difficult to predict what variants or versions of a proliferate kaleidoscope of mythology might have been introduced, and through what local mythic traditions they may have been perfused or varied along the way: of what syncretisms were the Papuan hero tales a synthesis, and themselves a syncretism? In fact, the Middle Eastern myth that the Papuan hero tales, and in particular, the Kiwai tale of Sido, most resemble, is neither Christian nor Islamic, but the ancient Mesopotamian Epic of Gilgamesh, known from the empires of Sumer and Akkad in the third and second millenia BC. The Gilgamesh Epic is either the original version of a myth that was later incorporated into other religions and other texts, or else it was merely an earlier adaptation of a myth that was already old by the time of Sumer and Akkad. Gilgamesh was a kind of superhuman, gigantic in his abilities and appetites – a dominator of men and seducer of women. To control him the gods create a wild man, Enkidu, whom Gilgamesh succeeds in overcoming and befriending. After Gilgamesh refuses to marry Ishtar, the goddess of love, she sends a bull to destroy him. Gilgamesh and Enkidu subdue the bull, but the gods decided that Enkidu must die. He falls ill, and dreams of the "house of dust" that he must enter; when Enkidu dies, Gilgamesh is overcome, and sets out on a journey across the world to find the secret of immortality. Guided by Utnapishtim, survivor of the deluge, he finds a plant that restores youth, but this is stolen from him by a snake while he is at a waterhole. Saddened and resigned, he returns to tell humanity of the land of the dead.

Like the Kiwai Sido, who was conceived of the ground by his father, Enkidu in the epic is made of mud. Sido's troubles, and fate, like those of Gilgamesh, arise from his spurning a woman - not the goddess Ishtar but the lovely Sagaru, his wife, to whom he refuses sex. When Sido is killed in a fight with her next lover, Meuri, it is the latter who grieves over him, much as Gilgamesh grieves over his friend and rival Enkidu. Sido then journeys over the earth to find a means of rejuvenating himself, but is finally frustrated at a famous waterhole on Boigu Island, where he is offered a drink from his own skull[30] (the Daribi story of Souw is even closer to the Gilgamesh epic in this respect, for in it the snakes and other hairless creatures appropriate Souw's immortal skin, thus cheating mankind of immortality). Finally, too, Sido, like Gilgamesh, becomes resigned to his (and humanity's) fate, and prepares the land of the dead for the many who are to follow him. (The similarity in name between the barmaid Siduri in the epic and the protagonist in the Papuan tales is interesting, but probably accidental.)[31]

Pointed similarities with the ancient Mesopotamian epic relate rather specifically to the tale of Sido and the other "eastern" stories seemingly derived from, or associated with it, rather than those of Torres Strait or the Marind-anim. There *are*, of course, themes and details shared by all of these stories. In the Gizra origin myth discussed by Laba, for instance, it is stated that all peoples, including Australian Aborigines, Torres Strait Islanders, the Gizra, and other Papuan peoples, originated at the place called Basir Puerk. Many of the Daribi Souw texts name a similar legendary or ancestral place, the kunai grass plain on the Tua River called Bumaru, associated with Souw in the stories, as the place of origin of all peoples.[32] As the Gizra account names Giadap as ancestor of dark-skinned peoples, and Muiam of those with lighter skins, so some of the Souw tales name Souw's daughter Yaro as ancestress of all light-skinned peoples, and her friend (or stepsister) Karoba as ancestress of dark-skinned peoples.[33]

Despite these similarities, the names of the Gizra protagonists, Giadap, his younger brother Muiam, and the single woman Kumaz (originator of death and musical instruments) do not seem to share cognacy with the Sosom-Soido-Hido-Iko-Souw series. Interestingly, however, the notion of a woman who was the originator of death and the founder of cultural practices is shared among the peoples of the Fly-Sepik Divide, around Telefolmin, in their common tradition of "The Old Woman". She is called Afek (by Telefolmin), Afekan (by Tifalmin), and Karigan (among the Faiwol). In many of the mythical accounts, including specifically those involving the origin of death, she interacts with her younger brother, who is portrayed as very clever, and who becomes the first man to die. This brother, quite similar to Muiam, the "younger brother" of the Gizra account, bears a name - Umoim at Telefolmin,[34] Wolmoiin among the Faiwol - that could easily be a cognate of "Muiam."

Is there yet another mythic "track," additional to the Sosom tales to the west, the Soido stories of Torres Strait, and Sido-Souw series to the northeast, radiating northward from the Trans-Fly and into the Star Mountains? The possibility bears exciting historical implications, but more will have to be known of the likelihood of intervening links before it can be entertained seriously.

Were such an interior connection of the Gizra myth to be established, we would have solid evidence of the radiation of mythic traditions in *all* directions from a focal centre (Basir Puerk?) of Indonesian trade connections in the southwest of Papua New Guinea. The possibility of ethnohistoric links to the "Mountain Ok" peoples of the Fly-Sepik divide recalls, however, the *caveat* discussed above. Peoples like the Telefol and the Faiwol have become famous recently in the ethnographic literature[35] for the epistemological sophistication of their conceptual orientation and ritual life. Since this conceptual and ritual world centres on the *ban*, or male cult-initiation system, which is, in turn, based on the mythic corpus of the "Old Woman" complex, it is evident that the use that these peoples have made of what may be a very widespread historical legacy is very much a product of their own creativity. This is no less true, of course, for peoples like the Kiwai, the Daribi, and the Gizra, but what it implies is that the historical source of such a complex is perhaps less important, in terms of the significance of the myths for the peoples themselves, than the ways in which this source has been interpreted and elaborated upon in each particular case.

Nonetheless, the likelihood that the origin traditions and even the secret knowledge of a number of Melanesian peoples owe their own origin to an early epoch of cultural contact is a matter of prime ethnohistorical importance. Whether the interconnecting routes of the heroes map out actual journeys in the past, or just simply the journeying of the stories themselves, they trace out a sphere of religious and conceptual communication. Whether the tales deal, like those of Sido, Souw, Soi, and Gilgamesh, with the loss of human immortality, or whether they concern the bringing of life and fertility like the stories of Soido and Sosom, they concern the central truths of life and death that can be found to animate the core symbolisations of most or all Papua New Guinea cultures.

Whether they actually communicate something to the indigenous peoples, or whether, as I suspect, they merely reveal to them aspects and implications of their thought (through the shock of alienation and the consequent self-consciousness) that would never otherwise have been realised, cultural contacts like the one that is in evidence here are extra-processual events. They are unusual impingements, and carry their own momentum. But this is no reason to conclude that such events were necessarily few in number, over long historical periods.

In his monograph on the Waropen people of Cendrawasih Bay, G.J. Held lists a number of honorific titles in use there that clearly and obviously derive from Moluccan originals,[36] and he notes that in Waropen mythology, a famous trader from Ternate, Raja Amos, was brought to the area by the culture-hero Kuru Pasai.[37] The Waropen possessed also large, whole specimens of what is apparently ancient Chinese porcelain,[38] used as brideweath. Granted that an area as far west as this fell well within the nominal domain and trading and tax-collecting ambit of the Sultan of Tidore,[39] and hence in a region of known contact with Indonesians, the parallels between this known instance of contact and those reported in Laba's account are intriguing.

Notes

1. Anthropological field research was carried out among the Daribi people of Mt. Karimui from November, 1963 to February, 1965, funded by the Bollingen Foundation and the University of Washington, and from July, 1968 to May, 1969, funded by the Social Science Research Council of New York and Northwestern University.

2. The texts and the routes, as well as those collected among the Polopa-Daribi of the Erave (identified there as Foraba), are published in R. Wagner 1972: 24–32.

3. van Baal 1966: 491–3.

4. Rivers 1904: 31.

5. van Baal 1966: 267

6. Landtman 1927: 1 01502.

7. Austen 1932: 468.

8. Landtman 1917: 95–116.

9. Landtman 1917: 116–9.

10. Landtman 1917: 118.

11. Landtman 1917: 119–24.

12. Landtman 1917: 123, variants G and H.

13. Rivers 1904 and Haddon 1908.

14. van Baal 1966.

15. Egloff and Kaiku 1978.

16. Wagner 1972: 21.

17. Landtman 1917: 110, variant B.

18. Landtman 1917: 116.

19. Wagner 1972: 19.

20. Russell et al 1971: 87.

21. Another Gope version is closer to the Kiwai tale than this, see Austen 1932: 474.

22. At Karimui she is called Yaro among the Daribi, and Yuaro by the Pawaian speakers.

23. Egloff and Kaiku 1978: 48.

24. Landtman 1917: 109–10, Episode 36.

25. Heider 1970: 144.

26. Arndt 1965: 242–3.

27. Wagner 1978: 65–90.

28. Heider 1970: 69.

29. In the 1960s, when I first became aware of the relationships among the Papuan Hero Tales, a former colleague, Dr. Phil Weigand, suggested that they might all have their source in epics dating from the conversion of Indonesians to Islam.

30. A photograph of the waterhole is published in Landtman 1917: 111.

31. Beardmore cited in Landtman 1917: 118, G. names the hero as Sidor. Perhaps more to the point of a discussion of the possible introduction of Middle-Eastern mythic themes is the Miriam Island name for the hero: Said.

32. Wagner 1972: 28. An aerial photograph of Bumaru appears in Wagner 1978: 122. c

33. Wagner 1967: 41.

34. Textual material and the source for these comments is contained in an unpublished paper by Dan Jorgensen, "Revelation and Transformation in Telefolmin," which was presented in the symposium on dynamism in Oceanic cultures at the annual Meetings of the American Anthropological Association, Washington, D.C., in December, 1982.

35. Jorgensen 1981 as yet unpublished, records the exegesis of the Telefol "mother house" at Telefolip. Some implications of the complex are articulated in Fredrik Barth 1980. See also Barbara Jones 1980.

36. Held 1957: 82.

37. Held 1957: 83.

38. Held 1957 depicted in plates 26 and 27, opposite page 98.

39. Given the well-known Melanesian tendency to reproduce an aspirated "t" as "s" (e.g. *tobago-sobago*), the resemblance between Tidore and Sido (Sidor) should not pass our notice.

Contribution 2

Oral traditions about early trade by Indonesians in southwest Papua New Guinea

Billai Laba

Introduction

Indonesian traders have sought natural products in the coastal areas of southwest Papua New Guinea in the past. There are no written records of this early trade. However, the oral traditions of the people of this area, plus linguistic clues, indicate that Indonesian traders once visited this area. The area concerned extends along the coast from the Wassi Kussa River in the west to Kura Creek, some forty kilometres west of Daru (Figure 64).

The area is inhabited by the Gizra who live in the lower Pahoturi River area, the Agob of the Pahoturi and the lower east bank of the Mai Kussa, and the Idi on the upper parts of the Mai Kussa and Wassi Kussa River system. Although the Kiwai once had a fishing camp at Mabudauan, they did not establish a permanent village until after the British established Mabudauan as the first District headquarters in 1889.[1]

Foreign objects and their names

The Gizra, Agob and the Idi people seem to have had contact, prior to the arrival of Europeans, with foreigners who used metal implements and books. The names used by the speakers of these three Papua New Guinean languages for metal implements, books and other objects were probably derived from certain Indonesian words. This is the case with metal implements. For example, a knife is called *turik* by the Gizra, Saibai and other Western Torres Strait Islanders. The Miriam speakers of Eastern Torres Strait call it *tulik*, and the Bine call it *turi*. *Turik* refers to an axe rather than a knife amongst the Agob, Idi, Nambu and Tonda. Likewise the word for axe in the Kiwai dialects of Tureture, Mawatta and Mabudauan is *tiriko*.

Matthew Flinders, the captain of the *Investigator*, reports that Mer (Murray) Islanders in Eastern Torres Strait, paddled to his ship shouting *tooree*, *toolick* in 1802. This was how they asked for knives and axes.[2] Hence these islanders and presumably others in Torres Strait knew about metal implements when Europeans such as Flinders began to visit their islands.

Other words are also used to refer to metal implements or iron. These may also have an Indonesian origin. *Malil* is a word for iron in Gizra, Western and Eastern Torres Strait. *Kamda* was another type of early metal axe. It was known in the Gizra village of Waidoro. The Tonda have a similar word, that is *kamba*. Both *kamda* and *kamba* may have been derived from the Malay word for axe (*kampak*).

Another word is *beta*. This was a heavy metal axe used in the past by the Gizra. The Nambu sometimes also call an axe *bila*. An Indonesian informant told me that *belah* in Malay means to 'split'.

Salmita is a general word for axe in the Togo and Kupere dialects of Gizra. The Tonda sometimes refer to a knife as *salmita*. It may be related to the word *scimitar*, which is the name for a curved sword.

Finally, in the Togo and Kupere dialects of Gizra, the word for hoe is *pambu*. The same word is used by the Agob and Idi, whereas the Tonda refer to a knife as *fambu*.

Most of the above words are probably not indigenous; it is likely they were introduced by foreigners during the period of early trade. Another example of widespread name similarities for a foreign item is the local names for tobacco. The different names given are listed in Table 1 below and seem to be closely related.

Figure 64: Southwest Papua New Guinea.

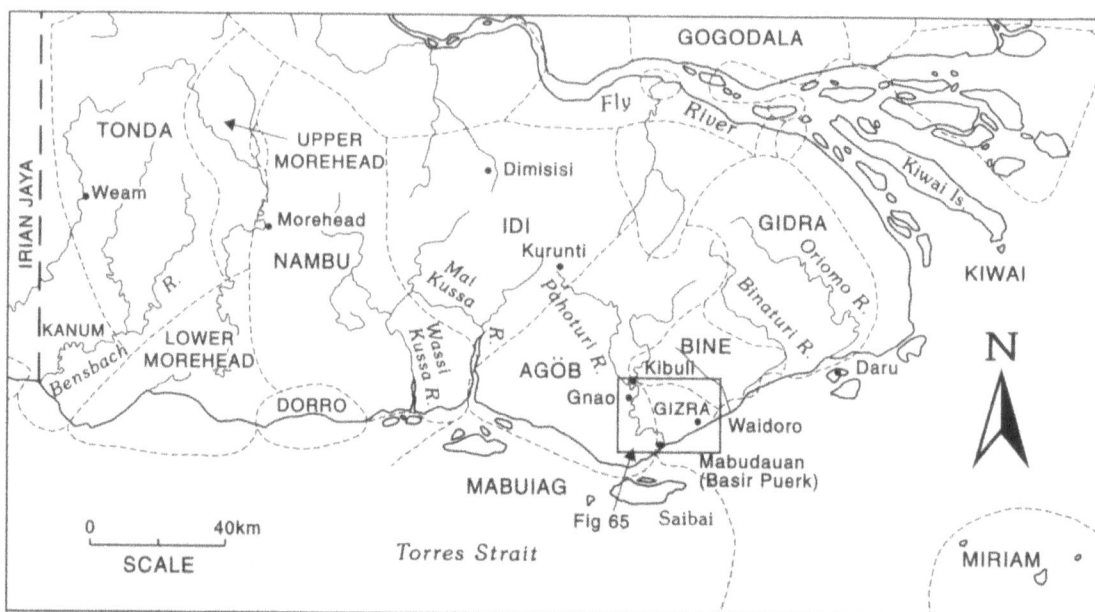

Table 1: Variant names for tobacco used in southwest Papua

names for tobacco	languages
suguba	Bine, Gidra, Gizra, Kiwai and Saibai Islanders
sakpa	Agöb, Idi, Tonda
sakop	Miriam (Eastern Torres Strait)
sukufa	Nambu
sakopa	Gogodala

It is no surprise that there are similarities between the names used on the mainland and in Torres Strait. The Gizra or Daudai-pam of the Papua New Guinea mainland formed the northern fringe of the Torres Strait trade system. There was also considerable social interaction, for example, the annual ceremony conducted by the Ait Algans of eastern Saibai. Each year they sailed to the mainland to join the Zibram of Zibar (Gizra people of Waidoro) for the ceremony called Buzural Terle. However, the focus of the early foreign trade seems to have been the mainland rather than the Torres Strait Islands, as the islanders know little about the now sacred *buk* (books).

Buk were once held at Basir Puerk as well as at Togo (now shifted to nearby Kulalae), Kupere, Waidoro and Dimisisi villages. We only know they existed and this knowledge has been passed down verbally through successive generations.

The incorporation of foreign introductions within the local mythology

Today many young Gizras are faced with such questions as, who brought the *buk*, where did they come from and what was written in them. The old people believe that the *buk* originated during the time that life was created at Basir Puerk (Mabudauan). According to the Gizra, Basir Puerk was the centre where three major mythical figures interacted. These were Giadap (the elder brother), Muiam (the younger brother) and Kumaz (a single woman). Kumaz is the originator of death and musical instruments, whereas Giadap is less powerful. Muiam was young, handsome, tattooed, straight-haired, light-skinned and was much more powerful than the other two. He lived on his own at a hamlet called KumKumpal at Basir Puerk. Although he was the younger brother of Giadap, Muiam was more intelligent and his activities were more complex than those of his elder brother.

Our origin myth states that the Zon Uglai (Australian Aborigines), the Siepam (Torres Strait Islanders) and the Gizra have a common birth place. This was Basir Puerk. According to the myth, the people who resemble Giadap are the Gizra people of Kupere and Togo, the Torres Strait Islanders and the Australian Aborigines. The Zibram of Waidoro, the Bine, Kiwai, Keremas, Motuans and other light-skinned people resemble Muiam, Giadap's younger brother. The overall belief is that these groups and their cultures emerged at Basir Puerk. Whatever sociomagical powers and beliefs the Gizra valued and used to master their environment, the other groups were likewise equipped. In other words, these people were bound by common beliefs and customs whether on land or in the sea.

The first Gizra villages were Kumazbasir, Nimon-muot and Solokono just north of Basir Puerk at Mabudauan hill (Numandorr), see Figure 65. Later the Gizra moved across the Pahoturi River to the area of their current settlements. They still regard Basir Puerk as their birthplace and ceremonial centre.

One of the activities which started because of the presence of Muiam at Basir Puerk was the ability to make metal implements. The Gizra believe that these were manufactured by a process which extracted iron from the granite rock at Basir Puerk.[3] It is also believed that when iron was being manufactured there, men of different races lived side by side.

Although Muiam dwelt in a hamlet called Kumkumpa[4] at Basir Puerk, he also travelled extensively along the coasts of southwest Papua New Guinea. I think this culture hero was a real person who once travelled as far east as the Gulf Delta. It must have happened long ago, as the accounts of his travels and activities have been passed on for many generations. They have won a prime place within the myths and legends of this coast. He was engaged in many different activities. Most of these were quite new to the local people and for this reason they believed his acts were supernatural.

He has various names in the myths of the coastal tribes. We call him Muiam. The Kiwai call him Sido.[5] The Gapo of Wabo call him Hido, whereas the Purari Delta people and Elema call him Iko.[6]

In most versions of the myth, at least one episode tells that the hero was the first man to have a sexual relationship with a female. He is then killed and as a consequence death becomes a reality. In many versions he is the originator of many things, including life and death. The hero comes from the west to the east and when he dies his soul goes back to the west and prepares a place for all mankind. Douglas Newton[7] stresses that Hido's path was subsequently taken by many migrants from Kiwai Island. Many elements of culture are shared as a result of this hero's activities and travels, for example, the widespread 'long-house cult'.

The Gizra believe that many activities, including the manufacturing of metal implements, came to an end due to European contact. The granite deposit then lay idle. Although the library at Basir Puerk was not used any more, two different men from each of the Gizra villages came everyday to guard it. The annual Dabu Terle (initiation ceremony) also continued. This ceremony used to last for six months and within this time the initiates roamed the area between Dabu and Basir Puerk, conducting all sorts of rituals and learning the secrets of their society.

Sites associated with these foreign introductions

Previously all Gizra villages consisted of three hamlets and each had a *kobo* (men's house). Out of the nine hamlets, there were only three leading ones. That is to say, each of these leading *kobo* had a *buk*. The

Figure 65: Basir Puerk and hinterland.

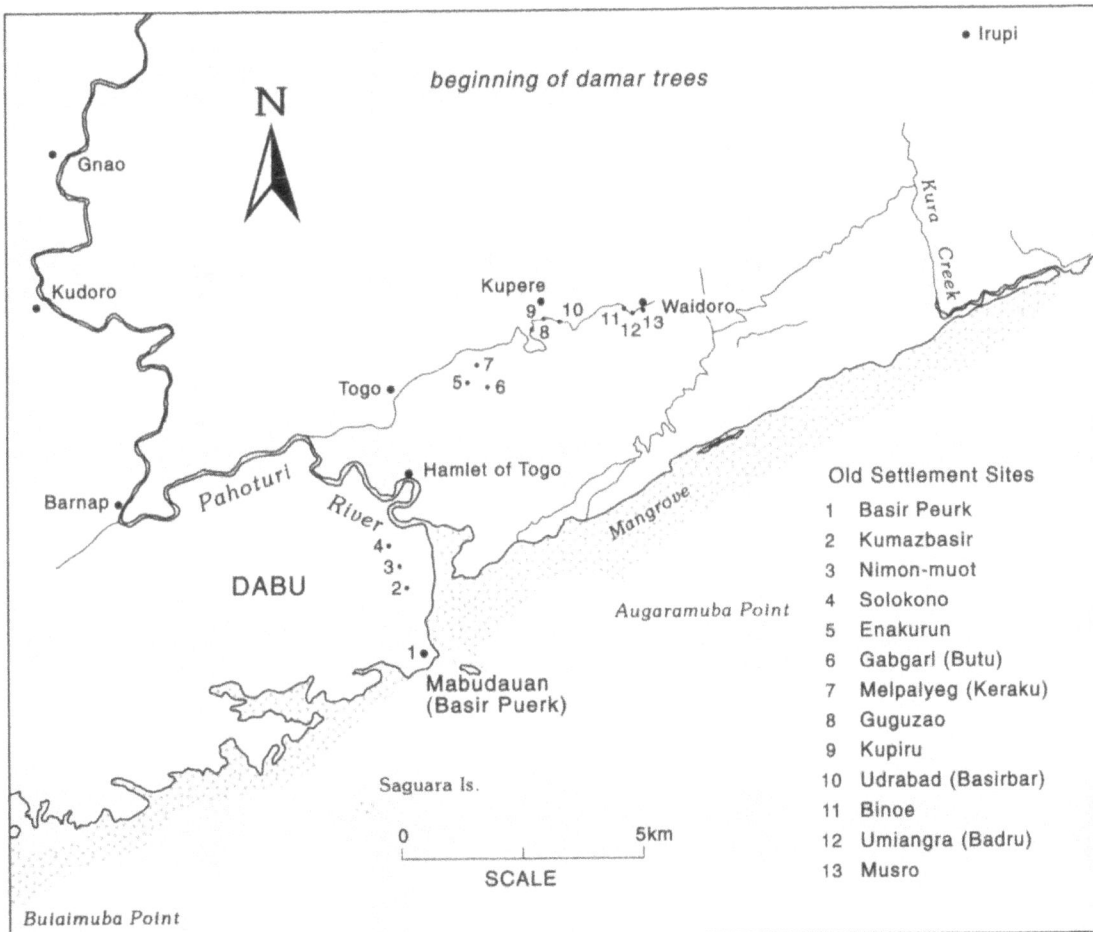

Old Settlement Sites

1 Basir Peurk
2 Kumazbasir
3 Nimon-muot
4 Solokono
5 Enakurun
6 Gabgarl (Butu)
7 Melpalyeg (Keraku)
8 Guguzao
9 Kupiru
10 Udrabad (Basirbar)
11 Binoe
12 Umiangra (Badru)
13 Musro

kobo at Zibar (Waidoro) was regarded as being much more powerful than the other two, as it also had a curved piece of *malil* (iron) which was placed underneath the *buk*. This symbolised the supernatural hero Muiam. Many mythical figures are portrayed by carved representations, but Muiam was never symbolised by any other form.

It is also claimed that there is a *buk* at Dimisisi in the Idi area. The local people say the *buk* is not a modern one, but was there for many years before European contact. It has been passed down by many generations and is believed to be associated with a very old boat. This is also very sacred and is located at the headwaters of the Mai Kussa River. The boat is in the water, but is tied to a tree at the bank of the river by a chain. The clan that is in charge of the *buk* also owns the sacred site where the boat is located. Access to this area is restricted to members of this clan. No other person can enter the area unless they have undergone certain rituals organised by the clan's elders.

In the Agöb area there is another sacred site near the headwaters of the Pahoturi River. Once again this area can only be entered by elderly male members and initiates (*kernge*) from the local clan. The boats are believed to possess supernatural powers originating from dead relatives (*mari*). In other words, one has to be transformed into the image of a dead spirit in order to see the boats or even to enter the area.

The local people and other nearby tribesmen believe that the boats are the 'Arks' belonging to Noah, that drifted there after the flood. The only reason why the people believe they are 'Arks' is merely because of the biblical stories they have heard. In reality they may be old boats used by early traders to this area. The explanation could be that the boats were not in good enough condition for the traders to use on their return journey, or perhaps they were left behind when the local people became hostile and forced the traders to leave hastily. They may have abandoned some of their boats and fled for their lives.

How the introductions may have come about and what happened when the traders came no more

It is possible the boats were owned by Indonesian traders from the Seram or Aru Islands who were in search of damar, a tree gum, as suggested by Pamela Swadling in Chapter 9. In the past damar was used like a candle. The name for this gum-producing tree in Agob and Idi is *yoto*. The Agöb, Idi and Gidra people used to collect damar and burn the gum to produce light at night. However, in the Nambu area of the Morehead District, the wood rather than the gum of the tree was favoured. The trees grow naturally and plentifully throughout the Oriomo Plateau.

The books may have been the diaries which the early traders distributed to the local headmen. These were then available for use during their visits to these areas. Basir Puerk is the traditional centre from whence cultural influences came forth in this region. At one time it may have been a trading post from which these foreigners operated into the hinterland. The people also believe that it was from this centre (Basir Puerk) that ideas and powers were transmitted to the *kobo* (men's houses).

These foreign items and influences were no longer reaching my area at the time of European contact. The metal implements have now rusted away. The original practical uses of the *buk* are forgotten, but their status within our society remains. I assume that metal implements were not the only trade items. There may have been others such as mirrors (*barida*) and glass beads (*kusal*). Some traces of these may be found by a thorough archaeological investigation of some of the early settlement locations of the Waidoro, Togo and Kupere. These would include the following sites: Barnap, Binoe, Gabgarl, Enakrun, Guguzao, Melpalyeg, Kupiru, Musro, Udrabad and Umiangra, which were last inhabited three generations ago.

Some *buk* may have been taken when Torres Strait Islanders made a retaliatory raid in about the 1890s. Others were probably lost during the frequent moves which had to be made to avoid the Tugeri raiders. This meant the *buk* would have been kept in poor storage facilities and were possibly exposed to the rain. The *buk* were last seen three generations ago and I assume that my people had them at least another three generations back from that time; otherwise the mythical associations about these objects would presumably not have arisen.

I am not in a position, since I have not been initiated, to understand the full sacred importance of the *buk*. There is an underlying belief that the *buk* were associated with the source of life. I and other young Gizra believe this not to be the case. We think that the myths and supposed powers of the *buk* and metal implements exist because they were first introduced long, long ago. Then they ceased to come. Some time afterwards Europeans came along.

Our old people claim we also had a school before Europeans came

Once there was a school in Zibar (*Waidoro*). In this school, students were taught the rituals and the secrets of the fertility of coconuts. It ceased operation due to the pregnancy of a young girl. A widespread belief among elderly Gizra men is that the names such as *urlpagi-siikull* (school),[8] *buk* (book), *barida* (mirror) and *malil* (iron) are not foreign but their own, because they had them before European contact.

Recent Indonesian traders from West Papua (former Dutch New Guinea)

Early last century, and in particular after the Second World War, some light-skinned foreigners entered my area. They rode on horseback and came from Dutch New Guinea. These foreigners were known to the Gizra and Agöb as 'Malayo'. Some Gizra people were given money in return for food, while others were given penknives. Later they were advised in Daru that the money was valueless in Papua and government officials inquired as to how Gizra people had obtained this foreign currency. The foreigners also taught the Gizra and the Kiwai people of Mabudauan how to play soccer and hockey. The local people can still recall some of the songs sung by the outsiders.

Here are two examples:

1. *Inu intu waraike*
   Sapelang jala a sapelang meri
   Dangan mari saian baia ... o
   O ... Arumbai e ... Malayo

2. *Alang alang dipania pania adi dipania tu*
   Kista Malayo
   Oli oli wanja wanja
   Wanja mela tu kosta Malayo

Some foreigners gave horses to their trade partners in the Weam area of the Morehead District. This was also the case in Ngao village in the Agöb area. Although the local people were taught how to ride horses and at times used them for carrying heavy loads, they remained frightened of them, probably because they had no previous experience with such big animals. The horses were also a nuisance because they fed on the leaves of garden crops and some developed horrible skin diseases. For these reasons the village people killed the horses in the Agöb area. However, some horses escaped and have been breeding wild. These wild horses can still be found in the Weam area of the Morehead District.

An informant from the Morehead area stated that his people referred to the foreigners as 'Dutchy from the Balanda Government'. The people believed the Dutch were moving their territorial boundary eastwards with the aim of bringing part of the Western Province under Dutch control. Many village people were given penknives as presents.

The names of many trade partners are still easily recalled, as well as the strange experiences they had with the horses and saddles.

Notes

1. A Gidra-speaking man called Bidebu played a significant role in the history of the Kiwai settlements of Tureture, Mawatta and Mabudauan. Bidebu controlled the area between the Oriomo and Binaturi (Badengle Tage) Rivers. His associations included links with the Bine-speaking people of Kunini, Tati, Glulu and Badu (Irupi), as well as with the Gizra village of Zibar (Jibaro-Waidoro).

   It was Kiwai people from Kadawa village on the south bank of the Fly River mouth who came to develop associations with the people of the Trans Fly coast. These Kiwai were led by Gamea. Bidebu after meeting Gamea assisted Gamea and his people. This is evident from the clan histories of the current Tureture, Mawatta and Mabudauan populations. Their lines have a Kiwai origin through Gamea, Gidra through Bidebu, as well as Gizra, Agöb and Torres Straits origins.

   The first Gizra to be associated with the Kiwai at Mawatta were the Waidoro. They met when the Kiwai went on fishing trips to Kura, Iarika-Zanarangbad, Dogai and Iamaz. Landtman (1917: 406–7) reports that Mainau arranged an ambush against the Gizra (Djibaru) in order to obtain heads for the marriage payment to the relatives of his son's Kiwai wife at Mawatta. Gamea's father Mainau was killed when the Gizra of Waidoro avenged this attack. The Gizra not only attacked Mawatta, but also the Bine at Masingara and the Torres Strait Islanders on Saibai and Yam Islands. It was sometime after this fight that the Kiwai came to Mabudauan. The Torres Strait Islanders also made a retaliatory raid and seized some of our sacred relics.

2. Haddon 1935 (1): 7–10.

3. The literal translation of Basir Puerk in Gizra is village swamp. This seems a misnomer as the area is slightly higher than the surrounding country and thus cannot be considered swampy. The Malay words *Pasir putih* not only have similar sounds to Basir Puerk, but also have a relevant meaning. Pasir means sand and putih is white. When looking at the coast from out to sea, the hillock of Mabudauan, with its stone outcrops, gleams like white sand. This makes it a very distinctive feature on the Trans Fly coast. Perhaps Pasir Putih was the original name for this place and over time the Gizra changed the name to words they knew, namely Basir Puerk.

4. Kumkumpal does not sound like a Gizra word. The literal translation of this name is the area where a lot of a particular type of ginger is found. Again this seems a misnomer as ginger is not found there. Perhaps the name is a corruption of the Malay word *kampong*, meaning village.

5. Landtman 1927.

6. Newton 1961.

7. Newton 1961.

8. The Malay word for school is *sekolah*.

Bibliography

Part A: Legislation and translation of German New Guinea colonial documents

British New Guinea

The Wild Birds Protection Ordinance, No. 2 of 1894. *Annual Report 1893–4*: vi and *The Laws and Ordinances of British New Guinea* 1898: 208.

The Bird Collectors Ordinance, No. 6 of 1897. *Annual Report 1897–8*: v and *The Laws and Ordinances of British New Guinea* 1898: 209–10.

Dutch New Guinea

Besluit van de Gouverneur-Generaal, Staatsblad van Nederlandsch Indie, 1909, No. 497 (decree introducing closed seasons and hunting licence fee).

Besluit van de Gouverneur-Generaal, Staatsblad van Nederlandsch Indie, 1911, No. 473 (decree extending 1909 restrictions to area under Tidore's jurisdiction).

Besluit van de Gouverneur-Generaal, Staatsblad van Nederlandsch Indie, 1931, No. 266 (decree protecting birds of paradise).

Indonesia

Act of the Republic of Indonesia, No. 5 of 1990: Concerning Conservation of Living Resources and their Ecosystems. Ministry of Forestry, The Republic of Indonesia.

Mandated Territory of New Guinea

Order requiring persons in possession of skins of birds of paradise, etc. to declare the same. *New Guinea (Rabaul) Gazette*, 15 August 1915.

Gun or shooting licence *New Guinea (Rabaul) Gazette*, 15 June 1915.

Order requiring persons in possession of the skins and plumage of birds of paradise, goura pigeons and herons to declare and register the same in certain cases. *New Guinea (Rabaul) Gazette*, 15 August 1915.

Customs Duty Ordinance 1916. *New Guinea (Rabaul) Gazette* 15 May 1916.

Birds of Paradise (Exportation) Ordinance 1920. *New Guinea (Rabaul) Gazette*, 28 February 1920.

Birds of Paradise Exportation (Amendment) Ordinance 1921. Amends 1920 Ordinance *New Guinea (Rabaul) Gazette*, 31 January 1921.

Birds and Animals Protection Ordinance 1922 (and subsequent amendments to 1933). *The Laws of the Territory of New Guinea 1921–45* (Annotated): 61–6.

Papua Government Gazette

The Wild Birds Ordinance, No. 15 of 1908. *Papua Annual Report 1908–9*: 3.

The Wild Birds Amendment Ordinance, No.@nbsp;13 of 1909. *Papua Annual Report 1908–9*: 4.

Birds Protection Ordinance, No. 9 of 1911. *The Laws of the Territory of Papua 1888–1945* (Annotated): 129–34.

Papua and New Guinea

Fauna Protection Ordinance, No. 19 of 1966. *Laws of the Territory of Papua and New Guinea* 1966 (Annotated): 87–93.

Exemptions and Declaration of Protected Fauna 1968 (under the Fauna Protection Ordinance of 1966). *Territory of Papua and New Guinea Government Gazette*, 31 October 1968: 842.

Fauna (Protection and Control) (Amendment) Act 1974. No. 42 of 1974. *The Laws of Papua and New Guinea* 1974 (Annotated: 288–292).

Papua New Guinea

Fauna Act (Protection and Control) 1976. Chapter No. 154 of the Revised Edition of *The Laws of Papua New Guinea*.

Fauna (Protection and Control) Amendment 1976. *Papua New Guinea Acts*, No. 16 of 1976.

International Trade (Fauna and Flora) Act 1979, No. 52 of 1979, Chapter No. 391 of the revised edition of the *Laws of Papua New Guinea*.

Translations of German New Guinea colonial records (and other documents included in these records)

The files on hunting and wildlife protection in German New Guinea (Jagd und Wildschutz Deutsch-Neu-Guinea) were obtained by Father J.J. Tschauder SVD and translated into English in 1989. Volume one of these translations covers the period 1891–1912, volume two 1912–13 and volume three 1913–14. Copies of these translations have been deposited in the New Guinea Collection of the National Library and in the Library of the Divine Word Institute in Madang.

Anon. 1911a. Footnote made in New Guinea on letter to Dr A. Hahl, Governor of New Guinea from Colonial Office, Berlin, September. Vol. 1: 43–44.

Anon. 1911b. Note by an official in the German Foreign Office. Vol. 1: 46.

Anon. 1912a. Notes by an official in the Foreign Office. Vol. 1: 105–6.

Anon. 1912b. Comments/notes on draft of 1913 Ordinance. Vol. 2: 110–18.

Anon. 1912c. Comments on proposed 1914 ban, by Colonial Office staff, Berlin. Vol. 2: 121–22.

Anon. 1912d. The murdered bird of paradise hunter. Article in *Berliner Lokal – Anzeiger*, No. 580, 13 November. Vol. 2: 137–140.

Anon. 1913a. Planters and bird of paradise hunters. Article in 12 January, *Hamburger Correspondent*. Vol. 2: 150–54.

Anon. 1913b. Letter to the State Secretary, Dr. Solf from the Kosmos Society der Naturefreunde, 4 March. Vol. 2: 177–78.

Anon. 1913c. Report to all friends of the Colonial Protect the Bird Movement about Dr Solfs support. Vol. 2: 214.

Anon. 1913d. The protection of the Birds of Paradise. Article in *Blätter für Naturschutz*, a monthly periodical of the Association to Protect Nature, No. 5, May 1. Vol. 2: 214–18.

Anon. 1913e. Protection of birds in the colonies. Article in *Deutsche Kolonialzeitung*, Vol. 30. 29 November. Vol. 2: 219–20, 222–25.

Anon. 1913f. Letter and resolution sent to the Secretary of the Colonial Office from the Colonial Committee for the Protection and industrial use of bird wildlife in the Colonies, 23 December. Vol. 2: 226–29.

Buckland. J. 1909. Lecture on the destruction of plumage birds. *Journal of the Royal Society of Arts*. December. Vol. 2: 157–69.

Busse 1911. Note. Vol. 1: 46–7.

Busse 1912. Notes on the Hunting Ordinance for New Guinea. Vol. 1: 84–91.

Conze 1913. Report to His Imperial and Royal Majesty, The Emperor of Germany and King of Prussia from the Colonial Office, 15 March. Vol. 2: 173–74.

Ebert 1912. Report to His Majesty, the Emperor and King from Commander of S.M.S. Cormoran. Vol. 1: 63a–67.

Hahl, A. 1910a. Letter to the State Secretary of the Colonial Office, Berlin, 3 November. Vol. 1: 24–26.

Hahl, A. 1910b. Letter to M. Thiel, Hamburg, 5 November. Vol. 1: 29–30a.

Hahl, A. 1912. Letter to Colonial Office, Berlin, 29 November. Vol. 2: 144.

Hahl, A. 1913a. Letter to State Secretary, Colonial Office, Berlin including copy of existing hunting licences and a petition from planters in Kaiser Wilhelmsland, 14 February. Vol. 2: 186–211.

Hahl, A. 1913b. Letter to State Secretary, Colonial Office regarding decree of 26 July regarding the protection of the bird of paradise, 25 October. Vol. 2: 225–6.

Hähnle, L. and R. Neuhauss 1913. Letter to His Imperial and Royal Majesty, The Emperor of Germany and King of Prussia from the Association for the Protection of Birds, 21 February, Vol. 2: 170–72.

Neuhauss, R. 1911. Article in *Der Tag*, Berlin. Morning edition, 28 September. Vol. 1: 39–42.

Neuhauss, R. 1912a. Mikulicz murdered. Article in *Berliner Lokal-Anzeiger*, 17 November 1912. Vol. 2: 140–2.

Neuhauss, Richard 1912b. Rebellion, murder, no end. Article in *Berliner Lokal-Anzeiger*, 1 December. Vol. 2: 145–9.

N.S. 1910. Letter to Imperial Government in Rabaul from Colonial Office in Berlin, 11 November. Vol. 1: 30a–32.

Ordinance 1891. Ordinance regarding the hunting of birds of paradise in the Protectorate of the New Guinea Company, 11 November 1891. Vol. 1: 6–7.

Ordinance 1892. Ordinance regarding the hunting of birds of paradise in Kaiser Wilhelmsland, 27 December 1892. Vol. 1: 4–5.

Ordinance 1907. Ordinance regarding the amendments to the 27 December 1892 Ordinance of the Landeshauptmann regarding the hunting of birds of paradise in Kaiser Wilhelmsland, 13 March 1907. Vol. 1: 23–4.

Ordinance 1911. Ordinance regarding the hunting of birds of paradise. 18 March. Vol. 1: 32–7.

Ordinance 1913. Ordinance regarding hunting in German New Guinea. Vol. 1: 70–100 (includes comments). Vol. 2: 194–198.

Preuss, P. 1912. Hunting and shooting birds of paradise in New Guinea. Article in *Kolonial Zeitung*, 23 November and 30 November. Vol. 2: 122–135.

Reichenow 1913. Letter from German Ornithological Society to Secretary of State, 13 December, Berlin. Vol. 3: 254–8.

Rose, F. 1891. Imperial Commissary Report, Stephansort, 11 November. Vol. 1: 1–3a.

Rose, F. 1892. Letter and notes taken from practical experiences of the Ordinance of 11 November 1891, 16 June. Vol. 1: 12–14.

Sarasin, P. 1913. Letter to the State Secretary, Dr Solf, from the French World Nature Protection Committee, 3 March. Vol. 2: 175–6.

Schillings, C.G. 1912. Article in *Magdeburgische Zeitung*, 10 April. Protect the birds of paradise in German New Guinea: The murder of the bird of paradise hunter Petersen. Vol. 1: 58–61.

Schillings, C.G. 1913. Letter to the State Secretary of the Colonial Office, Dr Solf, 7 March. Vol. 2: 178–9.

Schobel 1911. Notice. Vol. 1: 44–6.

Solf 1912a. Letter to Dr A. Hahl, Governor of German New Guinea from the Colonial Office, Berlin, 19 February. Vol. 1: 47–50.

Solf 1912b. Letter to Vice President of the German Colonial Society, 24 February. Vol. 1: 54–58.

Solf 1912c. Letter to Dr A. Hahl, Governor of German New Guinea, November. Vol. 2: 119–21.

Solf 1913a. Letter to Professor G. Schillings, Berlin, 25 January. Vol. 2: 143.

Solf 1913b. Letter to Dr Paul Sarasin, 25 March. Vol. 2: 176–7.

Solf 1913c. Letter to von Valentini Aide-de-Camp of His Imperial and Royal Highness, the Crown Prince regarding the petition of the Association for the Protection of Birds concerning the preservation of birds of paradise in German New Guinea, 26 July. Vol. 2: 183.

Solf 1913d. Letter to the Association for the Protection of Birds, Stuttgart, 26 July. Vol. 2: 183–4.

Solf 1913e. Letter to the State Secretary of the Foreign Office, 26 July. Vol. 2: 184–5.

Solf 1913f. Letter to Imperial Governor of German New Guinea, 26 July. Vol. 2: 185, 212–3.

Strauch 1912. Letter to Governors of German Colonies, 24 February. Vol. 1: 50–3.

Thiel, M. 1910. Letter to Dr A. Hahl, Governor of German New Guinea, 31 October. Vol. 1: 28–9.

Tschauder, J. J. 1989a. Translator's Note. Vol. 1: 26–7.

Tschauder, J. J. 1989b. Translator's Note. Vol. 1: 37.

Tschauder, J. J. 1989c. Translator's Note. Vol. 1: 42–3.

Tschauder, J. J. 1989d. Translator's Note. Vol. 2: 174

Tschauder, J. J. 1989e. Translator's Note. Vol. 2: 211.

Valentini, von 1913. Reply from Aide-de-Camp of His Imperial and Royal Highness, the Crown Prince to the State Chancellor of the Colonial Office, 26 July. Vol. 2: 182.

Vohsen, von Beck, Brass, Consul, M. Frankenschwerdt, Heinroth, Schweidnitz, and P. Staudinger 1913. Report on the second meeting of the Colonial Committee for the Protection and Commercial use of Birds, 12 December. Vol. 2: 230–4; Vol. 3: 235–42.

Part B: Alphabetical list by author

Agogino, G.A. 1979. Review of V. Watson and J.D. Cole, Prehistory of the Eastern Highlands of New Guinea. *Man* (n.s.) 14 (4): 756.

Agogino, G.A. 1986. Letter to Chris Ballard dated 17 October. (Copy deposited in New Guinea Collection. PNG National Library).

Alder, W.F. 1922. *The Isle of Vanishing Men:* A Narrative of Adventure in Cannibal-land. Century, New York.

Allen, B. 1976a. Information flow and innovation diffusion in the East Sepik District, PNG. Ph.D. thesis, Dept, of Human Geography, Australian National University, Canberra.

Allen, B. 1976b. Vanimo. In *An Introduction to the Urban Geography of Papua New Guinea*. Richard Jackson (ed.). Occasional Paper No. 13, Geography Department, University of Papua New Guinea, Port Moresby: 322–35.

Ambaiy, H.M. 1980. Some notes on the discovery of the archaeological evidence at Ternate. *Aspek-aspek Arkeologi Indonesia* 10: 1–25.

Ambrose, W.R. 1988. An early bronze artefact from Papua New Guinea. *Antiquity* 62: 483–91.

Anon. 1910a. The trade in feathers. *The Times* (London), 4 November, p. 16.

Anon. [Mattingley, A.H.] 1910b. The Tragedy of the 'Osprey' Plume: Photographed from life on the Murray River, Australia. *The Wild Life Preservation Society of Australia, Leaflet No. 1*.

Anon. 1920. Killed by Cannibals after surviving war: ex-lieutenant's fate, an island tragedy. *Sydney Morning Herald*, Thursday, October 21, p. 4.

Anon. 1985. Smuggler jailed. *Niugini Nius*, Thursday 21 February, p. 13.

Anon. 1990. Plucking profits from Irian Jaya: Big profits and weak enforcement have allowed an illegal trade in feathers and skins from Irian Jaya's birds of paradise to flourish. *The Times of PNG*, 22 November p.30 (from *Inside Indonesia*)

Araho, N., Torrence, R. and White, J.P. 2002. Valuable and useful: mid-Holocene stemmed obsidian artifacts from West New Britain, Papua New Guinea. *Proceedings of the Prehistoric Society* 68: 61–81.

Archbold, R. and A.L. Rand 1940. *New Guinea Expedition, Fly River, 1936–7.* McBride, New York.

Ardika, I.W. and P. Bellwood 1991. Sembiran: the beginnings of Indian contact with Bali. *Antiquity* 65: 221–32.

Aschenbach, J. 1982. U.S. scientist discovers the mystery birds. *The Times of PNG*, 26 March, p.4.

Arndt, W. 1965. The Dreaming of Kunukban. *Oceania* 35 (4): 242–3.

Austen, L. 1923a. Report of a patrol from the Tedi (Alice) River and the Star Mountains, Western District. *Papua Annual Report* 1921–2, Appendix 1: 122–41.

Austen, L. 1923b. The Tedi River District of Papua. *Geographical Journal* 62: 335–349.

Austen, L. 1925. Report of a patrol from Wukpit camp (Tedi River) to Star Mountains, 1922. *Papua Annual Report* 1922–23, Appendix 3: 27–37.

Austen, L. 1932. Legends of Hido. *Oceania* 2. (4): 468–75.

Avé, J.B. 1977. Sago in Insular Southeast Asia. In *Papers of the First International Sago Symposium*, K. Tan (ed.), Kuala Lumpur, Kemajuan Kanji: 21–30.

Baal, J. van 1966. *Dema*: Description and analysis of Marind-anim Culture. Martinus Nijhoff, The Hague.

Baal, J. van, K.W. Galis and R.M. Koentjaraningrat 1984. *West Irian: A Bibliography.* Foris Publications, Dordrecht.

Babcock, T. 1990. Introducing North Sulawesi. In Volkman and Caldwell (eds.) *Sulawesi: The Celebes.* Periplus, Berkeley: 189–91.

Bachtiar, H.W. 1963. Sedjarah Irian Barat. In Koentjaraningrat and H.W. Bachtiar (eds.), *Penduduk Irian Barat.* P.T. Penerbitan Universitas, Indonesia: 55–94.

Badner, M. 1972. Some evidences of Dong-son derived influences in the art of the Admiralty Islands. In Barnard, N. (ed.) *Early Chinese art and its possible influence on the Pacific Basin*, Vol. 3. Intercultural Press, New York: 597–630.

Barth, F. 1975. *Ritual and Knowledge among the Baktaman of New Guinea.* Yale University Press, New Haven.

Barton, F.R. 1908. Note on stone pestle from British New Guinea. *Man* 8: 1–2.

Beardmore, G.E. in *The Journal of the Royal Anthropological Institute* xix, : 465ff. quoted by Landtman 1917.

Beehler, B.M., T.K. Pratt and D. A. Zimmerman. 1986. *Birds of New Guinea*. Wau Ecology Institute Handbook No. 9, Princeton University Press, Princeton.

Beehler, B.M. 1993. Biodiversity and conservation of the warm-blooded vertebrates of Papua New Guinea. In Beehler, B.M. (ed.) *Papua New Guinea Conservation Needs Assessment*, Vol. 2. Department of Environment and Conservation, Government of Papua New Guinea, Port Moresby: 77–155.

Bell, H. 1969. Field notes on the birds of the Ok Tedi drainage, New Guinea. *The Emu* 69 (4): 193–211.

Bellwood, P. 1978a. *Man's Conquest of the Pacific: The Prehistory of Southeast Asia and Oceania*. Collins, Auckland.

Bellwood, P. 1980. The Buidane Culture of the Talaud Islands, North-Eastern Indonesia. *Indo-Pacific Prehistory Association Bulletin* 2: 69–127.

Bellwood, P. 1985. *Prehistory of the Indo-Malaysian Archipelago*. Academic Press, Sydney.

Bellwood, P. 1989. Archaeological investigations at Bukit Tengkorak and Segarong, Southeastern Sabah. *Indo-Pacific Prehistory Association Bulletin* 9: 122–62.

Bintarti, D.D. 1985. Prehistoric bronze objects in Indonesia. *Indo- Pacific Prehistory Association Bulletin* 6: 64–73.

Bodrogi, T. 1953. Some notes on the Ethnography of New Guinea: Initiation rites and ghost-cult in the Astrolabe Bay region. *Acta Ethnographica* 3: 91–184.

Boelaars, J.H.M.C. 1958. *Papoea's aan de Mappi*. De Fontein Utrecht, Antwerpen.

Boelaars, J.H.M.C. 1981. *Headhunters About Themselves: An ethnographic report from Irian Jaya*, Indonesia. Martinus Nijhoff, The Hague.

Borrell, O.W. 1990. A silver bracelet with an ancient Greek coin found in Wewak, East Sepik Province, Papua New Guinea. *Journal Royal Asiatic Society*, Hong Kong Branch. Vol. 28: 212–17.

Brookfield, H.C. with D. Hart 1971. *Melanesia:* A geographical interpretation of an island world. Methuen, London.

Brumund, J. F.G. 1853. The Kei and Arru Islands. *Journal of the Indian Archipelago* 7: 64–9.

Bruyn, J.V. de 1959. New archaeological finds at Lake Sentani. *Nieuw Guinea Studiën* 3: 1–8, plates.

Bruyn, J.V. de 1962. New bronze finds at Kwadeware, Lake Sentani. *Nieuw Guinea Studiën* 6: 61–62, plates.

Buccellati, G. and M.K. 1983a. Terqa: The first eight seasons. *Les Annales Archeologiques Arabes Syriennes* 33/2.

Buccellati, G. 1983b. Terqa: An introduction to the site. Preprint on the occasion of the symposium of Der-ez-Zor, October.

Bulbeck, F.D. 1986–7. Survey of open archaeological sites in South Sulawesi 1986–1987. *Indo-Pacific Prehistory Association Bulletin* 7: 36–50.

Bulmer, R. 1961. Man and birds in New Guinea: An anthropologist's comments on problems of nature conservation in the Central Highlands. Revised version of a talk given to the New Guinea Society, Canberra, on 14th May 1961. (Copy held New Guinea Collection. University of Papua New Guinea).

Bulmer. R. 1962. Chimbu plume traders. *Australian Natural History* 14 (1): 15–19.

Bulmer, S. and W.E. Tomasetti 1970. A stone replica of a bronze socketed axe from the Chimbu District of Australian New Guinea. *Records Papua New Guinea Museum* 1 (1): 38–41.

Busse, M. 1987. Sister exchange among the Wamek of the Middle Fly. Unpublished PhD thesis. University of California, San Diego.

Champion, I. F. 1966. *Across New Guinea: from the Fly to the Sepik.* Lansdowne Press, Melbourne.

Chaudhuri, K.N. 1965. *The English East India Company*: The Study of an Early Joint-Stock Company 1600–1640. Frank Cass and Company, London.

Cheesman, E. [1938a], *The Land of the Red Bird.* H. Joseph, London.

Cheesman, E. 1938b. The Cyclops Mountains of Dutch New Guinea. *Geographical Journal* 91: 21–30.

Cheesman, E. 1940. Two unexplored islands off Dutch New Guinea: Waigeu and Japen. *Geographical Journal* 95: 208–17.

Cheesman, E. 1941. The mountainous country at the boundary: North New Guinea. *Geographical Journal* 98: 169–88.

Cheesman, E. 1949. *Six-legged Snakes in New Guinea:* A collecting expedition to two unexplored islands. George G. Harrap, London.

Cheesman, E. 1960. *Time well spent.* Hutchinson, London.

Coates, B.J. 1990. *The Birds of Papua New Guinea*: Including the Bismarck Archipelago and Bougainville. Vol. 2. Dove Publications, Alderley, Queensland.

Coates, B.J. and E. Lindgren 1978. *Ok Tedi Birds.* Papua New Guinea Office of Environment and Conservation, Port Moresby.

Cobley, L.S. 1976. *An Introduction to the Botany of Tropical Crops*. Second Edition. Revised by W.M. Steele. Longman, London and New York.

Collins, J.T. and Voorhoeve, C.L. 1981. Moluccas (Maluku). In Wurm, S.A. and S. Hattori 1981.

Cooper, W.T. and J.M. Forshaw 1977. *The Birds of Paradise and Bower Birds*. William Collins, Sydney.

Crittenden, R. 1982. Sustenance, seasonality and social cycles on the Nembi Plateau, Papua New Guinea. Ph.D., Australian National University.

Crosby, E. 1976. Sago in Melanesia. *Archaeology and Physical Anthropology in Oceania*. XI (2): 138–55.

Curtin, P.D. 1984. *Cross-cultural trade in world history*. Cambridge University Press, Cambridge.

D'Albertis, L.M. 1877. *Journal of the Expedition for the Exploration of the Fly River*. Frederick White, Sydney.

D'Albertis, L.M. 1880. *New Guinea: What I did and what I saw*. 2 vols. Sampson Low, London.

Deck. D. 1990. Traditional use of bird of paradise plumes. *Post Courier*. 20 July, page 25.

Deklin, F. 1979. A review of Richard Parkinson's 1900 paper on the Aitape Coast: from a Wanimo viewpoint. In People of the West Sepik Coast, *PNG National Museum & Art Gallery Record* 7: 30–4.

Denham, T. 2011. Early agriculture and plant domestication in New Guinea and Island Southeast Asia. *Current Anthropology* 52, No S4, The Origins of Agriculture New Data, New Ideas (October 2011): S379-S395.

Depew, R. n.d. Birds of paradise, bird traders/hunters and their trade language in the Aekyom area, manuscript.

Diamond, J.M. 1982a. Rediscovery of the Yellow-Fronted Gardener Bowerbird. *Science* 216: 431–34.

Diamond. J.M. 1982b. Rediscovery of the Bowerbird *Amblyornis flavifrons*. *Newsletter of the Papua New Guinea Bird Society* 187–8: 38–9.

Doughty, R.W. 1975. *Feather Fashions and Bird Preservation: A Study in Nature Protection*. University of California Press, Berkeley.

Downes, M.C. 1977. Report of the consultant of the Wildlife Management Program for Papua New Guinea. *Wildlife Publication* 77/23, Port Moresby.

Downham, C.F. 1911. *The Feather Trade: some facts and fallacies in connection with the trade in fancy feathers*. F. Howard Doulton, London.

Drabbe. P. 1947–8. Folktales from Netherlands New Guinea. *Oceania* 18: 157–75, 248–70.

Drake, F. 1966. *The World Encompassed*. University Microfilms, Ann Arbor. First published in 1628.

Dumont d'Urville, M.J. 1839. *Voyage Pittoresque Autour du Monde*. Volume 2, Libraire L. Teure, Paris.

Dutton, T.E. 1973. "Cultural" items of basic vocabulary in the Gulf and other Districts of Papua. In K. Franklin (ed.) The linguistic situation in the Gulf District and adjacent areas, Papua New Guinea. *Pacific Linguistics Series C*, No. 26: 413–538.

Dutton. T.E. n.d. Manuscript on tobacco in New Guinea prepared in 1974. (Copy deposited in New Guinea Collection, PNG National Library).

Earl, G.W. 1840. Translator's Preface. In Kolff 1840: vii–xvi.

Earl, G.W. 1853. *The Native Races of the Indian Archipelago: Papuans*. Hippolyte Bailliere, London.

Egloff. B.J. 1972. The sepulchral pottery of Nuamata Island, Papua. *Archaeology and Physical Anthropology in Oceania* 7: 145–163.

Egloff, B.J. and Kaiku, R. 1978. *An Archaeological and Ethnographic Survey of the Purari River (Wabo) Dam Site and Reservoir*. Purari River (Wabo) Hydroelectric Scheme Environmental Studies (5), Waigani and Konedobu, 1978: Office of Environment and Conservation, Department of Minerals and Energy. Papua New Guinea.

Egloff, B.J. 1979. Recent prehistory in Southeast Papua. *Terra Australis* 4, Australian National University, Canberra.

Egloff, B.J. and Specht, J. 1982. Long Island, Papua New Guinea-Aspects of the Prehistory. *Australian Museum Records* 34 (8): 427–46.

Ellen, R.F. 1979. Sago subsistence and the trade in spices: a provisional model of ecological succession and imbalance in Moluccan history. In P. Burnham and R. Ellen (ed.) *Social and Ecological Systems*. Academic Press, London: 43–74.

Ellen, R.F. 1987. Environmental perturbation, inter-island trade and the relocation of production along the Banda Arc; or, why central places remain central. In *Human Ecology of Health and Survival in Asia and the South Pacific* edited by T. Susuki and R. Ohtsuka, pp. 35–61, University of Tokyo Press.

Ellen, R.F. and Glover, I.C. 1974. Pottery manufacture and trade in the Central Moluccas, Indonesia: the modern situation and historical implications. *Man* (N.S.) 9: 353–379.

Elmberg, J.E. 1968. *Balance and circulation*: Aspects of tradition and change among the Mejprat of Irian Barat. Ethnographical Museum Monograph 12, Stockholm.

Everill, H.C. 1888. Exploration of New Guinea... Captain Everill's report. *Transactions and Proceedings of the Royal Geographical Society of Australasia*, New South Wales Branch, Sydney. 3–4: 170–87.

Flinders, M. 1814. *A Voyage to Terra Australis* ... Nicol, London.

Forrest, T. 1969 [first published 1779] *A voyage to New Guinea and the Moluccas 1774–1776*. Edited with an introduction by D.K. Bassett. Oxford University Press, London.

Fraassen, Ch. F. van 1981. Introduction. In *The North Moluccas*: An Annotated Bibliography. K. Polman (ed.), Koninklijk Instituut voor Taal-, Land- en Volkenkunde, Bibliographical Series 11, Martinus Nijhoff, The Hague.

Galis, K.W. 1953–4. Geschiedenis. In W.C. Klein (ed.), *Nieuw Guinea*, Vol. 1: 1–65.

Galis, K.W. 1955. *Papua's van de Humboldt-Baai*: Bijdrage tot een Ethnografie. J.N. Voorhoeve, The Hague.

Galis, K.W. 1956. Oudheidkundig Onderzoek in Nederlands Nieuw- Guinea. *Bijdragen tot de Taal-, Land-, en Völkerkunde* 112: 271–284. (with a postscript by V.D. Hoop).

Galis, K.W. 1964. Recent Oudheidkundig Nieuws uit Westelijk Nieuw-Guinea. *Bijdragen tot de Taal-, Land-, en Volkenkunde* 120: 245–274.

Gash, N. and J. Whittaker 1975. *A Pictorial History of New Guinea*. Jacaranda Press, Milton.

Gell, A. 1975. *Metamorphis of the Cassowaries*. London School of Economics, University of London.

Gellibrand, T., I.S. McPhail, D. Attenborough and S. Breeden 1966. Why the killing? Naturalists write to *Wildlife in Australia* giving their views on the controversial proposal to permit the commercial exploitation of New Guinea birds of paradise. *Wildlife in Australia*: 46–7.

Gerbrands, A.A. 1967a. *The Asmat of New Guinea: The Journal of Michael Clark Rockefeller*. The Museum of Primitive Art, New York.

Gerbrands, A.A. 1967b. *Wowipits*: Eight Asmat Woodcarvers of New Guinea. Mouton and Co., The Hague.

Gilliard, E.T. 1969. *Birds of Paradise and Bower Birds*. Weidenfeld and Nicolson, London.

Gilliard, E.T. and Riboud, M. 1957. Coronation in Katmandu. *The National Geographic Magazine*. CXII (1): 139–52.

Glover, I.C. 1986. Archaeology in Eastern Timor, 1966–67. *Terra Australis* 11, Australian National University, Canberra.

Glover, I.C. 1990. *Early trade between India and South-east Asia: A link in the Development of a World Trading System.* Second edition. Centre for South-East Asian Studies, Hull.

Goloubew, V. 1929. L'age du bronze au Tonkin. *Bulletin de l'École Française d'Extrême-Orient* 29: 1–46.

Golson, J. 1972. Both sides of the Wallace Line: New Guinea, Australia, Island Melanesia and Asian Prehistory. In Barnard, N. (ed.) *Early Chinese Art and its possible influence in the Pacific Basin*, Vol. 1, Intercultural Press, New York: 533–95.

Goode, J. 1977. *Rape of the Fly.* Thomas Nelson in association with Robert Brown, Melbourne.

Haddon, A.C. (ed.) 1912. Reports of the Cambridge Anthropological Expedition to Torres Strait. Vol. 1: General Ethnography, Cambridge University Press, Cambridge.

Haddon, A.C. 1908. *Reports of the Cambridge Anthropological Expedition to Torres Straits* (6). Cambridge University Press, Cambridge.

Haddon, A.C. (ed.) 1912. *Reports of the Cambridge Anthropological Expedition to Torres Strait.* Vol. IV: Arts and Crafts, Cambridge University Press, Cambridge.

Haddon, A.C. 1935. *Reports of the Cambridge Anthropological Expedition to Torres Strait*, Vol. 1. Cambridge University Press, London.

Hahl, A. 1980. *Albert Hahl: Governor in New Guinea.* (Edited and translated by P.G. Sack and D. Clark) Australian National University Press, Canberra.

Hanna, W.A. 1978. *Indonesian Banda: Colonialism and its aftermath in the Nutmeg Islands.* Institute for the Study of Human Issues, Philadelphia.

Healey, C.J. 1980. The trade in bird plumes in the New Guinea region. In *Occasional Papers in Anthropology* 10, University of Queensland: 249–75.

Healey, C.J. 1986. The impact of man on birds of paradise in the Jimi valley. *Muruk* 1 (2): 4–33.

Healey, C.J. 1990. *Maring hunters and traders: production and exchange in the Papua New Guinea Highlands.* University of California Press, Berkeley.

Heaney, W. 1982. The changing role of bird of paradise plumes in bridewealth in the Wahgi valley. In Morauta, L., Pernetta, J. and Heaney, W. (eds). *Traditional Conservation in Papua New Guinea: Implications for Today.* Monograph 16, Institute of Applied Social and Economic Research, Boroko: 227–231.

Heekeren, H.R. van 1958. *The Bronze-Iron Age of Indonesia.* Nijhoff, The Hague.

Heider, K.G. 1970. *The Dugum Dani: A Papuan Culture in the Highlands of West New Guinea.* Viking Fund Publication No. 49, Wenner-Gren, New York.

Held, G.J. 1957. *The Papuas of Waropen.* Koninklijk Instituut voor Taal-, Land- en Volkenkunde, Martinus Nijhoff, The Hague.

Higham, C. 1989. *The Archaeology of Mainland Southeast Asia.* Cambridge University Press, Cambridge.

Historical Section of the Foreign Office, London 1920. *Dutch New Guinea and the Molucca Islands.* Handbook No. 87.

Höltker, G. 1951. Die steinvögel in Melanesien. In *Südseestudien,* Museum für Völkerkunde, Basel: 235–65.

Hopfner, G.K. 1977. A collection of ancient sago implements of the Indonesian Archipelago in the Museum of Ethnography, Berlin. In *Papers of the First International Sago Symposium,* K. Tan (ed.), 39–52, Kemajuan Kanji, Kuala Lumpur.

Hornaday, W.T. 1913. *Our Vanishing Wild Life: Its extermination and preservation.* New York Zoological Society, New York.

Hornaday, W.T. 1917. Great Seizure of smuggled plumage at Laredo, Texas. *Trade*: 180–84.

Horridge, A. 1981. *The Prahu: Traditional Sailing Boat of Indonesia.* Oxford University Press, Kuala Lumpur.

Horsbrugh, C.B. 1909. A journey to British New Guinea in search of birds of paradise. *The Ibis* 10: 197–213.

Hossfeld, P.S. 1965. Radiocarbon dating and palaeoecology of the Aitape fossil human remains. *Proceedings Royal Society of Victoria,* 78 (2): 161–65.

Hughes, I. 1977. New Guinea Stone Age Trade. *Terra Australis* 3. Australian National University, Canberra.

Huie, S.F. 1990. The Hidden Truths: Evelyn Cheesman. In *Tiger Lilies: Women Adventurers in the South Pacific.* Angus and Robertson, North Ryde, Australia.

Hurley, F.J.F. 1924. *Pearls and Savages.* G.P. Putnam's Sons, New York.

Innes Miller, J. 1969. *The spice trade of the Roman Empire, 29 B.C. to A.D. 641.* Clarendon Press, Oxford.

Ishige, N. 1980. The preparation and origin of Galela Food. In N. Ishige (ed), The Galela of Halmahera: A preliminary survey. *Senri Ethnological Studies* 7, National Museum of Ethnology, Osaka: 263–341.

Jackman, H.H. 1988. *Copra marketing and price stabilisation in Papua New Guinea*: A history to 1975. Pacific Research Monograph No. 17, National Centre for Development Studies, Australian National University.

Jacobs, M. 1972. German New Guinea. In Ryan, P. (ed.) *Encyclopaedia of Papua New Guinea*, Vol. 1. Melbourne University Press in association with the University of Papua New Guinea, Melbourne: 485–98.

Jones, B. 1980. *Consuming Society*. Unpublished doctoral dissertation, University of Virginia, 1980.

Jorgensen D. 1981. *Taro and Arrows: Order and Entropy in Telefol Religion*. Unpublished doctoral dissertation University of British Columbia.

Joyce, R.B. 1971. *Sir William MacGregor*. Oxford University Press, Melbourne.

Joyce, R.B. 1972. British New Guinea. In Ryan, P. (ed.) *Encyclopaedia of Papua New Guinea*. Vol. 1, 115–18, Melbourne University Press in association with the University of Papua New Guinea, Melbourne: 115–8.

Jukes, J.B. 1847. *Narrative of the surveying voyage of HMS Fly, commanded by Captain F.P. Blackwood ...* 2 vols. Boone, London.

Kachau, G., Saulep, R. and Pinjong, S. 1980. Yuon. In Traditional Settlement Histories and Early Historical Accounts of the Schouten Islands, East Sepik Province. *Oral History* VIII (2): 1–-18.

Kamma, F.C. 1972. *Koreri: Messianic movements in the Biak-Numfor Culture Area.* Martinus-Nijhoff, The Hague.

Kamma, F.C. and Kooijman, S. 1973. *Romawa Forja Child of the Fire: Iron Working and the Role of Iron in West New Guinea (West Irian).* Mededelingen van het Rijksmuseum voor Volkenkunde, No. 18, E. J. Brill, Leiden.

Kathirithamby-Wells, J. and J. Villiers 1990. *The Southeast Asian Port and Polity.* Singapore University Press, Singapore.

Kempers, A.J.B. 1988. The Kettledrums of Southeast Asia: A bronze age world and its aftermath. *Modern Quaternary Research in Southeast Asia* 10 (1986/1987) Balkema, Rotterdam.

Kirsch, S. 1991. The Yonggom of New Guinea: An ethnography of sorcery, magic and ritual. Unpublished PhD thesis. University of Pennsylvania, Philadelphia.

Kolff, D.H. 1840. *Voyages of the Dutch Brig of War Dourga through the southern and little-known parts of the Moluccan archipelago and along the previously unknown southern coast of New Guinea performed during the years 1825–1826.* Madden. London.

Kooijman, S. 1959 *The Art of Lake Sentani.* The Museum of Primitive Art, New York.

Kooijman, S. 1966. Introduction. In *Papoea-kunst in het Rjksmuseum.* Mertenloonstelling, Amsterdam.

Kops, B.G.F. de 1852. Contribution to the knowledge of the north and east coasts of New Guinea. *Journal of the Indian Archipelago* 6: 303–48.

Kwapena, N. 1985. *The ecology and conservation of six species of Birds of Paradise in Papua New Guinea.* Department of Environment and Conservation, Port Moresby.

Laarhoven, R. 1990. Lords of the Great River: The Magindanao Port and Polity during the Seventeenth Century. In Kathirithamby-Wells and Villiers 1990: 161–86.

Lam, H. J. 1945. *Fragmenta Papuana: observations of a naturalist in Netherlands New Guinea.* Trans, from Dutch by L. M. Perry. Jamaica Plain (Mass). Arnold Arboretum of Harvard University.

Landtman, G. 1917. *The Folk-tales of Kiwai Papuans.* Acta Societatis Scientiarum Fennicae, Vol. 47. Finnish Society of Literature, Helsingfors.

Landtman, G. 1927. *The Kiwai Papuans of British New Guinea.* MacMillan & Co. Ltd., London.

LeCroy, M. 1985. A Gift Fit for a King. Faces. American Museum of Natural History 2 (3): 5–8.

Lilley, I. 1986. Prehistoric exchange in the Vitiaz Strait, Papua New Guinea. PhD Thesis, Dept, of Prehistory, Australian National University.

Lyng, J. 1919. *Our New Possession* (Late German New Guinea). Melbourne Publishing Company, Melbourne.

Lyons, A.P. 1922. Report of an expedition to the upper Fly River for the purpose of inquiring into the alleged murders of a party of bird hunters consisting of Dreschler, Bell and others, conducted by the resident magistrate, Western Division. *Papua Annual Report* 1920–1: 112–24, Appendix 1.

Lyons. A.P. n.d. Field Journal No. 3. Facsimile copy hand transcribed by Mr J. Murphy of Brisbane. Copy held New Guinea Collection, University of Papua New Guinea.

MacGregor, W.M. 1889–90. Despatch giving details of an expedition undertaken to explore the course of the Fly River and some of its affluents. *Annual Report on British New Guinea* 1889–1890, Appendix G: 49–64.

MacGregor, W.M. 1892. Despatch Reporting Administrative Visit of Inspection to the Western Division. *British New Guinea Annual Report* 1890–91, Appendix L: 42–57.

Mackenzie, S.S. 1934. The Australians at Rabaul: The Capture and administration of the German Possessions in the Southern Pacific. *Official History of Australia in the War of 1914–18*, Vol. X, Angus and Robertson, Sydney.

Macknight, C.C. 1971–2. Macassans and Aborigines. *Oceania* 42: 283–321.

Macknight, C.C. 1976. *The Voyage to Marege*. Melbourne University Press, Melbourne.

Macknight, C.C. 1986. Macassans and the Aboriginal past. *Archaeology in Oceania* 21: 69–75.

Marshall, A. 1937. Northern New Guinea. *The Geographical Journal.* 89: 489–506.

Marshall, A. J. 1938. *The men and birds of paradise: journeys through equatorial New Guinea*. Heinemann, London.

May, R.J. 1989. The impact of early contact in the Sepik. In S. Latukefu (ed.) *Papua New Guinea: A century of colonial impact: 1884–1984*. The National Research Institute and University of Papua New Guinea, Port Moresby: 109–32.

Mclnnes, D.M. 1992. *A Tribute to the Brave*: 1941–1945 Papua New Guinea. South Pacific Post, Port Moresby.

McKillop, R. 1974. Papua New Guinea's Bootless Bay Railway. *Light Railways*, Autumn: 3–15.

Meek, A.S. 1913. *A Naturalist in Cannibal Land*. T. Fisher Unwin, London.

Meilink-Roelofsz, M.A.P. 1962. *Asian Trade and European Influence in the Indonesian Archipelago between 1500 and 1630*. Martinus Nijhoff, The Hague.

Mennis, Maiy 1979. The Kilibob and Manup myth found on the north coast of Papua New Guinea. *Oral History* VII (4): 88–101.

Mennis, Mary 1981. Oral Testimonies from Coastal Madang, Part 2. *Oral History* IX (1): 1–107.

Miklouho-Maclay (Mikluho Maklay) N. 1875. Incidents of travel in Papua – Koviay (New Guinea). *Proceedings of the Royal Geographical Society*, London: 517–21.

Miklouho-Maclay, N. 1982. *Travels to New Guinea*: Diaries, Letters, Documents. Progress Publishers, Moscow.

Militaire exploratie 1920. *Verslag van de militaire exploratie van Nederlandsch-Nieuw-Guinee, 1907–1915*. Landsdrukkerij, Weltevreden.

Molnar-Bagley, E. 1982. West Sepik History. *Oral History* X (3): 1–59.

Moore, D.R. 1978. Cape York Aborigines: Fringe Participants in the Torres Strait Trading System. *Mankind* 11: 319–25.

Muller, K. 1990a. *Maluku: The Moluccas*. Periplus Editions, Berkeley.

Muller, K. 1990b. *New Guinea: Journey into the Stone Age*. Passport Books, Lincolnwood, Illinois.

Mulvaney, D.J. 1989. *Encounters in Place: Outsiders and Aboriginal Australians 1606–1985*. University of Queensland Press, St. Lucia.

Murray, J.H.P. 1914. Visit to the Fly and Strickland Rivers. *Papua Annual Report* 1913–14: 17–25, plus map.

Naval Intelligence Division, The Admiralty, London. 1944-5. *The Netherlands and British East Indies and the Philippine Islands*. Allied Forces Southwest Pacific Area, Vol. 1.

Nelson, H. 1976. *Black. White and Gold: Goldmining in Papua New Guinea 1878–1930*. Australian National University Press, Canberra.

Nelson, H. 1989. Changing the Label. In S. Latukefu (ed.). *Papua New Guinea: A century of colonial impact 1884–1984*, National Research Institute and University of Papua New Guinea, Port Moresby: 19–36.

Newton, Douglas 1961. *Art Styles of the Papuan Gulf*. Museum of Primitive Art, New York.

Nicholson. M. 1987. *The New Environmental Age*. Cambridge University Press. Cambridge.

Nielsen, A.K. 1930. *In Het Land Van Kannibalen en Paradijsvogels*, N.V. EM: Querido's Uitgevers-Maatsch. Amsterdam.

O'Hanlon, M. 1989. *Reading the skin: adornment, display and society among the Wahgi*. British Museum Publications, London.

O'Hanlon, M. 1993. *Paradise: Portraying the New Guinea Highlands*. British Museum Publications, London.

O'Hare, M. 1986. Majapahit's influence over Wwanin in New Guinea in the Fourteenth century. B. Litt, thesis. Faculty of Asian Studies, Australian National University, Canberra.

Oliver, D.L. 1961. *The Pacific Islands*. Revised edition. Doubleday, New York.

Osborn, H.F. 1913. Our new campaign: to stop the importation of wild birds' plumage for millinery. *Zoological Society Bulletin* 16 (57): 994–6.

Parkinson, R. 1979. The Aitape Coast. In People of the West Sepik Coast, (translated from German by Father John J. Tschauder. SVD). *PNG National Museum and Art Gallery Record* 7: 35–107.

Peckover, W.S. 1978. The challenge for survival: birds of paradise and bowerbirds. *Wildlife Publication* 78/7, Port Moresby.

Peckover, W.S. 1990. *Birds of Paradise*, Papua New Guinea. Robert Brown and Associates, Coorparoo.

Petocz, R. 1989. *Conservation and Development in Irian Jaya*. E.J. Brill, Leiden.

Pouwer, J. 1955. *Enkele aspecten van de Mimika-Cultuur*. Staatsdrukkerij, The Hague.

Pouwer, J. 1970. Land tenure in West Irian, (trans. by A. Ploeg). *New Guinea Research Bulletin* 38: 24–33.

Pratt, A.E. 1906. *Two Years Among New Guinea Cannibals: A Naturalist's Sojourn among the Aborigines of Unexplored New Guinea*. Second edition. Seeley, London.

Pratt, A.E. 1911. Birds of Paradise. In C.F. Downham 1911: 46–55.

Prescott, J.R.V., Collier, H.J. and Prescott, D.F. 1977. *Frontiers of Asia and Southeast Asia*. Melbourne University Press, Melbourne.

Preswich, A.A. 1945. Early importations of birds of paradise. *The Avicultural Magazine*, Series 5, Vol. 10: 44–7.

Ray, S.H. 1912. Notes on the the languages in the east of Netherlands New Guinea. Appendix C in Wollaston 1912: 322–45.

Rhoads, J.W. 1980. Through a glass darkly: present and past land-use systems of Papuan sago palm users. PhD thesis, Australian National University, Canberra.

Rhoads, J.W. 1984. Pre-contact glass artefacts from Papua New Guinea. *South-east Asian Studies Newsletter* 14: 1–5.

Riesenfeld, A. 1951. Tobacco in New Guinea and the other areas of Melanesia. *Journal Rogal Anthropological Institute of Great Britain and Ireland*, 81: 69–102.

Ripley, D. 1950. Strange Courtship of Birds of Paradise. *The National Geographic Magazine* 97: 247–78.

Rivers, W.H.R. 1904. *Reports of the Cambridge Anthropological Expedition to Torres Straits* (5). Cambridge University Press, Cambridge.

Robinson, E.D. 1934–5. Special Patrol Report Yellow and Sand Rivers, No. 1/1934–5 Sepik District. PNG National Archives.

Roder, J. 1959. *Feldsbilder und Vorgeschichte des MacCluer-Golfes West-New Guinea*. L.C. Wittich, Darmstadt.

Roe, M. 1966. 'Hayes, Sir John (1768–1831)', Australian Dictionary of Biography, National Centre of Biography, Australian National University, http://adb.anu.edu.au/biography/hayes-sir-john-2173/text2789

Rowley, C.D. 1958. *The Australians in German New Guinea 1914–1921*. Melbourne University Press, Melbourne.

Rowley, C.D. 1966. *The New Guinea Villager*. F.A. Praeger, New York.

Rumbiak, A.M. 1984. Observations on the trade in birds of paradise in Bomakia, District of Kouh, Region of Merauke. *Report of Cenderawasih University Student Investigations sponsored by the World Wildlife Fund*. World Wildlife Fund, Jayapura.

Russell, D.A., Wigley, S.C., Vincin, D.R., Scott, G.C, Booth, P.B. and Simmons, R.T. 1971. BloodGroups and Salivary ABH Secretion of Inhabitants of the Karimui Plateau and Adjoining areas of the New Guinea Highlands. In *Human Biology in Oceania* Vol. I (2): 79–89.

Sack, P. and Clark, D. 1979. (editors and translators) *German New Guinea: The Annual Reports*. Australian National University, Canberra.

Sack, P. and Clark, D. 1980. (editors and translators). *German New Guinea: The draft annual report for 1913–14*. Department of Law Research School of Social Sciences, Australian National University, Canberra.

Sande, G.A.J. van der 1907. Ethnography and Anthropology of New Guinea. *Nova Guinea*. Vol. 3. E.J. Brill, Leiden.

Schodde, R. 1972 Birds of Paradise. In Ryan, P. (ed.) *Encyclopaedia of Papua New Guinea*, Vol. 1, pp. 86–89, Melbourne University Press in association with the University of Papua New Guinea, Melbourne.

Schoorl, J.W. 1957. *Kultuur en Kultuurveranderingen in het Moejoe gebied*. J.N. Voorhoeve, The Hague.

Schoorl, J.W. 1967. The anthropologist in government service. Anthropologists in the field. Jongmans, D.G. and P.C.W. Gutkind (eds). Van Gorcum and Comp. N.V., Assen: 170–92.

Schoorl, J.W. 1979. *Mensen van de Ayfat*. Katholieke University, Nijmegen.

Schoorl, J.W. 1993. *Culture and change among the Mugu*. KITLV Press, Leiden.

Schrieke, B.J. 1955. *Indonesian Sociological Studies*. The Hague.

Schultze-Westrum. T.G. 1969. Protection of birds of paradise in New Guinea. *World Wildlife Yearbook 1969*, World Wildlife, Morges, Switzerland: 300–04, 336.

Schurig, M. 1930. *Die Südseetöpferei*. Schindler, Leipzig.

Scott, P. (ed.) 1989. *The World Atlas of Birds*. Crescent Books, New York.

Scott-Norman, F. 1992. Big birds, big bucks. *The Australian Magazine*, Jan. 18–19, pp. 14–19.

Seiler, W. 1985. The Malay language in New Guinea. In *Papers in Pidgin and Creole Linguistics* 4, A–72: 143–153.

Singe, J. 1979. *The Torres Strait People and History*. University of Queensland Press.

Smith, P.M. 1976. Nutmeg. In Simmonds, N.W. (ed) *Evolution of Crop Plants*. Longman, London: 316–7.

Soejono, R.P. 1963. Prehistori Irian Barat. In Koentjaraningrat and H.W. Bachtiar (eds.) *Penduduk Irian Barat*. P.T. Penerbitan Universitas, Indonesia: 39–54.

Soejono, R.P. 1979. The significance of excavations at Gilimanuk (Bali). In Smith, R.B. and Watson, W. (eds.), *Early South East Asia*. Oxford University Press, New York: 185–98.

Solheim, W.C. and Ap, A.C. 1977. Pottery manufacture in Abar, Lake Sentani, Irian Jaya. *Irian*, Bulletin for Irian Jaya Development 6 (1): 52–70.

Solheim, W.C. and Mansoben, J. 1977. Pottery manufacture in Mansinam, Manokwari, Irian Jaya. Irian, Bulletin for Irian Jaya Development 6 (1): 46–51.

Sonnerat, M.P. 1781. *An account of a voyage to the Spice Islands and New Guinea*. Reprinted by W. Green, Bury St. Edmund's.

Specht, J. 1988. Pieces of Paradise. *Australian Natural History, Supplement* No. 1

Spennemann, D. R. 1985a. Einige Bemerkungen zum Dong-So'n Schiff vom Berge Dobo auf Flores, Indonesien. *Tribus* 34: 145–180.

Spennemann, D. R. 1985b. On the bronze age ship model from Flores, Indonesia. *The International Journal of Nautical Archaeology and Underwater Exploration* 14 (3): 237–241.

Spennemann, D. H. R. 1987. Evolution of Southeast Asian kettledrums. *Antiquity* 61: 71–5.

Spriggs, M. 1998. Research questions in Maluku archaeology. *Cakalele* 9 (2): 51–64.

Spriggs, M. and D. Miller 1979. Ambon-Lease: On study of contemporary pottery making and its archaeological relevance. In M. Millet (ed.) *Pottery and the Archaeologist*, Occasional Paper No. 4, Institute of Archaeology, University of London.

Spriggs, M. and D. Miller 1988. A previously unreported bronze kettle drum from the Kai Islands, Eastern Indonesia. *Indo-Pacific Prehistory Association Bulletin*, 8: 79–89.

Spring, S. 1977. Wildlife in Papua New Guinea, bird of paradise utilisation at the Goroka Show. *Wildlife Publication* 77/5, Port Moresby.

Steinberg, D.J. 1985. The Archipelago, 1750–1870. In Steinberg, D.J. (ed) *In Search of Southeast Asia: A Modern History*, University of Hawaii Press, Honolulu.

Stevens, H.N. and G.F. Barwick 1930. *New light on the discovery of Australia as revealed by the journal of Captain Don Diego de Prado y Tovar*. Series 2, No. 64, Hakluyt Society, London.

Stokhof, W.A.L. (ed.) with L. Saleh-Bronkhorst and A.E. Almanar 1980. Holle Lists: Vocabularies in Languages of Indonesia. Vol. 1. Introductory Volume. *Pacific Linguistics* Series D – No. 17.

Stokhof, W.A.L. (ed.) with L. Saleh-Bronkhorst and A.E. Almanar 1981. Holle Lists: Vocabularies in Languages of Indonesia. Vol. 3/2. Central Moluccas: Seram (ii). *Pacific Linguistics* Series D - No. 44.

Stokhof, W.A.L. (ed.) with L. Saleh-Bronkhorst and A.E. Almanar 1982a. Holle Lists: Vocabularies in Languages of Indonesia. Vol. 3/3. Central Moluccas: Seram (iii), Haruku, Banda, Ambon (i). *Pacific Linguistics* Series D - No. 49.

Stokhof, W.A.L. (ed.) with L. Saleh-Bronkhorst and A.E. Almanar 1982b. Holle Lists: Vocabularies in Languages of Indonesia. Vol. 3/4. Central Moluccas: Ambon (ii), Burn, Nusa Laut, Saparua. *Pacific Linguistics* Series D – No. 50.

Strachan, J. 1888. *Explorations and Adventures in New Guinea*. Sampson Low, London.

Stresemann, E. 1954. Die Entdeckungsgeschichte der Paradiesvögel. *Journal fur Ornithologie*, 95: 263–91.

Swadling, P. 1981. *Papua New Guinea's Prehistory: An introduction*. National Museum and Art Gallery in association with Gordon and Gotch, Port Moresby. Revised with some editions 1986.

Swadling, P. 2005. The Huon Gulf and its hinterlands: a long-term view of coastal-highlands interactions. In *A Polymath Anthropologist: Essays in honour of Ann Chowning*, C. Gross, H.D. Lyons and D.A. Counts (eds.), Research in Anthropology and Linguistics Monograph Series 6, University of Auckland.

Swadling, P. 2013. Prehistoric stone mortars. In *Melanesia Art and Encounter*. L. Bolton, N. Thomas, E. Bonshek, J. Adams and B. Burt (eds.), The British Museum Press: London: 78–82.

Swadling, P. 2016. Mid-Holocene social networks in Far Eastern New Guinea. *Journal of Pacific Archaeology* 7 (1): 7–19.

Swadling, P. 2017. Early art in New Guinea: Glimpses from prehistory. In *New Guinea Highlands: Art from the Jolika Collection*. J. Friede, T.E. Hays and C. Hellmich (eds.), Fine Arts Museums of San Francisco, de Young: 13–55.

Swadling, P. and Hide, R. 2005. Changing landscape and social interaction: looking at agricultural history from a Sepik-Ramu perspective. In *Papuan Pasts: cultural, linguistic and biological histories of Papuan-speaking peoples*, A. Pawley, R. Attenborough, J. Golson and R. Hide (eds), Pacific Linguistics, Australian National University, Canberra: 141–57.

Swadling, P., Araho, N. and Ivuyo, B. 1991. Settlements associated with the inland Sepik-Ramu sea. *Indo-Pacific Prehistory Association Bulletin* 11 (2): 92–112.

Swadling, P., Wiessner, P. and Tumu, A. 2008. Prehistoric stone artifacts from Enga and the implications of links between the highlands, lowlands and islands for early agriculture in Papua New Guinea. *Journal de la Société des Océanistes* 126–127: 271–292.

Thomson, D.F. 1953. War-time exploration in Dutch New Guinea. *The Geographical Journal*: 1–16.

Tichelman, G.L. 1963. Ethnographic bronze objects from the Lake Sentani District. *Sixth International Congress of Anthropological and Ethnological Sciences*. Paris, Musée de l'Homme: 645–51.

Torrence, R. and P. Swadling 2008. Social networks and the spread of Lapita. *Antiquity* 82: 600–16.

Torrence, R., Swadling, P., Kononenko, N., Ambrose, W., Rath, P. and Glascock, M.D. 2009. Hid-Holocene social interaction in Melanesia: New evidence from hammer-dressed obsidian stemmed tools. *Asian Perspectives* 48 (1): 119–148.

Townsend, G.W.L. 1968. *District Officer: From untamed New Guinea to Lake Success, 1921–46*. Pacific Publications, Sydney.

Trend, M. 1988. This Foolish Day's Solemnity' in *The Spectator*, 31 December: 29–31.

Trenkenschuh, F. 1970. Border areas of Asmat - The Mimika. In *An Asmat Sketch Book* 1, F. Trenkenschuh (ed.), Asmat Museum of Culture and Progress: 124–33.

Urry, J. n.d. Goods for the oriental emporium: the expansion of trade in the Indonesian archipelago and its impact on the outer periphery 1650–1850. manuscript.

Vanderwal, R. 1973. The Torres Strait: protohistory and beyond. *University of Queensland Anthropology Museum Occasional Papers* 2: 157–194.

Veur, P.W. 1966a. *Search for New Guinea's boundaries: From Torres Strait to the Pacific*. Australian National University, Canberra.

Veur, P.W. 1966b. *Documents and correspondence on New Guinea's boundaries*. Australian National University, Canberra.

Veur, P.W. van der 1972. Dutch New Guinea. In *Encyclopaedia of Papua New Guinea*. Vol. 1, P. Ryan ed., Melbourne University Press in association with the University of Papua New Guinea: 276–283.

Villiers, J. 1981. Trade and Society in the Banda Islands in the Sixteenth Century. *Modern Asian Studies* 15 (4): 723–50.

Villiers, J. 1990. The cash-crop economy and state formation in the Spice Islands in the fifteenth and sixteenth centuries. In *The Southeast Asian Port and Polity: Rise and Demise*. J. Kathirithamby-Wells and J. Villiers (eds), Singapore University Press: 83–106.

Voorhoeve, C.L. and Wurm, S.A. 1981. Western Province. In Language Atlas of the Pacific Area: Part 1: New Guinea Area, Oceania, Australia. S.A. Wurm and Shiro Hattori (ed.) Australian Academy of the Humanities in collaboration with the Japan Academy, Canberra.

Wagner, R. 1967. *The Curse of Souw: Principles of Daribi Clan Definition and Alliance*. University of Chicago Press, Chicago.

Wagner, R. 1972. *Habu: The Innovation of Meaning in Daribi Religion*. University of Chicago Press, Chicago.

Wagner, R. 1978. *Lethal Speech: Daribi Myth as Symbolic Obviation*. Cornell University Press, Ithaca.

Waiko, J.D. 1993. *A short history of Papua New Guinea*. Oxford University Press. Melbourne.

Wallace, A.R. 1857. On the great Bird of Paradise, *Paradisea apoda*, Linn.; 'Burong mati' (Dead bird) of the Malays; 'Fanéhan' of the Natives of Aru. *The Annals and Magazine of Natural History* 20: 411–16.

Wallace, A. R. 1860. Notes of a voyage to New Guinea. *Journal Royal Geographical Society*. 30: 172–7.

Wallace, A.R. 1862a. Narrative of search after Birds of Paradise. In *Proceedings of the Scientific Meetings of the Zoological Society of London*: 153–61.

Wallace, A.R. 1862b. On the trade of the Eastern Archipelago with New Guinea and its Islands. *Journal of the Royal Geographical Society, London* 32; 127–37.

Wallace, A.R. 1879. New Guinea and its inhabitants. *Contemporary Review* 34: 421–41.

Wallace, A.R. 1986 [first published 1869]. *The Malay Archipelago*: The Land of the Orang-Utan and the Bird of Paradise. Introduction by J. Bastin. Oxford University Press.

Wang Gungwu 1958. The Nanhai Trade: A study of the early history of Chinese trade in the South China Sea. *Journal of the Malayan Branch of the Royal Asiatic Society* 31, Part 2, No. 182: 1–135.

Warren, J.F. 1981. *The Sulu Zone 1768–1898*: the dynamics of external trade, slavery and ethnicity in the transformation of a Southeast Asian maritime state. Singapore University Press.

Warren, J.F. 1990. Trade, slave raiding and state formation in the Sulu Sultanate in the Nineteenth Century. In Kathirithamby-Wells and Villiers 1990: 187–211.

Whittaker, J.L., Gash, N.G., Hookey, J.F. and Lacey, R.C. 1975. *Documents and Readings in New Guinea History, Prehistory to 1889*. The Jacaranda Press, Queensland.

Wichmann, A. 1917. Bericht über eine im jahre 1903 ausgeführte reise nach Neu-Guinea. *Nova Guinea*, Vol. 4. E.J. Brill, Leiden.

Wiltgen, R. 1971. Catholic mission plantations in mainland New Guinea: their origin and purpose. In Inglis, K. (ed.) *The history of Melanesia*. Australian National University and University of Papua New Guinea, Port Moresby: 329–62.

Wirz, P. 1922. *Die Marind-anim von Holländisch Sud-Neu-Guinea*. Friederichsen, Hamburg.

Wit, F. 1976. Clove. In *Evolution of Crop Plants*. Simmonds, N.W. (ed). Longman, London: 216–8.

Wollaston, A.F.R. 1912. *Pygmies and Papuans*: the Stone Age today in Dutch New Guinea (with appendices by W.R. Ogilvie-Grant, A.C. Haddon and S.H. Ray). John Murray, London.

Wright, H.R.C. 1958. The Moluccan spice monopoly, 1770–1824. *Journal of the Malayan Branch Royal Asiatic Society* 31 (4): i–v, 1–127.

Wu, D.Y.H. 1977. The migration of Chinese to New Guinea and its settlement history. In Wurm, S.A. (ed.) *New Guinea Area Languages and Language Study Vol. 3*. Language Culture, Society and the Modern World, Fascicle 2, *Pacific Linguistics Series C* No. 40: 1047–53.

Wurm, S.A. and Hattori, S. 1981. *Language Atlas of the Pacific Area*. Australian Academy of the Humanities in collaboration with the Japan Academy, Canberra.

Yonge, C. M. 1930 *A Year on the Great Barrier Reef*. London: Routledge and Kegan Paul.

Zieck, J.F.U. 1973. *Massoy Bark in Papua New Guinea*. Forest Products Research Centre, Department of Forests, Technical Paper No. 1, Port Moresby.

Zieck, J. 1975. *Copal Industry in Papua New Guinea*. Dept, of Primary Industry, PNG Office of Forests, Port Moresby.

Zeick, J. 1978. Distribution of the most important resin producing tree species in Papua New Guinea, map, PNG Office of Forests, Port Moresby.

Index

Giadap 295, 301–302

Gidra 162, 301, 304

Gilimanuk 57

Gilliard, E.T. 80, 104, 240

Gira River 52, 280

Giulianetti, A. 77

Gizra 155, 159–162, 295–296, 299–307

glass 53, 194, 206, 272
  beads 27, 54, 59, 155, 206, 209, 305
  bracelets 57, 206, 209
  earrings 206

glut 36, 38, 40, 275

gold 31, 37, 180, 249, 267, 280
  mining 267
  prospecting 76, 247, 263

Goldie, A. 76

gong(s) 31, 150, 168, 181, 281

Goodfellow, W. 96

Gope 288–292

Gorong, *see traders*, 33, 36, 124, 137–139, 142–143, 146–147, 153, 166, 169

Gould, J. 74

goura 88, 93, 125, 214, 235, 236, 255–257, 267

Granada 43

Great Banda 30, 41

Greece 53

green snails 219, 253

Grunungen, van 187

guide(s) 130, 180, 190, 193, 243

Guinea 46

Gulf Delta 302

Gulf of Carpentaria 157

Gulf of Papua 155

Gulf Provinces 285

gulls 91

gunpowder 37, 147, 168

gun(s) 92, 101, 104, 137, 147–148, 184, 191, 196, 220, 243, 247, 266, 283

Gunung Baik 139

Hague, The 65

Hahl, A. 76, 219, 221, 231, 235, 241, 252, 254

Hahn, W.J. 241, 251

Halmahera 21, 26, 29–30, 45, 75, 115, 118–119, 122, 272, 282

Hamburg 241

handkerchiefs 143, 168

Hanna, W.A. 40

Hansa Bay 246

Hansemann, A. von 224, 225

Haruku 33, 41

Hasan, B. 119

HatiHati 146

hats 17, 83–88, 92

Hatzfeldthafen 246

Hatzfeldthafen Plantation 241, 251

Hawaiian Islands 91

Hayes, J. 114, 273

head-hunting 116

Helwig, J.O. 65, 74, 169

hemp 251

heritage 21, 92, 93

Hernsheim Company 241, 280

hero traditions 158, 285–297, 302

herons 92–96, 104, 257

Herzog Range 246

Hido 158, 288, 291, 302

highlands 15, 51–52, 99, 156, 164, 282, 292

hiri 164

Hitu 36

Hoedt, D.S. 74

Hoefnagel, J. 65

Holland 43, 64

Hollandia, *see Jayapura*, 91, 99, 187–188, 205, 213–217, 220–221, 224, 255

Hong Kong 235, 243, 257

hongi, see raiding, 112, 116, 118–119, 125, 139, 146–147, 149, 211

Horsbrugh, C. 266

www.ingramcontent.com/pod-product-compliance
Lightning Source LLC
Chambersburg PA
CBHW050038220326
41599CB00041B/7204